THE COMPLETE FINANCIAL GUIDE TO THE 1990s

THE
COMPLETE
FINANCIAL GUIDE
TO THE
1990s

GARY L. KLOTT

TIMES BOOKS

RANDOM HOUSE

Library of Congress Cataloging-in-Publication Data

Klott, Gary L.
    The complete financial guide to the 1990s / by
Gary Klott.
      p.   cm.
    ISBN 0-8129-1814-2
    1. Finance, Personal—Handbooks, manuals, etc. 2. Investments—
Handbooks, manuals, etc. 3. Corporations—Finance—Handbooks,
manuals, etc. I. New York times. II. Title.
HG179.K576   1990
332.024—dc20   89-40189

Manufactured in the United States of America

9 8 7 6 5 4 3 2

First Edition

To my brothers, David and Richard

ACKNOWLEDGMENTS

Writing is said to be a lonely profession, but in truth it is always crowded with ideas and help from others.

My special appreciation to:

The WEFA Group, the econometric forecasting concern, for their economic projections, with particular thanks to economist Lawrence W. Chimerine; John Savacool, director of real estate and construction services; Sungchul Kim; Roger C. Bird; and Sally Dodge.

Dr. Nestor E. Terleckyj of the National Planning Association and president of NPA Data Services, Inc., for projections on regional economic growth trends.

Steven B. Enright, director of financial planning at Seidman Financial Services, for his assistance in formulating retirement and college savings projections, and also Douglas Mollin, assistant director of financial planning.

My special thanks to the experts who read through portions of the manuscript at various stages and offered valuable suggestions. Among them were George W. James, president of Airline Economics, Inc., a consulting firm in Washington, D.C.; Frank Y. Fradin, associate laboratory director for physical research at the Argonne National Laboratory; Douglas C. Birdsall, president and chief executive officer of Travelmation Corporation, a travel management firm in Stamford, Connecticut; David Rosen, vice president of electronic entertainment at LINK Resources Corporation, a consulting and market research firm; Scott Jones, president of AUS Consultants of Philadelphia; Charles Peck, senior research associate at The Conference Board, a business research group; Richard J. Stricof, a tax partner at the accounting firm of BDO Seidman; Herbert M. Paul, senior partner of the New York accounting firm of Mahoney, Cohen, Paul & Company; Christopher Hartwell, an attorney with the Palo Alto, California, law firm of Wilson, Sonsini, Goodrich & Rosati; David S. Rhine, a tax partner at BDO Seidman; Gurdon H. Buck, an attorney with the Hartford, Connecticut, law firm of Robinson & Cole;

Andrew E. Zuckerman, an employee benefits expert at the accounting firm of Grant Thornton; Randall McCathren of Bank Lease Consultants, Inc., of Nashville, Tennessee; Glenn E. Davis, a tax partner at BDO Seidman; Frank Poirier, assistant national director of management consulting services at Seidman; Thomas D'Amato, a Seidman partner; and Stephen T. Gorman, director of financial planning in Boston for Seidman Financial Services.

For their technical expertise, I wish to thank Sandra Shaber, an economist specializing in consumer affairs at The Futures Group, a management consulting firm; Carol D'Agostino, senior research associate at LINK Resources; Christopher N. Caton, director of forecasting at Data Resources, an economic consulting firm in Lexington, Massachusetts; Elizabeth A. Deakin, assistant professor, Department of City and Regional Planning at the University of California at Berkeley; Herschel Shosteck, of Herschel Shosteck Associates Limited, a cellular telecommunications consulting firm in Silver Spring, Maryland; James H. Kennedy, editor and publisher of the *Directory of Executive Recruiters* (Kennedy Publications); James M. McCarthy, fiber optics industry analyst at the U.S. Department of Commerce; Christine Paulson, policy analyst at the Education Commission of the States; Orrin H. Pilkey, Jr., professor of geology at Duke University; David A. Lins, professor of agricultural finance at the University of Illinois, Urbana/Champaign; State Farm Insurance; and William T. Brack, an attorney with the Washington, D.C., law firm of Williams & Jensen.

For special research materials, my appreciation to Peter A. Morrison, director of the Population Research Center at the Rand Corporation; Susan Call of the market research firm of Frost & Sullivan, Inc.; The Joint Center for Housing Studies of Harvard University; the Office for the Study of Automotive Transportation at the University of Michigan; and Neal H. Rosenthal, Alan Eck, and Suzanne Sadowski of the U.S. Bureau of Labor Statistics.

To Robert D. Hershey Jr., Washington correspondent at *The New York Times*, for his friendship, encouragement, and late-night debates on the future.

To my agent, Mel Berger of the William Morris Agency, for his valued advice and help in shepherding this project. And to my attorney, Kenneth P. Norwick, for his wise counsel over the years.

To Jonathan B. Segal, for his enthusiastic support and help in conceiving this book, and to Hugh O'Neill, former editorial director at Times Books, for all his efforts in seeing this book to fruition. To Ruth Fecych, for her patience and valued editing on this book and my two previous books. To Nancy Inglis, for her caring efforts in guiding my three books through the final stages of production. My thanks also to Kathie Gordon for her editorial services, to Susan Luke for her assistance on the project, and to Robert Bull, for his creative artwork and design.

My everlasting gratitude to Tanya L. Hildebrand, for her constant encouragement, advice, and her endless sacrifices made throughout the writing of this book.

To Maren and Evy, my heartfelt appreciation for all their cheerful support.

To my mother and father, who encouraged me always to be prepared for the future. And to my brothers, David and Richard, both tax lawyers, for a lifetime of encouragement, inspiration, and advice. This book is dedicated to them.

CONTENTS

the Work Force • A Maturing Work Force • A New Attitude Toward Older Workers • Disability No Longer as Much of a Handicap

The Best and the Worst Jobs in the 1990s: An Occupation-by-Occupation Guide

An Industry-by-Industry Guide to Trends Shaping Business in the 1990s

Nowhere for Taxes to Go But Up • Coping with the Threat of Higher Income Tax Rates • Capital Gains Taxes: Prospects for Lower Rates • Take Deductions Now Before They Disappear • Focus on Economics, Not Tax Benefits of Investments • Don't Bet Your Home on the Mortgage Deduction • The Threat to Preferred Stock Prices • Taxing Cash-Value Life Insurance Policies • Taxing Away More Social Security Benefits • Motorists Face Higher Gasoline Taxes • Cost of Smoking and Drinking Going Up • Filing Your Return by Computer: Is It Worth the Cost? • Tax-Exempt Bonds: A Hedge Against Higher Rates

The Moderate-Growth Scenario • Why Inflation Is Expected to Remain Moderate • Investment Implications of Mild Inflation • A Rising Standard of Living • Unemployment: Easing Concerns • A Higher Savings Rate—Finally? • A Less Lavish Shopping Spree • A Rebound in Productivity • The Comeback of "Made in America": Narrowing the Trade Gap • Why the Economy Should Be Less Vulnerable to Recession • Looming Threats: What Could Go Wrong

THE COMPLETE FINANCIAL GUIDE TO THE 1990s

1

WHAT LIES AHEAD IN THE 1990s

Welcome to the 1990s, a decade where traditional assumptions used to guide careers, run a business, make sound investments, buy a home, or secure a comfortable retirement will be rendered obsolete. It is the dawn of a new era that will change the way you look at the world, invest your money, plan your career, manage your business, and conduct your financial affairs.

Powerful demographic, technological, social, and economic currents are converging to reshape the workplace, the marketplace, the investment landscape, the job market, and the very fabric of everyday business and personal life.

Forget all you learned from the 1980s about the kinds of products consumers wanted, which investments seemed the most promising, which businesses offered the best growth prospects, what skills employers were searching for, what cities or countries were growing the fastest, or what it took to climb the corporate ladder.

The 1990s will require an entirely new perspective, new strategies, and new skills, because the decade ahead promises to be far different from the one just past. American business and society are being transformed in fundamental ways. The occupations, investments, and businesses that offer the best opportunities will be different ones from those of the past.

Sweeping changes in the demographic makeup of American society, new technologies, increasing foreign competition, and other political, economic, and social trends are altering the employment outlook in virtually every occupation. They are also shifting the relative merits of individual investments, the fates and fortunes of every industry, the skills needed to climb the corporate ladder, the criteria for selecting a home, and the way you deal with your banker, your employer, your insurance agent, the IRS, and even members of your family.

Signs of a new age are already emerging. The huge baby-boom generation, which spent the 1980s crowding trendy restaurants, discos, jogging tracks, and BMW showrooms, is now staying home, raising children, playing golf, and driving minivans. Employers accustomed to long lines of job applicants to pick and choose from are now struggling with labor shortages. Madison Avenue, which used to ignore the over-fifty crowd in favor of more youthful audiences, is now casting aging celebrities instead of shapely teenage models in more and more ads. In the workplace, clogged corporate ladders are making job promotions more elusive than ever. In the job market, the doctor shortage is turning into a doctor glut, and teachers, who couldn't find jobs a few years ago, are now being showered with offers. America's throwaway mentality is being transformed by mandatory-recycling laws. New cars and planes are being fitted with all-plastic bodies instead of steel ones. Gold, long treasured for its rarity, is no longer so rare. The Cold War, which guided superpower relations since World War II, is drawing to a close. And Communist leaders, trying to rejuvenate their sagging economies, are now quoting Adam Smith instead of Karl Marx.

RISING TRENDS OF THE 1990s

- Environmental clean-up
- Waste disposal
- Health-care services
- Biotechnology
- Retirement communities and nursing homes
- Home entertainment
- Space commercialization
- Infrastructure rehabilitation
- Health and convenience foods
- Space-age materials
- Time-saving services
- Cost-saving devices
- Highway and air traffic congestion
- Recordable compact disks
- Computers playing more central role
- Telecommunications, fax machines, electronic mail
- Information services
- Golf, bicycling, walking, cross-training
- Energy prices
- Service sector
- Pharmaceuticals
- Child care
- Elderly care
- Alternative fuels
- Flexible compensation
- Flexible work hours
- Digitalization
- Foreign competition
- Children's goods
- AIDS cases
- Elementary and high school enrollments
- Continuing education
- Taxes
- Cellular phones

THE FUTURE ISN'T SHAPED IN A VACUUM

The seeds of change have already been planted.

Demographic trends that will radically alter the makeup of American society and reshape consumer spending patterns were set in motion long ago. Many of the technologies that will have a major impact on jobs and industry in the 1990s are already in advanced stages of development. New industrial powers that will make foreign competition even fiercer and force more changes in the workplace of the 1990s are already emerging in the shadows of Japan and South Korea, behind the crumbling Iron Curtain, and in Western Europe, where efforts are under way to create the world's largest single market by the end of 1992.

Indeed, while the future holds many uncertainties, much is already known about what lies ahead in the 1990s. The future isn't shaped in a vacuum.

What lies ahead in the 1990s and what you can do to prepare for, cope with, and capitalize on the coming changes are the twin focuses of this book.

MODERATING OR DECLINING TRENDS OF THE 1990s

- Alcohol consumption
- Tobacco use
- Vinyl LPs
- College enrollments
- Discos
- Real estate
- Early retirement offers
- Network TV audiences
- Births
- Economic growth rate
- Defense industry
- Convenience stores
- Inflation
- Jogging, aerobics
- Manufacturing jobs
- Pesticides
- Consumer electronics
- Video rental stores
- Mainframe computers
- Divorce
- Job promotions
- Job security
- Messenger services

DEMOGRAPHIC CHANGES OF THE 1990s

- Middle-aging of the baby-boom generation
- Expanding elderly population, particularly those over 85
- Shrinking young adult population
- Fast-growing ethnic population
- Increasing school-age population
- Declining births
- Divorce rate leveling off
- Singles, one-parent families, childless couples growing faster than married couples
- Slower overall population growth
- More women entering the labor force

JOB MARKET OF THE 1990s

Fast-growing professions	Declining occupations
Health care	Manufacturing
Engineering	Farming
Computers	Unskilled labor
Service industries	Automatable clerical jobs

2

THE WORKPLACE
REVOLUTION

GOOD-BYE TO THE TRADITIONAL ORGANIZATION

From the executive suite to the factory floor, the American workplace is undergoing fundamental change. It is revolutionizing the nature of jobs, the way workers are paid, when they work, where they work, their prospects for advancement, and the security they can expect from their employers.

The traditional organization—where dedication and hard work have long been rewarded with promises of steady advancement, annual raises, and lifetime security—is crumbling. In an age of corporate takeovers, restructurings, technological change, and fierce foreign competition, employees can no longer count on security from a single employer. Finding a good job and hanging on to it until retirement is becoming the exception rather than the rule.

Corporate organizations are being overhauled and put on a crash diet. Jobs are being shuffled, redefined, and scrapped. Layers of management bureaucracy are being peeled from the corporate hierarchy, shoving long-time white-collar employees out into the street and leaving survivors with new opportunities, but heavier workloads and fewer rungs on the corporate ladder available to climb.

Even what a worker earns is becoming more uncertain. Annual raises are being replaced by new compensation schemes linking workers' pay to the fates and fortunes of the company.

At the same time, the workplace is becoming more accommodating to the individual needs of a more diverse work force. Workers are being unshackled from the rigid nine-to-five schedule, the traditional forty-hour work week, the need for all work to be done in the office, and a corporate culture intolerant of family responsibilities conflicting with company needs. Corporations are increasingly allowing workers to set their own hours, choose their own benefits from a menu of options, work from home, work part-time, share a job with a coworker, and take official time off to have a child.

And as automation and computerization spread further into the workplace, the nature of jobs is changing, as are the criteria for what it takes to be successful. Bank tellers are becoming "customer service representatives." Factory floor workers are no longer assembly-line workers but technicians who monitor and repair the sophisticated robots that now do more and more of the assembling. Professionals and managers, being fitted with their own computer terminals and telecommunications gadgetry, are increasingly doing the kinds of clerical tasks that their secretaries used to perform.

As the Congressional Office of Technology Assessment observed in a recent report on America's economic transition: "Managers, physicians, laborers, clerks, salespeople, and many others will find their jobs redefined. They will face changes in their power to command wages, in the stability of their positions, in the safety and stress of their work, and in the texture of their daily working life. There will be new opportunities for pride and enjoyment in the workplace, and new opportunities for frustration and alienation."

If there is an underlying theme to corporate strategy in the 1990s, it is *flexibility*. To be able to respond swiftly in a more competitive and rapidly changing environment, companies are redesigning their organizations to provide flexible staffing, flexible compensation, flexible work rules, flexible commitments, flexible inventory systems, flexible strategic plans, flexible hours, and flexible job definitions.

As John D. Ong, chairman and chief executive officer of the B.F. Goodrich Company, said in a speech on the future of the workplace: "Technological innovation, foreign competition, and shifts in consumer preferences add up to a workplace in which change is the only constant."

For workers, a new set of strategies for keeping their careers on track will be required in the face of rapid change and greater uncertainty.

JOB SECURITY: A VANISHING DREAM

In the rubble of the corporate upheavals of the 1980s lie the shattered dreams of loyal employees who thought their future was secure in the company's future.

Gone are the days when employees could expect job security in exchange for dedication and hard work. In a world of corporate takeovers, buyouts, downsizing, and restructuring, job security is a vanished dream.

The long-standing, if unwritten, promise of protecting loyal workers through thick and thin is a covenant companies have found they can no longer keep. It is the sunset of a long tradition.

In offices and factories across the country, American workers are facing wrenching dislocations as companies are merged, bought out, de-merged, restructured, automated, and downsized in their effort to compete in a world of rapid technological change and ever-growing competition from abroad and in newly deregulated markets at home.

While laying off workers has been a fact of life for a long time in many parts of the business world, it is the new willingness of some of the most successful and paternalistic companies to slash jobs at all levels that has fundamentally changed the nature of employer-employee relationships.

A few companies, like IBM, still maintain no-layoff policies. But the long-held belief that working for a successful industrial giant guarantees a steady job through good times and bad was shattered after hundreds of leading companies slashed their payrolls in the past few years. Among them were such respected names as AT&T, CBS, Eastman Kodak, Exxon, Time, and General Electric.

In the 1980s, more than two million workers were displaced each year, according to estimates by some labor economists.

Companies are growing less and less reluctant to let people go when their services are no longer needed, no matter what their stripe. Managers and professional workers, whose jobs used to be protected even when conditions required massive layoffs of their blue-collar colleagues, are now equally vulnerable. By some estimates, more than a million managers and professionals lost their jobs in the 1980s.

And despite the layers of bureaucracy that have already been peeled away (estimates are that as many as a third of management positions were eliminated in the past decade), some management experts believe the executive ranks at many companies still need to be cut much further in order to compete in the 1990s. Streamlined management structures make for more nimble organizations, more able to respond quickly to rapidly changing markets.

Even labor unions, which now represent only 17 percent of the labor force (compared to 33 percent in 1960), haven't been able to stop the hemorrhaging of jobs. Despite the large wage concessions they granted in the 1980s in hopes of saving jobs, only a tiny fraction of labor contracts contain job security provisions. And even those provisions won't necessarily guarantee your job. Rather, they provide ways of easing the pain when you do lose your job, with severance pay, early retirement benefits, preferential rehiring rights, and company-paid job retraining. If your company is taken over, you may not even get those benefits. In many cases, job security provisions can be thrown out the door in the event of a takeover.

Even workers at the relatively few companies with no-layoff policies are finding that job protection goes only so far in an age of takeovers, where all bets are off, and restructuring, where keeping a job often means relocating or accepting a lower-level position.

As a result of the changing environment, the Labor Department estimates that the average American can expect to work for as many as six different employers during his lifetime and switch careers as many as three times. Even before the most recent wave of dislocations, long-term employment with a single employer was a rarity. According to Labor Department data from 1987, nearly 3 of 4 U.S. workers were with their current employer less than ten years. Fewer than 1 in 10 workers were with their employer twenty years or more.

The increasing job turbulence will be particularly hard on middle-aged and older workers, who tend to have large financial commitments and find it difficult to relocate, learn new skills, or change occupations. Older workers also have a harder time matching their previous salaries and benefits when looking for a new job. As a result, the traditional expectation of steadily increasing earnings through one's work life is being undermined.

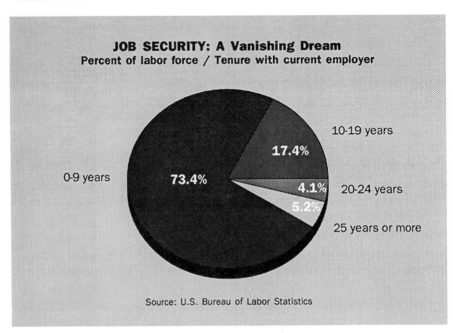

JOB SECURITY: A Vanishing Dream
Percent of labor force / Tenure with current employer

0-9 years 73.4%

10-19 years 17.4%

20-24 years 4.1%

25 years or more 5.2%

Source: U.S. Bureau of Labor Statistics

All of this has eroded the concept of corporate loyalty; commitments between employees and employers will now be viewed as fragile, tentative, and illusory. Job security lasts only as long as the employee continues to provide worth to the company. And an employee is loyal only until a better opportunity comes along. There are already signs that the new crop of younger managers is more self-oriented and less dedicated to the organization.

PROMOTION BOTTLENECK ON THE CORPORATE LADDER

Not only is job security a vanishing dream, but promotions will also become more elusive in the 1990s. It will be an era of diminishing opportunities.

The reason: growing competition for a shrinking number of man-

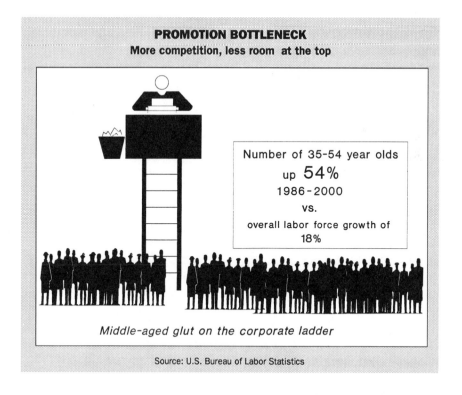

PROMOTION BOTTLENECK
More competition, less room at the top

Number of 35-54 year olds
up 54%
1986-2000
vs.
overall labor force growth of
18%

Middle-aged glut on the corporate ladder

Source: U.S. Bureau of Labor Statistics

agement positions. The huge crop of educated baby-boomers and women who entered the labor force in the 1970s are now crowding a corporate ladder that has fewer rungs on it, the result of drastic downsizing of the management ranks in recent years.

While career "plateauing" has always been a concern, managers will see their careers peaking at earlier ages, and the lack of promotional opportunities will become a leading source of frustration in the management ranks for years to come.

In contrast to the management boom times of the 1950s and 1960s, when promotion opportunities expanded so rapidly that many people were promoted beyond their abilities, the 1990s will see a reversal. Qualified and able managers will be "underpromoted."

Bureaucrats in the federal government will find the same kind of bottlenecks to promotion. A recent government report on the future of federal services observed: "As competition increases among the greater number of qualified candidates for fewer job openings, career plateauing becomes a very real danger, with many federal employees forced to stay at promotional and pay levels for longer periods of time."

As an indication of the growing crowding on the corporate ladder, the 35–54 age group, the biggest group vying for management positions, will swell 54 percent between 1986 and the year 2000, compared to 18 percent growth in the overall labor force. (Broken down, the 35–44 age group will grow 42 percent, and the 45–54 age group will increase 72 percent.)

Companies are going to have to create a new environment that takes these promotion realities into account by attaching less importance to promotions, while providing new challenges and rewards to those stuck in the promotion bottleneck. One option is to provide managers with more challenging opportunities through "lateral promotions." Another is to put the best nonmanagerial professionals and technicians on the same pay scale as managers.

Regardless of what steps are taken, the lack of promotion is bound to lead to more restlessness and frustration among valued employees, many of whom will search elsewhere for more promising opportunities.

JOB-SURVIVAL CREDO FOR THE 1990S: BE FLEXIBLE AND ALWAYS BE PREPARED FOR THE WORST

In this new era of turbulent change and fewer guarantees, employees at all levels need to develop new strategies for surviving and for advancing their careers in the face of uncertainty. Dedication and hard work alone no longer guarantee financial security and success, as those who were victims of the mergers, restructurings, and technological changes of the 1980s can attest.

Since corporations can no longer be counted on to ensure an employee's future, employees themselves have to take steps to secure it. Today's climate calls for developing new attitudes and skills that make you more flexible and marketable.

In the business organization of the 1990s, survivors are the ones who can demonstrate flexibility in the face of constant change, who can learn new skills as jobs are redefined, and who are not afraid to abandon comfortable routines for challenging new opportunities when they arise.

Long-term success also means always being prepared for the worst. By cultivating outside contacts and developing professional skills that can be marketed elsewhere, you will be paving the road to new opportunities should prospects at your company dim. If you think of yourself as an independent contractor rather than an employee, control of your future will be in your hands rather than dependent on the whims and fortunes of a single company. Your future will be secured even if your company's isn't.

Employees should take a lesson from Hollywood actors who move from studio to studio, loyal only to themselves and their craft. On their own initiative, they polish their skills, keep their bodies trim so they look good on camera, make the rounds of late-night talk shows to enhance their reputations, and read *Variety* every day to keep abreast of casting opportunities. All of this enhances their marketability. Who they work for on their next film depends only on which studio offers the best deal.

Following are some tips on how to secure your career and keep it from plateauing.

Gaining a New Perspective: Come to grips with the new realities of the employer-employee relationship and always be prepared for the worst.

Don't Be Lulled into a False Sense of Security: If your organization has already undergone restructuring and downsizing, don't be lulled into thinking that the bloodbaths have come to an end. Management ranks at many companies are still bloated. Cost-cutting and restructuring will be an ongoing necessity for years to come.

Maintain Outside Contacts: Always have an iron in the fire by cultivating outside contacts.

Join a Professional Association: Become active in your professional or trade organization. You'll meet lots of contacts and hear about lots of job opportunities.

Become Financially Secure: Build a nest egg of at least six months' income to tide you over in the event you lose your job. Many financial advisers used to recommend only three months' income, but that's not enough in this age of corporate turmoil. Management job searches can easily last five to six months and if you're short of money, you may be forced to accept a job that you really don't want or risk landing in serious financial straits.

Become Distinguished in Your Field: Develop a reputation in your field. Write an article for a professional journal, give lectures, or teach a course in it. Prominence often brings new opportunities to your doorstep.

Don't Become Too Specialized: Don't overspecialize to the point where your career becomes dependent on one company. Make sure your skills are transferable to other companies in your field or even other industries.

Learn New Skills: If your field is on the decline or vulnerable to automation, don't wait until you're out of a job or at a dead end to learn new skills. Go to night school.

Assess the Vulnerability of Your Job: Is your job crucial to the bottom line or is it vulnerable in the event that staff cuts need to be made? If you're vulnerable, consider the possibility of a new assignment into a more secure position or one that is more readily marketable elsewhere.

Be Flexible: Be flexible enough to move out of your particular specialty and assume a different assignment at your company that offers greater promise for advancement or that equips you with more marketable skills in the event you need or want to find a job elsewhere. Find out what areas of your company are growing and are in need of additional talent. Another department may provide a stepping-stone to advancement that your current job doesn't.

Relocate to Better Opportunities: If you are willing to relocate, find out what positions might be opening up at your company's other offices. Volunteering for a transfer to another city can be a quick way to get a career off dead-center these days because many people, particularly those with working spouses, are turning down attractive and challenging assignments in other cities.

Be Cautious of Group and Long-Term Projects: If you have a choice, try to steer clear of group assignments in which your personal contributions won't receive due notice. Also be selective about taking on long-term projects where the prospective payoff may not be worth the time spent. Results are what counts in this new era and companies value people who demonstrate constant achievement.

Seize Opportunities When They Arise: If you are the survivor of a downsizing, make the most of the new opportunities at your doorstep. A reduced staff leaves more interesting and demanding challenges for those who remain. Don't wait for those tasks to be assigned. Ask to take on additional responsibilities. This will help you gain more visibility and show off your skills and initiative. It's also a chance to broaden your horizons and tackle assignments outside your immediate specialty. Those added skills will not only increase your worth at the company but make you a more marketable commodity should you need or want to go elsewhere.

Early Warning Signs of Trouble: Keep a close eye on how your company is faring and how your particular division is doing. Your future is wrapped up in their prospects. If your company or division is having financial troubles, or if your company is mentioned as a takeover target, those are early warning signals that your own job could be in jeopardy.

Monitor Your Company's Health: Monitor your company as if you were an investor. Investors with only a few thousand dollars to spare spend far more time researching a company than do employees who have their full-time earnings at stake. Scour the business pages of newspapers and business magazines for articles about your company and, if its stock is publicly traded, ask your stockbroker for research reports on your company. Independent appraisals of your company can give you insight into how secure your job is and whether you should be looking elsewhere. Even if your company isn't a takeover candidate, your job could still be at risk if the company is preparing to take over another in the same line of business. If such a merger is in the works and it appears likely that operations will be combined, are you confident that you could survive the competition for jobs from your counterparts at the other company?

Assess Prospects on the Inside: Regularly assess your company from an insider's vantage point to determine whether you should at least be checking out opportunities elsewhere. Is your firm overstaffed and ripe for trimming? Are you a potential victim? Does the firm have a history of cost-cutting layoffs or does it have a long record of protecting jobs? Is there room for advancement? Or are you a victim of the baby-boom bulge in management ranks with too many people vying for too few positions?

Attend Conventions and Meetings: Attend professional meetings, seminars, conferences, and conventions. You'll learn about the latest developments in your field and make some new contacts during coffee breaks, at lunch, and after the formal presentations. Don't be afraid to chat with the speakers and panel participants after each session.

Keep an Eye on the Job Market: Periodically survey job opportunities outside your company to see whether your pay and promotions are keeping up with those of others in your field. If few opportunities are available in your field, investigate further. That could be a sign that your field is becoming crowded or that your specialty is no longer in demand.

Don't Let Your Skills Fall Behind: Keep your professional skills up-to-date. Attend night classes and symposiums. If your knowledge and skills become stale, you are vulnerable.

Reexamine Your Family Budget: Don't stretch your finances to the point where you would be in trouble if you lost your job and were forced to accept a lower-paying one. Middle-level managers were among the most devastated by the cutbacks of the 1980s because they lived as though their jobs would last forever and their salaries had nowhere to go but up. They thought wrong. Don't buy a house that's so expensive that you have to stretch to make the monthly payment. Build a cushion into your financial commitments. Lowering your standard of living is not easy or pleasant. But the new realities of the job market demand it.

Listen to All Offers: If another employer wants to talk to you, always listen. Tell them you are happy where you are, but always listen. They may offer a deal that is hard to refuse or a contact that may be worth pursuing later.

Think Hard Before Leaping: Don't jump hastily at the first job offer you get. It may be flattering and it may seem like a job you want. But weigh all the implications carefully before committing. Getting a job offer, particularly if it's unsolicited, may be the kind of ego massaging that you lack from your current employer. But the ego massaging may not last long after you get to the new job—and even if it does, ego therapy may not be enough to make the job worth taking. Also keep in mind that while corporate loyalty is vanishing, too much job hopping is still frowned upon. A long list of jobs on your résumé can make you look opportunistic, restless, or as if you have trouble getting along with your bosses.

Keep Your Résumé Updated: Keep your résumé up-to-date in case you receive word of a promising job opportunity or you need to move quickly to find another job. Updating your résumé is also a way to periodically assess your accomplishments and shortcomings.

Don't Quit Your Job Before You Have Another: Don't quit your job before you have a firm offer from another employer. It's much easier to search for a new job while you're still employed, both from a financial perspective and for appearance' sake.

Keep Your Job Search Secret: Don't let your bosses know you're looking for another job. Your position could be imperiled if they found out. Don't let your colleagues know, either. Trusted confidences can't always be trusted, and word travels quickly through the corporate grapevine.

Try Entrepreneurship as a Sideline, First: If you want to start your own business, can it be done as a sideline business first? If so, you can test the waters without giving up the security of your current job. But make sure your sideline doesn't jeopardize your job. Some employers have strict rules about what outside activities are permitted.

GAINING JOB SECURITY THROUGH AN EMPLOYMENT CONTRACT

Employment contracts used to be the legal preserve of movie stars, network newscasters, and sports celebrities. But in the wake of the business and management upheavals of the 1980s, more corporate executives are pressing for employment contracts in order to guarantee the kind of financial and job security that the corporate culture used to provide implicitly.

Employment contracts don't provide the same long-term security that many corporations used to bestow tacitly on their management ranks.

Employment contracts usually guarantee your salary for only two to five years. The contract doesn't take away your right to voluntarily quit during that period (the thirteenth amendment to the U.S. Constitution forbids involuntary servitude), but the employment contract may contain a provision prohibiting you from working for a competitor during the remaining term of the contract.

Though employment contracts are becoming more common, they are still largely reserved for top technical talent and executives at the apex of the corporate pyramid.

Nevertheless, middle managers and other professionals can often get an employer's promises put in writing by asking for an "offer letter." These letters are much less formal and much easier to obtain and negotiate than an employment contract. Most companies now provide them to employees who ask. When you are offered a job and you settle on terms, ask whomever you are dealing with if he or she would kindly put in a letter the terms that you have just agreed on, and say you'll resign from your current job as soon as you receive it. (If the letter doesn't include all you expected, you can try to negotiate revisions.) Offer letters should describe your title, duties, compensation, fringe benefits, retirement benefits, perks, and, if you're relocating, details on what moving expenses will be reimbursed. Offer letters usually don't provide the kind of legal or job security protection that an employment contract does. But if you feel you have the leverage, you can try to negotiate a termination provision in the offer letter so that the company is obligated to give you a specified amount of notice or severance pay if you're let go (such as one or two years' compensation).

Even if you don't get an employment contract or offer letter, save all the "new employee" literature you receive from the company when you begin the job, as well as any subsequent pamphlets, letters, personal evaluation reports, and memos. In recent years, many courts and juries have been interpreting these documents as contractual obligations, including language that implies long-term employment opportunity so long as your performance is satisfactory. The legal concept of "at will" employment, under which an employer has the right to fire you anytime and for any reason, has been eroded by the courts—as reflected by the increasing number of "wrongful discharge" suits won by employees. That's why a lot of companies are rushing to revise employee manuals to delete any explicit or implicit representations about long-term employment commitments.

As a result, you will increasingly need to rely on offer letters and employment contracts to nail down commitments. Following are some tips for dealing with employment contracts.

- Don't discuss the idea of an employment contract until you have a firm job offer. Discussing it in advance may spoil your chances. Many companies do not like the idea of employment contracts.
- Employment contracts should fully spell out what salary and benefits you will be entitled to, including bonuses and severance pay. The contract should also stipulate your title and job description. That's so if they don't like your work the company can't demote you to a job sweeping floors in hopes that you'll quit in disgust.
- Watch out for provisions that might hamper your employment opportunities should you leave the firm. A lot of companies want to prevent you from working for a competing firm. If your job is designing computers, you could find yourself unable to work in your field.
- Be particularly cautious of the section dealing with conditions under which you can be fired. It should be as specific as possible.
- Get a lawyer to advise you on the contract. Even if the negotiations are between you and your boss, be assured that the company's lawyers are going over the contract, if not actually drafting it. If your attorney is not familiar with employment contracts, ask for a referral to a lawyer who is expert in the field. The money you may spend is well worth the expense because you're dealing not only with your immediate job but also with your future career prospects and financial security. Why? Because some employers will try to coax you into signing contracts containing complex non-compete clauses that could severely limit your future job prospects. While non-compete clauses don't always hold up in court under antitrust laws, you might have to spend a lot of time and legal fees trying to resolve the issue. It's much cheaper to have a lawyer go over the contract before you sign it.

WHEN THE HEADHUNTER CALLS, DON'T HANG UP

If you've got a good reputation, chances are you'll get a call one day from a headhunter offering you the promise of a better job, greater challenges, more prestige, and a lot more money. Headhunters, or executive recruiters, scour the corporate terrain for talented executives and professionals to find suitable candidates for corporate clients with positions to fill.

Flattery usually goes a long way. But employees who are satisfied with their current positions and have a sense of great loyalty to their companies tend to dismiss the overture without giving the caller a chance to give his pitch. They may be hanging up on a terrific opportunity.

Always listen, but don't volunteer much information until you're sure who you're talking with. Even if you recognize the recruiting firm's name, you might tell the caller that you're unable to talk at the moment but you'll call him back. That will give you time at least to check the phone number that the caller gives you against the firm's listing in the telephone directory. If colleagues are within earshot of your desk, tell the recruiter you're unable to speak freely at the office and ask if he can be reached at home during the evening or on the weekend.

Ask the recruiter whether he has a specific position in mind or whether he's just feeling you out to see if you might be in the market for the right position. If he's just fishing, don't talk long. Tell him to give you a call when something specific comes up. After all, what's there to talk about if you don't know what the opportunity is?

If there is a specific job, say you might be interested in finding out more about it—even though you haven't been looking and you're content with your current position. The recruiter probably won't tell you the name of the company, but he should be able to give you sufficient information about the job to determine whether it's worth scheduling a face-to-face meeting.

Keep in mind that legitimate recruiters don't ask for a cent from the heads being hunted. They get paid by the corporate client to find the right person. (The bounty typically runs one third of the first year's compensation for the position being filled.) So if a recruiter asks for money, ask him what kind of headhunter he really is. Chances are he makes more money extracting fees from individuals than recruiting for corporations.

BIDDING ADIEU TO YOUR COMPANY: A GUIDE TO EXITING WITH GRACE

Saying good-bye to a company is getting to be a more frequent ritual in this age of declining corporate loyalty. Regardless of whether you are being laid off or heading for greener pastures of your own volition, leaving a company these days demands greater diplomacy than ever.

Odds are growing that you will be working with some of your old bosses and colleagues again someday, somewhere. In an era of rampant internal and external upheavals, you could well find your new company merging with your old one. Or your old boss might need to hunt for greener pastures, and wind up in your new backyard. Hence the importance of leaving your company on good terms, exhibiting the same grace you would on your first days of a new job. It is said that first impressions are lasting ones. But so are parting impressions. Superiors may well remember you most for what you said and how you acted as you left. Here are some tips on exiting with grace:

- Whatever you say or do, always keep in mind that you don't want to burn any bridges. One day you may want to return to the company, perhaps in a higher position. Even if you vow never to return, mergers and executive mobility could well place you in another working relationship with former colleagues.
- Don't use your good-byes to complain about everything that was wrong with the company and your bosses. While such parting shots may be good for the soul, they can come back to haunt you later in your career. Instead, stress the positive aspects of your stay with the company.
- If you have just been laid off, hide your ill-feelings and make peace with your supervisors. When you go looking for another job, you'll need them for references.
- Even if you are asked for frank opinions in a farewell interview, try to keep things peaceful and friendly. Rarely do criticisms made during exit interviews lead to significant organizational changes. But your criticisms could end up hurting you. So don't make disparaging remarks about your supervisor, even if the interviewer promises confidentiality. If your supervisor is told the next day to straighten up, he or she will assume the reprimand stemmed from criticisms you made during your exit interview.
- Don't even speak disparagingly about the company or your superiors to your fellow workers. Your sentiments may spread much farther than you intended. People leaving a company are popular subjects for the gossip mill, and gossip often makes its way into the management ranks. What's more, gossip mills tend to carry exaggerated versions of what was originally said, so the words filtering up to your bosses will likely be worse than the sentiments you actually expressed.
- Don't slack off during your final days on the job. If you do, that's how you may be remembered. Keep working hard through the last day. Demonstrating your dedication to the company when you don't

have to gives new meaning to the word *dedication*, and that's how you want your bosses to remember you.

- If you are leaving of your own volition, give as much notice as possible so that the company has some time to make alternate arrangements. Tell your superiors that you are willing to do whatever is necessary to smooth the transition, such as completing a project you have under way or training a replacement.
- Don't boast about your new job. Boasting will only bring resentment from colleagues. Even if the sky is falling at your company and everybody is trying to bail out, others will be jealous of the fact that you found a good job.

STRESS: A HEIGHTENED CONCERN IN THE 1990s

Stress has always been an inescapable part of modern-day life, but the workplace environment of the 1990s promises to intensify those strains. Corporate upheavals, cost-cutting, fiercer competition, spreading computerization, heavier workloads, and clogged promotion ladders are magnifying tensions and multiplying the sources of stress.

Corporate mergers and downsizing have left both workers and their bosses anxious about the security of their jobs. Even survivors of cutbacks are worried about whether their jobs might be sacrificed in the next cost-cutting effort or rendered obsolete by technology or foreign competition.

Burnout has been a problem in business for years, but the pressure-cooker environment now facing managers is likely to increase the risks. Competition is fiercer. Decisions have to be made faster. Issues confronting managers are more complex and technical. Promotions are harder to come by. And staff cutbacks have left managers working harder and longer than ever to pick up the workload left by those who were laid off. Weary from the enormous workloads and with little time to recharge, they have trouble getting inspired for the next project. And cellular phones have made it impossible for executives ever to escape completely from the tumult.

With companies forced to dip further down into the labor pool to find workers, many supervisors may soon suffer from the kind of stress factors usually found only in Third World countries where managers are forced to cope with workers who lack the skills and education needed for the job.

Computerization of the workplace is also breeding new sources of stress. While computers can eliminate tedious tasks and make jobs more interesting and challenging, they also can increase the complexity and number of tasks confronting workers, speed up the pace at which the work has to be done, and give employers new ways to increase surveillance of workers.

As computer-based communications networks proliferate, managers and professionals may find themselves suffering from information overload, forced to sift through more memos, more documents, and more data to get at what is relevant. Many will no longer have secretaries to help. Instead they will need to draft their own documents, sort through electronic mail directories for their memos, and rely on voice mail systems to answer their phone and take messages.

Computerization is also speeding up the work process and placing greater demands on people to get things done sooner. The proliferation of fax machines, for instance, has redefined the concept of timely response. With the capability of transmitting documents in seconds, clients now expect immediate responses as well.

Computer monitoring is another source of increasing tension. Employers can now use the employee's own computer terminal to spy on him. Supervisors can monitor every minute of a worker's time. Computers can be set to record how many keystrokes a keypunch operator types each minute and how long the machine was idle. Electronic cash registers can be set to record the number of transactions a cashier handles each hour.

For the growing numbers of women entering the labor force, the strains are compounded as they struggle with the stresses of their job and the responsibilities of raising children and, increasingly, caring for an aging parent.

More and more companies are offering stress-management programs to improve their employees' well-being and reduce the toll that stress can take on the bottom line. Employee stress can lead to increased medical costs, higher absenteeism, lower productivity, and higher turnover. For individuals, stress can not only lead to unhappiness and fatigue but also to more serious physical problems, including ulcers and heart disease.

One way to ease the stress arising from job insecurity is to develop skills that will make you indispensable, or marketable elsewhere. Knowing that you will always be able to find a good job in your profession is a better form of security than any you could ever get from a single employer. Another is to become financially secure so that if worse comes to worst you won't need to worry that your family will be in financial trouble. That is why at least a six-month reserve is so important. Knowing that you will be able to pay the bills no matter what happens should be a source of comfort.

Building a nest egg for emergencies should be every household's first financial priority. If you don't have such a reserve, budget for it immediately. You never know when an emergency will arise. Do whatever is necessary to build the fund quickly. When you sit down to pay your bills each month, write a check to your savings account; pretend it's just another big expense. If you lack the discipline to do something like that, have your credit union withhold 10 percent of each paycheck until you build a big enough reserve. If you can't afford 10 percent, try 5 percent. If you can't afford 5 percent, look for ways to cut back on expenses. You don't have to become a monk, but most everyone should be able to find a way to save some money. Take a less lavish vacation. Buy a less expensive car or keep your car a year or two longer. Dine out less often. Buy more thoughtful—but less expensive—gifts for friends and relatives. And if the urge strikes to go impulse-shopping on a Saturday afternoon, take in a matinee movie instead.

Your emergency funds should be kept in safe, liquid investments that you can rely on in case of emergency, such as money-market funds, Treasury bills, bank accounts, or other short-term investments. Don't put your emergency funds in long-term investments or riskier ventures. If an emergency arises, you will need to get at the money quickly. If you invest the funds in stocks and the market happens to be down when the emergency arises, you'll be forced to sell at a loss.

FLEX-TIME: WHEN BEING LATE TO WORK IS NO LONGER A CRIME

The traditional nine-to-five workday is rapidly withering away. In an effort to help workers balance family needs with their jobs and to help alleviate rush-hour congestion, a growing number of companies are introducing flexible work schedules, giving employees the freedom to set their own hours—within limits.

By some estimates, about one in four employers already offers some form of "flex-time," and the policy is certain to spread rapidly to other companies in the 1990s as growing numbers of women with small children or elderly parents to care for enter the labor force and as commuting becomes an even bigger problem.

How much leeway employees have in setting their work hours varies widely from company to company. IBM employees can adjust their schedules to start work up to an hour earlier or an hour later than normal.

Equifax, Inc. allows many workers the freedom to put in their 7½ hours anytime between 7:30 A.M. and 6:30 P.M. At some other companies, employees are allowed to put in their forty hours for the week by working three- or four-day weeks.

Flex-time has not only created happier workers but also increased productivity. Tardiness and absenteeism have been reduced since workers can now adjust their schedules to accommodate what had previously caused them to arrive late or take a day off. Flex-time also has allowed some businesses to expand their customer-service hours since some of their workers come in earlier than normal and some stay later than normal.

Flex-time doesn't fit the demands of every organization. Some operations demand workers be together during fixed hours. It's hard for a small office operation to run smoothly if a receptionist is allowed to come in two hours after the doors open or if the secretary doesn't arrive until well after the boss begins work.

Most companies insist that choosing a flexible schedule won't hurt careers. But before taking advantage of a flex-time arrangement make sure that the company culture is in tune with the written policy. Attitudes don't always run in sync with new policies, and your standing may be hurt if supervisors still cling to the traditional standards for measuring commitment. Many companies are trying to get supervisors to be more supportive of these new policies and more sensitive to the family needs of employees.

JOB-SHARING: ONE JOB, TWO PEOPLE

Job-sharing, where two people working half-time share one full-time position, is a small but growing phenomenon in the workplace as more women opt for part-time work commitments and as labor shortages force some employers to make accommodations.

In a job-sharing arrangement, two people share the responsibilities and duties of a single job. In some arrangements, one person works mornings, the other afternoons. In other cases, each worker may put in 2.5 days a week, work alternate weeks, or even alternate quarters.

Job-sharing gives employees a way of meeting child-care or elderly-care commitments without dropping out of the work force or leaving the company for a part-time job elsewhere.

One recent survey showed job-sharing programs were offered by 16 percent of American companies, including such well-known names as Levi Strauss & Company and Quaker Oats. During the last recession, some companies implemented job-sharing arrangements as a way to avoid massive layoffs.

More employers may be a bit more open to the idea of job-sharing, given all the recent publicity about it, but few encourage job-sharing. Most companies don't like job-sharing because it can mean two benefits packages, two desks, two phones, the time and expense of training an extra worker, and the fear that if they give the nod in one situation a flock of employees will be knocking on their door demanding the same.

For employees, job-sharing means reduced salaries and sometimes reduced benefits. Part-time commitments may also reduce your standing at the company and diminish your prospects for advancement.

There is also the risk that the person who is sharing your job may want to become full-time, in which case you could end up losing your part-time job.

Nonetheless, job-sharing appears an attractive option when compared to the alternatives of leaving a company you like for a part-time job elsewhere or dropping out of the labor force altogether.

Selling Your Employer on a Job-Sharing Arrangement

Trying to sell your boss on a job-sharing arrangement isn't easy, but it's likely to be easier with your current employer than with one who doesn't know your work. Your employer knows your talents and commitments and perhaps those of the person with whom you'll be sharing the job. Following are some tips on how to go about it.

- Find out if your company has a formal policy on job-sharing. If so, you're halfway there.
- Find out if anyone else at the company has made a similar arrangement. If so, find out what it took.
- Prepare a written proposal so that your employer can see in detail how the job-sharing arrangement would actually work.
- Explain how the company would benefit from the arrangement and how it won't cost them much, if anything, more. Figure out how you can split the salary and, if necessary, how benefits can be divided. For instance, if your spouse has a health insurance policy that can cover you, you could agree to give up your health benefits in exchange for some benefit that your job-sharing partner is willing to give up. Some companies are generous and don't reduce the basic benefits of job-sharing employees.

- Instead of each of you working 2.5 days a week or the equivalent, you might propose working three days a week each, giving the company an extra day for the same salary. The day on which you both work is used partly to brief the other on what's going on and what needs to be done.
- Point out that two people can be more productive than one.
- Point out that no longer will the company be left out in the cold on vacations. The job would be done by the other worker, at least on a half-time basis.
- If you can't get a job-sharing arrangement, there may be alternatives that can help accommodate your outside needs, such as flexible work hours, personal leaves, parental leaves, and part-time work.

THE SHORTENING WORK WEEK

The traditional forty-hour work week is already a thing of the past for most Americans. It's now closer to thirty-five hours, and dropping.

But don't start making plans for a lot of extra hours of leisure time in the near future because there is no productivity miracle in sight that would allow for a much further shortening of the work week by the turn of the century without a decline in the standard of living. Nor is there any move afoot to make a less-than-forty-hour work week the official standard.

Shrinking work weeks have not been the result of any wondrous boost in productivity of the American work force. Rather, the shorter average work week is due largely to the economy's increasing shift toward service businesses, which traditionally tend to have shorter work weeks than manufacturing and which tend to have more people working part-time.

In the retail and wholesale business, for example, the average work week is only 31 hours. In the finance, insurance, and real estate sectors, the average is about 36 hours.

As a result, the average work week for people working in the private sector (not counting farmers) has shrunk from 40 hours in 1948 to an estimated 34.7 hours in 1989. By the turn of the century, economists at the WEFA Group predict that the average work week will be about 33 hours.

Even if the forty-hour week remains the official standard, the move to fewer hours in most industries could lead to legislative reforms of worker benefits. If full-time workers are putting in only thirty or thirty-five hours, companies will have a harder time justifying giving part-time workers fewer fringe benefits. The Bureau of Labor Statistics considers thirty-five hours a week the official boundary between full- and part-time employment.

GOING TO WORK BY STAYING HOME

Linked to the outside world by personal computers, facsimile machines, multiline telephones, and other electronic gadgetry, millions of Americans are going to work these days by staying at home.

Spare bedrooms, dens, basements, garages, attics, and kitchen tables are becoming the workplace for a rapidly growing number of people who use their home as their primary base of operations for full-time jobs, a place to run a sideline business, or, for executives and professionals, a refuge to which they bring work home at night.

By one estimate, more than 26 million Americans now work at least part-time out of their homes, and their numbers should continue to swell in the 1990s as more people seek to balance work with family responsibilities, and as more employers accommodate the trend. Such leading corporate giants as IBM, Pacific Bell, and J. C. Penney have programs allowing some workers to do their jobs at home.

It is an ironic twist in the nation's economic evolution that the twentieth century began with the flight of workers from homes to urban factories, and is ending with millions of jobs being shifted back to the home front.

The work-at-home movement not only presents a new alternative for workers, but also a potential way to help ease growing labor shortages and traffic congestion. The movement also holds important implications for the real estate industry, because every home-based business reduces the demand for office space. In addition, local zoning officials will increasingly face the thorny issue of how to balance the competing demands of home-based workers with the complaints of neighbors who don't like the extra traffic that certain types of home businesses generate. Home offices also represent a fast-growing market for makers and sellers of computers and other office equipment.

The Forces Behind the Home-Office Boom

The work-at-home movement is a reflection of the changing nature of work, technological advances, demographics, and social trends.

Many white-collar, technical, professional, and clerical office jobs require little face-to-face contact or teamwork in an office setting. And with advances in computer and telecommunications technology, it no longer matters whether these workers are sitting in an office down the hall or electronically linked from a remote mountaintop cabin in Colorado. Such sophisticated office electronics, once affordable only by larger businesses, have dropped into the price range of a growing number of individuals.

But technology is only accommodating the movement to home offices, not driving it. There are several more fundamental forces at play.

- The number of women entering the labor force is increasing, and working at home provides a way to balance their careers with child-rearing obligations. Working at home is increasingly an option for women during maternity leave.
- As elderly care becomes a burden to a rapidly growing number of workers, home offices will become a solution for some of those who need to stay close to home.
- Many of the fastest-growing occupations of the 1990s are the ones best suited to work at home, including computer programming, consulting, accounting, engineering, sales, public relations, and investment management.
- The explosion in entrepreneurial activity, which is frequently home-spun, is another factor. Entrepreneurs often find that setting up shop in their refurbished basement or garage is an affordable way to launch a small business. Silicon Valley is full of success stories about companies, such as Apple Computer, whose fledgling beginnings were in someone's garage.
- Growing traffic congestion will lead more people to try to avoid going to the office at all, or at least to work part-time at home, in order to avoid the rush-hour snarls.
- Government is helping accommodate the home-office trend by easing restrictions on home-based work. Despite fierce opposition from labor unions concerned about the potential for exploitation, the government recently lifted a forty-seven-year-old ban on manufacturing many apparel items at home, including mittens and gloves, embroidery, buttons and buckles, handkerchiefs, and some jewelry.
- Cutbacks in the management ranks have left survivors with heavier workloads, forcing executives to take more work home at night.
- Employer attitudes toward working at home are gradually changing, if slowly. For corporations, permitting work at home is one way to accommodate their employees' child-care and elderly-care needs

without having to resort to subsidies or pay for the cost of private day care, or even risk losing the employees. It is also a way of recruiting workers who otherwise wouldn't be available to work, such as mothers of small children. J. C. Penney, for instance, recruited home-based workers to help handle mail orders. Technology permits phone orders to be diverted to employees at home. Control Data Corporation and Metropolitan Life launched programs to help disabled workers. At Pacific Bell, as many as one thousand employees are taking advantage of a program that allows them to work at home when their tasks permit it. IBM recently announced a work-at-home program to accommodate certain employees on leave who want to work part-time but can't make it into the office regularly. The state of California has a pilot "telecommuting" project with about 150 government employees trained to work at home.

In all, more than five hundred corporations have programs permitting some work to be done at home by employees, according to LINK Resources Corporation, a market research and consulting firm that surveys the trend each year.

Employers also see home offices as a way to trim overhead costs— saving on office space and other amenities—and often labor costs. Many home-based workers, particularly those working on a piece-rate basis, are paid less and receive fewer fringe benefits than their colleagues at the office. When a job moves from the office to the home, companies will sometimes redesignate the worker's status from full-time to part-time or independent contractor. Employees in those classifications usually aren't eligible for the same benefits as full-time workers.

Home offices also provide a quick and inexpensive way to establish a business presence in new markets. A New York firm can set up a regional sales office in Los Angeles overnight simply by hiring someone willing to work out of his or her home. No need to lease downtown office space at $30 a square foot or spend thousands of dollars furnishing it. Some newspapers seeking to establish news bureaus in other cities are locating them right in the reporter's home rather than in an office, a cheaper alternative and often a preference of reporters who find they can get a larger home or apartment at the newspaper's expense by stuffing a few file cabinets and electronic paraphernalia into a spare bedroom.

What has encouraged some companies is the discovery that telecommuters tend to put in more hours than they did at the office and are more productive. Their quality and quantity tend to be better, according to some studies.

While millions more Americans could find themselves working at home in the 1990s, it's not likely that there will be any wholesale shift of jobs from the office to the home, leaving downtown office buildings half empty.

Most of those with home offices work at home only part of the time, spending the rest of their work week in a conventional office setting. And that is where most of the recent growth has been, as well. The annual survey by LINK Resources estimated a total of 26.6 million home offices in 1989, but only 6.7 million of them were used on a full-time basis. Of these full-time users, 3.9 million were self-employed workers,

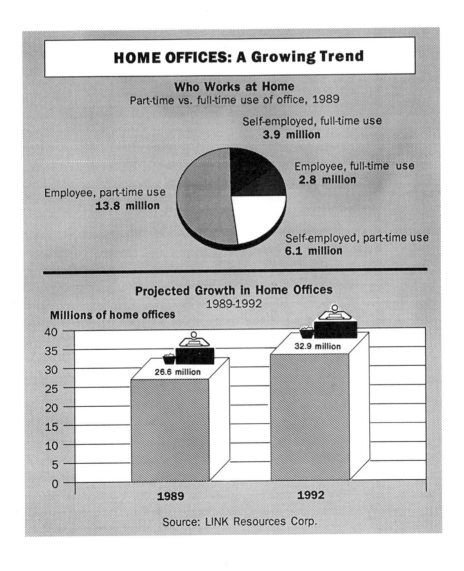

HOME OFFICES: A Growing Trend

Who Works at Home
Part-time vs. full-time use of office, 1989

Self-employed, full-time use
3.9 million

Employee, full-time use
2.8 million

Employee, part-time use
13.8 million

Self-employed, part-time use
6.1 million

Projected Growth in Home Offices
1989-1992

Millions of home offices

26.6 million

32.9 million

1989 **1992**

Source: LINK Resources Corp.

and 2.8 million were corporate employees. The other 19.9 million persons with home offices (6.1 million self-employed and 13.8 million employees) worked out of their home offices only part-time.

The move to greater full-time use of home offices is likely to be slow because corporate culture is slow to accept the idea of having employees out of immediate and visible reach. Workers are not beating down their boss's door either for a chance to work at home. Many people don't like the idea of being stuck at home day and night, preferring to share in the social and intellectual stimulation of a group office setting.

Nonetheless, millions more home offices will continue to spring up in neighborhoods across the country in the 1990s. LINK Resources predicts there will be 32.9 million home offices in 1992.

The Advantages of Working at Home

For working mothers, as well as the growing number of fathers who are taking on child-care responsibilities, working at home is one way to maintain a career while rearing young children; the same is true for those caring for an elderly parent. Working at home usually permits flexible scheduling. So you can take time out to be with your children, providing a richer and fuller relationship with them than if they were placed in a day-care center.

Others find the flexible schedule a liberating experience, allowing them to sandwich work around other pursuits, such as going to school.

If you plan to start a business, using your home as a base of operations is a low-overhead way to launch it. A variety of businesses are well suited for home-based operations, including child care, secretarial services, sales, consulting, investment management, free-lance writing, painting, tutoring, engineering, answering services, designing, accounting, sewing, research, photography, catering, and others.

For professionals, a home office can mean unparalleled opportunity to concentrate on the work at hand without all the distractions common in traditional office settings—no colleagues coming over to your desk to interrupt with the latest office gossip.

Working at home also means an end to the time, the expense, and the aggravation of commuting, which promises to be of increasing anguish and expense in the 1990s as traffic congestion worsens. All you need do is walk a few steps from your breakfast table to your office desk.

Working at home can also cut down on some other expenses, including the considerable cost of child care. Clothing costs can also be reduced since you no longer need to "dress for success" every day when you're at home and out of sight of customers, clients, bosses, and colleagues.

The Drawbacks of Working at Home

Etched in the minds of many who yearn for the chance to work at home is the image of a well-tanned Wall Street money manager lounging by his pool, tapping on a computer terminal linked to stock exchanges around the world. This picture has, in fact, appeared more than once in magazines.

But working at home is not always so paradisiacal. For many people, the idea of working at home is a recipe for boredom, cabin fever, and social and intellectual isolation. It's the same kind of feeling they get after being stuck home sick for a few days.

Many of those who have tried working at home for a while begin to miss the intellectual stimulation, and the daily interaction with coworkers that plays such an important role in the social lives of Americans.

What seems to be a preference of many home workers is the option to mix working at home with work at the office. Others want the option to return to work full-time at the office in the future.

Working at home isn't necessarily the solution to child care either, as many women have discovered. Younger children don't fully understand the concept of work and why you can't devote all your time to them since you're home. As a result, many women working at home either wind up getting child-care help or saving their work for times when the other spouse is home or when the child is sleeping. Even if your children are of school age, don't count on having peace and quiet year-round. They'll still be around on holidays, when they're home sick, and all summer long.

Indeed, home offices can lead to tensions in family life. An office takes away a room in the home that might be used for something else by other members of the family, like a separate bedroom for your teenagers. They may also resent the idea that your home office makes it difficult to live a normal life at home while you're working or parading clients through the living room.

Trying to draw a clean line between work and home life is not easy. Family and friends may feel that since you're home all day you have the flexibility to do some favors for them. A neighbor may ask you to accept a delivery or even baby-sit for a little while. A spouse may ask you to do the shopping or pick up the laundry.

If you're running a business, projecting a professional image is tougher with a home office. Bear in mind that many businesses pay premium prices to have their offices located in a prestigious building with a prestigious address. Operating out of a home doesn't project the same kind of prestige or stability. And home is far from an ideal place to bring customers and clients.

For professionals, working at home usually leaves them out of the promotion pipeline. People who work at home normally aren't considered to have the same kind of commitment and management skills as the faithful who show up at the office every day.

Some people have a more fundamental problem. They don't have the self-discipline to work as well at home. They need the support team of colleagues, the deadline pressures of a fixed schedule, supervisors watching over them, and protection from the various distractions of home life, such as TV soap operas and unfinished household chores.

For others, a home office poses the danger of work becoming obsessive. With your work site so close at hand, it's hard to escape the pressures of mounting paperwork or unfinished projects. It is a workaholic's paradise.

While you may save on commuting, dry cleaning, and perhaps even child-care expenses, there is another side to the balance sheet. Home workers usually have to pay for their own office furnishings, and sometimes even their own computer terminals. Working at home also means higher utility bills since you wouldn't use as much electricity or need as much heat or air conditioning if you were away from home all day. In addition, home workers sometimes get stuck footing the bill for business calls made from home, and they usually end up getting paid less than their peers at the office. And while the tax deductions for home offices can be lucrative they are not always easy to obtain.

TIPS FOR RUNNING A HOME OFFICE

Meet Your Clients Elsewhere: Try not to meet your clients at home. It's not a businesslike setting and it can invade your family's privacy. Meet your clients at their offices; it will be more convenient for them. Another option is to meet them for lunch or cocktails. If your business entails frequent client meetings, consider joining a private club in the city that has quiet areas for business meetings.

Zoning: Before you start a home-based business, find out whether your business is permitted under the local zoning laws. If it's not, find out how you might qualify for a variance or exception to the ordinance. If your business is permitted, keep in mind that zoning laws can be changed. If your business starts to bring lots of customers and delivery trucks to your house all day, your neighbors would have good reason to take their complaints to the local zoning board. So it's best to keep a low profile and good relations with your neighbors—especially if your home isn't zoned for business. Zoning officers don't usually have the time to prowl around for unzoned home offices that aren't bothering anybody. But beware that some localities have nabbed people for zoning violations when they applied for a business license at town hall with a home address listed.

Revise Homeowner's Insurance: Get your homeowner's policy revised to provide adequate coverage for your home business. Special riders are usually required to cover fully your computer and other business equipment. Personal liability coverage usually needs to be expanded as well, in case a client or business associate slips on your steps. Most basic homeowner's policies exempt accidents related to your business.

Choosing an Address: Think twice before using your home address for business. Some people don't want their customers and clients to know they're working out of their home. They want to maintain a professional image. Another reason for using a different address is to protect your family's privacy. You don't want a disgruntled customer knocking on your door at midnight. A post-office box is the most common solution.

In some cities, you can contract with a private mail service (often an adjunct of a telephone answering service). You use their address as your mailing address and the firm forwards your mail to your home.

If you do decide to use your home address and you live in an apartment, consider listing your apartment number as a "suite" number to project a more professional image (e.g., "Suite 12" instead of "Apt. 12.").

Stationery: An inexpensive way to enhance your business image is to spend some extra money at a professional printer for well-designed stationery and business cards.

A Second Phone Line: Unless you are assured of uninterrupted use of your home phone, get a separate line for your business. If there are other family members hanging around the house during business hours, a single line is bound to lead to embarrassing situations and family squabbles. With a separate line, you won't have to worry about your business callers being greeted by your four-year-old child or always getting a busy signal because your teenager spends countless hours chatting with friends. The cost of adding a second line is a relatively small price to pay for keeping up a professional image for your business, as well as keeping peace with your family.

Phone companies generally require you to have a business line, which can cost a bit more than residential service. But you'll be entitled to have your business listed in the Yellow Pages.

A second line may also be needed if you frequently tie up your phone with facsimile transmissions or spend a lot of time communicating with a modem to your company's computer or outside databases. Adding a second line will assure that you'll have at least one line free for customer or client calls. The extra cost of a second line will be paid for many times over when customers can get through to you for a sale.

If you can get by with a single line, adding "call waiting" will allow you to accept an incoming phone call while you're on the line with someone else. That will prevent customers from being frustrated by a busy signal. However, if you use the line for facsimile transmissions or computing with a modem, call waiting will disrupt your transmission.

If you stick with one phone line, make sure other family members are trained how to answer during business hours. It will prevent embarrassing situations.

Answering Machines: Buy an answering machine or contract with an answering service if you plan to be away from your office during the day. Clients may get tired of trying to get hold of you if there's no answer. For the most flexibility, get an answering machine that is accessible from a remote phone. So if you're traveling about town for a few hours, you won't have to wait hours to get your messages and your clients won't have to wait hours to hear back from you. Check your messages frequently.

An answering service is more expensive but the advantage is in having a real person answer your phone. When shopping around for a service, make sure it has enough staff to answer your phone promptly. Not all do.

Another option is to subscribe to "voice mail" service, which many local phone companies are starting to offer. With voice mail, you can instruct the phone company's computer to answer your calls using your own prerecorded message. The phone company then makes a digital recording of any incoming messages. What the phone company will do that an answering machine can't is give you a clue as to who called in but didn't leave a message; the phone company records the time of the call and the caller's telephone number.

Another new telephone company service that may be of value for home-office workers who want some capability to screen incoming calls is "caller identification." This service lets you know who might be calling before you pick up the phone. When your phone rings, caller ID will show the telephone number of the caller on a small liquid-crystal display. Some newer phones have LCD screens built in; otherwise, you can rent an attachment from the phone company. This service will help you screen out unwanted callers if you're busy on a project.

If you need to be in constant contact with your clients, consider a pocket paging service or a cellular phone.

Drawing the Line: From the start, make sure it's clear to everyone in your household as well as to friends and neighbors that work is work and that you need to be as free from distraction as you would be at the office. Set a firm work schedule and insist that nothing else interfere. Just because you're working at home doesn't mean that you're available to do household chores or walk the neighbor's dog.

Set a Schedule: To avoid having your work spill too much into your family life, set business hours and then try to stick by them. When your office and home are under the same roof, it's especially important to establish a regular routine so that you and your family know when you are working and when you are "home."

Facsimile Machines: Fax machines have recently become an essential tool of business. As a rule of thumb, if you need to send documents quickly to clients at least once a week, or if you need to receive documents from them, it pays to buy a fax. They start at under $500. But if you only need to send an occasional fax, you can get by without a machine by taking your documents down to your local print shop, private mail service, or other outlets that now offer fax services at relatively low cost, usually $3 for the first two pages plus the cost of the telephone call. You can also receive transmitted documents through these services, but it's not convenient and it's not a way to impress your clients. (For more on fax machines, see chapter 22, Consumer's Guide to Personal Electronics in the 1990s.)

Tax Deductions for Your Home Office

If you qualify, a home office can be a lucrative reservoir for tax deductions. Homeowners can claim deductions for depreciation, utilities, and other operating expenses attributable to that part of the house. Renters get to deduct a proportionate amount of rent. But the government makes it hard for most of the 26 million Americans with home offices to qualify.

Employees hardly ever qualify for home-office deductions unless they work exclusively at home or run a sideline business out of their home. Self-employed people don't have much trouble qualifying so long as their primary base of operations is their home.

There are several tests to pass. First, your home office has to be used "regularly and exclusively" for business. The office doesn't have to be a separate room. It can be a corner of a studio apartment or even a corner of your bedroom. But whatever space is designated as your home office, no other use can be made of it. If you bake pies for a living, you can't claim your kitchen as your home office since you also use the kitchen to cook meals for your family. One exception to the exclusivity rule is the use of your home for a child-care business.

Second, your office has to be your "principal place of business" or a place to "meet or deal" with customers or clients. Employees who work part-time out of their home have a tough time meeting the principal-place-of-business test because their desk at their employer's office is usually considered their principal place of business. Most employees can't pass the meeting-or-dealing test either because it's rare that employees have clients or customers coming over to their house. Talking to them on the phone from your home office isn't sufficient to pass the test, according to court rulings.

Use of your home office also has to be for the convenience of your employer. But even if your boss requires it, bringing paperwork home at night from your downtown office is probably not going to get you a home-office deduction because you won't pass the other tests.

Employees who run a sideline business out of their home, however, can qualify for home-office deductions because you are allowed to have a principal place of business for each job. So if you teach school during the day and moonlight as a free-lance computer programmer, you can claim your home office as the principal place of business for your sideline computer business. But if you own a computer shop downtown and use your home office to work on paperwork related to the computer shop at night, you probably won't be entitled to a home-office deduction because your downtown computer shop is considered your principal place of business.

In a few cases, the courts have shown mercy in applying the principal-place-of-business test. In one case, some musicians with the Metropolitan Opera contended they should be allowed home-office deductions because they spent more time practicing at home than they did performing at Lincoln Center. A federal appeals court agreed. The court also agreed with a college professor who contended that he spent 80 percent of his time researching and writing at home and that his office at the university wasn't suitable.

Home Offices Are a Growing Market

Office-product firms will find a burgeoning multibillion-dollar market in home offices. It should be one of the fastest growing markets for manufacturers and sellers of personal computers, fax machines, personal copiers, and other office supplies. In 1988 LINK Resources estimated the size of the market at $5.7 billion.

Major companies are already targeting the market with special products and marketing efforts. Long-distance telephone companies are offering budget-priced "800" phone services in hopes of capturing the home-business market. Sharp, Panasonic, and Canon have formed home-office divisions; and Scholastic Inc.'s *Family Computing* magazine changed its name to *Home Office Computing*.

Office-supply firms can tap into the market by stocking lower-cost equipment and office furniture that fits the smaller space requirements of home offices.

WHAT KIND OF WAGE INCREASES CAN BE EXPECTED IN THE 1990s

Even as companies struggle to contain costs in a world growing ever more competitive, employers will be under pressure to pay higher wages in order to attract and retain enough good workers in the face of a tighter labor market.

Nowhere are the signs of wage pressures more visible than in the fast-food industry. Scrounging to hire enough workers from a shrinking pool of younger people, fast-food chains are advertising starting salaries far in excess of the minimum wage plus an array of fringe benefits—a compensation package unheard of in the industry until recently.

Other industries, such as health care and computers, are facing similar pressures, bidding up wages in order to lure nurses, computer programmers, and other skilled workers in short supply.

As unemployment continues to decline, wages are expected to rise about 6 percent a year during the 1990s, according to the WEFA Group, a leading economic-forecasting firm. That is slightly ahead of inflation and well ahead of the pace of wage increases in the mid-1980s.

In an earlier era, labor shortages of the magnitude expected in the 1990s would lead to forecasts of much larger wage hikes. But this is clearly a different age. The bargaining power of American workers is diminishing.

Global competition has put a lid on what American workers, whether

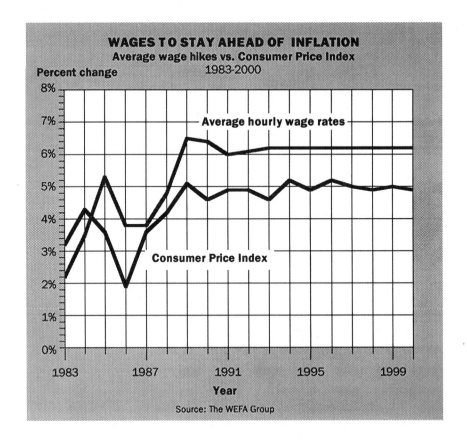

union or nonunion, can ask for without threatening their own jobs. Wages of U.S. workers are now influenced more by what goes on in Tokyo or Seoul or Bonn than at the bargaining table in Detroit or New York or Pittsburgh. And wage competition from foreign countries will intensify in the 1990s as the working-age population in developing countries mushrooms. Between 1985 and 2000, according to the Hudson Institute, there will be 600 million new job seekers in the global labor market.

With vivid memories of the cutbacks of the 1980s, workers themselves have become more gun-shy about pressing their wage demands too far. Even in the management ranks, few executives are stomping into their boss's office to demand a big increase in pay. After seeing their contemporaries axed in the recent downsizing push, managers fear that the answer might be more than no.

For all the restraint and cost-cutting, many companies are discovering that the wages they pay are still too high to remain competitive. To reduce labor costs further, they are investing heavily in laborsaving technology. A fast-growing number of companies are also implementing innovative compensation schemes that make wage increases more contingent on how the company fares.

THE ANNUAL RAISE: A VANISHING EXPECTATION

The annual raise, long considered a natural entitlement, is rapidly being replaced—at least, in part—by one-shot bonuses and other pay schemes linked to the fates and fortunes of the company. In an era when competitive pressures are driving employers to find new ways to cut costs and enhance productivity, the trend toward alternative pay schemes is spreading like wildfire.

By limiting across-the-board wage increases and substituting pay schemes based on profits or individual or group performance, corporations find that they not only can pare one of their biggest fixed expenses but also help motivate employees and improve productivity. Big Japanese companies routinely employ this kind of incentive pay system. Bonuses often account for as much of 40 percent of a Japanese worker's pay.

For American employees, these new compensation strategies can help put their own company in a better competitive position, and to that extent they enhance the workers' own fortunes and job security. Middle-level managers and rank-and-file workers get to share in the improving fortunes of the company, just as top executives have long been able to do through stock options and performance bonuses.

But these new pay schemes also mean greater uncertainty for employees—the kind of uncertainty that salesmen have long faced in working on a salary-plus-commission basis. No longer can employees count on steadily rising wages. And even when their pay does go up, these new pay schemes don't always affect other elements of an employee's compensation packages in the same way that traditional pay raises do.

One-Shot Bonus: An example is the lump-sum cash bonus, offered by a growing number of companies in lieu of annual raises or merit increases. These one-shot payments, almost unheard of a decade ago, are now widespread.

Companies like them because they don't raise the employee's base pay for purposes of computing other compensation ingredients, such as vacation pay, overtime, and some fringe and pension benefits.

A Piece of the Profits: There are a variety of ways employers are linking compensation to the fortunes of the company. Profit-sharing plans are the most common, and have been around many companies for years. Employees get a piece of the profits sometimes in the form of a year-end cash bonus. In most cases, however, the employee's share of profits is held in trust by the company until the employee retires or leaves the firm.

A more limited version of profit sharing, known as "gain sharing," is being considered by a growing number of companies. With gain sharing, employees get only that share of the profits resulting from improvements in productivity. In other words, if a company making raincoats had a good year just because it rained a lot everywhere, employees wouldn't be entitled to any of the profits under gain-sharing. But if profits soared because everybody worked harder and faster to turn out more and better-quality raincoats, employees would share in the gains because it was their extra effort that helped add to the bottom line.

Many of the new pay schemes base bonuses on group or individual performance, rather than the overall profitability of the company. At the Du Pont Company, for instance, an incentive pay plan was recently implemented in its fiber department, where workers will get more or less than everyone else at the company, depending on how profitable the department is. This is how the plan works: Fiber-department employees will get smaller raises each year than employees elsewhere in the company, so that by the end of a five-year phase-in, the base pay of fiber-department employees will be 6 percent less than everyone else's. If the department meets its annual profit goals, employees get that 6 percent back. If fiber-department profits surge and exceed 150 percent of the goal, they will get a bonus that will put them 12 percent above others in the company. However, if profits fall short of their department's goal, employees will find their pay lagging behind everyone else's pay.

Workers as Part-Owners: Employee ownership of their company's stock has exploded since 1974, when Congress passed legislation allowing tax deductions for corporations that buy stock for their workers through Employee Stock Ownership Plans. The Labor Department estimates that more than 30 percent of workers in large and medium-sized corporations are now covered by ESOPs. In recent years, some ESOPs were set up in exchange for pay concessions from workers. In other cases, ESOPs were made a part of the company's employee retirement plan with the hope of spurring productivity and greater loyalty among workers. If employees are made part-owners of the company through stock ownership, they have a new incentive to help the company increase the bottom line. Indeed, studies have found instances where productivity skyrocketed 200 to 300 percent after an ESOP was in place.

Skill-Based Pay: As an incentive to encourage employees to learn a wide variety of skills, a small but growing number of companies is paying workers based on what they know. The more skills they master, the more they get paid. The goal is to create a more flexible work force in an era when constant adaptation to changing technology and markets is pivotal to corporate success.

Two-Tier Pay: A pay scheme implemented widely in the airline industry in recent years is the "two tier" pay system, where workers hired after a certain date get less than workers with more seniority.

Many employers and employees like the two-tier system because labor costs can be reduced without resorting to layoffs or asking senior workers to take a pay cut. Only new hires bear the brunt of the burden, like pledges at a fraternity house.

But pledge week doesn't last forever. As time goes on, workers on the lower pay tier are likely to grow resentful of a system that offers them much different rewards for the same work. There's little incentive built into the system for improving productivity.

That discontent will place unions in the thorny predicament of representing two classes of workers with very different goals in labor negotiations. Lower-tier workers will be pressing to get their wages up to the higher tier, while higher-tier workers, who tend to be older, will likely want negotiations to focus more on the issues of job security and pension benefits.

RELOCATION: PERSUADING EMPLOYEES TO PICK UP AND MOVE

At a time when the business environment demands ever greater flexibility and mobility, employees are growing more resistant to the idea of making a move for their company. And the dilemma will only get worse as the work force grows older and the number of two-earner couples increases.

Baby-boomers are approaching their forties and, after being footloose for the past fifteen to twenty years of their work life, now relish stability. They are raising families, are finally settled in communities, and have spouses with established careers of their own.

Even where relocation is the instant ticket to promotion, employees are increasingly telling their employers no and taking their chances. Many are refusing because relocating would mean disrupting their spouse's career. Gone are the days when wives didn't work and were always ready to follow their husbands wherever their jobs required. Today, many men on the corporate ladder have wives who are in the midst of climbing their own corporate ladder, becoming partners at law firms, tenured professors at colleges, or cultivating businesses of their own that have taken years to build up.

Even when a spouse is prepared to make a sacrifice, employees are balking at moves that threaten their current standard of living. Growing numbers of employees are refusing transfers to cities with high living costs, such as New York City, Los Angeles, Boston, and San Francisco. As a result, companies are being forced to entice them with bigger raises, cost-of-living payments, and help in financing their new home.

All of this comes at a time when promotion lines are clogged and relocating may be the only available ticket to advancement.

Employees should start thinking about the possibility of a transfer long before they get asked to move. Before you take a job, you should ask whether you're expected to relocate and what might be in store for you.

If relocation is a way of life at your firm, don't wait for your boss to come to you with your marching papers. Discuss your preferences with your superiors well in advance. If you put your bid in early, you may be able to get your choice of London or Paris rather than the company's new office in San Salvador.

WHAT TO CONSIDER IF YOU'RE ASKED TO MOVE

When your superiors ask you to relocate, whether to say yes or no depends on many factors, including how it will impact your family and how it will affect the rest of your career. Here are some of the questions to consider in making your decision.

- Is your spouse in a position to move?
- Would your spouse's career disruption be worse than the problems you would face if you turned down the transfer? Or would you be hurt more by turning down the transfer? Which decision will leave the family in better shape? Consider both the short-term and the long-range implications.
- Will your spouse be able to find a comparable job in the new location that will pay just as well? Or will the move result in a lower standard of living for your family? Will the company help the spouse find a job and help make up for any loss in income resulting from the move?
- How long will the assignment last?
- Will your career be better off by relocating? Does the move mean a promotion? What might be in line for you after the assignment? Is this move a path to bigger and better things? Or is it a dead end? Make sure the transfer is not an effort by the employer to move you out of the mainstream. Consider looking elsewhere if you are no longer on the promotion track.
- Is the transfer mandatory? If so, what other options do you have if you can't or don't want to make the move? Can you find a comparable job with another company in your current location? Can the employer be persuaded to change his mind based on your spouse's job situation? Can the move be postponed to give your spouse time to make other arrangements? Or could you turn down this transfer and accept a different assignment later that would be preferable to you and your family? Could you be transferred to a location where your spouse's company also has an opening?
- What is the cost of living in the new location? Will your company make up for any differential? Or will the move force you to accept a lower standard of living?
- If your spouse can't move, could you manage a long-distance marriage for a while in order to accept a short-term assignment? If so, would your employer be willing to pay for regular visits back home and the cost of maintaining two homes?
- Don't automatically shy away from foreign assignments. In the past, employees on the corporate ladder frequently viewed foreign assign-

ments as an obstacle to career advancement. They feared being for-
gotten by top management sitting continents away. But as business
becomes more international in scope, foreign experience is becoming
a valued asset for those who aspire to lead their companies in an age
of global markets. Before volunteering for a foreign post, find out
how colleagues fared after returning from overseas duty. Foreign
experience doesn't benefit careers at all companies.

NEGOTIATING A BETTER RELOCATION DEAL

When your marching orders come through, sound out other employees
who have been relocated to learn what kind of assistance they received
from the company for their move. Large corporations usually have standard relocation policies detailing what they'll pay and what they won't.
But many of them also leave room for negotiation. If they think enough
of you, they may be willing to negotiate almost anything reasonable to
keep you satisfied. What companies will automatically offer employees
may be much less than what they will provide if the employee specifically
asks for it. That's why you should sound out a few employees to see
what each of them was able to coax from the company. The expense of
moving your household goods is only the beginning. You will need much
more assistance from your company to compensate for the move. And
employers are providing it. On average, companies pay $35,000 to re-
locate an employee who owns a home.

Ask for a Raise: Moving time is a propitious time to ask for a raise. If
your move involves a promotion, a raise should be automatic. At the
least, you should ask for a big enough increase in salary to cover any
higher cost of living. Remember to consider any higher state and local
taxes you will be paying.

Helping Your Spouse Find Work: A growing number of companies have
formal programs for helping spouses find work in the new location. Typically, the firm contracts with an outplacement counselor. If the company
doesn't offer assistance for your spouse, impress upon them that this is
a big roadblock. If they still balk, think about how the company might
be able to help on an informal basis, like making a few phone calls to
some well-placed contacts in the local area about job leads. Larger firms
have all sorts of contacts. Those contacts may not have a job open in
their own firm, but they can still help provide leads to jobs elsewhere.

For instance, if your spouse is a real estate agent, your firm could contact the local broker it used to lease the office you'll be working in. If that broker doesn't have an opening, the broker may still be able to provide some tips about where an opening might exist.

Selling Your Home: If you own your home, the company should help you get the house sold one way or another. If you don't sell it yourself, most companies will either buy it from you or arrange for some third party to do it at the appraised market value. (Two appraisals are usually made to fix a price.) If you sell the home on your own, the company should pay brokerage fees. If your home was sold for less than what you paid for it, ask the company to make up the difference. After all, their job transfer is preventing you from waiting to sell until the housing market recovers.

Looking for a New Home: One or two company-paid house-hunting trips to your new job location is typical, as are temporary living expenses at the new location while you wait to move into your new home or continue your search for one.

Buying a New Home: Most companies pay closing costs on the new home, including points, attorney fees, etc. Some companies will also help you finance a down payment for the new house, through either an interest-free or low-interest loan. Also try to get the company to pay any difference in interest rates between your new and old mortgages.

Housing Differential: Housing costs have been climbing rapidly in many cities. So if you're lucky enough to have a low housing payment now, your relocation to a city with high home prices could send your monthly payments soaring. Ask your company for a mortgage differential. Be aware that most companies will pay the differential only for a few years. So if your new assignment is likely to be long-term, make sure the home you buy will still be affordable after the company stops subsidizing your monthly payments. If the company won't provide a mortgage differential, make sure the higher housing costs of your new location are reflected in your raise.

"Curtain Fee": Ask for a bonus or "curtain fee" to defray the incidental expenses of setting up a new household, such as draperies, new shelving, and new carpeting. Keep in mind that this curtain fee is subject to tax, so ask for an additional allowance to defray fully the extra federal, state, and local taxes you'll pay. The goal is to come out even on a move, not lose money.

Other Taxes: Whatever reimbursements you receive from your employer can do significant damage to your tax return. Employers are required to include all the reimbursements on your W-2 wage statement and all of it has to be declared as income on your tax return. While most of the income can be offset by claiming the moving expense deduction, you can still come up short. There are no limits on how much you can deduct for moving household goods and traveling to your new home, but all your other relocation expenses are limited to $3,000. And of that $3,000, no more than $1,500 can be deducted for house-hunting trips and temporary living expenses. If you were reimbursed for more than that, you'll end up paying taxes on it. What's more, if you don't itemize deductions you can't take advantage of the moving-expense deduction. So make sure your employer provides an additional reimbursement for any extra taxes incurred—including the tax you'll have to pay on the additional reimbursement.

Capital Gains Taxes: If you're moving to an area where housing prices are lower, you could run into a capital gains tax problem, which few companies will help mitigate. The federal income tax law allows you to defer capital gains tax on profits from the sale of your home so long as you buy another home within two years that costs at least as much. So if you're selling a $200,000 home in New York and find a comparable one for $80,000 in Phoenix, you may be delighted. But keep in mind you will have a capital gains tax to pay out of your profits.

LANDING ON YOUR FEET: IF YOU LOSE YOUR JOB

Getting laid off no longer carries the stigma it did in the days when executives and professionals felt the ax only if they embezzled a lot of money or were grossly incompetent. Massive layoffs of white-collar workers have become commonplace in an age of corporate belt-tightening and mergers. Below are some ways to handle matters should a pink slip arrive on your desk.

Stay in Control: If you've just been fired, your inclination is to lash out at anyone in sight who may have been the least bit responsible. That is a natural reaction, but one that will do you more harm than good (a few unkind words, even in the heat of passion, are enough to burn bridges). When your boss first calls you on the carpet, you won't be in an emotional state to negotiate anything rationally in terms of severance, references, or wrapping up your stay with the firm. Nor will you be prepared in terms of what to ask for. Request a follow-up meeting so you have a chance to cool down and think about what you want and need.

Outplacement Counseling: Ask for outplacement counseling. Most large corporations offer such counseling to fired managers. Outplacement counselors will help map out a game plan for you, help you put together a résumé, and help prepare you for job interviews.

Getting Letters of Reference: Ask your supervisors for letters of recommendation before you leave. Written references may be enough to satisfy the needs of some prospective employers. Even if they still want to talk to your former supervisors, written recommendations are not a wasted effort. Writing a recommendation letter helps fix in your supervisors' minds your positive contributions. Don't be afraid to give your supervisors a written outline of your accomplishments to help them in drafting the reference letter.

Ask for a Delay: Try to negotiate a delay in your departure date. Some companies will give employees, particularly those with long or distinguished service, extra time on the payroll to look for another job.

Get Your Act Together: Make sure you have your emotions under control before you start looking for another job. Contacting other companies while you're distraught or before you have your sales pitch polished could spoil your best prospects. Losing your job and then trying to find a new one is bound to be a traumatic experience. Even getting fired from a job you hate can be traumatic because it's a blow to your ego and throws a monkey wrench into your plans. But dwelling on your plight won't help overcome it. Understand that what happened to you is happening to a lot of other talented people. Then focus on the task at hand: finding a new job.

Job Hunting as a Full-Time Pursuit: Searching for a new job should be your full-time occupation. Don't spend time cleaning out the attic or playing golf every day. Discipline is crucial. Get up at your normal time and spend the full day on your job hunt.

THE COMPLETE FINANCIAL GUIDE TO THE 1990s

Health Insurance Coverage: Arrange to continue health insurance coverage under your company's plan so that you'll be protected in case of illness or injury between jobs. Under a recent change in the law, companies that employ twenty or more people are obliged to continue your group health coverage—if you want it—for at least eighteen months. You will have to pay the premiums. The company's obligation to continue group coverage was included in the Consolidated Omnibus Budget Reconciliation Act of 1986, commonly known among company benefits managers as COBRA. Before COBRA, the best option employees faced was to convert their group coverage to an individual policy. But group coverage is usually cheaper and more comprehensive than a conversion policy. So you'll get more for less by sticking with your employer's group plan under the COBRA provision. If your spouse works and has a company health plan, another possibility is to see whether you can be included under the plan. It may be cheaper than continuing your own policy. But make sure there won't be any gaps in coverage (such as for pre-existing conditions) for yourself or for the rest of your family if you discontinue your own policy. Also make sure that you can count on your spouse's policy for the duration of your job hunt. In other words, is your spouse's job secure? If there's any doubt, find out if your spouse would be able to continue coverage under COBRA if worse came to worst. If the spouse works for a company with fewer than twenty employees, the company would not be obliged to continue coverage.

Check Your Contacts: Call everyone you know to see if they've heard of any job openings or if they know someone else you could contact for a lead.

Consider Relocation: Decide whether you would be willing to relocate. If you expand your geographic horizons, your job opportunities widen.

Broaden Your Sights: Consider all your talents and interests and think about how far afield you would be willing to go. Widening your sights expands your opportunities. For example, if you are a radio announcer, would you be willing to work in programming or advertising sales? Or if you work for a clothing manufacturer selling apparel to department stores, consider the option of becoming a buyer for a department store.

Job Interviews: In job interviews, don't talk badly about your former employer. Such disparaging talk usually backfires and casts you as a disgruntled employee in the eyes of a prospective employer.

Don't Become Discouraged: Accept the idea that you're going to be told no time and again in your job hunt. Keep searching until you have a firm job offer. Don't stop when a company starts to show strong interest in you. No matter how close an offer seems, keep looking; all too often tentative prospects fall through. If you have sent out résumés and have additional job interviews lined up, you won't be so despondent if you get rejected. Other irons will still be in the fire.

3

THE NEW TECHNOLOGIES
OF THE 1990s

HOW COMPUTERS WILL CHANGE THE WORKPLACE AND YOUR HOME

However quickly computers have evolved and spread into the American workplace and home, the revolution has, in many respects, just begun.

Computers will get smaller, smarter, faster, and easier to use. They will spread into more homes, more offices, and more appliances. They will be used to make more decisions, automate more jobs, and make libraries full of information and entertainment instantly available at the touch of a key. Desktop computers will become as powerful as today's giant mainframe computers that fill air-conditioned rooms. And personal computer systems will contain enough storage capacity on a single disk to store a small home library.

The computer industry should continue to be one of the fastest-growing industries of the 1990s. But most analysts predict the rate of growth will be much slower than in the 1980s when computers first became common fixtures in the workplace. Software sales are expected to grow faster than computer hardware as users seek new applications for the systems already in place.

For many companies and individuals, computers have done little more than serve as glorified typewriters and financial calculators. But in the 1990s, computers will play a more central role.

Computers will increasingly be used to automate all phases of manufacturing. More and more products are being designed by engineers directly on computer screens instead of on drafting tables. Instructions can then be sent electronically to the factory floor, where computer-driven automated assembly lines will become more and more commonplace. Advances in computers have endowed a new generation of factory robots with the ability to handle many tasks with the dexterity of humans.

Computers are also being used to automate trading of some financial products, such as currency futures. Instead of humans waving their arms and shouting bids in trading pits, the new systems electronically match buyers and sellers on computer networks that can run twenty-four hours a day and be linked around the world. While the major financial exchanges are not likely to give up their floor trading activities any time soon, some of them do see computers offering a way to expand their trading to off-hours.

Even supermarkets are experimenting with automated checkout counters where customers scan their own products. The system's computers check to make sure that customers don't cheat, and then tote up their bill.

In the music world, computer synthesizers and "samplers" allow a keyboard player to replicate the sound of any instrument or even a symphony orchestra with uncanny precision, and are increasingly replacing dozens of musicians in recording studios and on the concert stage.

Computer disk drives with vastly expanded storage capacity are paving the way for a new medium to develop in the 1990s, combining video, sound, and text. Look up an article on President John F. Kennedy, and you can read about his life, see a picture of him, and hear a recording of his inaugural speech.

Computers will not just be sitting on desktops; already on the market are portable computers that let you take notes with an electronic pen, and hand-held models that can slip into your vest pocket. Computer power will also be infused into more and more appliances to make them smarter, such as VCRs that can be programmed by telephone. "Smart" credit cards, which contain a computer chip instead of a magnetic strip, are already being used in Japan and in France for various financial transactions. They can be used instead of cash to operate pay telephones, parking meters, and vending machines. Marine Corps recruits at the Parris Island training base in South Carolina now get smart cards instead of cash on payday; when they buy merchandise at a base store, the amount of the purchase is automatically deducted from their account.

As telephone companies extend fiber-optic cable to office buildings over the next several years, businesses will be able to communicate visually on their computers while talking on the phone. An architect in New York will be able to show his client in Los Angeles the blueprint he has just completed on his computer screen. And if the client doesn't like it, the architect can make changes on the spot and the client can watch as the changes are made on his own computer screen. No need to ship blueprints back and forth and no need for anyone to fly cross-country for a personal meeting. With cameras installed, they'll also be able to see each other's faces in a corner of the screen.

New technology will put more resources at the disposal of professionals and managers than ever before, and give them better tools to analyze the data. Desktop computers and databases are giving managers access to more and better information, from up-to-the-minute status reports on factory operations to data on business conditions halfway around the world. More powerful electronic spreadsheet programs are helping managers better analyze data; desktop publishing programs let them turn out polished reports without the need for an artist or even a print shop. Doctors are getting help in making diagnoses from artificial-intelligence programs that incorporate the expertise of medical specialists.

Electronic mail systems, facsimile machines, and voice mail systems provide ways to get business done more quickly; no need to wait for overnight mail or spend as much time playing telephone tag. The electronic global village is finally coming of age.

Why You May Lose Your Personal Secretary

At the same time, professionals and managers will increasingly find themselves performing many of the tasks that their secretaries used to perform. Executives who never would have thought of typing their own reports and memos are now routinely drafting them as personal computers spread to virtually every desktop, and the use of electronic mail for interoffice and intraoffice communication becomes more commonplace. As voice mail spreads to more and more offices, many executives and professionals will also find themselves without a switchboard operator or a secretary to take telephone messages or screen incoming calls. Some firms are already experimenting with computer programs that can schedule meetings without having to check with your secretary to see if you're available; the system automatically checks appointment calendars in each person's computer and then picks the best time.

With managers and professionals doing their own typing, with voice mail systems automatically intercepting phone calls and "groupware" arranging appointments, private secretaries will likely become a less common fixture in lower- and middle-level management offices. Many professionals and managers have already lost their personal secretaries, and as office automation spreads further, more and more of them will see their private secretaries taken away—even if they still want one around for other duties, like keeping unwanted phone callers at bay. Increasingly, secretaries who used to work for just one person are being shared among several workers. In the 1990s, having your own secretary will be an even more exclusive status symbol.

Eventually, voice-operated typewriters and computers will eliminate many more secretarial positions, although widespread use isn't expected until the turn of the century. Researchers are making significant progress in developing computers that can recognize naturally spoken language from a variety of different speakers. So far, their vocabularies are relatively limited. Some systems are able to recognize in excess of 20,000 words, but only if the words are separated by pauses and spoken by one particular person who has "trained" the computer to recognize his or her distinct voice patterns. Even so, voice-recognition systems are likely to gain wider commercial application in the next several years, including use as dictation machines, as their capabilities grow.

Automating Clerical Jobs out of Existence

Office automation is threatening other clerical jobs as well. Spreading use of dictation machines is rapidly making stenographers obsolete in many offices. Widening use of voice mail systems suggests that businesses will also be able to get by without as many human telephone operators.

Word processors and typists are threatened as managers and professionals do more of their own word processing on personal computers. Posing an even bigger threat is optical character recognition (OCR) technology, where a device "reads" a printed page into a computer. Advances are occurring rapidly and are expected to be in widespread use in the next several years. These systems would dramatically reduce the typing load. OCR systems with very high accuracy rates are already available for under $5,000. Voice-operated typewriters and computers will ultimately eliminate many more jobs.

Keypunch operators, who transfer data from paper into computers, face the same technological threats, as well as the trend toward data being inserted directly into the computer system by others. Salespeople are inputting orders directly into the computer system. Bank customers are conducting more and more of their transactions using ATM machines rather than paper deposit and withdrawal slips. Even taxpayers are starting to file their returns electronically with the IRS.

Facsimile machines and electronic mail are eating into the business of messenger delivery services, overnight mail services, and even the post office. Mail-room jobs are threatened by spreading use of in-house electronic mail systems as well as the growing use of mail-room robot systems.

Despite a growing economy and exploding demand for information, automation is spreading so rapidly that the decades-long expansion in office employment may be nearing an end. In a comprehensive study on office automation, the Congressional Office of Technology Assessment concluded that growth in office jobs is likely to slow in the 1990s and that "some decline in office employment could begin by 2000." This would have a dramatic effect on office building construction.

While clerical positions are threatened the most by technology, lower- and middle-level managers are also vulnerable. Fewer clerical workers implies that fewer supervisors and managers will be needed to manage those workers. In addition, computers are taking over the functions of many managers whose jobs involve collecting and analyzing data.

Computers Making Professional Decisions

Computers are also allowing many management and professional functions to be performed by lower-level (and lower-paid) workers. Secretaries and other clerical workers, armed with desktop computers as powerful as those on board the rockets that took man into space, are being given assignments that used to be reserved for professionals. For these clerical workers, the computer age does open up more challenging and interesting opportunities.

Whereas yesterday's computers were able to automate many clerical functions, today's computers are beginning to take over or assist in higher-level decision making, embodying the knowledge and reasoning power of a team of medical specialists or rocket scientists to help solve problems.

Getting computers to simulate human intelligence has been a goal that has long eluded computer scientists, and they are probably decades away from computers that can emulate the human mind. But in the past decade, computer programmers have made major strides in getting computers to mimic some of the decision-making processes of human beings and putting them to everyday use in corporate America.

Anyone who has seen a computerized chessboard in action will begin to understand what "artificial intelligence" is all about. Computer programmers can endow the computer with some of the expertise and reasoning power of human experts, be they chess grand masters or NASA scientists, to help solve problems, whether the next move in a chess game or the go-ahead for a rocket launch.

Artificial intelligence is spreading rapidly in government and the corporate world. About 80 percent of major U.S. corporations have implemented some 1,500 "expert" systems, according to the Commerce Department.

Commercial applications of expert systems can be found in most every industry. Computers instilled with the knowledge of medical specialists help doctors make diagnoses. The New York Stock Exchange has a program to detect insider trading. At American Express, a computer system contains the expertise of in-house specialists who approve unusual credit requests from cardholders. Some law firms are using expert systems to help speed the drafting of corporate bylaws, estate documents, loan agreements, and other routine legal matters. These law-firm systems use the collective wisdom of the firm's legal minds to produce rules of thumb to address legal problems based on facts of particular cases. They are particularly useful for law firms that tend to produce a large volume of documents relating to relatively routine matters.

Impending retirements of high-level managers, scientists, and engineers at NASA have forced the space agency to rely more on artificial intelligence to help run missions. The collective wisdom of seasoned flight controllers has been embodied in these new systems, some of which are designed to take action automatically when the computer deems it necessary and not just to carry out programmed instructions.

Artificial intelligence is also critical to advances in factory robots, which are still found mainly in the automobile industry but are expected to spread to other industries in the 1990s.

Many companies were slow to embrace artificial intelligence, and the market has taken much longer to develop than many in the industry anticipated. Some artificial-intelligence firms have downsized their operations or even completely abandoned the field. But that is likely to change. According to a Commerce Department analysis, artificial intelligence is expected to become commonly used in desktop computing in the 1990s to help solve major strategic problems in various businesses.

Computers as Language Translators

As business becomes more global, some companies are turning to computers and artificial intelligence to break the language barrier. Though they often require a little assistance from human translators to fix colloquialisms, computers that translate text from one language to another are advancing in terms of both speed and accuracy. Japanese manufacturers use these computer systems to translate user manuals and other technical documents for many of the products they export.

How Computers Spy on Workers

With computers has come the capability of employers to monitor more closely the performance of their employees. Anyone who works at a computer terminal can be continuously monitored. Computer systems can be programmed so that supervisors have a record of how many keystrokes you type each shift or how long the machine sits idle.

Electronic cash registers can record the number of transactions a cashier handles each hour. Some restaurants have systems to monitor which waiters are pushing the more expensive daily specials and which aren't.

Telephone call-accounting systems have spread rapidly in the workplace as concern has risen about the expense of personal calls being made. These systems give managers data on each call made—the time, the duration, the number called, the originating extension, and the estimated cost. Telephone bills are a major expenditure for many businesses, and firms that sell call-accounting software have promoted them as being effective ways to cut costs. Indeed, at some workplaces, call-accounting

ELECTRONIC WORK MONITORING

Job	What is measured	How obtained
Word processors	speed, errors, time working	keystrokes counted by computer
Data-entry clerks	speed, errors, time working	keystrokes counted by computer
Telephone operators	average time per call	each call timed by call distribution system
Customer-service workers	time per customer; number and type of transaction	each call timed by call distribution system; transactions counted by computer
Telemarketing	time per customer; sales volume	each call or transaction timed; sales tabulated by computer
Insurance claims clerks	number of cases per unit of time	time spent on each form tabulated by computer
Mail clerks	letters or packages per unit of time	collected by sorting machine
Bank proof clerks	checks processed per unit of time	collected by proof machine

Source: U.S. Office of Technology Assessment

has uncovered a large number of calls to off-track betting and "Dial-a-Porn," as well as many personal long-distance calls. According to the Congressional Office of Technology Assessment, anecdotes of abuses uncovered with call-accounting equipment abound, like that of the secretary who made a one-hour long-distance call every lunch hour in order to listen to a soap opera on her mother's television.

According to a study by the Office of Technology Assessment, more than six million employees are monitored by computers.

While employers have long used various means of monitoring individual performance, computers allow for more extensive, intrusive, and continuous monitoring. In contrast to most traditional methods of monitoring, such as a supervisor standing behind you for a few minutes, computers allow nonstop monitoring. It is as if the supervisor stood behind you throughout the workday.

Anyone who works on a computer terminal is also vulnerable to electronic eavesdropping. When computer terminals are hooked into a central mainframe, a sales manager could snoop through one of his salesman's computer files to see what he's up to or a newspaper editor could snoop through a reporter's files to check an embarrassing first draft of a story. If an employer were to come and rummage through an employee's file drawer, the employee would be outraged. But today, an employer can effectively do the same by rummaging electronically through the employee's computer files, and the employee would have no way of detecting the intrusion. Every report, memo, and note sitting in the person's computer file becomes open for inspection to anyone with the right password.

Some companies are being careful not to go too far with computer monitoring because it's been found to lead to increased stress and turnover among employees.

Nevertheless, coping in the era of computer monitoring means never putting anything in a computer that you're afraid to have anyone else see, like a nasty note about a colleague or a supervisor. And unless you know better, always assume that a record of your phone calls is being made.

The Paperless Office: Getting Partway There

When computers began proliferating, many people saw the stage being set for electronic, paperless offices. To date, the computer revolution has turned out to be a bonanza for the paper industry rather than its death knell. Computer printers, fed by crates of paper and tractor feeders, spew out seemingly endless reams of printed data. Fax machines add to the sea of paper.

But in the next several years, paper will play an ever-diminishing role in the office. Companies with the heaviest paperwork burdens are doing the most computerizing. As computers proliferate to the point where almost every worker has one and the storage capacity of computers increases, it will become easier to pass electronic documents back and forth than to use paper. Paper may be nice to read and handle, but paper is cumbersome to edit and amend and to transport around the office and around the world.

Businesses want instant communications and their frustration with the lengthy delays of transporting paper is evidenced by the explosive growth of facsimile machines and electronic mail. Electronic mail lets you send a written message almost instantly to another computer. It's faster and cheaper than overnight mail services. It's also more private than sending it by fax.

Electronic Mail versus Overnight Couriers: While this expanding stream of data transmissions should enrich telecommunications companies, electronic mail and facsimile machines are already hurting overnight mail delivery services and messenger services. The spectacular growth in overnight mail delivery has slowed dramatically. According to the market research firm of Frost & Sullivan, electronic mail will eventually replace 25 to 35 percent of the business that has been controlled by overnight couriers. The inroads made by electronic communication have forced overnight delivery services to shift their marketing emphasis to larger shipments. Package shipments have been growing rapidly with the trend by businesses to "just-in-time" inventory management. Just-in-time delivery is a practice borrowed from the Japanese as a way to reduce inventory costs. Rather than keeping expensive parts on hand and taking up valuable space, companies don't want them until they're needed. But then they need the parts fast. Electronic transmission is also driving air courier services to expand aggressively to overseas markets, which should eventually lead to global door-to-door delivery networks, linking most of the industrialized world. Anticipated growth in mail-order sales and electronic home shopping should also help package-delivery services such as United Parcel Service and Federal Express.

Home Libraries on Disk: Getting rid of paper means having enough storage in the computer. To be sure, no matter how much memory a computer system has it never seems to be enough to handle the ever-increasing needs. But storage capacity is increasing exponentially.

Already available for personal computers are "erasable optical disk" drives, which use a laser beam to record vast amounts of information— the equivalent of 250,000 pages of typewritten material can be stored on a single disk. Students could store all the class notes and term papers ever produced during their academic career. Writers could have instant access to all the articles they ever wrote. Another large storage device that should become more common in the next few years is called CD-ROM, which stands for compact disk–read only memory. It is the erudite cousin of the audio compact-disk player. You can't write or edit information on a CD-ROM disk, but the contents of an entire encyclopedia can fit on a single disk, including illustrations and sound. CD-ROM is ideal for storing reference works. Searching through disks for a particular item takes only seconds. With CD-ROM, lawyers could bring a law library with them into the courtroom or an accountant could carry the complete tax code to a client's offices.

Choosing Hairstyles and Home Decoration by Computer

Do you have trouble visualizing what a new hairdo would look like on you? How a nip and tuck by a plastic surgeon might alter your appearance? Or how your living room might look filled with all the furniture that your interior decorator just showed you in a catalogue? At hundreds of beauty salons across the country, a hair stylist will point a video camera at you and then superimpose different hairstyles on the screen. Similar computer systems now let plastic surgeons give you a preview of facial alterations. Landscape architects can show what your house would look like with new shrubs. And interior decorators can show you what your living room would look like with Art Deco furniture, then with the touch of a key, change the furniture to Early American, then move it around the room. These new systems exemplify how the power of computers will be infused into more and more aspects of everyday life in the 1990s.

Videotex: Connecting to the Outside World

Futuristic visions of your home linked electronically to the rest of the world to make airline reservations, shop, order groceries, trade stocks, get the latest news, pay bills, and talk to other people are already a reality. They've been a reality for years; it's just that consumers have been slow to take to the idea. Businesses have been the main users of online database systems for a fast-growing number of purposes such as to research legal cases, track market information, check credit reports, and access government documents.

But as computers spread to more and more households and the cost of videotex services comes down, more Americans are likely to conduct some of their transactions electronically.

There will be no shortage of companies trying to spur public interest in videotex. In addition to such existing general-interest videotex services as CompuServe (owned by H&R Block) and Prodigy (jointly owned by Sears and IBM), the telephone companies want to get into the business. AT&T recently received permission to enter electronic publishing. The local phone companies are also trying to get permission so they can offer an electronic version of the yellow pages and a host of other information services. They have been trying to persuade the government to drop the restrictions that bar the regional phone companies from providing the content of information services; all they can do now is transmit the information provided by others.

Newspaper publishers and other companies involved in information services are lobbying to keep the phone companies out of the business for fear that they could use their monopoly position in their respective local markets to unfair advantage.

While newspapers in their present form are likely to remain the dominant print medium for general news information in the 1990s, electronic publishing could nibble away at the historical franchise that newspapers have held on a number of specialized types of information, such as stock quotes, classified ads, movie reviews, arts and entertainment listings, TV schedules, and sports scores. Electronic media are particularly well suited to information that requires regular updates, such as airline schedules, stock quotes, weather, and sports statistics.

Newspaper publishers increasingly see electronic publishing as a source of new revenue at a time when readership levels have been declining, the industry's daily circulation has been stagnant, and advertising growth rates have been slowing.

Videotex isn't likely to become a mass-market medium anytime soon. Many Americans still get stumped in front of a bank ATM, let alone trying to operate a computer. Though the number of homes equipped with a personal computer should grow rapidly in the years ahead as more people become computer literate at work and at school, fewer than one in four households had a computer at the start of the 1990s. And only about 1.5 million consumers subscribed to a videotex service.

That's why some electronic publishers will also be focusing heavily on audio services. Audio information services require only a Touchtone phone. The customer presses a few buttons on the keypad to get a stock quote, listen to a capsule movie review, or order merchandise. Nintendo, the Japanese maker of electronic games, plans another route; it is trying to develop a network in which its best-selling video game unit could function as a personal computer to tap into an array of videotex services. Fax machines are yet another route: several newspapers, including *The New York Times* and the *Hartford* (Connecticut) *Courant*, have launched fax editions.

The world's largest and most successful videotex system is run by the national phone company in France. Its system has more than four million users and offers more than 7,500 services. One reason that it gained such wide acceptance in France is that the phone company offered terminals to the public free or for a low monthly rent.

Whether or not the local phone companies are allowed to enter information services, transacting business by computer is bound to become more widespread because of the convenience. In Santa Monica, California, for instance, residents can now electronically tap into a computer at City Hall to see whether the municipal library has a certain book, check the bus schedule, find out about City Council actions, and obtain information about how to get city permits. Or, if they like, they can send angry messages to City Council members or department heads.

GUARDING AGAINST COMPUTER "VIRUSES"

The expanding use of computers in the 1990s is likely to make computer "viruses" a growing threat. As several much-publicized incidents over the past few years have dramatically illustrated, computer viruses can wreak havoc on computer systems and destroy valuable data.

While the incidents that have drawn the most attention involved large government, corporate, and research systems and networks, home computers are also vulnerable. Viruses, which are rogue sets of instructions planted inside otherwise normal programs, can be picked up from many common sources, including public-domain programs, pirated software, electronic bulletin boards, and disks borrowed from a friend or colleague. Viruses are designed to replicate themselves and spread from computer to computer by attaching themselves onto healthy programs. Home computers that are never hooked into electronic networks and are used only to run packaged software don't run much risk of catching a virus. Instances of commercial software becoming infected at the factory are extremely rare.

Some viruses are merely annoying, designed by a hacker to print some message on your screen; others are toxic, designed to change data or erase files. Some viruses strike immediately; others are time bombs, lurking silently inside a disk until it's set to go off, sometime in the future, perhaps weeks from now or years from now.

There is no foolproof way to protect completely against computer viruses. But there are several steps you can take to minimize the threat.

- Make frequent backup copies of your files and data. If a virus strikes, at least you'll have other copies of your files to turn to.
- Although they are not 100 percent effective, a growing number of commercial software programs can help you detect and/or destroy common virus infections.
- Avoid pirated software and public-domain programs, which are common breeding grounds for viruses.
- Don't exchange software programs with other people.
- Be cautious of electronic bulletin boards. If you're not willing to give up bulletin boards, stick to reputable ones.
- If you download computer programs from an electronic bulletin board or can't stay away from public-domain software, check the software through a virus detection program before running it on your system.
- Buy software programs only from reputable dealers and make sure the software package is sealed. Buy software as you would a bottle of medicine: If the package is opened, assume that someone may have tampered with the contents.
- Be alert for signs of viral infection, such as slower computer operation or unexpected shrinkage in memory.
- To protect your original software disks from becoming infected, always set the "write-protect" tab on the disk when copying the program to your hard disk drive.
- If you lend somebody a disk, tape over the write-protect tab so that any virus that that person's computer may have won't be automatically transferred to your disk. Of course, this won't prevent a person from intentionally tampering with your disk (he can just peel away the tape), but it will help prevent an unintentional viral transfer from occurring.

- Keep your computer and disks secure so that no one can tamper with them. If someone can gain access to your computer or files he can infect your computer with a virus or simply erase or damage your files.

Computer Security Businesses: The threat of computer viruses and other forms of sabotage is making a growth industry out of businesses that can find ways to make computer systems more secure. But how quickly the computer security industry grows is likely to depend on how many publicized incidents there are. Businesses get scared after an incident, but they tend to relax if there is no further trouble.

THE ENTERTAINMENT WARS

The big battle in the entertainment industry of the 1990s may not be between cable TV, broadcasters, and videocassettes, but rather between the nation's phone companies and the rest of the industry. What could revolutionize the TV industry would be the entry of your local telephone company into cable TV. Phone companies are waging a massive lobbying campaign on Capitol Hill to get Congress to lift the restrictions that bar them from moving into the cable-TV business. Cable operators are lobbying just as hard to keep the phone companies out.

With their vast switching capabilities and budding fiber-optic networks, telephone companies have the potential to give each viewer the freedom to order up almost any movie or program he likes and have it transmitted to his TV set whenever he likes. Pick from the world's library of films, dial up the phone company, and within moments it could be on your screen.

Because fiber-optic cables have far more capacity than the copper coaxial cable that cable-TV companies use, the phone companies could provide video entertainment and information services that cable can't. By adapting the switching technology used to direct millions of telephone calls from one point to another, the phone companies could offer personalized programming and services, from full-motion videophones to "movies on demand," and could theoretically provide hundreds of channels of entertainment.

The copper telephone wire that extends into everyone's home can't carry video programming. But fiber-optic cable can. Seeing optical fiber as the best way to expand capacity, phone companies have installed thousands of miles of fiber-optic cable in their networks. Since optical fiber can carry enormous volumes of voice, data, and video signals, the phone companies would like to capitalize on their investment in fiber-optics technology by offering an array of new services to residential customers, such as videophones, push-button home-shopping, all sorts of information services, and video programming, which could be transmitted in movie-theater-quality, high-definition television (HDTV); unless the cable companies string more wire, most may have to cut back on the number of channels they carry in order to transmit HDTV, which requires a wider bandwidth. (For more on HDTV, see chapter 22.) Fiber optics is trouble for cable companies because it has far more capacity and can transmit in greater quality than cable TV's coaxial copper wiring.

Because of the enormous expense, phone companies aren't rushing to rewire existing homes. Nor are new homes generally being wired with optical fiber because it's still more expensive than copper wiring. But costs are expected to become competitive in the next few years, and installing optical fiber to residential areas might well accelerate if the phone companies received approval to enter the cable business.

Phone companies are spending millions of dollars testing the idea in their research labs and with in-home tests in communities like Cerritos, California, and Heathrow, Florida. They are experimenting with movies on demand, electronic yellow pages, online classified advertising, remote control of appliances, remote meter-reading, and more.

In 1984, Congress enacted legislation barring the phone companies from offering video programming in their local areas for fear they would inhibit the growth of the cable business, then in its infancy. In addition, the court decree governing the breakup of the Bell System barred the Baby Bells from providing information services anywhere in the United States. The Federal Communications Commission recently endorsed the idea of letting phone companies offer cable service, provided there were safeguards to prevent anticompetitive behavior by the phone companies. Congress was preparing to review the issue. Now that the cable business is prospering, some members of Congress think that it's time to open cable to competition in order to spur more advances in home entertainment and information services. Others fear the phone companies would wind up monopolizing the cable business.

The cable industry is not alone in its lobbying campaign. Newspaper publishers and business information companies are also lobbying to keep the local phone companies out of the information and entertainment business, fearing that they could use their financial strength to dominate the communications industry.

Even if the phone companies were given the legislative and regulatory go-aheads, it would take several years for them to install the technology and extend fiber-optic cable to a significant number of residences. Only about 5 percent of homes will have fiber-optic cable installed by the year 2000, according to a LINK Resources forecast. In all, rewiring America with fiber-optic cable will command an investment estimated at $200 billion and take decades to complete. In any event, Congress would probably take steps to ensure that cable companies had ample time to devise new strategies and technologies to compete, including the possibility of linking up with a phone company in a cable venture.

Pay-Per-View

As political and legal storms gather over phone-company involvement, cable viewers will get a primitive version of video-on-demand with "pay-per-view." More and more cable systems are starting to offer this service, which gives subscribers a chance to watch recently released movies, live performances, and sporting events for fees ranging from $4 to $40 each. Viewers order from a monthly menu by either pressing a button on their cable box or calling a special number. The program is then descrambled on the subscriber's set and the charge shows up on his monthly cable bill.

In contrast to video-on-demand, pay-per-view subscribers are offered a very limited selection of programs that are shown only at fixed times.

Pay-per-view has been slow to develop because only a fraction of cable companies have the equipment needed to scramble and descramble programs for individual subscribers. Channel capacity has also been a problem; many cable companies don't have enough capacity to devote more than one or two channels to pay-per-view, so the selections are limited.

But pay-per-view has the potential to be enormously lucrative for cable operators and pay-per-view networks, as well as movie studios, sports promoters, and those who own the rights to Broadway plays and other live performances that are tapped for pay-per-view broadcast.

In a limited way, phone companies stand to benefit, too. Many are serving as the middlemen, taking orders for pay-per-view program requests from cable subscribers and then passing those orders on to the cable companies.

Eventually, cable companies will equip all subscribers with a device that lets them order a program electronically at the touch of a key.

Pay-per-view could hurt pay cable programming services such as

Home Box Office and Showtime, which don't run movies until well after they've been released in video stores and on pay-per-view.

Video Rental Outlets

Video rental stores are also likely to suffer from pay-per-view. With pay-per-view, you don't have to drive down to the video store to get recent movie releases or find that all the copies of a popular video have been rented out. So far, movie studios have not released movies for pay-per-view broadcast until after they have been released in video stores. But that could change in the future.

Video stores would have enough to worry about even if it weren't for pay-per-view and the long-term threat from telephone companies. The era of rapid growth in the video rental business has ended now that VCRs have nearly saturated American homes. At the same time, competition has intensified. Not only have the number of video rental stores exploded in the past several years, but supermarkets, convenience stores, gas stations, and other retailers have also gotten into the video rental and sales business.

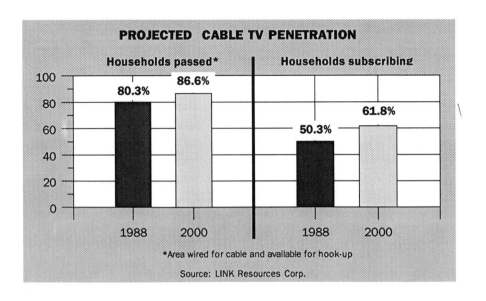

PROJECTED CABLE TV PENETRATION

Households passed*

Households subscribing

*Area wired for cable and available for hook-up

Source: LINK Resources Corp.

Cable versus the Broadcasters

Cable television, meanwhile, continues to expand into more and more homes. By 1988 cable TV had reached a majority of American households, with some 46 million subscribers. By the year 2000, cable-TV subscribers are expected to number 65.5 million households, or about 62 percent of all American households, according to LINK Resources Corporation. Expanding cable viewership has made cable network programs a viable advertising medium, and ad revenues can be expected to rise as cable's share of the viewing audience increases.

With the growth of cable television, as well as VCRs, broadcast television has watched its share of viewers and advertising erode. Network television, which drew 92 percent of prime-time TV viewers as recently as 1978, saw its share of prime-time viewership plunge to below 68 percent in 1989. Many industry executives and analysts predict the networks' share will drop below 60 percent or even 55 percent in the next several years as more homes subscribe to cable and as cable networks invest more heavily in original programming.

Cable versus Radio

Cable is also moving in on radio's turf by starting to offer subscribers several channels of compact-disk-quality music. Three digital music networks have been signing up cable companies to carry the service. Subscribers pay about $5 to $8 a month to receive eight or more channels of uninterrupted music; each channel carries a different type of music and is piped into the subscriber's home through the same cable that carries the TV channels. (Subscribers also have to buy or rent a $100 digital tuner from the cable company.) Because the music is digitally encoded—just as compact disks are—the music can be transmitted without distortion. Previous audio efforts on cable have failed, but none of them transmitted pure digital sound.

If successful, the new digital services could eat into radio station listenership as well as CD sales.

Home Satellite Dishes

For many years now, home satellite dishes have been a part of the rural landscape, giving homeowners in remote areas where cable TV hasn't arrived access to a broader selection of programming. But as dishes get smaller in size and lower in price, dishes could spread into suburban and urban areas where cable already reaches. Some satellite companies already have plans for programming directly to the home-satellite audience, a development that has some cable operators worried. The key is a new generation of high-powered "Ku-band" satellites from which broadcasts could be received at home on small, flat antennas costing only a few hundred dollars rather than the costly, huge parabolic dishes that are needed to pick up today's "C-band" satellite broadcast signals. (C-band satellites transmit at lower power levels than Ku-band satellites.)

Home satellite TV is not likely to play as big a role in the United States as it may in Europe, which is not as extensively wired for cable TV. But cable operators in the United States that have limited channel capacity or offer poor service could find satellite-to-home programming services nibbling away at their customer base. Satellite transmission offers viewers in most locations far better picture quality than they can receive from terrestrial broadcast signals or cable. When HDTV finally arrives, satellite operators will be able to implement HDTV programming much faster and more easily than either cable or local TV stations.

For now, dish owners are finding a shrinking supply of free programming to pluck from the sky. If you lived on a farm or didn't mind filling up your backyard with an unsightly ten-foot satellite dish, you used to be able to intercept Home Box Office and more than a hundred other TV channels (as well as dozens of radio stations) beamed from orbiting satellites. All for free. Satellite dish manufacturers could hardly keep up with the demand. Some two million private satellite dishes sprang up across the American landscape, making backyards look like Nike missile sites.

Cable industry lobbyists stormed Capitol Hill begging Congress to outlaw the dishes. Congress, fearful of disenfranchising dish-owning constituents, refused. So cable programmers started scrambling their pictures, and sales of home satellite dishes plummeted. Today you can still pluck scores of channels from the skies, but the major cable services, like HBO, Showtime, and the Cable News Network, scramble their signals. In all, more than forty programmers now scramble their satellite transmissions.

To get the signal descrambled, you need to pay a fee to a program packager. Sales of home satellite dishes have picked up again now that packaged program costs have dropped to rates that are comparable to or even lower than cable subscriber rates.

But most analysts don't see every backyard and apartment balcony growing satellite dishes in the 1990s. By late 1989, about 3 percent of households owned a satellite dish, compared to about 2.3 percent in 1988. That share is expected to rise to 5.8 percent by the year 2000, according to LINK Resources. But David Rosen, vice president of electronic entertainment at LINK, sees the potential for home dishes to spread to 18 percent of households by the turn of the century if satellite pay networks offer special programming, improved HDTV picture quality, and promote interest in the service by "seeding" the market with free or low-cost foot-long antennas.

Such systems are nearing reality. Four major media companies—NBC, Hughes Communications, News Corporation, and Cablevision Systems Corporation—recently announced a joint venture to launch a home satellite TV service by late 1993 that will allow subscribers to receive up to 108 channels on a $300 dish small enough to be mounted on a windowsill.

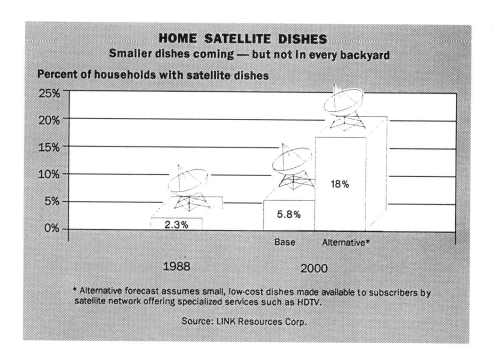

HOME SATELLITE DISHES
Smaller dishes coming — but not in every backyard

Percent of households with satellite dishes

2.3%

5.8%

18%

Base   Alternative*

1988   2000

* Alternative forecast assumes small, low-cost dishes made available to subscribers by satellite network offering specialized services such as HDTV.

Source: LINK Resources Corp.

Movie Theaters Face New Challenges

The imminent demise of movie theaters has been predicted for decades. When television was invented, most everyone wondered why anybody would pay 25 cents to go to a movie theater when they could watch TV at home for free. Then came videotape recorders and video rental stores. Yet movie theaters have managed to survive.

But despite all the talk about how movie theaters have defied predictions of doom and new box-office money records have been set, growth in attendance has been anemic. The number of tickets sold has hovered around the one-billion-a-year mark for more than two decades. Meanwhile, competition has increased; the number of movie screens has grown 35 percent over the past decade, sending profit margins tumbling. Nonetheless, new movie houses continue to be built.

Why are they putting up all those screens? For forty years the Hollywood film studios had been barred for antitrust reasons from owning movie theaters; then the Reagan administration began giving them exemptions to the ban. So, to ensure they had places to exhibit their films, the studios started acquiring movie chains.

It's all good news for the movie-going public. Theater owners have been battling for customers in a stagnant market by refurbishing their theaters, installing lavish sound systems, and adding more screens. Movie ticket prices, after rising to $7.50 in some cities, have shown signs of stabilizing.

Movie theaters face new challenges in the 1990s to keep their audiences. Young adults, who are big theatergoers, are declining in numbers. Meanwhile, aging baby-boomers aren't going out as often as they used to; they're getting more of their entertainment from the expanding offerings on broadcast and cable TV, VCRs, and laser-disk players. What's more, the advent of HDTV will make cinema-quality viewing possible right in your living room.

Busy Times for Hollywood

With all the new entertainment media, Hollywood should be a busy place in the 1990s as it tries to fill an insatiable demand for new motion pictures and TV programming.

Cable TV networks have already announced plans to spend billions of dollars on original programming. Many suppliers to the home video market are so hungry for material that they are prebuying motion pictures, paying up to half the film's production cost; some are making commitments even before they know who the stars will be.

All these new outlets mean that filmmaking won't be quite as risky as it used to be. Even if a movie doesn't make money at the box office, there is still hope for revenues from videocassettes, pay-per-view, pay cable networks, TV broadcast networks, local TV stations, and foreign sales.

But making money in Hollywood is never easy. For one thing, some of these new markets offset revenues from traditional outlets; network television sales, for instance, are no longer as lucrative as they once were because broadcast TV audiences are smaller and the films have already been shown before on cable and videocassette. For another, box-office success is still the main determinant of how well a movie fares in the ancillary markets. A film that does poorly in movie theaters usually won't be in great demand at video rental stores, either, or be able to earn much from the sale of TV broadcast rights. And the odds of a hit in Hollywood are far worse than at casinos in Las Vegas or Atlantic City. Profits for private investors in motion pictures—even on box-office hits—tend to be elusive. The cost of producing, distributing, and promoting films has skyrocketed. So have the demands by actors, directors, and other creative talent for a share in gross revenues. In the large movie partnerships sold to individual investors by Wall Street brokerage houses, the brokers take a sales commission up front and the people running the partnership take administrative and management fees up front. By the time everyone gets paid off, there's often little or nothing left for the investor. Even investors in partnerships with some box-office hits in their portfolio have been disappointed by the returns; the profits from the hits were offset by losses from other films in the package. Of course, these investors can still brag at cocktail parties about all the films in which they have a direct stake. And some movie partnerships guarantee that investors will at least get their original outlay back eventually. But investors who bought shares of stock in successful Hollywood movie studios have fared far better financially.

BIOTECHNOLOGY: COMING OF AGE

Manipulating the building blocks of life through biotechnology holds the potential to create some of the most extraordinary technological marvels of the decade.

The fledgling industry has already given birth to a host of new drugs, diagnostic aids, and animal vaccines. But the revolution has only begun. Biotechnology offers promise for creating new drugs for diseases that have long eluded treatment, new generations of animals that grow faster and leaner, new breeds of plants that are more nutritious and resistant to disease, and new ways to protect crops without the need for chemical pesticides.

Under development are drugs to help treat a wide variety of diseases, from AIDS to cancer; products that make cows produce more milk, sheep produce more wool, and fish grow bigger; tomatoes that stay fresh for weeks in grocers' produce bins; plants that require less irrigation; microbes that eat toxic waste and oil spills; and a range of products that would eliminate the need for chemical pesticides.

Despite all its promise, investors haven't always been patient with the pace of the industry's progress, the regulatory hurdles, patent problems, lower-than-expected sales of some products, and public concern over unpredictable health and environmental consequences of tinkering with genes in animals and plants.

But after years of costly research and development, genetic engineering seems to be on the threshold of a more prosperous era. A steady stream of biotechnology products is expected to appear in the 1990s. The market value of new biotechnology products, estimated at more than $1 billion in 1989, is expected to reach several billion dollars by the early 1990s, according to Commerce Department analysts. By early in the next century, they estimate, the market could be worth $15 billion to $40 billion.

The industry is large, consisting of over four hundred biotechnology companies, plus more than two hundred manufacturing firms that have diversified into biotechnology. Most biotechnology firms aren't profitable yet, relying for their survival mainly on research contracts, venture capital, and funding by larger companies.

Most of the research is focused on developing health-care products, but biotechnology will also be making visible contributions to agriculture in the 1990s.

Scientists can make genetic changes that endow an animal or plant with specific traits suited for particular purposes, changes that sometimes would be impossible even through natural evolution or breeding. Genetically improved breeds of livestock that can grow faster, are more disease-resistant, and contain less fat and lower cholesterol are expected to appear on the market in the next several years. So are plants with better resistance to diseases and insects.

Advances in biotechnology will greatly enhance farm productivity, but portend gluts on the world agricultural market and more family farmers driven out of business. American farmers are hoping that biotechnology will give them a competitive edge in the world market, but the technology is likely to be picked up quickly by farmers in other countries.

The potential impact of biotechnology on farm productivity was illustrated recently when dairy farmers mounted a campaign to ban a new drug that has been shown to increase milk production by 10 to 25 percent when administered to cows. Dairy farmers saw their livelihood threatened by the prospect that the drug would vastly increase milk supplies and thus bring lower prices.

Biotechnology is also seen as key to the replacement of chemical pesticides, which are coming under increasing public and governmental scrutiny as a health and environmental threat.

Further into the future is the prospect of manipulating human genes to cure genetic diseases. To that end, researchers across the country are involved in a federally funded effort, known as the human genome initiative, to identify and map every one of the estimated 100,000 genes in the human body.

SPACE-AGE MATERIALS

A quiet revolution is under way in the materials used to make everything from cars to planes. Traditional materials—such as steel, aluminum, and copper—are slowly being replaced in industry by reinforced plastics, advanced ceramics, and other space-age materials that are stronger, lighter, and longer-lasting. General Motors has introduced all-plastic bodies in a line of 1990 minivan models. Beech Aircraft recently began producing an executive jet made of plastic composites. Engine parts are increasingly being made of ceramics. Army engineers are testing plastics for use as heavy armor. And copper is being replaced by plastic in plumbing fixtures, and by optical fiber in telecommunications transmission wires.

According to a recent study by the Congressional Office of Technology Assessment, the value of components produced from advanced materials in the United States is expected to grow from less than $2 billion a year to nearly $20 billion by the year 2000.

Steel and other metals are not going to disappear overnight. These metals are still lower in cost than advanced materials. And the threat of these materials eating into their business led metals producers to develop improved alloys. But new plastics, ceramics, and other advanced materials are expected gradually to become the fabric of choice for more and more types of manufactured products because of their superior qualities.

Used in car bodies, reinforced plastic offers several advantages over metal. Plastic can be made just as strong as or stronger than metal, but plastic is much lighter, making the car more fuel-efficient. Plastic won't rust, so the body will last longer. Nor will minor scratches show up on plastic since the color is mixed right into the plastic; so there's no need for repainting. These new plastics pose a threat to the long-term survival of car paint shops.

A new generation of aircraft is also making extensive use of plastic composites, which make the plane lighter and more fuel-efficient.

Even homes may be suited to plastic construction. In Pittsfield, Massachusetts, the plastics division of the General Electric Company has built a 3,000-square-foot "house of the future" to demonstrate the possibilities of plastics as a major building material. Plastics are already common in building construction, in insulation, plumbing fixtures, and siding. But builders see many other potential applications in the home, including foundations, molding, interior walls, windows, and roofing.

The military also has been expanding its use of plastics in everything from helmets and flak jackets to aircraft wings and ship panels.

At the same time, advanced ceramics are showing up in cookware, artificial tooth implants, scissors, knives, and car engines. Ceramics are replacing metal in car engines because they're as strong as metal but they're lighter, which helps improve fuel efficiency. Ceramics can also withstand much higher temperatures than metals; that's an important trait since engines burn cleaner at higher temperatures. So increasing the burning temperature would reduce auto emissions and help alleviate the nation's pollution problem. What's more, ceramics wear better than metal, which means engine parts won't wear out as quickly.

One problem that engineers are trying to overcome is the inherent brittleness of ceramics, which keeps them from being used to replace certain metal engine parts. But engineers see ceramics gradually being used for more and more engine components.

THE COMMERCIALIZATION OF SPACE

Outer space, long the preserve of government, is the next frontier for American business in the 1990s.

Commercialization of space promises to be a multibillion-dollar-a-year business almost overnight. Private companies recently began launching unmanned rockets and have a heavy backlog of commercial payloads awaiting launch.

Other commercial space ventures are involved in gathering data from "remote sensing" satellites about weather, geography, and natural resources and then selling the information to governmental agencies and companies involved in mineral exploration, fishing, forestry, agriculture, environmental monitoring, and land use. There is also long-term promise in the commercial manufacture of certain drugs, computer chips, and other products that can only be created in the near-weightlessness and vacuum of outer space.

In an effort to hasten the commercialization of space, the Reagan administration put NASA's space shuttle off limits to commercial payloads and directed the military and other government agencies to use commercial launch companies whenever possible.

Those directives, along with delays in NASA's shuttle program, sent corporations and foreign governments knocking on the doors of private space companies to launch their telecommunications satellites. More than twenty launches are scheduled in the next several years by the major rocket manufacturers, McDonnell Douglas, Martin Marietta Corporation, and the General Dynamics Corporation. These companies have a lot of experience in the business as primary suppliers to NASA and the military.

Demand for satellite launchings is expected to be strong in the early 1990s because of the growth in telecommunications and the need to replace many satellites currently in operation that are nearing the end of their designed lives. Rocket companies charge $40 million to $100 million to launch a commercial satellite.

Smaller space-transportation companies are counting on growing demand for a new generation of small, lightweight, and low-cost satellites. These satellites, used for purposes such as navigation and tracking fleets of trucks, can operate in low orbit. Thus, launching them doesn't require rockets as large or as expensive as those made by the big manufacturers to hurl heavier payloads more than 22,000 miles into space.

But while the backlogs will keep American space companies busy for the next few years, they will be facing growing competition for new business in the 1990s. The primary competitor is Arianespace, a French-led consortium of European nations. The Soviet Union and China are also offering commercial launch services. China has been trying to attract business by quoting prices much lower than U.S. and European space companies charge. Japan is also expected to enter the international competition in the early 1990s.

Space companies also have terrestrial competition from fiber optics.

Although demand for information services is exploding, demand for communications satellites isn't expected to grow as quickly because of the expanding use of fiber optics by communications companies for voice, data, and video transmissions.

Remote Sensing: The remote-sensing side of the space business has developed more slowly than expected. But a new generation of commercial remote-sensing satellites offering improved resolution and sensors should help stimulate demand; the new generation will be able to resolve objects of less than 5 meters compared to the 30-meter resolution offered by the older generation of U.S. commercial satellites. This capability has drawn interest from the news media, which could use remote-sensing satellites to provide pictures of inaccessible news events, such as the dramatic satellite photos that were taken of the damaged Chernobyl nuclear plant. But American firms involved in the business face growing international competition from remote-sensing satellites operated by France, Japan, Canada, and Brazil.

Space Manufacturing: Space-based manufacturing offers long-term promise in developing new pharmaceuticals, high-strength metals, and pure crystals for microelectronics. But most experts don't see any significant commercial production in space until after the 1990s.

SUPERCONDUCTIVITY

In laboratories around the world, researchers are struggling to develop a technology that has the potential to revolutionize electronics and make possible such old fantasies as electric cars, ultrafast computers, 300-mph trains, power lines that can carry electricity without energy loss, and nuclear fusion reactors. A series of dramatic breakthroughs in the mid-1980s brought new hope and attention to the technology of superconductivity. Scientists compared the potential impact of superconductors—materials that offer no resistance to the flow of electricity—to the advent of transistors.

But some recent results of laboratory research have tempered expectations about how quickly the technology might develop and even its ultimate potential. Commercialization of superconductivity is moving forward slowly, with some limited applications expected over the next several years. Scientists believe that large-scale commercial applications, the ones that have so captured the public's imagination, are at least a decade or two away. Scientists aren't even sure yet whether they will ever be able to deliver the full potential of superconductivity.

All the common materials used to carry electricity, from the copper wiring in your home to the silicon in your computer, offer some degree of resistance. Resistance creates a lot of problems. Whenever there's resistance, energy is wasted in transmission. In high-power tension wires, for instance, 15 to 20 percent of the energy transmitted is wasted fighting the friction. Resistance also creates heat, which means you can't pack circuits too close together or they will melt away.

Superconductors, with their inherent capability to transmit electricity without resistance, offer the potential for substantial energy savings. Superconductors would also make for far more efficient motors, perhaps cutting their size in half. Since an electric current could flow forever without resistance, superconducting coils could store large amounts of electricity indefinitely, making possible efficient batterylike storage systems for electric cars to run on and for utilities to draw on during peak periods. Since no heat would be created, superconductors would also allow microchips to be packed closer together in computers to make them

DEVELOPING SUPERCONDUCTOR COMMERCIAL APPLICATIONS

ESTIMATED TIME FRAME:

Less than five years

Computer wiring	Interconnecting chips to speed up computers
Sensors (SQUIDS)	For underground exploration of minerals, detecting submarines from the sky, and neural impulse in the human brain

Over ten years

Magnet system	For possible use in sorting scrap metal for recycling, removing sulfur from pulverized coal, cleaning up waste water

Long term

Transmission lines	Carry electricity without loss of power
Energy storage	Stored power could be used by utilities to provide electricity during peak hours
Motors and generators	Smaller and lighter motors and generators for use on ships, submarines, or utilities
Superconducting computer	Extremely fast, small computers

Source: Office of Technology Assessment, 1988

smaller and run faster. Superconductors can also produce magnetic fields far stronger than anything previously encountered, paving the way for more sensitive medical diagnostic systems, magnetically levitated trains, and the clean and inexhaustible energy that could be created by nuclear fusion reactors.

To date, scientists have been able to achieve superconductivity only at frigid temperatures, requiring substances to be constantly bathed by expensive cooling systems. Thus their applications have been limited to specialized uses, such as imaging devices for medical diagnosis and an experimental levitated train in Japan.

Widespread commercial applications will ultimately depend on discovery of room-temperature superconductors, the Holy Grail of scientists. Although researchers have made progress in finding materials that are superconductive at higher and higher temperatures, they still require cooling systems. What's more, scientists aren't sure whether these new compounds can be fabricated into wiring or can handle enough current to make them practicable. Most recently, scientists discovered that these new compounds ceased to be superconductive when exposed to large magnetic fields while carrying large currents—a potential roadblock to many large-scale commercial applications, since they would either require or create powerful magnetic fields.

As a result, superconductor applications in the 1990s are likely to be in only highly specialized areas. One of the more immediate applications is a sensing device, or "squid," which doesn't require large amounts of current. Squids, which are used to detect extremely sensitive magnetic fields, such as those caused by a submarine, have applications in the military as well as in oil and mineral exploration. In medicine, squids can be used to detect brain signals in order to diagnose neurological disorders.

Some laboratories are also trying to develop superconductors for computers to make them run faster. To get around the fabrication problem, researchers are engineering thin layers or films of superconducting material to coat the computer chips. But their cost would make them prohibitive for most computer applications at present.

4

REAL ESTATE IN THE 1990s: END OF THE BOOM

THE HOUSING MARKET OF THE 1990s

After the rapid and seemingly endless upward spiral in home prices over the past two decades, the party is coming to an end. The halcyon days of sure and quick profits in real estate are over.

The recent weakness exhibited in real estate values in many parts of the country is not a temporary phenomenon. Demographic and economic trends point to a much slower rise in home prices through the 1990s. Most housing analysts expect homeowners will be lucky just to keep pace with inflation.

Demand for homes ultimately comes down to demographic factors, and the long-term demographic trends don't bode well for housing. New households are being formed at a slower rate and the number of young adults of home-buying age is shrinking. The bottom line is that there simply won't be as many people demanding homes in the 1990s.

Fueling the explosive rise in home prices in the 1970s and 1980s was the influx of the huge baby-boom generation into the housing market. Inflation may have helped bolster the run-up in prices, but it was fundamentally the rapidly growing number of young people entering the real estate market that created the boom. Seventy-six million young people needed a place to live and the surging demand outstripped the supply. So prices rose.

But now the baby-boom generation is matured and mostly housed. In its wake is the much smaller "baby-bust" generation, born between 1965 and 1976.

As a result, new households will be formed at an average rate of 1.17 million a year, according to Census Bureau projections. That's fully one-third lower than the rate of the 1970s and 13 percent lower than the 1980s rate.

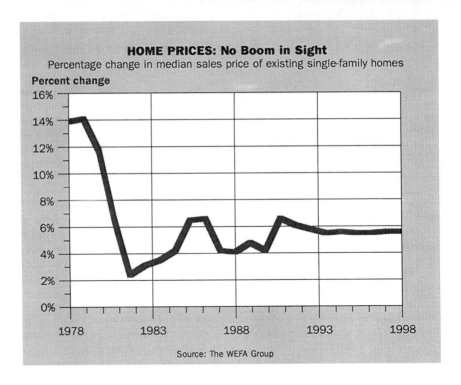

HOME PRICES: No Boom in Sight
Percentage change in median sales price of existing single-family homes

Percent change

Source: The WEFA Group

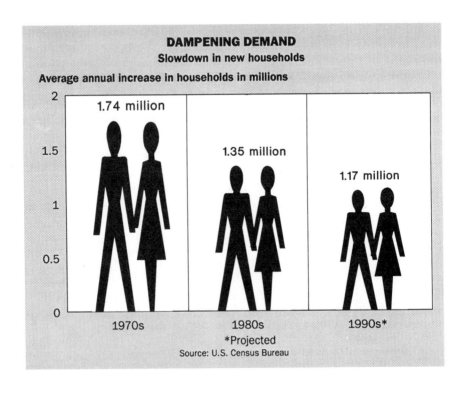

DAMPENING DEMAND
Slowdown in new households

Average annual increase in households in millions

1.74 million

1.35 million

1.17 million

1970s   1980s   1990s*

*Projected
Source: U.S. Census Bureau

Slackened Demand for Starter Homes

Starter homes are likely to be the hardest hit by the demographic changes. The number of households headed by persons aged twenty-five to thirty-four—the primary market for starter homes—will shrink from 21 million in 1988 to 18 million in the year 2000, according to Census Bureau projections. At the same time, many baby-boomers will be moving out of starter homes into larger homes.

Consequently, starter homes are expected to be in excess supply and should give first-time home buyers a larger and more affordable selection. It will be a buyer's market.

Stronger Demographics in Trade-Up Housing

By contrast, upscale housing should be the most resilient end of the market as baby-boomers reach their peak earnings years and seek to trade up to larger homes with more amenities. Rather than the first-time buyer, it will be the trade-up buyer that dominates the housing market in the

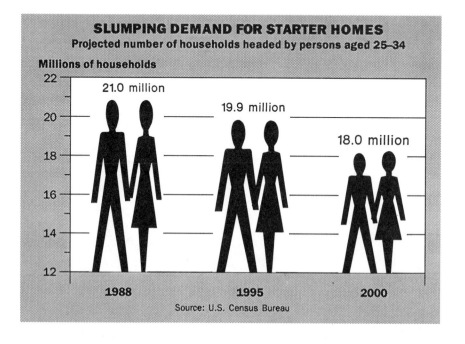

SLUMPING DEMAND FOR STARTER HOMES
Projected number of households headed by persons aged 25–34

Millions of households

21.0 million

19.9 million

18.0 million

Source: U.S. Census Bureau

1990s. The number of households headed by persons in the thirty-five-to-fifty-four-year-old age bracket, the potential market for trade-up housing, will swell from just over 33 million in 1988 to nearly 47 million in the year 2000.

But that doesn't assure booming prices for upscale homes. In recent years, home builders have been focusing on the upper end of the market and signs of overbuilding are evident in many cities.

Affordability Factors

Aside from demographics, the upward spiral in home prices was bound to slow because fewer and fewer people were able to afford ever higher prices. Home prices were climbing faster than personal income, and it was only a matter of time before the bubble burst.

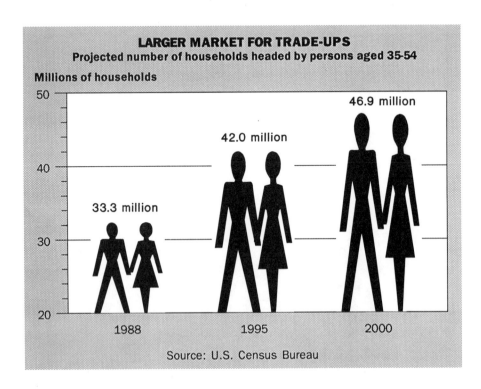

LARGER MARKET FOR TRADE-UPS
Projected number of households headed by persons aged 35-54

Millions of households

46.9 million

42.0 million

33.3 million

1988 1995 2000

Source: U.S. Census Bureau

HOW MUCH HOUSE YOU CAN AFFORD

Assumes monthly payments cannot exceed 28 percent of gross income. Figures assume buyer makes 15% down payment and property taxes and insurance average 30 percent of monthly loan payment.

Purchase price	$90,000	$125,000	$150,000	$200,000	$250,000

Mortgage rate	Minimum annual gross income needed to qualify				
8%	$31,274	$43,436	$52,123	$69,498	$86,872
9%	$34,294	$47,631	$57,157	$76,209	$95,261
10%	$37,403	$51,949	$62,339	$83,118	$103,898
11%	$40,590	$56,374	$67,649	$90,199	$112,748
12%	$43,841	$60,890	$73,068	$97,424	$121,780

Home buyers are no longer allowed to stretch their income as far as they did during the 1970s and early 1980s when the average monthly payment sometimes climbed as high as 35 percent of gross income. Lenders now impose much tighter standards. As a rule, monthly payments can't exceed 28 percent of gross income. For down payments of 10 percent or less, monthly payments usually can't exceed 25 percent of gross income.

The Tax Reform Act of 1986 also raised the out-of-pocket costs of home ownership. For a homeowner who used to be in the 40 percent tax bracket, the out-of-pocket cost of a $1,000 monthly payment rose from $600 to $720 as his tax rate fell to 28 percent.

Prices of luxury homes may also be under pressure from a 1987 tax law change that limits mortgage-interest deductions to the first $1 million in debt used to acquire, construct, or substantially improve a principal residence and a vacation home.

Threat from Dumping of Foreclosed Real Estate

Another threat to home prices in some areas is the $200 to $300 billion of residential and commerical real estate sitting in the portfolios of hundreds of insolvent savings and loans. Part of the massive federal plan to bail out ailing thrifts is for the government to seize control of the foreclosed real estate and sell it off. These properties include single-family homes, condominiums, apartment buildings, office buildings, shopping malls, hotels, and raw land. Federal regulators are mindful of the threat posed to property values by dumping so much onto the market, and they have been trying to figure out how to carry out sales in an orderly fashion. But even if sales are stretched over several years, the impact on property values is still likely to be significant. Just the knowledge that so much real estate will be coming onto the market should be enough to depress prices in some markets. Southwestern real estate, which slumped along with the depression in the oil industry, is likely to suffer the most since much of the foreclosed property is located in that region. It was the slump in Southwestern real estate that led to the financial troubles of many savings and loans.

Should prices plummet from the dumping of foreclosed properties, it could pose an attractive buying opportunity for first-time home buyers.

NEW PERSPECTIVES ON HOMES FOR THE 1990s

With the housing market seemingly headed for less robust times, homes need to be thought of more as shelter than as an investment. It may seem an old-fashioned view; but in today's weaker housing market, profits can no longer be counted on to be sizable enough—or certain enough—to make homes a reliable investment for speculation.

Homes may still be a good long-term investment. If home prices keep up with inflation, as many economists expect, 5 percent annual appreciation is not bad, particularly since you're highly leveraged and the profits are sheltered from taxes.

But the market's no longer strong enough to justify stretching your financial resources to buy more home than you really need. The extra expense is now a much riskier investment. It may not pay off. What's more, it's a mistake to think you can't lose money in buying real estate. As illustrated by the recent slump in home prices in Denver, Phoenix, Manhattan, Boston, and other markets, you can lose money.

Nor is it safe to borrow heavily against the equity in your home. In a weaker housing market, you can't be assured that the equity will always be there to bail you out of a big debt burden. Should you need to sell at a time when prices are depressed, the proceeds may not be enough to pay off all your second mortgage debt.

When home prices were rising rapidly, home buyers didn't need to concern themselves much with how long they were going to live in the home. Even a couple of years of appreciation in some markets was more than enough to offset all the expenses associated with buying and selling real estate. But with the prospect of more modest appreciation in home values, it will take longer to recoup the 6 percent sales commission, the "points" paid to finance the home, closing costs, and other expenses. So if you expect to live in a home for only a few years because of a probable job transfer or plans to move to a bigger house, be aware that appreciation may no longer be rapid enough to offset the thousands of dollars in buying and selling costs. Unless your company picks up the tab for all such costs in a relocation, it's easier to lose money these days on short-term transactions.

RENTING VERSUS BUYING

Whether to buy or rent is as much a life-style decision as an economic choice. If home ownership is your vision of the American dream and you can afford it, then that may be enough justification to buy. That's the way most people viewed housing in the old days, before soaring home prices left everyone thinking that home ownership was not only the American dream but also the investor's dream.

But the investment dream is fading. Home ownership in the 1990s isn't likely to provide anywhere near the double-digit returns of the 1970s. And in many markets, appreciation is not expected to be great enough to offset the higher out-of-pocket costs of buying a home—at least in the short run.

Real estate agents always like to make the pitch that, even if your home doesn't appreciate much, you're not throwing money down the drain in rent; you're building equity and earning tax deductions. But those advantages are overrated. In the early years of a mortgage, only about 5 percent of your monthly payments goes toward building equity; so instead of throwing money down the drain in the form of rent to your landlord every month, most of your money's going down the drain in the form of interest to your banker. Either way, a lot of money's going down the drain; it's just different drainpipes.

Nor do the tax deductions for mortgage interest and property taxes automatically make home ownership inherently cheaper than renting. All they do is help reduce the out-of-pocket cost of mortgage interest and property tax payments. But the tax deductions don't necessarily reduce the costs enough to make home ownership more economical than renting. It depends mainly on the particular market and how high rents are relative to home prices.

If you figure in the tax savings, along with all the costs of owning a home, you'll find that renting is cheaper than buying in many markets.

In the past, rapid appreciation in home prices more than made up for the extra cost. But a repeat isn't likely in most markets. So whether it's worth spending the extra money is primarily a life-style decision and secondarily an estimate of the appreciation potential in your local area.

To estimate whether buying or renting makes financial sense, compare the costs over the period of time you expect to remain in the home. In toting up the cost of ownership, make sure to include interest and principal payments, property taxes, insurance, maintenance, utilities, closing costs, and brokerage commissions. Then subtract any expected gain on the sale of the home as well as tax savings from mortgage interest and property tax deductions. In calculating rental costs, make allowance for increases in rents and utilities each year. Also make sure to account for interest you could earn on money that you don't have to tie up in a down payment.

NEW CRITERIA FOR CHOOSING A HOME IN THE 1990s

Location is the key to property values. But what may look like a desirable location today may not be tomorrow. There are several trends afoot in the 1990s that promise to change the character and desirability of many neighborhoods. They range from a new law forcing the closure of scores of military bases to the impact of growing traffic congestion.

Closing Military Bases: From Fort Dix in New Jersey to the famed Presidio in San Francisco, eighty-six military bases across the country are to be shut down over the next few years, with varying impacts on the local economies and real estate markets. The closures were scheduled to begin in 1990, with the process taking four or five years to complete. In smaller communities, where the military has been an important prop to the local economy, property values could be hurt as thousands of military and civilian jobs are lost. In other communities, the question is what use will be made of the bases after the military moves out. Federal agencies have first dibs on the property, followed by state and local governments and then private developers. Proposals for the sites include new prisons, amusement parks, shelters for the homeless, new housing developments,

FORECASTS OF LOCAL HOME PRICES
Annual average percentage appreciation in existing single-family homes
(Metropolitan Statistical Areas)
1988-1998

BELOW 3%

Albuquerque
Austin
Baltimore
Baton Rouge
Birmingham
Columbia, S.C.
Dallas-Fort Worth
Gary-Hammond,
Ind.
Knoxville
Las Vegas
Memphis
Mobile, Ala.
Monmouth-Ocean,
N.J.
Nashville
New Bedford-Fall
River, Mass.
New Orleans
Oklahoma City
Providence, R.I.
Tucson, Ariz
Tulsa
Wichita

**WORST
MARKETS**

3-4%

Allentown-
Bethlehem, Pa.
Boston
Columbus, Ohio
Dayton
El Paso
Flint
Grand Rapids,
Mich.
Greensboro, N.C.
Greenville-
Spartanberg, S.C.
Indianapolis
Johnson City-
Kingsport, Tenn.
Kansas City
Lansing, Mich.
Little Rock, Ark.
Norfolk-Newport
News, Va.
Raleigh-Durham,
N.C.
Richmond-
Petersburg, Va.
San Antonio
Scranton-Wilkes
Barre, Pa.
Springfield, Mass.
Worcester-
Fitchburg, Mass.
Youngstown-
Warren, Ohio

4-5%

Akron
Bergen-Passaic,
N.J.
Charlotte-Gastonia
Chicago
Cincinnati
Fresno, Calif.
Harrisubrg-
Lebanon, Pa.
Los Angeles-Long
Beach
Minneapolis-St.
Paul
Newark
Omaha
Oxnard-Ventura,
Calif.
Phoenix
Portland, Oreg.
San Diego
San Francisco-
Oakland
San Jose
Seattle-Everett

5-6%

Anaheim-Santa
Ana, Calif.
Bridgeport-
Stamford, Conn.
Charleston, W.V.
Denver-Boulder
Detroit
Honolulu
Jacksonville, Fla.
New York City
Philadelphia
Stockton, Calif.
Tacoma
Wilmington, Del.

6-7%

Albany-
Schenectady
Atlanta
Cleveland
Louisville
Miami-Hialeah
Milwaukee
Nassau-Suffolk,
N.Y.
New Haven-
Waterbury, Conn.
Pittsburgh
Riverside-San
Bernadino, Calif.
Rochester, N.Y.
Salt Lake City
St. Louis
Syracuse, N.Y.
Toledo
Washington D.C.

ABOVE 7%

Bakersfield, Calif.
Buffalo
Fort Lauderdale,
Fla.
Hartford-New
Britain, Conn.
Houston
Jersey City
Middlesex-
Somerset, N.J.
Orlando
Sacramento, Calif.
Tampa-St.
Petersburg
West Palm Beach,
Fla.

**BEST
MARKETS**

Source: The WEFA Group

and college campuses. Some of them may not be what you had in mind as a neighbor or the type of development that would foster higher property values—including proposals that would create a flood of new housing in the area. If you are looking for a place to live in the vicinity of a closing military base, find out what the property is likely to be used for and whether that's something you want to live next door to. Be aware that the list of base closings is likely to grow beyond the original eighty-six that have already been approved by Congress. The Defense Department recently proposed closing an additional thirty-five installations.

School District: Homes in good school districts are likely to fetch a premium in the 1990s as the children of the baby-boom generation create a surge in school enrollments. Baby-boomers, who placed great emphasis on advancing their own education, can be expected to be equally concerned about their children receiving a quality education.

Traffic Congestion: Growing traffic congestion during the 1990s is a problem that will lead to longer commutes and heavier traffic along most thoroughfares. In shopping for a home, it's not enough to merely assess current commute times and how much traffic now passes in front of the house. Rather, it's essential to gauge what traffic conditions will be like in the future. Homes that front on throughways are bound to see traffic worsen as freeways and other main arteries become clogged and motorists seek alternate routes. This should place a premium on homes located on streets that don't permit through traffic, particularly cul-de-sacs, which offer the best protection from traffic. Proximity to mass transportation or work locations will also be of increasing importance as traffic congestion lengthens commute times.

High home prices have led a growing number of Americans to remote suburban developments in search of affordable housing. But while they may figure that a one- or two-hour commute is worth the sacrifice, increased traffic will make the journey a much longer one in the future. If those bedroom communities become intolerable commutes, their only salvation is the hope that industry will someday move in. But banking on that someday is a risky speculation. (For more on traffic congestion and home values, see chapter 18.)

Aircraft Noise: Although the new generation of commercial aircraft is quieter, air traffic noise could become an even worse problem in the 1990s for residents near major airports and along flight paths as air travel grows. As a result, assessing the impact of aircraft noise when looking for a place to live is critical. Not only can aircraft noise make life miserable for you and your family, but it can also affect the value of your home. (For more on aircraft noise and property values, see chapter 19.)

"Adults Only" Developments: If you're looking to live in a residential development that is free of the sights and sounds of children, be aware that federal law no longer permits discrimination in renting or selling a home to families with children. Retirement communities are exempt from this 1989 modification to the Fair Housing Act. But the guidelines for exemption are strict. Generally, a retirement complex qualifies for exemption only if 80 percent of the apartments are occupied by at least one resident who is age fifty-five or older and the development provides facilities and services specially designed to meet the needs of older persons. (Some other types of senior citizens' housing can qualify for exemption if all residents are age 62 or older or if the project is funded by government programs for the elderly.) So if you're looking to live in an adults-only complex, make sure the development adheres to the guidelines needed to qualify for the exemption; otherwise you could find children living next door.

If you decide to buy a home in an all-adult development, be aware that the new age restrictions may limit the market for your home should you later wish to sell or rent it. In the past, homeowner association rules in all-adult communities often allowed owners to sell or rent their unit to adults of any age, so long as they didn't have children. But with the new law's exemption requirements, you may no longer be able to sell or rent to adults of any age. If your all-adult complex intends to keep its exemption, you will likely be forced to sell or rent only to families with one resident age fifty-five or older.

"Impact Fees": The price spread between new and previously owned homes is widening sharply in many communities, and it's not just due to higher labor or material costs. Rather, it's the result of a growing movement by local governments to hit developers rather than taxpayers for the cost of building new roads, sewers, schools, parks, and other public facilities. "Impact fees" are especially prevalent in Florida and California, but they are spreading rapidly to other parts of the country. Local governments see impact fees as politically more palatable than hiking property taxes on every homeowner in the community. Impact fees typically run a few thousand dollars per home, but in some areas they run as high as $10,000 to $20,000 a home. While the fee is assessed on developers, the costs are usually passed on to the home buyer in the form of a higher price. Bear in mind that these fees may be hard to recover fully when it comes time to sell the home, particularly if there are comparable homes in the vicinity that were built before the impact fees were imposed and had municipal services financed by local taxes.

Garbage: Over the next few years, hundreds of communities across the country will be running out of places to put their mounting trash and are searching frantically for new sites for landfills and incinerators. In looking for a place to live, find out whether your prospective neighborhood is a potential site.

Prisons: Prison overcrowding is another crisis facing state governments, and many of them are under court order to build new ones. Find out if your neighborhood is on the list of sites being considered for a new prison.

The Earthquake Threat: In earthquake-prone regions, home buyers are likely to be more sensitive to seismic considerations in the wake of the major earthquake that damaged or destroyed thousands of homes in northern California on October 17, 1989. Homes that are located on or near fault lines or that are built on landfill or soft soil are likely to sell

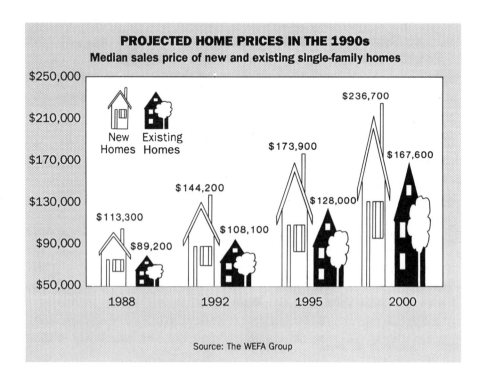

PROJECTED HOME PRICES IN THE 1990s
Median sales price of new and existing single-family homes

Source: The WEFA Group

for less than homes built on solid ground. Similarly, high-rise buildings, both residential and commercial, that were designed using the latest engineering technologies to withstand earthquakes are likely to fetch premiums over older buildings.

The San Francisco earthquake, measuring 7.1 on the Richter scale, underscored the serious seismic threat facing California—as well as many other regions of the country—and the importance of earthquake insurance. While earthquakes are more frequent in California, major earthquakes have occurred or could occur in many other parts of the United States, including the Northeast, the Mississippi Valley, South Carolina, Utah, the Pacific Northwest, and Alaska.

Seismic trends lead geologists to believe that the United States is headed into another cycle of major earthquake activity. In California, seismologists say that during the next thirty years both Los Angeles and San Francisco are vulnerable to an even more destructive quake than the one that struck the San Francisco Bay area in 1989. Seismologists have also placed high odds on a destructive earthquake occurring in the eastern United States over the next two decades, although they're not sure where. In fact, some of the most intense earthquakes ever recorded in the United States occurred in the East, including New Madrid, Missouri (the most intense on record in the U.S.); Charleston, South Carolina; and one near Boston, Massachusetts. Earthquakes in the East can be even more destructive than ones of similar magnitude in California because Eastern quakes tend to shake a much larger area and because few structures have been designed to withstand earthquakes.

Yet relatively few homeowners carry earthquake insurance—even in California. Standard homeowner's insurance doesn't cover damage caused directly by an earthquake. An earthquake endorsement needs to be purchased. Many homeowners dismiss earthquake coverage as too expensive and the deductibles too high. But without it, you could face huge losses if the damage is extensive; if you decide to walk away from the mortgage rather than rebuild, you lose whatever equity you built up in the home. In the highest-risk areas, including northern and southern California, earthquake insurance premiums run $1.50 to $4.00 per $1,000 of insured value, or about $300 to $800 a year for a $200,000 frame home. (Masonry homes cost far more to insure.) In most areas of the country, premiums on a frame home run as low as 22 to 30 cents per $1,000 of insured value.

Earthquake insurance usually carries a 5 to 10 percent deductible, meaning that on a $200,000 home, the policy won't cover the first $10,000 to $20,000 in damage. There is also a separate deductible on the home's contents.

Eroding Shorelines: In U.S. coastal areas, nature is taking a toll in another way: Shorelines are eroding at a rate of two to five feet a year along the Eastern Seaboard and the Gulf of Mexico, according to geologists, and the problem will grow worse as more and more buildings go up in coastal areas. (Eventually, global warming, resulting from the greenhouse effect, will accelerate the erosion as polar ice packs melt, sending sea levels rising.)

As a result, beachfront living, a dream of many Americans, is becoming more costly and hazardous. For property owners, an eroding shoreline can mean the expense of erecting a seawall, of replacing the sand every several years, or in some situations, of moving the entire home further inland. Moreover, an eroding shoreline exposes seaside homes to greater danger in heavy storms. Barrier islands face the greatest risk, but other coastal locations are also vulnerable, as was illustrated in 1989 by the widespread destruction caused by Hurricane Hugo along the South Carolina coast.

If your mind is set on living near the water, the home should be situated at a high elevation and at the greatest distance possible from the sea, according to Dr. Orrin H. Pilkey Jr., professor of geology and director of the program for the study of developed shorelines at Duke University. Also make sure that there is a reliable route available for evacuation in case of an emergency. Before buying, find out the erosion rate of the shoreline and the potential for flooding and wave damage in a severe storm. Flood maps of the area prepared by the Federal Emergency Management Agency should be available for public inspection at city and county government offices. Your state coastal commission should also be able to answer some of your questions.

If you do buy coastal property, get flood insurance. Standard homeowner policies don't cover flood damage. Flood insurance is available from the federal government under the National Flood Insurance Program. But it's available only to residents of communities that adopt prudent land-use control measures. Your insurance agent should be able to supply you with information on the government's flood insurance program.

ADJUSTABLE-RATE VERSUS FIXED-RATE MORTGAGES

After you find the house you like, the next major trauma is finding a mortgage you can live with. It's a natural instinct for people to lean toward the security of a traditional fixed-rate mortgage. And that's what you should stick with if you live on a fixed income or if you have any doubts about being able to afford a rise in monthly payments. It's also the best bet if you plan to keep the house a long time. Fixed-rate mortgages offer peace of mind that your monthly payments will remain the same for the life of the loan, regardless of what happens to interest rates. So for people who fear they'll have trouble sleeping at night worrying about how Federal Reserve policy is going to affect their next mortgage payment on an adjustable-rate loan, a fixed-rate mortgage is probably worth the price. Fixed-rate mortgages typically carry interest rates that are 1.5 to 3 percentage points higher than the initial rate on adjustable-rate mortgages.

That rate differential is why a lot of people choose adjustable-rate mortgages. The lower rate and lower monthly payments enable many home buyers to qualify for the size loan they need. On a $100,000 mortgage, a two-point rate differential can translate into savings of more than $140 a month.

Adjustable-rate loans also appeal to a lot of people whose job requires them to relocate frequently and who thus intend to own their home for only a few years. They figure they can take advantage of the lower rates of an adjustable-rate loan without much risk. Most adjustable loans have caps on how far the interest rate and monthly payments can change in any given period, so by the time any real damage was done by a spurt in interest rates, they'd be moved out of the house.

Even those who plan to keep their home longer than a few years

MONTHLY MORTGAGE PAYMENTS (30-YEAR TERM)

Loan Amount	$75,000	$100,000	$150,000	$200,000	$250,000	$300,000
Rate			Monthly payment			
8.0%	$550	$734	$1,101	$1,468	$1,834	$2,201
8.5%	$577	$769	$1,153	$1,538	$1,922	$2,307
9.0%	$603	$805	$1,207	$1,609	$2,012	$2,414
9.5%	$631	$841	$1,261	$1,682	$2,102	$2,523
10.0%	$658	$878	$1,316	$1,755	$2,194	$2,633
10.5%	$686	$915	$1,372	$1,829	$2,287	$2,744
11.0%	$714	$952	$1,428	$1,905	$2,381	$2,857
11.5%	$743	$990	$1,485	$1,981	$2,476	$2,971
12.0%	$771	$1,029	$1,543	$2,057	$2,572	$3,086
12.5%	$800	$1,067	$1,601	$2,135	$2,668	$3,202
13.0%	$830	$1,106	$1,659	$2,212	$2,766	$3,319

may not find the risks all that great with an adjustable-rate loan. Caps can prevent the mortgage rate from rising more than about 2 percent a year, or more than 5 or 6 percent over the life of the loan. Thus the risk is limited and tolerable so long as the borrower's income keeps rising enough to cover higher mortgage payments if interest rates do go up.

What's more, a lot of people figure that even if interest rates did shoot up, everything would balance out over time. They might even come out ahead, since rates on adjustable loans can go down as well as up. Indeed, if you can find an adjustable-rate loan with an initial rate that's substantially lower than on a fixed-rate mortgage and with a cap limiting how much the rate can rise each year and over the life of the loan, the adjustable loan may well turn out to be a better deal.

If inflation and interest rates remain moderate through the 1990s, as most economists expect, adjustable-rate mortgages would end up costing borrowers much less than fixed-rate loans. But interest-rate forecasts are not reliable enough to bet much money on, particularly when you're committing to a sizable loan that extends for thirty years.

So it's risky to decide what kind of mortgage to choose based on interest-rate hunches. An adjustable-rate mortgage is a safe bet only if you're confident your income will rise enough to handle higher mortgage payments under the worst-case scenario. If you're not sure that you'd be able to handle payments if rates rose as high as the loan cap allowed, then an adjustable-rate mortgage can be as risky as some of the legendary poker games in the Wild West. Homes were gambled away there, too. The only difference was that they bet their homes on a hand of cards rather than on long-term interest-rate forecasts. If you can't make the house payment because of rising interest rates, you lose the bet; the lender can foreclose on your home.

Which brings us back to the security of the fixed-rate mortgage. If the only reason you're opting for an adjustable-rate loan is that you can't afford the monthly payments on a fixed-rate mortgage, then you can't afford the house. Find a less expensive one.

What to Look for in an Adjustable-Rate Mortgage

To limit the cost and the risk of an adjustable-rate mortgage, you'll need to do more than compare the initial interest rate on the loan. Most initial rates are set artificially low as a promotion; they're teasers and only last for a year or so before they go up. So in shopping for an adjustable-rate mortgage, find out what the rate would be like after the first adjustment period, as well as what features the loan contains to minimize your costs and protect you against a rapid and steep rise in interest rates.

Interest-Rate Caps: Make sure the loan includes caps to limit how much the interest rate can rise each year and over the life of the loan. Caps protect you against any sudden or sharp rise in interest rates that might make monthly payments unaffordable. Look for caps that limit rates to a rise of no more than about 2 percent a year and 5 or 6 percent over the life of the loan.

Payment Caps: Beware of loans that cap monthly payments but not the interest rate. If interest rates rise, your monthly payment may not increase by as much as the rise in interest rates would dictate. But you'll get hit for the extra interest later. Any excess amount above the cap is tacked onto the unpaid balance of the loan. So during a period of rising interest rates, your loan gets bigger. This is called "negative amortization." To pay off the extra amount owed, either you'll find your monthly payments staying higher long after interest rates have gone back down or you'll find extra payments tacked onto the end of your loan term. If your unpaid balance keeps growing, you could wind up owing more than when you took out the loan. That's no problem if the value of your home continues to climb; you can recover the balance when you sell the house. But if real estate prices don't rise enough to keep pace with your rising mortgage balance, you may not be able to recover all of it on the sale.

Adjustment Period: This determines how often the lender can change your interest rate and monthly payment. Most loans make adjustments once a year. Others do it every six months, three years, or five years. (Good loans will adjust both the rate and monthly payments at the same time.) In comparing adjustment periods, bear in mind that the more frequently the rate gets adjusted, the more steeply your monthly payments will increase during a period of rising rates. On the other hand, a more frequent adjustment period allows a decline in interest rates to be reflected sooner on your mortgage payments.

Index: Find out what index the lender uses to base rate adjustments on the loan. This may seem like a technical matter, but which index is used can have a significant impact on the bottom line. Some indexes are more volatile than others. Volatility is helpful when interest rates are declining but it can make monthly payments more expensive when rates are climbing. The most common index used is based on yields of one-year Treasury bills. Unfortunately, it's also the most volatile. The slowest-moving index is the cost-of-funds index, which is used widely in California but takes second place elsewhere. Regardless of which type of index is used, make sure it's not one that the bank itself controls; otherwise, the bank could manipulate the index for its own advantage. The commonly used one-year Treasury bill index is compiled by the Federal Reserve and the cost-of-funds index is prepared by the Federal Home Loan Bank Board.

Margin: This is the fixed percentage amount that your lender will add to the index to determine your mortgage rate each adjustment period. So look for a low margin of 2 to 2.5 percent.

Prepayment Penalty: Make sure there is no penalty for paying off all or part of the loan balance early. If there is, you would face a stiff penalty if you later wanted to refinance or if you wanted to accelerate payments in order to build equity faster and save on interest costs.

Assumability: This feature allows the loan to be taken over by a future buyer of your home. If the terms of your loan are good, it can be an attractive selling feature.

Conversion Provision: Some adjustable loans contain a provision allowing you to convert to a fixed-rate mortgage during the first five years. It's a nice feature to have since it allows you to switch to a fixed-rate loan for less than the cost of refinancing. But the convertible feature isn't free. It normally entails a slightly higher rate or up-front fees.

40-YEAR MORTGAGES: NOT MUCH SALVATION

In the desperate search for ways to make home ownership affordable, 40-year mortgages are beginning to attract interest among home buyers. By stretching the life of the loan to forty years, from the traditional 30-year term, monthly payments are lower. In some cases, the lower monthly payment is the difference between qualifying for a loan and falling short of the income-eligibility guidelines.

But 40-year loans don't provide nearly as much salvation as many people think. On a $150,000 mortgage carrying a 10 percent interest rate, the difference in monthly payments between a 30-year and 40-year loan is about $42. That's a savings of only 3 percent. Obviously, 3 percent

40-YEAR MORTGAGES

Little salvation for home buyers

Comparing terms on a $150,000 mortgage

	30-YEAR mortgage	40-YEAR mortgage
Monthly payment	$1,316	$1,274
Total interest paid over life of loan	$323,889	$461,385
Principal paid off after five years	$5,139	$1,837
Mortgage Rate	10%	10%

doesn't go very far toward helping home buyers qualify for financing or easing the burden of high monthly payments.

What's more, to get that $42 savings on your monthly payments, you pay a steep price in the long run. With a 40-year mortgage, you build equity much more slowly and you pay much more interest than on a 30-year loan. In the example of the $150,000 mortgage, total interest on a 40-year loan runs over $137,000 more than on a 30-year mortgage. In addition, more of each monthly payment goes toward interest on a 40-year loan, which means you're paying down principal at a much slower rate, as you can see in the example of the $150,000 mortgage.

THE 15-YEAR MORTGAGE:
HOW TO SAVE $188,000 ON A $150,000 MORTGAGE

Rather than stretching mortgage payments out over thirty or forty years, a growing number of home buyers are opting for 15-year mortgages. With a 15-year mortgage, you can build equity much faster and reduce interest charges over the life of the loan by more than half. Yet your monthly payments are only about 20 percent higher than on a 30-year mortgage.

Most lenders offer 15-year home loans. In fact, they usually give better deals on 15-year mortgages; interest rates are often a quarter- to a half-percentage point lower than on 30-year mortgages.

Consider a $150,000 mortgage. Monthly payments on a 30-year mortgage at 10 percent interest run $1,316. On a 15-year mortgage with a 9.75 percent rate, the monthly payment would run $1,589. That's $273, or 21 percent more than on the 30-year loan.

30-YEAR vs. 15-YEAR MORTGAGE

Comparing terms on a $150,000 mortgage

	30-YEAR mortgage	15-YEAR mortgage
Monthly payment	$1,316	$1,589
Total interest paid over life of loan	$323,889	$136,028
Principal paid off after five years	$5,139	$28,486
Mortgage Rate	10%	9.75%

But by paying 21 percent more, you can slice interest charges by 58 percent. You save nearly $188,000 in interest charges over the life of the loan.

Equity builds much more quickly, too, since more of each monthly payment goes toward principal. At the start, principal represents about 23 percent of monthly payments on a 15-year loan compared to 5 percent on the 30-year loan. After five years, you will have paid off $28,486 in principal with a 15-year mortgage compared to only $5,139 on a 30-year loan.

How to Get the Benefits of a 15-Year Term with Your 30-Year Mortgage

Homeowners with 30-year mortgages don't need to go through all the trouble and expense of refinancing in order to get the benefits of a 15-year mortgage. Nor is taking out a 15-year mortgage when you buy a home always the right decision.

With a 30-year mortgage, you can achieve interest savings and equity buildup similar to a 15-year loan simply by writing a bigger check to your lender each month. It's that easy. No need to change the terms of the loan to do it. At the same time, sticking with a 30-year mortgage gives you the flexibility to go back to making smaller payments should some unanticipated expense arise that makes it hard for you to keep up with the larger payments required by a 15-year schedule. All you'll miss out on by opting for a 30-year loan is a slightly lower interest rate available on 15-year mortgages.

To make a 30-year mortgage provide the benefits of a shorter-term loan, all you need do is make bigger monthly payments and have the extra amount apply to the loan principal. Before making the larger payment, however, ask your lender if there is any special way it should be done. He may tell you to attach a note to your check specifying that the extra amount is to be applied to the loan principal. Also make sure your mortgage loan doesn't carry any penalties for prepayments.

VACATION HOMES: A BUYER'S MARKET

To many Americans, owning a ski chalet in Vail or a beachfront condo in Hawaii is a paradisiacal dream. But as many vacation-home owners have learned in the past few years, paradise can be a terrible investment.

After a speculative binge in the 1970s and early 1980s, overbuilding and tax-law changes sent vacation-home prices plummeting in some of America's best-known resort areas in the mid-1980s. Many areas have yet to show much sign of recovery, with prices still down 20 to 50 percent from their early 1980s peak.

Demographics bode well for the vacation-home market in the 1990s with the large baby-boom population reaching its peak earnings years. But that may not be enough to foster another buying boom. For one thing, prices of principal residences have climbed so high that many people who might otherwise be candidates for second homes are stretching just to make payments on their first home.

For another, many markets remain glutted with properties. Vacation-home owners began bailing out while Congress was drafting the Tax Reform Act of 1986. While the mortgage interest deduction was retained for first and second homes, the reduction in personal income tax rates effectively raised the out-of-pocket cost of owning a second home. In addition, Congress curtailed the tax benefits for upper-income taxpayers who rent out their vacation homes, turning many profitable operations into money losers. A year later, Congress capped the amount of mortgage interest that could be deducted on first- and second-home purchases to the first $1 million in debt, sharply raising the real cost of owning two homes in high-priced areas.

With all these cutbacks in tax benefits, it's small wonder that vacation-home prices remain depressed. With fewer tax benefits, prospective buyers aren't as numerous nor are they willing to pay as much as when tax benefits were more generous. What's more, the potential for further cutbacks in tax benefits is a looming threat to the vacation-home market. Although congressional tax writers say they have no plans to change the rules, the search for ways to trim the federal deficit has led to fears that vacation-home interest deductions would be a prime target in any major revenue-raising effort.

So if you want to buy a vacation home, buy for pleasure, not for profit.

RENTAL PROPERTIES: A MIXED PICTURE

Overbuilding and fewer tax benefits have also hurt the market for rental properties. Many cities are glutted with apartments. And upper-income landlords are no longer able to deduct more than they receive in rents. For many properties, those excess tax deductions (known as tax losses) were the difference between making money and losing money.

Demographics also suggest a bleak picture: The number of persons between the ages of twenty and thirty-four, the group most likely to rent, is declining.

Nonetheless, a case can be made for becoming a landlord, particularly if you're eligible to claim excess tax deductions and you live in a market where vacancy rates are relatively low and rental demand is strong.

Tax benefits, although reduced by the Tax Reform Act of 1986, can still be lucrative for all but the wealthiest landlords. So long as you play an active role in managing the property and your adjusted gross income (as calculated on your personal income tax return) doesn't exceed $100,000, you can use up to $25,000 a year in tax losses from your rental property to offset other personal income. If your income is between $100,000 and $150,000, you are still eligible to use some tax losses. (The $25,000 allowance is reduced 50 cents for each dollar that adjusted income exceeds $100,000.) Even if rental income isn't sufficient by itself to make the rental unit profitable, the tax benefits may help to make it so.

There are also reasons to suggest that the rental market will improve in the next several years. One reason is the current slowdown in apartment construction due to the cutback in tax benefits and to high vacancy rates. As fewer apartments are added to the supply, vacancy rates will gradually fall, allowing rents to be raised at a faster pace.

Demographics may not be as bleak for the rental market as the shrinking numbers of young people suggest, either. Offsetting the declines are increasing numbers of adults living alone and households headed by single parents. Another group of renters is also projected to grow: middle-aged adults without children. High home prices and stricter lending standards are also keeping would-be homeowners in the rental market longer.

Qualifying for Landlord Tax Breaks: To be eligible to claim up to $25,000 a year in tax losses from a rental property, the law requires you to "actively participate" in managing the property. Actively participating doesn't mean you personally have to scrub the hallways and interview prospective tenants. You can hire other people to do the dirty work, such as a rental agent to find tenants and a maintenance service to handle cleaning and repairs. But you personally have to make management decisions, such as approving capital expenditures and establishing rental terms.

You can own the rental property with other partners, but you can't own less than a 10 percent interest if you want to claim tax losses. Investments in large real-estate limited partnerships, where the "general partner" makes all the decisions and the "limited partners" do no more than invest their money, are not eligible for the special tax treatment. (Two exceptions are limited partnership investments in low-income housing projects and renovations of historic structures.)

LAND: TRICKIER TIMES FOR SPECULATION

Some of America's greatest fortunes have been made from land speculation, and no doubt many more investors will get rich in the future as development spreads to parcels of land they purchased at good prices.

But it will be harder and trickier to make a buck in land speculation in the 1990s. In most parts of the country, development is slowing, and that means slowing demand for land. Fewer homes will be built because of the slowdown in new households, and those that are built sit on smaller lots. Fewer office buildings will be built because of the current glut and because future demands for office space will not be as great. Fewer shopping malls will be built because most of the good sites have already been taken and the mergers of department-store chains have made fewer anchors available.

A moderate inflationary outlook also reduces the prospect that investors will be rushing to buy up land as a hedge against inflation.

Spreading Anti-Growth Sentiment

In fast-growing areas of the country where development is brisk, investors not only face high prices for land but also the substantial risk that local communities will suddenly call an early end to the party. Anti-growth sentiment is spreading. Tired of traffic jams, overcrowded schools, and other problems stemming from unfettered development, voters have approved ballot initiatives imposing tight restrictions on residential and commercial development in scores of communities across the country. In California alone, nearly sixty communities have adopted slow-growth measures.

Besides quality-of-life considerations, greed has motivated many homeowners to join the slow-growth movement. Prices of existing homes are driven up when curbs are placed on new housing construction. Similarly, owners of existing office buildings like growth controls because rents are driven up by the shrinking supply of new office space. In the long term, however, growth controls can hurt a community's economy. New jobs and tax revenues are sacrificed if businesses are driven away by high office rents and limited space for expansion and if new residents are kept away by high home prices.

Hardly anything could be worse for land values than new restrictions on development. If voters pass a local ordinance preventing developers from building homes or office buildings or shopping centers on your vacant patch of real estate, your land suddenly becomes much less valuable. Waiting for the growth controls to be lifted may be like waiting for Godot. Essentially, you're betting that the problems that originally prompted the development restrictions—such as traffic congestion—will be resolved. That's a long-shot bet.

FARMLAND

With the farm economy emerging from the depths of depression, farmland prices are also showing signs of revival. Farmland may seem a bargain given that acreage is selling for a fraction of the price it sold for as recently as 1982. But despite signs of recovery in the farm community, the 1990s aren't likely to be a return to the banner days of the 1970s when farmland values quadrupled.

A lot has changed since then. For one thing, the agricultural export market doesn't offer the same opportunities for expansion as it did a decade ago. Many of the countries that American farmers used to sell crops to have become self-sufficient.

Farmers also face the prospect of smaller government subsidies. Budgetary pressures are growing each year to reduce farm subsidy programs, a move that would cause commodity prices to fall further and make it even tougher for family farmers to survive.

Over the longer term, biotechnology promises to make farming much more productive, allowing crops to be grown for less money on less land. While such promises may not be realized until after the turn of the century, farmland is a long-term investment, and prices reflect the long-term earning potential of the land.

THE OFFICE BUILDING GLUT

America has such a glut of office buildings that it will take years to absorb the excess supply in most markets. Nationwide, vacancy rates average around 16 percent in downtown business districts and more than 20 percent in the suburbs. Most real estate experts think it will be the mid-1990s before the glut is brought under control. In such overbuilt markets as Denver and New Orleans, it could take much longer.

Even when the excess supply is absorbed, demand for office space in the 1990s won't be as strong as it was during the 1970s and 1980s. The labor force is still growing, but at a much slower rate than it did when baby-boomers were entering the work force. The trend toward telecommuting and home-based businesses will also have some marginal impact on the demand for office space. So will the spreading automation and computerization of the workplace. Automated teller machines, for example, mean you don't need as many brick-and-mortar bank branches. Nor will businesses need as much office space, as more of their files and data are electronically stored. Storage is already much cheaper in computers than in filing cabinets.

Even in markets where demand for office space is strong and vacancy rates are declining, office buildings won't be as profitable for investors as they were a few short years ago.

The main reason is the cutback in tax benefits. Before the Tax Reform Act of 1986, real estate tax benefits were so lucrative that many investors who poured money into an office building venture could wind up with a profit even if the building remained half empty. Tax losses from the partnership could be profitably used to shelter their personal income from taxes. Tax reform changed that. Now the tax losses can't be used to shelter your salary or any other income except from another tax-shelter investment. Only when the tax shelter is sold or otherwise disposed of can the unused losses be claimed in full.

Another reason that office building projects are riskier today is urban sprawl. Investing in a downtown office building no longer provides the same potential for charging ever higher rents. Downtown business districts are not the indispensable locations they used to be. If rents get too high, businesses are no longer reluctant to move at least part of their operations to cheaper quarters. Top management may choose to remain downtown, but back-office staff can be housed in cheaper suburban offices thanks to advances in telecommunications and computerization. In Manhattan, for example, many Wall Street firms have moved their back-office operations across the river to suburban New Jersey.

5

BANKING AND BORROWING MONEY IN THE 1990s

THE NEW BYWORD: DEVELOP A BETTER RELATIONSHIP WITH ONE BANK

After years of running around from bank to bank in search of the last iota of yield, it may finally be time to settle down and become friendlier with one banker.

In the early 1980s, after the government lifted restrictions on how much interest banks could pay on customer accounts, the byword became: Shop around. And so consumers shopped around town—and even out of town—looking for the bank with the best deal. The result for many investors became a string of banking relationships; perhaps a certificate of deposit at one bank, a checking account at another, a money market account at a third, and a few IRAs split among others.

But after a decade of chasing around and scattered accounts, the new strategy should be: Develop a better relationship with one bank. Once you find one you like, there are advantages in consolidating your accounts that can outweigh the extra interest you might earn from scattered accounts.

One reason is the proliferation of fees. Banks are imposing stiff fees on more and more accounts and the only way to avoid them is to keep more money in the bank. It's becoming commonplace for banks to charge fees of $60 to $120 a year on checking and savings accounts that don't meet minimum balance requirements. Thus, if your interest-bearing checking account is below the minimum because you invested $5,000 in another bank's certificate of deposit, you may be losing money on the deal. The fees on your checking account may more than offset the slightly higher yield earned on the other bank's CD.

These fees provide considerable incentive to make sure your accounts always have sufficient funds in them. Many banks also waive fees for customers who maintain more than one account at the bank and whose combined balances exceed the minimums. Either way, avoiding fees usually means consolidating your banking business.

Besides escaping fees, larger account balances usually earn higher yields. For example, if you have an interest-bearing checking account with a $5,000 balance, you will often earn a slightly higher rate than customers with smaller balances.

By consolidating your accounts you'll also become a more important customer to the bank, and banks tend to give their bigger customers preferred treatment. One typical benefit is immediate crediting of checks deposited in your account. No waiting for your check to clear before you have use of the money or before it starts earning interest. And when the need arises for a loan, valued customers can often extract better terms. If you find a bank where you can develop a personal relationship with one of its officers, you will inevitably find such a relationship can help grease the way through the bureaucracy when you need it.

Of course, once you have enough money in your primary bank to avoid account fees and build a good enough relationship to satisfy your future banking needs, there's no harm in investing some of the money you want to keep liquid elsewhere to get a higher yield on money market funds or CDs. But ultra-high CD yields won't be as prevalent in the 1990s as they were in the 1980s. The government's massive effort to bail out the savings-and-loan industry includes steps to rein in some of the reckless practices that led many thrifts to offer high yields in order to attract funds.

If you have substantial funds, a second banking relationship can be beneficial in the event your personal banker leaves the bank. At least you'll have an established relationship with an officer at your other bank to rely on.

Federal Deposit Insurance: There are limits to how much you should keep in any one bank or thrift. Federal insurance covers deposits only up to $100,000. That limit applies to the total of all accounts under the same name at any one institution. So if you have $75,000 invested in a CD, $25,000 in your money market account, and another $15,000 in your checking account at the same institution, $15,000 of your money (plus interest) could be lost if the institution failed.

There are ways to extend the $100,000 limit at one bank. For example, if you're married, you and your spouse can have up to $300,000 protected if you establish accounts under your own name, others in your spouse's name, and still others as joint accounts. Just keep in mind that you can have no more than $100,000 in deposits under the same name.

Individual Retirement Accounts and Keogh Plans are insured separately and each is eligible for $100,000 of protection. So if you had

$100,000 in IRA funds invested at the bank, you could still have another $100,000 in regular accounts at the bank and all of it would be covered by deposit insurance even if it was all in your own name.

HOME-EQUITY LOANS: THE WIDENING ADVANTAGE

Home-equity loans are becoming a more important source of borrowing as the tax deduction for most other types of consumer loans vanishes. Ever since the Tax Reform Act of 1986 targeted consumer interest deductions for extinction, homeowners have been rushing down to their local bank for a home-equity loan to finance everything from college educations to Caribbean cruises. In general, interest on home-equity loans up to $100,000 is fully deductible. Interest on other types of consumer loans is only 10 percent deductible in 1990 and nondeductible thereafter.

Beyond the tax advantages, tapping into the equity in your home can give you enormous borrowing power at interest rates that are usually much lower than on unsecured personal loans. The tax deductions make the real cost of home-equity loans even lower. Home-equity loans are also convenient and flexible. You can draw on your home-equity loan in full or in part, as you can on a revolving credit line at a department store, and take ten to fifteen years or longer to pay it back. To make a purchase, all you need do is write a check against your home-equity line of credit. Some banks give you a credit card to tap your credit line.

But the dangers are as great as the attractions. If you fall behind in your payments, you could lose your home. The collateral for your home-equity loan is your house. That makes home-equity loans riskier than other types of consumer loans. If you buy a car with a conventional automobile loan, all you stand to lose is the car. If you buy a car with a home-equity loan, you could lose the roof over your head.

If there is a consumer danger lurking in the 1990s it is the proliferation of home-equity loans and the ease with which so many Americans are tapping their home equity. Without discipline, it's easy to get deep into debt and stay in hock longer since payments can be stretched over many years. If you have trouble keeping control with a regular credit card, imagine the temptation to use a home-equity credit card that gives you many times the borrowing capacity and the option to pay off the debt over ten years or longer. If you buy a car with a home-equity loan and no one's forcing you to pay the loan off in a few years, it's conceivable that you'll still be paying for the car long after you get rid of it, and when it comes time to buy a new one you just go deeper into debt. Compounding the dangers is the loan's variable interest rate, which moves in lockstep with the prevailing level of interest rates. If interest rates go up, you could have trouble making the higher monthly payments. The interest rate on the loan is adjusted monthly and floats about 1 to 3 percentage points above the prime rate. It is rare to find a fixed-rate home-equity loan.

Although home-equity loan rates are lower, most other types of consumer debt are fixed-rate, giving you protection against any run-up in interest rates. Home-equity loans also entail many of the same up-front expenses as first mortgages. Most banks charge a loan origination fee equal to 2 to 3 percent of your home-equity credit line, plus closing costs of $200 to $400.

Nonetheless, if used with care, home-equity loans can be a cost-effective way to borrow for a college education or for home improvements, or to consolidate loans. Risking your house to finance a car or take a vacation, however, is certainly questionable. And you shouldn't overlook other sources of financing that sometimes provide a better deal—such as low-rate car loans that auto manufacturers occasionally offer or below-market-rate student loans offered by individual colleges and under government-sponsored programs.

When shopping for a home-equity loan, here are some points to consider:

Interest-Rate Cap: Try to find a loan that has a cap on how high the variable interest rate can be raised. Many home-equity loans don't have the same kind of caps commonly found on adjustable-rate mortgages, making you vulnerable should interest rates shoot up. Try to find one with a cap that allows the interest rate to rise no more than about 5 percentage points over the life of the loan.

Up-Front Fees: Look for a loan with minimal up-front fees and "points." It's a fiercely competitive market so you should be able to find a bank that offers significant savings on these charges. Points are the origination fees that banks charge to make the loan. Each point equals 1 percent of the loan amount. So if you take out a $50,000 home-equity loan that carries a two-point loan origination fee, you're charged $1,000 up front for the loan. That's in addition to closing costs that usually range from $200 to $400. By shopping around, you should be able to find a better deal.

Annual Fees: Besides up-front costs, some banks assess annual fees that continue for the life of the loan. Try to find one that keeps the fees to no more than about $25 a year.

Prepayment Penalty: Make sure the loan doesn't contain a prepayment penalty. So long as there is no penalty, you have the option to cut your interest expense by paying the loan off early or by making larger monthly payments than required.

Balloon Payments: Be wary of loans that require a large "balloon" payment at the end of the loan term. These balloons are common in home-equity loan arrangements where you're only required to pay interest during the course of the loan term. At the end of the term, your principal is due in one lump sum. This arrangement keeps your monthly payments lower, but it means coming up with a large amount of money at the end. If you can't come up with the balloon payment or find refinancing, you'll either forfeit your house or be forced into a quick sale. If you opt for a balloon loan, ask the lender to agree in writing that the bank will refinance the final balance or extend the loan term if it becomes necessary. That way you're protected in case you can't come up with the cash to make the balloon payment.

Interest-Only Loans: Not all interest-only loans contain balloon provisions. Some banks allow you to pay interest only for the first five or ten years and then give you another ten or twenty years to pay back the principal. This arrangement holds down the size of your monthly payment. But keep in mind that interest-only loans are more expensive in the long run, no matter when the principal comes due.

Home-Equity Loans Versus Second Mortgages

While most of the marketing attention by banks has been on home-equity loans, traditional second mortgages may be more appropriate for some people. A home-equity loan is technically a second mortgage but it is different from the traditional variety.

A home-equity loan commonly refers to a line of credit that you can draw on in full or in part whenever you like. By contrast, a traditional second mortgage provides you with a fixed sum for a fixed period of time, usually five to fifteen years. You get a lump-sum check for the full amount when you sign the papers. Thus, a second mortgage might be preferable if you need the money all at once for some purpose—such as to build an addition onto your house—and you don't want to be tempted with a line of credit readily available for other purchases.

A home-equity loan is preferable if you need funds for various purposes over a period of time, such as to pay college tuition one year at a time.

With either type of loan, banks will usually lend you up to 70 to 80 percent of the market value of your home minus whatever you still owe on your first mortgage.

For tax purposes, interest paid on home-equity loans and second mortgages of up to $100,000 is fully deductible—so long as all your qualified mortgage debt doesn't exceed the fair market value of your home. For example, say the market value of your home is $220,000 and you owe $120,000 on your first mortgage. You could claim interest deductions on a home-equity loan of up to $100,000. But if you owed $170,000 on your $220,000 house, no more than $50,000 in home-equity debt would qualify for the mortgage deduction. (Home-equity debt that was used to finance substantial improvements to your house doesn't count against the $100,000 limit.)

The deduction does help reduce the cost of the loan. For someone in the 28 percent tax bracket, for example, the deduction would bring the effective cost of a 10 percent home-equity loan down to 7.2 percent. That is about half of the cost of an unsecured personal loan, which won't be deductible at all because of the phaseout of personal interest deductions.

SHOPPING WITH AN ATM CARD:
ANOTHER STEP TOWARD A CASHLESS SOCIETY

In what could push America another step closer to a cashless society, ATM cards—the same card you use to get cash out of your bank's automated teller machine—are being accepted by a rapidly growing number of service stations, grocery stores, fast-food restaurants, and other retailers.

For consumers, ATM cards can be a convenient substitute for cash, particularly at stores that don't accept credit cards and won't honor your personal check.

Here's how it works: At the checkout counter, your card is inserted in a terminal and the cashier enters the total amount of the sale. For security purposes, you enter your personal identification code (the same one you use to get cash at the ATM) on a special keypad at the counter. Then the transaction is electronically relayed along the ATM network to your bank and the amount of the purchase is immediately withdrawn, or debited, from your checking account and transferred, or credited, to the merchant's bank account. (Some systems are not so elaborate and the transaction isn't completed until the following day, sometimes later.)

Retailers like ATM cards because their cash flow improves, they don't have to mess with all the paperwork required for credit card transactions, and they don't have to worry about bad checks. As a result, some 50,000 retail outlets had systems in place to accept ATM or other debit cards in 1988, compared to only about 2,000 in 1985. Gasoline stations and supermarkets account for most of the installations, known as "point-of-sale" (POS) systems.

Bankers like POS transactions, too, because they're much cheaper to process than checks. Processing a check costs the bank as much as 80 cents each, while an electronic transaction costs them as little as a dime.

What's in it for the consumer? At service stations, customers who use their ATM card get the same discount on gasoline as cash customers. So your ATM card offers the convenience of a credit card and the price advantage of cash.

Most retailers, however, don't give customers any price break for using ATM cards. So what's the incentive to use them? They can still be handy in situations where you are short of cash and the merchant doesn't accept credit cards or checks. Fast-food restaurants are one example. Supermarkets that won't accept your personal check are another.

But ATM cards may be slow to catch on at stores that accept personal checks or credit cards because consumers get the benefit of the "float" on checks and a grace period for payment of credit card charges. Thus, it may take a price incentive—such as the discount that oil companies offer—to get customers to use their ATM card instead. But many retailers aren't sure they want to encourage customers to use ATM cards. Some merchants fear that customers won't do as much impulse buying if they can't pay the purchase off in installments as they can with credit cards. Other merchants aren't in any hurry to join a POS system because they don't want to pay all the costs of installing and maintaining the equipment.

For now, the POS system itself is fragmented, with a few dozen local debit-card systems scattered across the country. As a result, many ATM cardholders face a fairly limited selection of merchants that accept the card.

Although ATM cards could well move the country another step closer to a cashless society, few bankers see the ATM debit card replacing cash or checks or credit cards anytime soon. Rather, debit cards are likely to be just one more card in your wallet, giving you another method of paying for groceries, gasoline, or a fast-food snack.

Before using your ATM card as if it were cash, find out whether your bank assesses any fees each time you use your ATM card in a retail transaction. If bankers start assessing the same fee for retail transactions as many of them now do for ATM cash transactions, the ATM card could prove the most expensive way to make some purchases.

"AFFINITY" CREDIT CARDS: A WAY OF GIVING—OR GETTING TAKEN?

Want a chance to help your favorite cause every time you make a credit card purchase? Or earn a frequent-flier mile on your favorite airline for every dollar charged? Those are the pitches for "affinity" credit cards that have won a place in the wallets of millions of Americans.

Banks and other financial institutions began peddling the concept only a few years ago and already there are a few thousand different Visa and MasterCard affinity cards on the market.

An affinity group is any group with a common bond, whether alumni of a particular college, members of a nonprofit organization, donors to a particular charity, or members of a frequent-flier program.

Generally, each time you use your credit card, a small cut (usually .5 percent of the purchase price) goes to the affinity organization. So everyone benefits each time you use your card. Your charity gets financial help. You get to feel good about helping your favorite cause when you spend money. (In the case of the frequent-flier programs, you help yourself, usually getting one frequent-flier mile for each dollar purchased.) And the credit card company is happy too.

But think twice before committing. Keep in mind that credit cards vary widely in terms of their interest rate, annual fees, and size of the credit line offered. So if you can get better terms on a nonaffiliated card, there is a cost involved in choosing the affinity card.

What's more, the amount of money that goes to the charity may be small. Some groups get only a flat fee of several dollars for each member that signs up for the affinity credit card, but no cut of each purchase you make.

Furthermore, no donations passed on to the charity by the credit card marketer for your participation are eligible for a deduction on your tax return.

So you may find that the best way to help yourself and your favorite cause is to find the credit card with the best terms and simply write a check to the charity. Your charity will be happy. You will get the best credit card deal. And by contributing directly to the charity, your donation will be eligible for a charitable deduction on your tax return. (Keep in mind that charitable deductions can be claimed only if you itemize deductions on your tax return. Also be aware that contributions made to certain types of nonprofit groups, such as political organizations, are not eligible for the charitable deduction.)

Airline cards can be a good deal if you charge a lot and travel a lot on that particular airline. Compare the annual fees, the finance charges, the credit line you're being offered, and any special features to see if it's worth switching.

SECURED CREDIT CARDS:
FOR PEOPLE WHO CAN'T QUALIFY THE NORMAL WAY

With the credit card market now saturated, a small but growing number of banks have decided to solicit people who couldn't qualify for a credit card before. It's not that these banks have decided to forego credit standards. Rather, they have come up with a new credit card arrangement in which the credit line is fully backed by the customer's deposits at the bank.

These "secured" credit cards were designed for people who can't qualify for a regular credit card because they ran into financial trouble in the past or because they don't have a credit history yet. While the number of banks now offering secured credit cards is relatively small, more are expected to do so in the future because there are millions of potential candidates for them. It is the one segment of the credit card market that hasn't been tapped.

In order to qualify for a secured credit card, the bank requires you to maintain a minimum deposit at the bank—typically $500 to $1,000. In exchange, the bank gives you a credit line equal to your deposit or a portion of it. That deposit is considered collateral for your credit line, so you are not allowed to withdraw the money. If your credit card payment is delinquent, the bank dips into your collateral. That's why the bank feels safe issuing the cards to people who aren't the greatest credit risks.

Secured credit cards don't carry exorbitant finance charges or fees. In fact, they are sometimes lower than on regular credit cards. But if you qualify for a regular card, don't rush to swap it for a secured card. Some banks pay a below-average interest rate—or no interest—on funds you are required to keep in the collateral account. So the advantage of a lower finance charge or annual fee may be more than offset by the lower interest rate on collateral deposits. But the secured credit card can be a salvation for individuals with a tarnished credit history who need a credit card and want to rehabilitate their credit record.

Despite the safeguards built into the secured credit card, banks don't approve everyone who applies. Therefore, it pays to check eligibility requirements before you waste your money on an application fee.

HOME BANKING: PAYING BILLS VIA YOUR PC

Consumers widely embraced automated teller machines, but bankers have had limited success getting customers to accept the next generation of automated bank services: electronic home banking.

Customer interest has been so disappointing that a few dozen banks that flirted with home banking dropped their systems. Mass acceptance of home banking faces formidable barriers. At $5 to $15 a month, home banking is not cheap. Nor does it satisfy all your banking needs. You still have to trek down to your local bank branch to get cash and deposit checks. You may also have to go down to your bank to apply for a loan, invest in a CD, or open a new account. And you still have to pay some bills the old-fashioned way.

Yet bankers continue to be hopeful. While home banking is not expected to enjoy the same widespread acceptance as the automated teller machine, the service is likely to draw more interest in the future as home computers proliferate and as home banking systems improve and expand their services. Now a puny $16 million business, home banking will grow to $426 million a year by the year 2000, according to a LINK Resources projection.

Despite its limitations, home banking does have its advantages. With your home computer, you can pay most of your bills at lightning speed, transfer funds from one account to another, check your account balance, and, on some systems, get stock quotes and buy and sell stocks.

Electronic bill paying is the key attraction of most systems. All you need do is tell the computer what bills you want to pay, how much to pay, and when you want them paid. The home banking service does the rest. No need to write checks, lick the stamps, and then schlepp down to the mailbox. For bills that recur on a regular basis, such as your mortgage payment and car loan, you can usually arrange to have the system pay them automatically. No more muss and fuss and no more worry about missing a payment. Well, almost no muss and fuss. One shortcoming of home banking is that you can only pay bills to those merchants that are on a preauthorized list. While some home-banking systems have arrangements with thousands of local and national merchants, you will inevitably find the need to send out checks to merchants not on the list, such as the small mail-order firm you bought tomato seeds from.

The price for paying bills electronically is not cheap, either. If you have only a few bills to pay, any savings in postage will hardly offset the cost.

But home banking systems do offer convenience and they are headed in a direction that will allow you to conduct more of your banking business from your computer keyboard.

In deciding whether to sign up for a particular home banking service, find out whether most of the bills you need to pay are included in the bank's preauthorized list. Also find out how long it takes the bank to process and pay the bills once you authorize payment; the longer it takes, the less interest you earn on your funds. That's because many banks will debit your account on the date you instruct the home banking service to send out payment, which can be several days before the money actually winds up in the hands of the merchant. Under a typical home banking arrangement, the bank reserves the right to take up to five business days to process and deliver the payment to the merchant. For example, if you have a bill due on the 15th of the month, you would have to designate the 10th (or earlier, if a weekend or holiday falls in between) as the "pay date." The bank would then debit your checking account on the 10th even though the merchant might not receive payment from the bank until the 15th.

In addition, find out if you have to pay any extra fees to connect to the system. To access some home-banking systems, you need to go through a videotex service, most of which impose hourly access charges. Also check the banking system's hours to make sure they are convenient. Not all of them operate twenty-four hours a day.

SAVING AND BORROWING IN THE FACE OF THE SAVINGS-AND-LOAN CRISIS

The temptation to pour money into whatever savings institution across the country offers the highest yields has proved irresistible for millions of Americans over the past decade. It didn't matter that the best deals tended to be at thrift institutions in the worst financial shape. Nor did it matter that the government was closing one almost every week. If the institution became insolvent and was forced to close its doors, investors were assured that their deposits were fully protected by federal deposit insurance up to $100,000. It seemed like a no-lose situation.

Yet there are risks in banking at a weak institution that can cost you money, inconvenience, and enough hassles to make you wonder why you ever thought it was worth sending money to some faraway institution for a slightly higher rate.

If federal regulators decide to liquidate a thrift, claims forms are sent out to depositors within a day or two. So local customers can get their money back quickly. All they need do is walk down to the thrift and present their claim form. But depositors who don't live close by may have to wait a week or longer to get their refund processed through the mail. In the interim, you lose interest on the money because interest payments stop the day the thrift is closed down.

Your loss can be more than just a few days' interest. If interest rates have fallen since you made your original investment, getting your money back early means you are stuck reinvesting it at a lower rate. For example, say you deposited $10,000 in a weak savings and loan because it offered a 10 percent yield on CDs while most others were paying only 9 percent. That's an extra $100 a year in interest. But if your thrift goes bankrupt and interest rates have fallen to 7 percent, your decision to go with the risky thrift will now cost you $200 a year in foregone interest. Why? If you had originally deposited your money in a healthy institution instead of the sick one, your money would still be earning $900 a year, rather than the $700 you must now settle for because rates have fallen while your thrift went bankrupt.

What happens if your ailing thrift is merged with another institution rather than liquidated? The acquiring institution is obligated to honor the rate on your CD for only 14 days. During that time, the institution gives you the option of accepting a lower rate (more in line with what other banks and thrifts are paying) or withdrawing your deposit without penalty.

Don't borrow from a troubled savings institution, either, no matter how attractive the terms. Home-equity loans are the most vulnerable. If the government shuts down the institution, your unused line of credit is likely to be canceled. That would put you in a bind if you were counting on that line of credit to finance some upcoming expense, such as your child's college tuition. You would be forced to go through the costly process of taking out a new line of credit someplace else. Other types of loans are not usually affected unless you're behind on payments.

Regardless, the prudent strategy is simply to avoid dealing with a weak institution and to confine your business to local institutions that you know are strong. If you're not sure, you could ask to see a copy of the institution's financial report, but few people are capable of properly analyzing one. The easiest way is to ask your accountant to recommend a strong institution.

If you're intent on shopping around for high yields, some financial publications, including *Money* magazine, carry lists of financial institutions offering the highest yields along with ratings of their financial soundness.

6

DEMOGRAPHIC TRENDS OF THE 1990s: THE MIDDLE-AGING OF AMERICA

THE NEW FACE OF AMERICA

America will experience a demographic upheaval in the 1990s that will reshape consumer spending patterns, the political agenda, social relationships, and the fates and fortunes of many industries.

The nation, whose postwar economy, culture, and institutions were predicated on a fast-growing, youthful, and family-oriented society, is becoming a slow-growing, aging, and more ethnically diverse society that is moving further away from the traditional family mold.

America's youth-oriented culture will give way to more mature tastes and priorities as the huge baby-boom generation reaches middle age and the elderly population swells. Younger people will make up a smaller and smaller fraction of the populace because of declining fertility rates over the past two decades.

Not since the Depression years of the 1930s has the population grown as slowly as it is expected to in the 1990s. But today's slow growth is due to life-style decisions and new family patterns rather than economic hardship. American households, meanwhile, are becoming ever more diverse; singles, childless couples, and single-parent households are growing faster than the traditional married-with-children family.

These demographic currents have profound implications for many aspects of economic, social, and political life in the 1990s, and will fundamentally alter the outlook for a broad spectrum of investments and industries. A slower-growing population, for instance, portends troubles for businesses whose fortunes have long depended on new mouths to feed, families to house, or babies to diaper. An aging population promises surging demand for health-care services, pharmaceuticals, retirement housing, and a host of other specialized products and services designed to meet the special needs of the elderly. And a maturing baby-boom generation, which is now busy raising families, portends less spending at discos and trendy restaurants and more on children's piano lessons and take-out foods.

THE MIDDLE-AGING OF THE BABY-BOOM GENERATION

No group has had a bigger impact on American business and culture in the postwar era than the baby-boom generation. Born between 1946 and 1964, baby-boomers number 76 million and account for nearly one-third of the U.S. population. The generations that came before them and after them are small by comparison. The baby-boom generation, now aged twenty-six to forty-four, will be in the thirty-six-to-fifty-four age group by the year 2000.

Because of their huge numbers, baby-boomers have reshaped industry, popular culture, and institutions for more than four decades as they moved through each phase of life. When they were born, anything that had to do with babies became a growth business, from baby food to

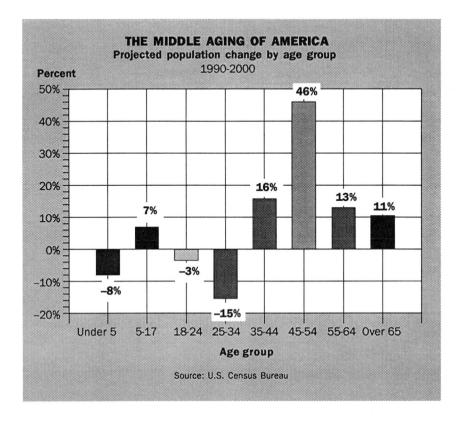

THE MIDDLE AGING OF AMERICA
Projected population change by age group
1990-2000

Source: U.S. Census Bureau

strollers. When they reached school age, education became a growth business and new schools had to be built at a record rate. When the baby-boomers reached their teenage years, movie theaters overflowed, sales of record albums soared, and college admission offices were deluged with applications. As young adults, baby-boomers created soaring demand for new housing, new automobiles, and vintage wines.

As they move into middle age, baby-boomers promise to be the dominant demographic force shaping the 1990s. Late to marry, they have been settling down and having children, adopting life-styles and spending patterns much different from those of their free-spending, freewheeling days in the 1970s and 1980s.

Their impact will be even larger than their one-third share of the population suggests. Baby-boom households will include almost half the population and account for roughly half of personal income. They should be the fastest-growing income group as they move into their peak earning years and reap the financial rewards of having two spouses working in many households. Baby-boomers also stand to inherit enormous sums from their parents, including homes that are owned free and clear and that have appreciated greatly in value over the past two decades.

Their shifting spending patterns promise to be a boon to many industries, from home entertainment to children's wear. But because the generation after them is much smaller, the aging of the baby-boomers means dimming prospects for many industries that prospered from a more youthful baby-boom generation—just as maternity wards were left with empty beds after the baby boom ended and schools were shuttered after the baby-boom generation received its diplomas.

Raising Children: When baby-boomers weren't shopping for BMWs or designer jogging suits, they managed to create a baby boomlet of their own. Demographers refer to the baby-boomers' children as the "echo boom" or the "baby boomlet." Even though baby-boomers are having smaller families than their parents did, the sheer size of the baby-boom generation was enough to create a large number of offspring. As a result, many of the school classrooms that were shuttered when the baby-boom generation graduated will now have to be reopened for the echo-boom generation. Elementary and high school enrollments are projected to surge during the 1990s. Perhaps the most fundamental change in spending patterns that is expected to occur among baby-boomers in the 1990s is the shift from self-indulgent spending to indulging their children. A wide range of companies that make children's goods should benefit, including those that make musical instruments, children's books, en-

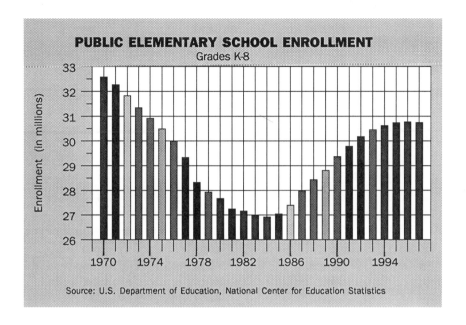

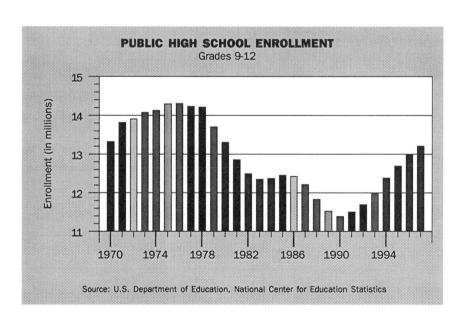

cyclopedias, school supplies, and children's shoes and clothing. So should pediatricians, music teachers, and summer camps.

Cocooning: Having spent the 1970s and 1980s in the social fast lane, baby-boomers are finally settling down, raising children, and staying home. Even those without young children no longer seem to have the inclination or the energy to go out as often as they used to. Marketing surveys consistently show that the over-thirty crowd is spending much less time going out than a few years ago and now clings to more traditional home values. Fashionable restaurants and bistros in many cities are already reeling from the impact of an aging baby-boom generation. Takeout and home delivery are replacing sit-down for many baby-boomers weary of years of endless socializing. Baby-boomers are also doing more of their entertaining at home, hosting quiet dinner parties rather than going to a local restaurant with friends. They are therefore likely to spend more of their income making their home a more comfortable refuge—upgrading their home entertainment systems, home furnishings, kitchen and bathroom fixtures, and table settings, and even remodeling. Many baby-boomers can also be expected to trade up to bigger homes, strengthening the market for "move-up" housing. (See chapter 4 for more on the impact on real estate.)

Saving More: Baby-boomers, notorious for their carefree spending and borrowing, are approaching the age when people tend to save more in order to build nest eggs for their children's college educations and their own retirement. A rise in savings would be a boon to financial services firms, from banks and brokerage houses to mutual funds and life insurance companies. But whether baby-boomers will soon abandon their spendthrift ways and follow the savings habits of their Depression-era parents remains to be seen. Nevertheless, some financial services firms are targeting advertisements to older baby-boomers, suggesting ways they can build bigger nest eggs.

Feeling the Effects of Age: Baby-boomers are approaching the age when the incidence of health problems increases, creating growing demand for health-care services of all types. Vision problems require more frequent visits to the eye doctor; dental problems require more intensive treatment; years of jogging wear down the knees; and years of listening to loud rock music take their toll on the ears. Of more serious concern, the risk of heart attack, stroke, and diabetes grows. Health consciousness among baby-boomers is high and they are likely to become even more sensitive to the importance of a good diet and physical exercise as they attempt to minimize the effects of age. Baby-boomers should provide a growing market for high-fiber, low-sodium, low-cholesterol, and low-fat foods. All sorts of weight-loss products and services should also be in strong demand as baby-boomers try to battle middle-age spread.

Tempered Fitness: The baby-boomers' obsession with physical fitness is not likely to wane as they reach middle age, but it is shifting to sports that are less strenuous on aging bodies. Many baby-boomers have already traded in their jogging shoes and aerobic tights for golf clubs, bicycles, swimming goggles, and fitness-walking shoes. Cross-training is also gaining popularity as a way to avoid burnout and injury.

Targeting a More Mature Market: The aging baby boom will force a major refocus in marketing strategies. Advertising used to target the youthful eighteen- to thirty-four-year-old audience. But that focus will need to shift to more mature audiences since the middle-aged will be the biggest single consumer market in the 1990s. And baby-boomers' tastes will change with age. While middle-aged people tend to spend more on apparel, for example, they will be buying fewer blue jeans and more business suits.

Family Vacations: Baby-boomers, who grew up in the jet age, have not given up their penchant for travel just because they're having children. They're simply bringing their children along. Walt Disney is not the only beneficiary. Many hotels, resorts, and cruise-ship operators are offering day-care services and special children's programs to attract the huge baby-boom crowd. Even Club Med, a mecca for swinging singles during the 1970s and 1980s, saw that baby-boomers were no longer so swinging or single and turned dozens of its resorts into clubs with activities designed for families.

GROWING IMPACT OF WORKING WOMEN

The movement of women into the labor force over the past three decades has led to revolutionary changes in economic and social life in America. As more women enter the labor force in the 1990s, the impact on lifestyles and spending patterns should become even more pronounced.

Household Services: With fewer women staying home, demand is growing for businesses that perform household chores such as house cleaning, cooking, and laundry, as well as child care. For most Americans, today's version of household help isn't a nanny or a full-time maid, but rather a local day-care center, a franchised maid service that will send someone to their home to clean up once a week, the corner dry cleaner or a laundry service that makes pickups and deliveries, and the take-out section at the supermarket or a restaurant located on the way home from work.

Convenience and Service: Growing numbers of two-career couples, single-person households, and single-parent families mean time is becoming an ever more precious commodity and virtually anything that can

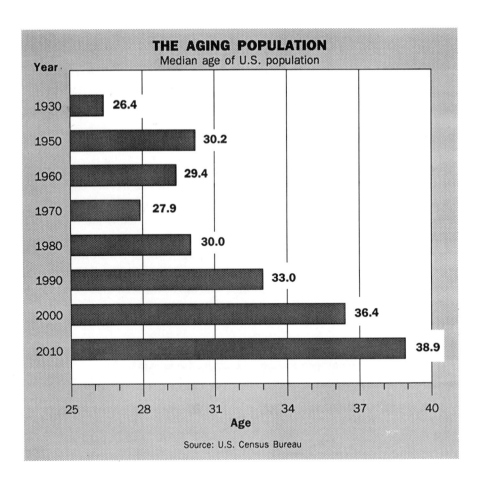

THE AGING POPULATION
Median age of U.S. population

Year	Age
1930	26.4
1950	30.2
1960	29.4
1970	27.9
1980	30.0
1990	33.0
2000	36.4
2010	38.9

Source: U.S. Census Bureau

save time should be in growing demand in the 1990s, such as take-out food, home delivery, microwave meals, and mail-order shopping. An entire new industry of mostly smaller entrepreneurs is emerging in many cities to cater to the needs of Americans suffering from a poverty of time. For a price, there are people who will stand in line for you at the passport office, walk your dog, shop for groceries, water your lawn, feed your fish and parakeets while you're on vacation, and deliver meals cooked at your favorite local restaurant. As an example of how some entrepreneurs have capitalized on the trend to break into a market that was already saturated and competitive, some businesses now offer home delivery and pickup of video movie rentals for a surcharge of around $1.50. Service and convenience are the new bywords in business. It's not that Americans don't care about price anymore; they do. But busy consumers are now more acutely aware of the trade-offs of time, effort, and money. With growing numbers of dual-income couples, Americans have more money to spend but less time to spend it. So at a time when people are busier than ever trying to balance work and family obligations, consumers are attaching a higher priority to service and convenience, as evidenced by the growing popularity of businesses offering such services as ten-minute oil changes, one-hour film developing, same-day laundry service, walk-in medical care, and while-you-wait shoe repair.

Extended Business Hours: With increasing numbers of women joining the labor force, retailers and other businesses that cater to consumers will be under pressure to extend their hours during the week and open their doors on weekends. Businesses that stick with 10:00 A.M.-to-5:00 P.M. weekday hours risk losing business since more and more people will be working during the day. More and more grocery stores and pharmacies are moving to twenty-four-hour schedules. Most shopping malls are open nights and weekends. Even banks are beginning to abandon their traditional "bankers' hours." In California, major banks recently opened their doors on Saturdays. It's not just a matter of keeping up with some competitor down the block who is staying open longer, either. Retailers have new competitors. Mail order, home shopping TV programs, and computer-based services are all growing quickly because they offer consumers the convenience of shopping twenty-four hours a day. Door-to-door sales is also becoming an anachronism since fewer people are home when salespeople come knocking. Avon sales representatives now show up at the office to peddle their wares during coffee breaks. And Tupperware parties are held at the office before everyone goes home.

Reliability and Quality: Because time is precious, consumers are willing to pay more these days to get quality and reliability in a product, be it a car or a dishwasher. Quite simply, people don't have time to take things to be repaired or take a day off from work to wait for a repairman at home. Reliability also means that if something does go wrong, the company will stand behind the product and provide quick and dependable service.

Shorter, More Frequent Vacations: The traditional three-week summer vacation is giving way to shorter and more frequent getaways throughout the year. The trend toward shorter vacations is the result of the difficulties that two-career families have in trying to coordinate a long vacation with their increasingly complicated schedules. Taking shorter but more frequent vacations is also a way of breaking up the pressures of modern life. Helping spur the movement to shorter vacations is the anxiety produced by the uncertainty and turmoil in the workplace. Mergers, acquisitions, restructurings, downsizing and changing job descriptions have made many people nervous about taking a long vacation for fear that something might happen to their job while they're away. If the office was able to function well for three weeks without them, maybe the company will decide it can do without them altogether. Travel industry statistics show significant growth in three-night weekend trips. Many people are taking advantage of special weekend discounts offered by a growing number of hotel chains, which have plenty of empty rooms available from the time business travelers check out on Friday afternoons until they start checking back in on Sunday afternoons.

BABY BOOMLET ENDING

As baby-boomers move beyond their childbearing years, the baby boomlet will come to an end. The number of births is expected to level off and then decline through the end of the century. Fewer babies portend declining sales in the future for the baby goods industry, from baby foods to diapers.

The number of children under the age of five is projected to decline steadily in the 1990s, from about 18.4 million in 1990 to 16.9 million in the year 2000. By contrast, the number of 5-to-9-year-olds will rise from 18.4 million in 1990 to 18.8 million in 1995 and then decline to 18.1 million in the year 2000. The 10-to-14 age group will continue to grow throughout the decade, from 17.3 million in 1990 to 18.8 million in 1995

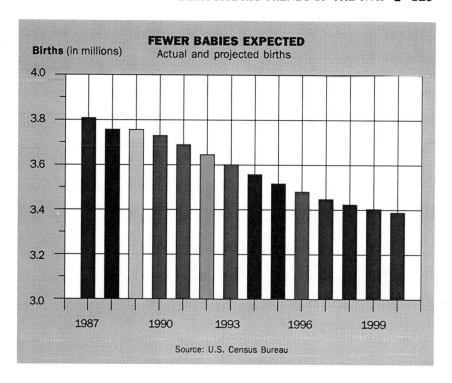

FEWER BABIES EXPECTED
Actual and projected births

Births (in millions)

Source: U.S. Census Bureau

and to 19.2 million in 2000. The number of 15-to-18-year-olds will grow slowly through the mid-1990s—rising from 13.5 million in 1990 to 14.2 million in 1995—and then rise quickly, reaching 15.2 million in 2000.

SHRINKING NUMBERS OF YOUNG ADULTS

While the ranks of the middle-aged will explode, young adults are shrinking in number.

Following on the heels of the baby-boom generation, the "baby bust" generation will cause the eighteen-to-thirty-four-year-old age group to shrink 10 percent during the 1990s. The baby-bust generation comprises those born between 1965 and 1976, a period when the birth control pill came into wide use, people married later, and women delayed having children in favor of careers.

The baby bust is now aged 14 to 25 and will be 24 to 35 years old in the year 2000. Their smaller numbers are expected to shrink college

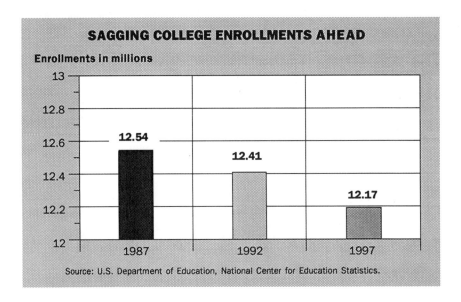

SAGGING COLLEGE ENROLLMENTS AHEAD

Enrollments in millions

Source: U.S. Department of Education, National Center for Education Statistics.

enrollments and give employers a smaller pool of entry-level workers to draw from.

Their dwindling numbers also mean new challenges for businesses that depend heavily on the young-adult market, such as discos, fast-food restaurants, and those who make or sell blue jeans, beer, and albums.

Fewer young adults also means fewer first-time home buyers or first-time renters for apartments—perhaps even fewer than their numbers suggest. The reason is that an increasing number of grown children are living with their parents, partly because of the high cost of housing. Among 20-to-24-year-olds, over half of young men and nearly one-third of young women are living with their parents, according to Census Bureau estimates. In the 25-to-29 age group, more than 1 in 6 men and 1 in 12 women are still living with their parents.

One positive effect of a shrinking young-adult population is the prospect of a lower crime rate in the 1990s, since teenagers and young men account for most crime.

SLOWING HOUSEHOLD FORMATION

Fewer young adults also portends that new households will be created at a slower rate in the 1990s. Fewer new households means slowing demand for housing and everything else that goes into setting up a new household, from appliances and furniture to drapes and carpeting. To keep sales from slumping, manufacturers face the challenge of trying to encourage people to replace what they have or trade up.

The Census Bureau estimates that new households will average only 1.2 million a year in the early 1990s and 1.1 million a year in the late 1990s. That compares with an annual rate of more than 1.3 million in the 1980s and over 1.7 million in the 1970s.

THE SHRINKING HOUSEHOLD

Small families are now the norm in American society, a trend that is projected to become more firmly entrenched in the 1990s. Family size has dropped sharply in recent years because couples are choosing to have fewer children and because a high divorce rate and record numbers of children born to unmarried mothers are swelling the number of single-parent families.

As recently as the early 1960s, three to four children per family was the norm. Today, two children is the norm. The fertility rate has been cut in half over the past three decades, with women now having an average of 1.8 children during their lifetimes. Demographers don't expect the birth rate to change much during the 1990s, either, because little change is seen in the forces that have led to a lower fertility rate—later marriages, high divorce rates, more women entering the labor force, birth control, and the growing perception that two children are enough of an economic burden. According to government surveys, most young women expect to have no more than two children, and a growing number of women aren't bearing any offspring. As many as 25 to 30 percent of women now in their twenties may never have children, estimates Peter A. Morrison, director of the Population Research Center at the Rand Corporation.

Besides the trend toward fewer children, families are becoming smaller because of divorce and soaring illegitimacy rates. Single-parent families now represent about 20 percent of American families and nearly one of every four babies born today is born out of wedlock.

As a result, the size of the average family is expected to continue shrinking in the 1990s, from 3.17 persons in 1988 to 3.07 persons by the year 2000.

Smaller families, along with the growing number of single adults, will push the size of the average household down to 2.48 persons by the year 2000, from 2.64 in 1988.

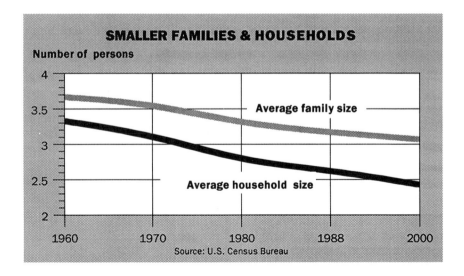

With fewer mouths to feed, jumbo "family" packages are no longer as relevant in marketing grocery items and other products. Smaller households also means that larger apartments and houses with a lot of bedrooms won't be as much in demand as they used to be. A five-bedroom house isn't necessary when you have only two children.

With fewer children to rear, many parents can be expected to spend more money on each child—buying them better clothing and toys and taking them on more expensive vacations—than was possible when families were larger.

NONTRADITIONAL FAMILY IS THE NORM

American households are also becoming more diverse, moving further away from the Ozzie-and-Harriet mold. Though politicians continue to extol traditional family values, the nontraditional family is the norm. Only 27 percent of American households are made up of a husband, a wife, and one or more children.

American family life has moved so far away from tradition that stepfamilies, single-parent households, and childless couples now rival the number of households where children are living with both their biological mother and father. If present trends persist in the 1990s, the majority of children born over the past decade can expect to spend part of their youth living in a broken home; living with both their natural mother and father throughout childhood is becoming the exception rather than the rule.

It's not that traditional values have been abandoned. Most Americans still expect to get married and have children, but they are spending more years in single life before getting married, and they are staying married for shorter periods and having fewer children. As a result, single-parent households, single persons living alone, and unmarried couples living together represent a growing proportion of American households. Married couples represent a dwindling share.

An aging baby-boom generation has led demographers to expect the divorce rate to level off or even decline in the 1990s. Divorce is less likely once people reach middle age. Growing concern about AIDS is likely to bolster the trend. Nevertheless, most demographers believe the probability of divorce will remain about 50 percent.

The erosion of the traditional family has led to a widening gap between the financial status of married couples and single-parent households headed by women. Female-headed households tend to have limited incomes and often live below the poverty line.

Extended Families: While "immediate" families are becoming smaller, "extended" families are becoming larger and more commonplace as a result of remarriages and longer life spans of older generations. More and more, children are finding the circle of family relationships enlarged by stepparents, and the survival of more grandparents, and even great-grandparents. This enlarged family circle has helped increase spending on children at a faster rate than the number of births would suggest. More relatives means more people sending a child toys and greeting cards on birthdays and holidays.

Singles: Being single is also becoming a more common way of life, largely the result of later marriages, more divorces, and more widows. Today, single persons living alone account for one of four American households, and that number is expected to keep growing. Consequently, single people will be a substantial and growing force in the marketplace. Single people spend heavily on convenience items, luxury goods, and travel, and also tend to rent rather than buy homes.

New Life Insurance Assumptions: Traditional assumptions on life insurance are changing with the nature of families. Life insurance takes on diminished importance in a world of singles and two-career couples. Coverage offered under employer-sponsored group plans may be all the life insurance needed in many situations. Single persons who have no children or elderly dependents to support could easily justify doing without life insurance or with just enough to cover funeral expenses and any debts. Childless couples could also get by with little insurance if both have reliable jobs and earn good salaries. There's no longer the same need for the husband to take out a big insurance policy to provide for the long-term financial security of a wife who has her own career and would be able to take care of herself financially and probably remarry. Large amounts of life insurance, however, remain critical for single parents and couples with children to support. Life insurance is also becoming more important for anyone who is providing financial support to an elderly parent. If your elderly parents are relying on you to provide financial help as they grow older, life insurance is needed to fulfill that obligation in the event of your untimely death.

When shopping for a policy, first determine the amount of coverage you need. Then decide what type of policy you want and can afford. Don't skimp on the amount of coverage your family needs just because an insurance agent tries selling you on the advantages that "cash-value" policies—such as whole life or universal life—have over "term" policies. Premiums on term policies, which provide solely life insurance protection, start off low and rise sharply with age, but they are far less costly than cash-value policies at the time in most people's lives when large amounts of insurance are most often needed. Premiums on cash-value insurance, which combines life insurance protection with a savings plan, typically remain fixed over the life of the policy but they start off five to seven times higher than term insurance. Consider a cash-value policy only if you can afford the premiums on the full amount of coverage your family needs and you find the investment features of the policy attractive.

One feature that more and more life insurance companies are likely to offer in the future is a provision allowing death benefits to be paid out to a living policyholder who is terminally ill or permanently confined to a nursing home. This "living benefit" option came in response to the growing number of elderly persons in need of expensive, long-term nursing care and the rising number of AIDS victims who are left impoverished by the disease. Prudential Insurance, the nation's largest insurer, recently made the feature standard on its policies. While this provision can be a godsend for a dying policyholder, keep in mind that most people buy life insurance as financial protection for survivors. If you use up the money before death, you may impoverish your spouse and children.

Disability Insurance: While life insurance is becoming less relevant in more households, disability insurance is becoming more important. For instance, single people may not have to worry about providing for anyone should they die, but they do have to worry about providing for themselves should they become disabled and not be able to work for a prolonged period. Single parents have the greater worry about who will provide for both themselves and their children should injury or illness keep them from working. In all family situations, disability coverage is probably the biggest gap. Odds are much greater that you will become disabled than that you will die during your working years. And disability can leave a family in much worse financial shape than death can. In either case, the income is gone. But if you die, at least there's one less mouth to feed.

Although most of the work force has some disability coverage separate from Social Security disability benefits, employer-paid group policies often fall short of what is needed to protect you and your family adequately in the event you became disabled for a prolonged period. And Social Security eligibility is strict; most people who try to claim disability are rejected. To protect against a permanent work disability, you need coverage that will replace most of your salary at least until you reach age sixty-five, when company pension and Social Security retirement benefits take over. If your company's disability plan is inadequate, you should seriously consider a supplemental policy. Disability policies are expensive—often costing in excess of $1,000 or $1,500 a year—but you can substantially reduce the premiums by designating a longer waiting period before monthly benefits are scheduled to start after a disability. Make sure the policy is guaranteed renewable so the company can't cancel you, or raise your premiums unless it boosts everyone's premiums. Be aware that disability insurance usually won't replace more than 60 or 70 percent of your salary. Insurers want to make sure that you have some incentive to return to work when you're able.

THE GRAYING OF AMERICA

America's elderly population is swelling. Longer life spans and declining birth rates will make the elderly an ever-growing share of the population over the next several decades. As their numbers increase, the elderly will command ever-increasing attention from business, politicians, and families.

The graying of America creates a growing and lucrative market for businesses that can help the elderly lead healthier, more independent, and more pleasurable lives.

An aging population will create surging demand for health-care services, skin-care products, pharmaceuticals, retirement housing, travel services, and many products that are designed with the special needs of senior citizens in mind.

On average, older Americans today are healthier, more active, and financially better off than any previous generation. Medical advances have increased life expectancy in the twentieth century by nearly thirty years, the largest gain in human history. And though the financial status of the nation's elderly is widely disparate, company pensions, Social Security, and personal savings allow a great many elderly Americans to live their

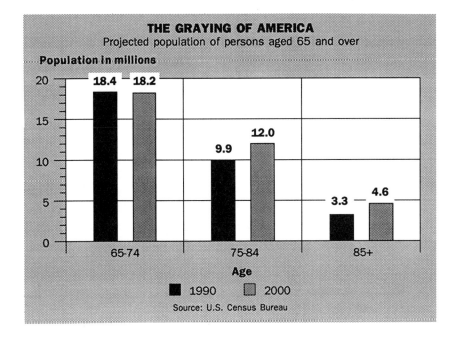

THE GRAYING OF AMERICA
Projected population of persons aged 65 and over

golden years in relative financial comfort. Americans over age fifty control about half of the nation's discretionary income.

Senior citizens tend to be in relatively good health and active at least in the early years of retirement, and they tend to spend a good deal of their time and money in leisure pursuit. The travel industry has been a major beneficiary of the burgeoning elderly market.

The graying of America will occur gradually. During the 1990s, the over-65 population will grow only about 10 percent overall, and their share of the population will rise only from about 12.7 percent now to 13 percent in the year 2000. Not until baby-boomers start retiring in the year 2010 will the ranks of the elderly start exploding.

One segment of the elderly population, however, is already exploding: those over 85. Their numbers are projected to grow 42 percent in the 1990s, from 3.3 million to 4.6 million in the year 2000. By contrast, the 75-to-84 age group is expected to grow 21 percent while the 65-to-74 age group is projected to shrink by 1 percent.

Demand for health care grows with age and the need is greatest for those over 85, particularly for nursing-home care.

Retirement Havens: Regions that have served as magnets for retirees, such as Florida, Arizona, and Hawaii, will benefit from the aging of America—but not as much as commonly perceived. It is a myth that most senior citizens pack up their households and head to retirement havens to live out their years. In fact, most people retire right where they live. Fewer than 6 percent of the population over the age of 65 moved between 1986 and 1987, and a majority of them moved only to another home in the same county.

Senior Citizen Discounts: In an effort to capitalize on the burgeoning elderly population, more and more businesses are likely to offer discounts to senior citizens. Many businesses offer discounts not just to retirees who have turned sixty-five, but also to working people in their fifties. Discounts arranged through the American Association of Retired Persons offer benefits to people as young as fifty. So even if you aren't retired, but you're over fifty, ask if a senior citizen discount is available whenever you make a purchase.

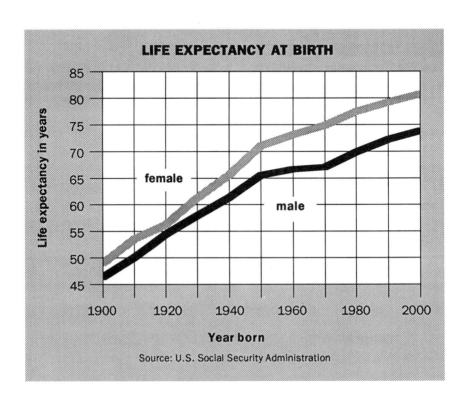

LIFE EXPECTANCY AT BIRTH

Life expectancy in years

female

male

Year born

Source: U.S. Social Security Administration

Political Influence: The political influence of elderly Americans should continue to strengthen as their numbers grow. Elderly Americans tend to have a high turnout rate in political elections and are active in lobbying efforts. Senior citizens' issues, from health care to Social Security, will increasingly become the focus of national political debates.

Retirement Housing: A growing elderly population should create growing demand for retirement housing. Developers are building several types of rental and ownership communities. Many of them offer a wide range of recreational facilities, housekeeping, and health-care services. In some cases, all the services are included in the monthly rent or monthly service fee. In others, you're charged for what you use.

Life-Care Communities: The ultimate in services is the "life-care" or "continuing-care" community. For an up-front endowment fee and monthly maintenance fees, residents are guaranteed housing, meals, recreation programs, housekeeping, full medical services, and, if necessary,

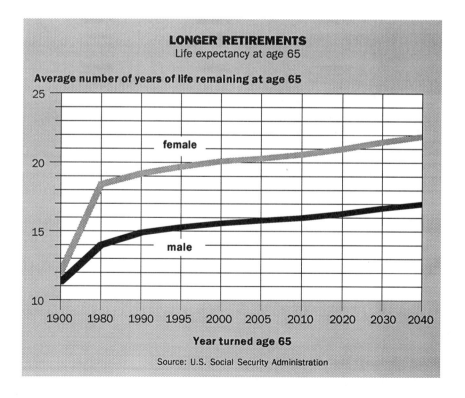

LONGER RETIREMENTS
Life expectancy at age 65

Average number of years of life remaining at age 65

Year turned age 65

Source: U.S. Social Security Administration

nursing-home care for the rest of their lives. Depending on the development and the size apartment you want, entrance fees range from around $30,000 to more than $300,000, while monthly maintenance charges range from $700 to more than $2,000 a month. Most life-care communities are "all-inclusive," meaning the monthly fees include all residential and medical services; everything from maid service to bypass surgery to long-term nursing-home care is included in the fee. Other communities try to hold down monthly fees by offering nursing care and other personal services on a fee-for-service basis. But this erodes the "total security" concept. Life-care communities normally attract people in their mid- to late seventies. Already there are more than 800 life-care communities around the country, and hundreds more are expected to be built during the 1990s. The Marriott Corporation hopes to have 200 life-care retirement communities by the year 2000.

The industry has had its share of troubles. Several operators have gone bankrupt and others have run into serious financial problems for one reason or another. Many of them had good intentions but they simply couldn't attract enough residents or they found nursing-care costs were higher than originally projected. If financial troubles plague a life-care community, it's not just the operators who suffer; residents can face higher monthly fees and cutbacks in services they were promised. Many states now have laws regulating life-care communities. But not all laws offer sufficient safeguards to protect your investment. Nor do life-care communities always hire actuaries to review financial projections and assess whether enough is being set aside to handle future expenses. An actuarial report is the only way to tell if the community is likely to have sufficient funds to cover future health-care costs. So ask to see a copy of the actuary's report. If the report says that fees are probably going to have to be raised a lot higher in order to cover future expenses, troubles may lie ahead for your pocketbook as well as for the financial health of the life-care community.

If a life-care community is to provide you with lifetime security and all the services promised, it has to be on solid financial footing. Otherwise, you could be risking a substantial part of your life's savings.

Consult with an accountant or lawyer who is familiar with life-care communities so you can get a professional appraisal of the actuary's report. Also ask them to give you the ins and outs of the contract you're signing. For instance, what portion of your entrance fee, if any, would you be entitled to get back if you wanted to leave the community? What assurance is there that you will receive all the promised services? How high are fees likely to be raised?

Also consider the option of taking out long-term nursing-care insurance and living in a less costly retirement development that doesn't offer nursing-home care.

Long-Term-Care Insurance: With longer life spans creating a greater risk that you will outlive your financial resources, insurance products that protect against that possibility should gain greater appeal. Annuities that promise to pay out monthly sums for the rest of your life—no matter how long you live—are one example.

Long-term-care insurance is another. A lot of people don't buy it because they think Medicare pays for all nursing-home care. It doesn't.

Medicaid, a joint federal and state welfare program, does cover nursing-home costs, but only for the poor, meaning you'll have to be poor or become impoverished in order to qualify. If you face this dilemma you should contact a lawyer who is familiar with Medicaid and local law. It may be possible to juggle assets between family members in order to qualify for Medicaid before the costs of nursing-home care do the impoverishing.

Long-term-care insurance is a way to guard against that fate, although it's expensive. Long-term-care insurance runs from about $500 to more than $2,500 a year, and the policies are often so riddled with loopholes that many policyholders entering a nursing home aren't able to collect.

Some policies stipulate that nursing-home costs are covered only if you had an illness that required hospitalization or "skilled" nursing care first. Many policies also exclude nursing-home care for "mental disorders," which could mean no coverage if you developed Alzheimer's disease.

Long-term-care insurance is fairly new, and insurers are still trying to feel their way in the market. For purposes of pricing, they have little experience to draw on in terms of what their claims might ultimately be. Nor do they have enough experience in marketing the product to know what kind of restrictions policyholders will or won't buy.

Better coverage is likely to be offered in the future as more insurers enter the market. Congress is also likely to continue debating the idea of providing some long-term-care assistance. It's a popular idea—more than one hundred bills have been submitted in Congress—but the stumbling block is the steep price tag. If you are approaching age sixty-five, there may not be time to wait to see what Congress does.

The best long-term-care policies available today are group policies, offered by a growing number of employers, which are cheaper and more comprehensive than what individuals could get on their own.

Everyone else will need to shop around for an individual policy, offered by more than one hundred insurance companies. Age is the biggest determinant of annual premiums. The younger you are, the lower the cost of the policy.

In comparing policies, examine the restrictions carefully:

- Make sure the policy is guaranteed renewable at the same rate so that you won't have your policy canceled or your premiums hiked should your health deteriorate.
- Coverage should apply regardless of whether you need to be in a hospital or skilled-nursing home first. Many people, including Alzheimer's patients, enter nursing homes without the need for prior hospitalization or skilled nursing care.
- Make sure the policy covers all three types of nursing-home care: "skilled" (which involves daily care performed by a licensed medical professional); "intermediate" (which requires only occasional medical care); and "custodial" (which is nonmedical care that assists patients with such personal needs as bathing, dressing, eating, and walking).
- Make sure the policy includes coverage for Alzheimer's disease.
- Coverage should include home health care, which is becoming an increasingly attractive alternative for older persons in need of long-term care.
- Make sure the policy provides adequate inflation protection. A policy that seems to offer adequate benefits today won't look as good in the future if the benefits aren't automatically adjusted to keep pace with the rising costs of long-term care. Health-care costs are rising even faster than overall inflation.
- Check the number of days you must be confined in a nursing home before the policy's benefits begin. This waiting period can range from 21 days to 365 days or more. The longer the waiting period, the lower your premiums. By opting for the longest waiting period that your personal assets can comfortably handle, you can significantly reduce the cost of carrying the insurance while still protecting yourself against the risk of a very long-term illness depleting your savings.

GROWING ETHNIC POPULATION

The ethnic diversity of America will become more pronounced in the 1990s. Minority groups are growing at a much faster rate than the white population as a result both of legal and illegal immigration and of higher birth rates.

Ethnic groups, while remaining a minority in terms of the rest of the population, are beginning to reach the size that attracts serious attention from mass marketers.

Hispanic Americans are the nation's youngest and fastest-growing ethnic group. Their numbers are expected to grow nearly four times as fast as the rest of the population in the 1990s. By the year 2000, the Hispanic population is projected to reach over 25 million, a 26.8 percent increase from 1990. By the turn of the century, Hispanics are expected to account for more than 9 percent of the U.S. population and they should surpass black Americans early in the next century as the nation's largest ethnic group.

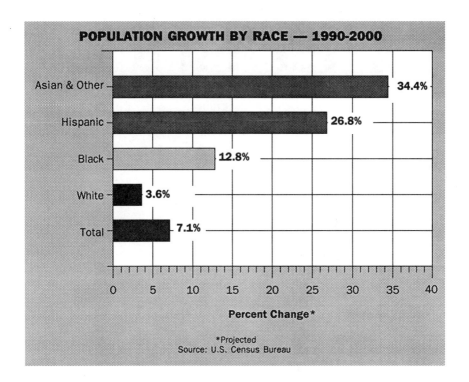

POPULATION GROWTH BY RACE — 1990-2000

Asian & Other — 34.4%
Hispanic — 26.8%
Black — 12.8%
White — 3.6%
Total — 7.1%

Percent Change*

*Projected
Source: U.S. Census Bureau

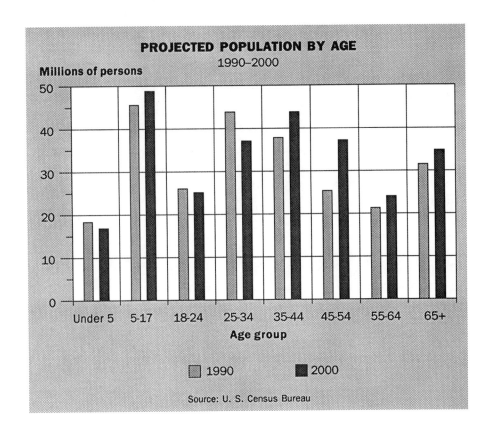

PROJECTED POPULATION BY AGE
1990–2000

Millions of persons

Age group

1990   2000

Source: U. S. Census Bureau

U.S. POPULATION PROJECTIONS

(Numbers in thousands)

Calendar Year	Population*	Births	Deaths	Immigration
1990	249,330	3,731	2,180	575
1995	259,238	3,517	2,275	525
2000	267,498	3,389	2,368	500

*As of Jan. 1
Source: U.S. Census Bureau

7

LOVE, MARRIAGE, AND FAMILY IN THE 1990s

LIVING TOGETHER: HOW TO HANDLE THE FINANCES

Living together before marriage and in between marriages is becoming the social norm. Nearly half of all young adults live together before their first marriage, according to a recent study, and cohabiting in between marriages is now the majority experience. Broader social acceptance as well as a more cautious attitude toward marriage in the face of a 50 percent divorce rate have swelled the ranks of unmarried couples living together by more than 60 percent since 1980. Census Bureau surveys peg the number of cohabiting heterosexual couples at 2.6 million.

Just because a relationship isn't bound by a legal marriage contract, don't assume that live-ins are immune to financial and legal complications. If you don't keep your finances carefully segregated you could wind up entangled in your companion's debt problems. Or if the relationship breaks up, sorting out who gets what can rival the acrimony and legal hassles of a bitter divorce.

Keeping Finances Separate

Live-in couples don't have any inherent responsibility for each other's debts. But once a couple starts mixing its finances, then one partner's troubles become the other's. For instance, if you obtain a joint credit card and your live-in companion goes on a buying binge, you can be held liable for the entire balance even though you personally didn't spend a cent. Or if both of your names are on a joint bank account, your companion can withdraw money from the joint account at will without your consent. What's more, should your companion run into trouble with the Internal Revenue Service, all the money in your joint account can be seized. It doesn't matter that part of the money was yours.

If those aren't enough reasons to dissuade you from joint accounts, consider the headaches you'll face every April 15 trying to sort out the tax liabilities for interest earned on a joint bank account. Unmarried couples aren't eligible to file joint tax returns.

So the best way to keep financial problems from spoiling a romance is to avoid joint credit cards and joint bank accounts. Maintain separate accounts. There are other ways to share common expenses than through a joint account. For instance, each of you can alternate weeks paying for groceries out of your separate accounts. For other miscellaneous expenses, you can jot down on the receipt who paid for the item and then toss it in a cookie jar. At the end of the month, you can split the expenses and settle up. As for rent payments, if your name is on the lease you can write the landlord a check on your separate account for the full amount and have your companion pay his or her share by writing you a check.

How to Handle Purchases

Buying furniture, a TV, a car or other household items together might seem a logical and even romantic notion. But it can lead to problems down the road should the relationship break up. To avoid feuding later over who gets what, each partner should own things separately. You can still share the burden; one buys a washer, the other a dryer; one buys a CD player, the other buys the FM tuner; etc. That way, if the relationship breaks up, there's no joint property to bicker over. But save the receipts in case there's a squabble over who purchased a particular item.

Buying a House Together

More and more unmarried couples are pooling their money and investing in a house, figuring that lack of a marriage certificate isn't any reason to keep them from realizing the advantages of home ownership. But the American dream of owning a home can quickly turn into a nightmare if the relationship comes to an end. When there's nothing left of the relationship but the house, what do you do with the house? If you wanted to stay in the house, would you have the income to support the entire monthly payment plus buy out your partner's share? Or would your partner have enough money to buy back your share and support the entire monthly payment?

Selling the house and splitting the proceeds may seem a logical solution, but it can be costly. If the market happens to be depressed at the time, you and your partner could face substantial losses.

Two people who want to invest in a $175,000 house together but are not willing to commit to each other in a marriage contract should think twice about one or the other. If you insist on buying a house together, consult a lawyer to work out the details of joint ownership.

Medical Power of Attorney

Should one of you wind up in the hospital with some illness or injury, you'll find that "significant others" normally don't count for much in medical matters. In some situations, hospitals restrict visitors to members of the immediate family. So a live-in companion might not even be able to get in to see his or her loved one. Furthermore, should one of you become seriously injured or sick and medical decisions need to be made, a relative can be consulted but an unmarried partner has no say. As a remedy, you should each consider getting a medical power of attorney drawn up so that you're able to visit each other in the hospital and, if desired, make medical decisions if the need arises.

Bequeathing Your Earthly Possessions

If you're living with someone for whom your affection stretches to the point of wanting to bequeath some of your earthly possessions, get a will drawn up, or, if you have one, revise it. In the absence of a will, a spouse would be taken care of but live-in companions have no legal right to any part of your estate. Your next of kin would inherit the property. Consequently, your companion could be left without a home, furniture, or any other property you intended to share together.

Get Promises in Writing

If your companion promises to "provide for you" in exchange for your helping out in a business or performing household services, get it in writing. Oral and implied promises are difficult to prove even in the wake of the California Supreme Court's landmark ruling in the "palimony" suit against the late actor Lee Marvin. For one thing, not every state subscribes to the *Marvin vs. Marvin* decision, which upheld implied contracts and even tacit understandings between unmarried couples. For another, even where the *Marvin* decision has been upheld, courts are aware of the potential for fraudulent claims by a spurned lover. They want solid evidence that there really was some sort of agreement to share money or property.

PRENUPTIAL AGREEMENTS: IS IT SAFE TO SAY "I DO" WITHOUT ONE?

For a couple en route to the altar, hardly anything could be more unromantic than discussing a prenuptial agreement. It makes vows of "till death do us part" ring hollow. But with one of every two marriages ending in divorce and the well-publicized marital split of boxing champion Mike Tyson and TV actress Robin Givens serving as a dramatic reminder of how stormy things can get in the absence of a prenuptial agreement, many people with sizable assets at stake are understandably skittish about heading to the altar without some legal protection.

Not everyone needs a prenuptial agreement to outline who gets what earthly possession should the marriage wind up in divorce court. Prenuptial agreements may do more harm than good in first marriages when neither partner is bringing much in the way of assets or business interests to the marriage. So when there's nothing much to protect, all the agreement usually ends up doing is causing ill feelings.

Yet the realities of modern marriage may well warrant serious consideration of a prenuptial agreement by people other than Hollywood celebrities, shipping magnates, and other traditional candidates. Anyone with substantial assets, an established business, or sizable income prospects may be a candidate for a prenuptial agreement. So is anyone with financial obligations to children from a previous marriage or to aging parents. Without a prenuptial agreement, income or assets that you planned on sharing with those family members could wind up being split with a spouse in a divorce settlement or in the event of your untimely death. People who have already been through a bitter divorce and didn't like the way the court divided the property are common candidates for prenuptial agreements when they remarry.

You don't have to be rich to be a prime candidate for a prenuptial agreement. Anyone covered by a pension plan at work is bringing to the marriage a potentially valuable asset that could be subject to division in a divorce.

Even students who are paupers now may be candidates if they are working on a postgraduate degree that promises to enrich them later.

California law holds that medical licenses, advanced degrees, and other training acquired during a marriage constitute community property. In New York, appeals courts have ruled that a medical license and advanced academic degrees constitute marital assets that are subject to division in a divorce. Other states could well follow California and New York.

If you don't have a prenuptial agreement, assets accumulated during a marriage are split up according to state law. Most states have "equitable distribution" laws, which means that all property accumulated during a marriage is divided up by the court regardless of who has title to the property. The court determines who deserves what, and what the court decides isn't always what both parties consider equitable. In community property states—Arizona, California, Idaho, Louisiana, Nevada, New Mexico, Texas, Washington, and Wisconsin—marital assets are divided down the middle.

If a marriage goes kaput, prenuptial agreements can ease the financial and psychological trauma of breaking up. With a property settlement already outlined, you will avoid the laborious and expensive process of trying to segregate property that was mixed together during the marriage.

A confidential visit with your lawyer should give you a better idea as to whether your particular circumstances warrant a prenuptial agreement and the consequences of not having one. Make sure the lawyer is familiar with premarital agreements, and is licensed to practice in the state where you will live. Matrimonial laws vary greatly from state to state.

A prenuptial agreement is not something to slap in front of your fiancé a few minutes before the ceremony begins. Not only is it likely to be an unwelcome surprise for your spouse-to-be, but courts don't look kindly on agreements that were signed under duress. Prenuptial agreements have to be bargained in good faith with plenty of time for both sides to review them. Each side should also have his own lawyer. Some states insist on it. Full disclosure also applies. If you conveniently forget to tell your spouse that in addition to being a schoolteacher you've got a million dollars stashed away in a Swiss bank account from trading commodity futures, the agreement won't be worth the price of a pork belly. A prenuptial agreement can be tossed out in court for failure to disclose all assets.

CHILD CARE: BALANCING WORK AND FAMILY LIFE

Finding affordable and decent child care is a growing concern among working parents as more and more women enter the labor force.

Full-time nannies cost around $250 to $700 a week, making them too expensive for most families. Live-in "au pairs" can be hired for less, but even if you find a good one, federal law lets au pairs work for a family for only one year at a time.

As a result, the trend has been toward formal day-care services rather than in-home care. But even day care can be costly, running $300 to $700 a month.

Employers are gradually, if slowly, recognizing the need to offer child-care assistance in order to recruit and maintain quality workers in a tight labor market. More than half of the scarce new entrants to the labor force in the 1990s will be women and the vast majority of them will be in their childbearing years.

Of the thousands of employers offering workers some kind of child-care assistance, only a fraction provide on-site day-care facilities. Companies are not keen on setting up their own day-care centers because of the expense of running what is a high-profile operation for a business. A substandard child-care operation can damage the image of the company as well as the morale of employees.

As a consequence, most companies offering child-care assistance do it by contracting with outside day-care programs or reimbursing employees for all or part of their child-care expenses.

$5,000 Tax Exemption for Employer Assistance

Employees are allowed to receive tax-free up to $5,000 in child-care assistance from their employer. None of the money is subject to income tax or Social Security tax.

"Flexible Spending" Accounts for Child Care

A cheaper and more common way companies support child care is by establishing special tax-free accounts for employees. Workers can earmark up to $5,000 of their salary for these "flexible spending accounts." Any salary earmarked is exempt from income tax and Social Security tax.

Employers like these accounts because they offer child-care assistance to employees without the company having to contribute a cent. The federal government provides the benefit in the form of a tax break.

In flexible-spending arrangements, employees have to tell their employer before the start of the calendar year how much they want deducted from their paychecks in the coming year. Be careful how much you decide to earmark to the plan because any unused funds remaining in the account at the end of the year are forfeited. That's why it's important to determine in advance what your day-care needs will be and to earmark no more than that amount.

Child-Care Tax Credit

Even if your company doesn't offer child-care assistance, you can still get help from the federal government by claiming the "child and dependent care" tax credit on your tax return. The credit, which is available to working parents who need to hire someone to care for their child or a disabled dependent while they are at work (or looking for a job), provides a partial rebate for up to $2,400 in expenses for the care of one dependent or up to $4,800 for the care of two or more dependents. The credit, which reduces taxes owed dollar-for-dollar, is worth between 20 and 30 percent of eligible expenses, depending on your income.

What Expenses Qualify for the Tax Breaks

Whether you're taking advantage of the child-care tax credit or the $5,000 exemption for employer assistance, eligible expenses are limited to the care of children under the age of thirteen (or a physically or mentally incapacitated spouse or dependent of any age). Eligible expenses include the cost of day care, nursery school, boarding school (except for tuition), and even the cost of sending your kids to summer day camp (overnight camp no longer qualifies). Eligible expenses also cover help hired to look after your children at home while you're off at work, including nannies, housekeepers, baby-sitters, maids, or cooks. Even payments made to a mother-in-law or other relative count, so long as the baby-sitting relative isn't someone whom you claim as a dependent on your tax return. About the only people who don't qualify as child-care givers in the eyes of the IRS are chauffeurs and gardeners. Even if they get along great with your kids, whatever you pay them won't qualify for a tax break.

Choosing Between the Tax Breaks

If you're eligible for both child-care tax breaks, you have to choose one or the other. Specifically, the law stipulates that any exemption you receive under an employer plan has to be offset against the child-care tax credit. So if you set aside more than $2,400 in a flexible-spending account for the care of one child (or $4,800 for two or more dependents), the child-care credit is entirely wiped out. In other words, there's no double dipping. You have to choose one tax break or the other. Which is better? As a rule, most middle- and upper-income taxpayers will fare better by choosing the employer tax exemption rather than the credit.

Disclosing the Identity of Your Household Help

In claiming either child-care tax break, the law now requires you to report the name, address, and Social Security number or tax identification number of your child-care help. That's no problem if it's a formal day-care center. But it could be a very big problem if you have an "off-the-books" arrangement with a private individual.

If your baby-sitter doesn't declare the income or is an illegal alien, making the disclosures on your tax return would be tantamount to turning your sitter into the IRS or immigration authorities. The disclosures may also invite tax troubles for yourself if you're not complying with the rules regarding payment of employer Social Security tax (FICA) and federal unemployment tax (FUTA) on behalf of the household help.

As a result of the new reporting requirements, a lot of working parents are probably going to decide to forgo the tax break rather than risk inviting troubles for their housekeeper—as well as themselves—because so many of these arrangements are off the books.

But if you claim a child-care tax break, make sure you get your housekeeper or the day-care center to fill out form W-10, which you can obtain from the IRS. The W-10 is only for your records and doesn't have to be attached to the return. But the form can be your insurance policy in case you're audited. If it turns out that the day-care provider gave the wrong information, you won't automatically lose your tax benefit. You can prove "due diligence" in trying to get the correct information by showing the IRS agent the W-10 form.

CARING FOR THE ELDERLY:
THE NUMBER-ONE FAMILY ISSUE OF THE 1990s

Nowhere will the graying of America hit home so painfully as in the growing number of elderly persons who become frail and enfeebled and require care by their children.

In the same way that child care became the central family issue of the 1980s, elderly care promises to become the focal family concern of the 1990s. As the elderly population mushrooms, more and more adult children will come face to face with the task of caring for an aging relative who may need financial as well as physical assistance.

For nearly 40 percent of these care-givers, the burden of helping their parents comes on top of career and child-care responsibilities. This is the first generation caught in this triple bind. In previous generations, women—who have long been the primary care-givers—didn't have careers and they had children at an earlier age. So by the time a parent was old enough to require assistance, women were unencumbered by a career or young children. Today most women are working and having children at a later age.

Protecting Against Financial Devastation

Issues of money and aging are so distressing that few families ever discuss them before a crisis actually emerges. But it's crucial for you to be aware of your parents' finances so that you and they can better prepare for any crisis and take steps to minimize any potential financial burden.

Looking over their finances will give you an idea of the extent to which you and your siblings may be called upon to provide assistance, and give you time to prepare. It also gives you a chance to see if your parents are effectively and prudently managing their own finances. For example, is their money tied up in risky investments at a time in their life when they should be adopting a more conservative approach in order to protect their nest egg? Or is their money sitting in low-yielding passbook savings accounts when they could be earning much more without assuming any greater risk by investing it in certificates of deposit or government bonds?

Make sure that each of your parents has a "durable" power of attorney drawn up so that you or someone else your parents trust will have the authority to look after their financial affairs if they're unable to do so should they become incapacitated. A durable power of attorney is different from a regular power of attorney, which isn't effective if a person becomes incapacitated. A durable power of attorney specifically stipulates that it won't be terminated if the person later becomes disabled or incompetent.

Also make sure that your parents have adequate health insurance to supplement Medicare, which leaves many expensive gaps. Many retirees are covered by their former employer's health plan. Otherwise, your parents should have a supplemental insurance policy, known as Medigap.

The most crucial step you can take may be to protect against the potentially ruinous costs of illnesses that require long-term care in a nursing home. Nursing-home expenses, which average $25,000 a year, can quickly exhaust an elderly person's entire savings. Medicare won't cover long-term nursing-home care. Nor will private health insurance or Medigap policies. Medicaid will, but to qualify, patients must exhaust virtually all their savings.

Long-term health-care insurance, although expensive, is one way to protect against the financial devastation of long-term care needs. If your parents can't afford the premiums, you and your brothers and sisters should buy the policy for them because you and your siblings could well end up bearing the financial burden one way or another. (See chapter 6, Demographic Trends of the 1990s, for more on long-term health insurance policies.)

Insurance is the only way to protect against such devastating expenses short of moving into a life-care or continuing-care residential community, where residents are guaranteed health care and housing for life in exchange for an endowment and monthly fees. (For more on such communities see chapter 6.)

When Your Parents Need Financial Assistance

If your parents need financial assistance, there are ways to minimize the burden.

Tax Benefits: If you supply more than half your parents' support, they are considered dependents, and that may make you eligible to write off some of the assistance you provide them on your tax return.

One tax benefit is the child- and dependent-care credit, which applies not only to children but also to the care of an elderly dependent. If you're working and can't personally care for an incapacitated parent who lives with you, hiring someone to look after your parent while you're working qualifies for the credit.

Another tax benefit is the itemized deduction for medical expenses. Medical bills incurred on behalf of an elderly dependent, including hospital and nursing-home care, may qualify for a medical expense deduction. To claim any medical expense deduction, total out-of-pocket medical expenses must exceed 7.5 percent of your adjusted gross income. Only expenses beyond the threshhold are deductible.

Renting to Your Parents: One way to provide income to your parents while gaining tax deductions for yourself is to buy their house and rent it back to them. This arrangement gives your parents the cash flow they need without having to move out. So long as you charge them "fair market" rent, you are entitled to claim the same tax deductions as a landlord who was leasing a rental property to a perfect stranger. In selling the home to you, your parents can reduce capital gains taxes by taking advantage of the special exemption available to homeowners age fifty-five and older. The one-time exemption allows elderly homeowners to shield up to $125,000 in profits from the sale of their principal residence, provided they owned and lived in the home for three of the five years prior to the sale. (An exception to the time test is made for homeowners who have become incapacitated.)

Reverse Mortgage: Elderly homeowners in need of income have a way to tap the equity in their home without having to sell it to you or anyone else. They can take out what is called a "reverse mortgage." They get monthly income for a specified number of years or for the rest of their lives. (For more on reverse mortgages see chapter 9.)

Making Them the Child-Care Providers: If you are part of the "sandwich generation," with young children in need of day care and parents in need of financial assistance, you can reduce the burden of both by letting your parents take care of your children. By so doing, money you otherwise would have paid to hire outside help would become supplemental income to your parents. Any money you pay your parents for baby-sitting may also qualify for the child-care tax credit. As previously mentioned, payments to a relative qualify for the credit so long as he or she isn't someone whom you can claim as a dependent on your tax return.

When a Parent Needs Care

When a parent becomes incapacitated in some way, a nursing home isn't necessarily the only option. There are less costly services and programs available that can let an ailing parent live at home, as most of them prefer.

Home Health Care: In-home health-care services are a rapidly growing alternative to nursing homes. Technology has made it possible to administer many treatments at home that used to be reserved to hospitals and nursing homes. Not only do home health-care services enable an elderly person to remain living at home, but the cost can be much less than nursing-home care. Health professionals can provide an elderly person with in-home nursing care, while home health aides can help a patient with personal hygiene, eating, getting around, and homemaking tasks.

Adult Day Care: Elderly people who aren't bedridden but still require some nursing care may be able to take advantage of a geriatric day-care center. Adult day care lets elderly people sleep in their homes but gives them a place to go during the day where they can receive full-time nursing services plus the companionship of others. Adult day care can be the solution in cases where an aging parent lives with you in your home but you're unable to personally care for him or her during the day because you're off working. Adult day care is less expensive than home health-care services. On average, adult day care costs around $30 a day, although many people qualify for financial assistance. Day-care directors can steer you to financial aid programs available in your community. Most day-care centers are affiliated with churches, hospitals, and other nonprofit community organizations.

Senior Citizens' Centers: If an elderly person doesn't require nursing care, a senior citizens' center may be the better choice. It's a place where an older person can spend the day with others in recreational pursuits. Senior citizens' centers don't provide full-time nursing care; they are usually staffed by social workers, recreational therapists, and other nonmedical personnel. Most centers are run by municipalities, religious organizations, and other community groups and are usually free or low-cost.

Meals, Transportation, Homemaker Services: Community organizations also provide a variety of services for older people who need help getting around town or with homemaking. Hot meals can be delivered to home-bound persons. Van service is available to take senior citizens to the doctor or shopping. Elderly persons living in their own homes can also get help with repairs and household chores.

Employer Programs: Another place to check for help is your company's personnel office. Employers are beginning to recognize the heavy burden that nearly one in four of their employees bear in caring for an elderly relative. Programs range from information and referral services to unpaid leaves and financial assistance. Companies aren't doing it just for altruistic reasons; elderly-care responsibilities lead to absenteeism, tardiness, unscheduled days off, and lower productivity. It's hard for an employee to concentrate at work while he or she is worrying about a parent's condition and how best to provide help.

Consulting a Professional to Guide the Way

How do you find your way through the growing maze of elderly-care services?

One source of help is the local Area Agency on Aging, a nonprofit organization that provides information and referral to services in your community. If you can't find a listing in your local telephone directory, contact the National Association of Area Agencies on Aging, 600 Maryland Avenue, SW, Suite 208, Washington, D.C. 20024, or call (202) 484-7520.

Another way to navigate through the jungle of options is to hire a private geriatric-care manager. These professionals aren't cheap—charging fees of as much as $50 to $100 an hour—but they provide personalized assistance in coordinating elderly-care needs. They will come and visit with your family, objectively assess your ailing parent's needs, suggest options, and then arrange care. They can be of particular help to you if your parent lives in a distant city. A private care manager in that city can do many of the things that you might do if you lived nearby and had time to coordinate arrangements and then monitor the care being provided. Hospital social workers should be able to refer you to a reputable care manager.

8

COLLEGE IN THE 1990s: WHAT IT WILL COST AND HOW TO SAVE FOR IT

Sending a child to college is becoming both a more expensive proposition and a more important obligation. Most of the new jobs of the 1990s and beyond will require at least some college education. So college can no longer be considered an option just for those who can afford it. It's essential to getting a good job in the future whether you can afford it or not.

Yet financing a college education has become an even tougher challenge. College costs have been rising faster than inflation, while federal aid has been slashed and changes in the tax laws have crippled some of the most popular ways of saving for a college education. Consequently, it will take more diligent efforts and new strategies to come up with enough money to put your child through school.

An array of new college savings innovations from Congress, state governments, and financial institutions may help. They range from plans that allow you to lock in tuition costs years in advance to new tax breaks for U.S. Savings Bonds.

WHAT COLLEGE WILL COST: A $40,000-TO-$100,000 BILL IN 2000

College costs outpaced inflation during the 1980s and education experts believe the same will hold true during the 1990s. If college costs rise just 6 percent a year, the average cost of attending four years at a private university will total nearly $100,000 for a child starting college at the end of the century. Four years at a state-run university will cost almost $40,000.

No one knows precisely how much college costs will rise, but some educated guesses need to be made in order to figure out how much you will need to save.

The chart on the next page projects college costs through the year 2011, when today's newborns will be graduating from college. The projections assume college costs will continue to rise at 6 percent a year. That is about one percentage point higher than the annual rate consumer prices are expected to rise during the 1990s, according to projections by the WEFA Group and by Data Resources, another leading economic-consulting firm.

Even at 6 percent, college costs will nearly double by the year 2000, and then double again by the year 2010. For example, the cost of one year's tuition, room, board, and fees is projected to run $8,476 for one school year at a public university in the academic year 1999–2000, and $22,627 at a private college. In the 1989–90 school year, costs averaged

THE FUTURE COST OF COLLEGE

Projected cost* of tuition, room, board & fees for each school year through 2012

School year	Public 4-year college	Private 4-year college
1989-90	$4,733	$12,635
1990-91	$5,017	$13,393
1991-92	$5,318	$14,197
1992-93	$5,637	$15,048
1993-94	$5,975	$15,951
1994-95	$6,334	$16,908
1995-96	$6,714	$17,923
1996-97	$7,117	$18,998
1997-98	$7,544	$20,138
1998-99	$7,996	$21,347
1999-2000	$8,476	$22,627
2000-01	$8,985	$23,985
2001-02	$9,524	$25,424
2002-03	$10,095	$26,950
2003-04	$10,701	$28,567
2004-05	$11,343	$30,281
2005-06	$12,023	$32,097
2006-07	$12,745	$34,023
2007-08	$13,510	$36,065
2008-09	$14,320	$38,228
2009-10	$15,179	$40,522
2010-11	$16,090	$42,953
2011-12	$17,056	$45,531

*Average annual cost, assuming 6% annual rise in costs.

Projections based on the 1989 annual survey of college costs by the College Board.

$4,733 at public universities and $12,635 at private colleges, according to the annual survey of college costs conducted by the College Board, the independent education and testing service in Princeton, New Jersey.

HOW MUCH TO SAVE EACH YEAR

Saving is the only way to ensure that you will have enough funds to send your child to college without going deep into debt. There's no way to guarantee that your young child will wind up with good enough grades to merit an academic scholarship or turn out to be a football star worthy of an athletic scholarship, and no way to know whether you will be poor enough for your child to qualify for financial aid.

HOW MUCH YOU NEED TO SAVE FOR COLLEGE

Chart shows how much you need to save annually to fully fund four years of tuition, room, board and fees at an average-priced public or private college. Figures assume: savings start in 1990 and continue through the child's junior year; savings earn 6% after taxes; college costs rise 6% a year.

Year child begins college	ANNUAL SAVINGS NEEDED	
	Public college	Private college
1991	$5,786	$15,445
1992	$4,757	$12,699
1993	$4,073	$10,872
1994	$3,585	$9,572
1995	$3,222	$8,601
1996	$2,939	$7,847
1997	$2,715	$7,248
1998	$2,533	$6,761
1999	$2,381	$6,356
2000	$2,253	$6,016
2001	$2,145	$5,726
2002	$2,051	$5,477
2003	$1,971	$5,260
2004	$1,900	$5,071
2005	$1,836	$4,904
2006	$1,781	$4,755
2007	$1,732	$4,623
2008	$1,688	$4,504

Source: Seidman Financial Services

The chart opposite will give you an idea of how much you need to save each year in order to fully finance four years of college tuition, room, board, and fees.

For example, if your child is due to begin college in 1997, you would need to save $2,715 a year starting now to finance four years at a public university, or $7,248 a year for four years at a private college. These figures assume you begin saving in 1990 and continue through your child's junior year in college.

The savings figures are based on the same college cost projections as contained in the first chart, which assumed college costs would rise 6 percent a year. The figures also assume your savings will earn 6 percent

THE 50% SOLUTION
College Savings Plan for Strained Budgets

If you can't set aside enough to fully fund a college education, this chart shows how much you need to save each year to come up with 50% of the costs.

This plan counts on other sources—financial aid, loans, earnings from your child's summer jobs, and scholarships—to finance the remaining 50%.

Year child begins college	ANNUAL SAVINGS NEEDED	
	Public college	Private college
1991	$2,893	$7,722
1992	$2,378	$6,349
1993	$2,037	$5,436
1994	$1,793	$4,786
1995	$1,611	$4,300
1996	$1,470	$3,924
1997	$1,358	$3,624
1998	$1,266	$3,380
1999	$1,190	$3,178
2000	$1,127	$3,008
2001	$1,072	$2,863
2002	$1,026	$2,739
2003	$986	$2,630
2004	$950	$2,536
2005	$918	$2,462
2006	$891	$2,378
2007	$866	$2,311
2008	$844	$2,252

Source: Seidman Financial Services

a year after taxes, a fairly conservative estimate since you can do better than that right now with tax-exempt municipal bonds.

Of course, you will need to monitor your investment return continuously as well as keep a close eye on college costs to make sure you're saving enough. If college costs rise faster than 6 percent a year or your savings earn less than 6 percent, you will need to adjust your savings accordingly. You will also need to add more to the pot if you want to build enough of a nest egg to allow your child to attend school for more than four years or to go to a school that costs more than the average.

As the chart implies, the earlier you start saving the easier it will be. The best time to start is when your child is born.

If your budget can't support the kind of savings needed to fully fund four years of college, don't give up. Set a more reasonable savings goal. The chart on page 161 below shows the amounts needed to build a nest egg that would cover half your child's college expenses. Of course, you would need to rely on other sources—such as student loans, scholarships, financial aid, and earnings from your child's summer jobs—to make up the rest.

The risk is that your child won't earn much from summer jobs and won't qualify for scholarships or financial aid. That would leave you with the option of either borrowing a lot of money or finding a less expensive school for your child to attend. But at least you'll have half the money needed in savings.

U.S. SAVINGS BONDS: A NEW TAX BREAK

U.S. Savings Bonds gain new luster as a way to save for a child's college education in the 1990s. So long as the money is used to pay for college, interest on newly issued savings bonds is tax-free for families earning up to $60,000. Households with incomes between $60,000 and $90,000 get a partial tax break.

The new tax break only adds to the attractive features of savings bonds that have made them popular investments for college savings in recent years. They are guaranteed by the federal government, they can be purchased for as little as $25, and the interest rate is adjusted every six months to keep you from falling behind if interest rates shoot up.

The new tax break applies to Series EE bonds purchased on or after January 1, 1990. The full tax break goes to families whose adjusted gross income is $60,000 or less on a joint return or $40,000 or less on a single or head-of-household return. Above those income levels, the tax break is gradually phased out. Once income exceeds $90,000 on a joint return ($55,000 for singles), the tax break is eliminated. After 1990, these income brackets will be indexed to inflation. Income eligibility is determined when the bonds are redeemed.

Another requirement is that the principal and interest can be spent only on college tuition and fees. Expenses for room and board or other expenses are not eligible. The tax break applies whether the college education is for your children, your spouse, or yourself.

Parents need to keep the bonds in their own name, rather than the child's. The reason is that you have to be age twenty-four or older when you buy the bonds to get the tax break.

What about a grandparent who wants to help a grandchild? The way the law is written, a grandparent who purchased bonds for a grandchild's education wouldn't be entitled to the tax break. The law stipulates that the tax break applies to dependents who can be claimed on your tax return. So except in the rare situation where the grandparents have custody of their grandchildren, grandparents should give the money to the parents and let the parents buy the bonds for the child.

If you don't qualify for the new tax break, U.S. Savings Bonds still offer tax advantages and other features that make them attractive college savings investments. They are exempt from state and local income taxes, and federal taxes can be deferred until the bonds are redeemed. If you buy them in your child's name and the bonds are redeemed after your child turns fourteen, the interest will be taxed at your child's tax rate, rather than your own. Once children reach age fourteen, all their income—including investment income—is taxed at their own rate.

The adjustable interest rate on Series EE bonds also provides a way to keep up with rising inflation, something you can't do with other fixed-income investments. So long as you hold the savings bond at least five years, your yield is guaranteed to be at least 6 percent, or more if interest-rate levels are higher. The interest rate is adjusted every six months to reflect changes in the yield on five-year Treasury notes. Specifically, the rate is set to yield 85 percent of the average market yield on five-year Treasury notes. (If you cash the bond in before five years, lower fixed rates apply.)

Unlike most other bonds, savings bonds don't pay interest until the bond is redeemed. The bonds mature in twelve years, but you can hold onto them and continue to earn interest for an additional eighteen years.

PAY NOW, GO LATER: PREPAID TUITION PLANS

In what could be the wave of the future in college financing, several states now offer plans under which parents can prepay their child's college tuition years in advance of enrollment and avoid worrying about whether their savings will grow fast enough to keep up with college-cost inflation.

These plans—known variously as prepaid tuition plans, tuition futures, and education trusts—have become popular because they eliminate uncertainty about whether your child will be able to afford college. Michigan, Florida, and Wyoming were the first to offer prepayment plans. Eight other states have enacted legislation authorizing similar plans: Alabama, Indiana, Louisiana, Maine, Missouri, Ohio, Oklahoma, and West Virginia.

In general, the plans work like this: Years before the child is scheduled to enroll, parents pay a fixed sum based on the child's age, current tuition rates, the state's estimate of how much those costs will rise in the future, and the expected return it will get by investing your funds. In return, your child is guaranteed four years at any public college in the state. It doesn't matter how much costs rise. If the state based your prepayment on projections that costs would rise only 6 percent a year and they actually turned out to rise 15 percent a year, that's the state's problem, not yours.

As an example of what these plans cost, when Michigan started its prepaid tuition program in 1988, charges ranged from $6,756 for an infant to $9,152 for a high school sophomore. That guarantees four years of tuition at any public college in the state. The average cost for four years at Michigan's colleges then ran in excess of $9,000.

In figuring how much to charge, states are not looking to lose money on the deal. They hope to earn enough by investing your cash payment to keep up with future tuition increases. Of course, you may be able to do just as well—or better—by investing the money yourself. But you won't know until it's too late because the value of the contract depends on how much tuition increases. If college-cost inflation stays moderate, you can do better. If it soars through the roof, you probably won't be able to come close to matching the return. What the state is offering is a guarantee: four years of tuition whether or not its investments keep pace.

But there are some considerable disadvantages to these plans. When you enter into a prepaid tuition plan you are locking your child into a limited choice of schools. And those choices may not fit their needs or desires when they reach college age. Knowing that their parents have already locked them into a state college, children might be discouraged from studying as hard as they would if there was the prospect of going to Harvard or Yale or Cal Tech. Or a musical prodigy might never have the chance to go to Juilliard because his parents' money was all tied up in a state plan.

The financial penalty for sending your child to a school not covered by the plan can be stiff. Participants in Florida's plan who want to withdraw their money early or send their child to an out-of-state school only get back their original investment minus a $50 handling fee. They sacrifice any interest earned on their funds.

Some plans are more liberal. Michigan gives participants who want to send their children to an in-state private college a sum equivalent to the average cost of in-state public colleges at the time. Children choosing an out-of-state college get a bit less. But participants are not allowed to pull their money out of the plan unless the child dies, becomes disabled, or doesn't go to college. So read the fine print carefully before you commit.

Another drawback to prepaid tuition plans is their tax treatment. In ruling on Michigan's arrangement, the Internal Revenue Service said that participants have to pay tax on the increased value of the tuition contract starting when the child enrolls in college. To give an example, assume a parent paid $10,000 for a prepaid tuition contract and the actual cost of four years of college for your child turns out to be $30,000. That $20,000 increase in value would be taxed over the course of your child's college education.

If you commit to a prepaid tuition plan, be prepared to save enough money on the side to pay those taxes when they come due. Also keep in mind that most prepaid college programs only cover tuition. So you will still need to save enough on your own to pay room, board, and other expenses.

Some educators are pushing for a national prepaid tuition program that would give participants the choice of hundreds of colleges across the country. Expanding the choice of colleges would certainly broaden the appeal of prepaid tuition plans and could even make them a common way of financing college educations in the future. For now, parents are stuck with the more limited choices available under the state programs, or the ones available under a few new private programs that are trying to get a wider selection of public and private colleges across the country to participate.

The Hemar Education Corporation, a private company involved in educational financing, was expected to be offering a plan for prepaying tuition at participating colleges in 1990. Under the plan, called the National Prepaid Tuition Plan, parents would make a cash payment to a participating college based on current tuition rates and that school would guarantee the child's tuition when he or she enrolled. As originally conceived, the plan would allow for the transfer of tuition credits if your child wanted to attend a different school participating in the plan. If your child didn't attend a school in the Hemar network, a sibling or first cousin could use the credit or you could get a refund of your original investment, but with no interest. The plan was initially backed by officials of eighteen private and state colleges. The tax treatment of the prepayment arrangement was under review by the Internal Revenue Service. Hemar, based in St. Paul, Minnesota, will administer the plan for participating colleges. For information call (800) 888-4846.

Another new private plan, called the College Prepayment Fund, allows parents to lock in tuition costs at one of the colleges participating in the program by investing in a mutual fund. Even if your mutual fund investment doesn't keep pace with the rising cost of tuition, the college you select guarantees to cover any shortfall. If the mutual fund outperforms tuition rises at that school, you get to keep any excess amount. The plan offers parents considerable flexibility, including the ability to change to a different participating school and the right to withdraw all your money, including earnings, whenever you want. One disadvantage is that you have to pay taxes on interest and dividend earnings each year. Kemper, a large financial services company, manages the fund, which imposes no fees to join or leave. The plan itself is administered by the nonprofit National Tuition Maintenance Organization, based in Ann Arbor, Michigan. The College Prepayment Fund started in late 1989 with fifteen colleges participating. For information, call (800) 288-6866.

TAX-EXEMPT COLLEGE SAVINGS BONDS

Other states are helping residents save for college by issuing a special class of tax-free municipal bonds, called "baccalaureate bonds." These bonds have been enormously popular among investors. Interest is exempt from federal, state, and local taxes; they can be purchased in relatively small denominations; and they sometimes come with attractive features not found on other municipal bonds.

Like U.S. Savings Bonds and other "zero-coupon" bonds, baccalaureate bonds don't pay interest until they mature. You invest a small sum now and it grows into a larger sum over the term of the bond. For instance, if you were to invest $6,249 in baccalaureate bonds paying 7.5 percent interest, you would have about $20,000 in interest and principal waiting for you by the time your two-year-old child is ready to enter college.

Baccalaureate bonds have a few advantages over other municipal bonds. Most baccalaureates cannot be called in early, so your yield is guaranteed for the life of the bond. Other municipal bonds usually contain provisions allowing issuers to call in the bonds after ten years. If, at that time, interest rates have dropped, you are stuck reinvesting your funds at a lower rate.

Baccalaureates also tend to have higher credit ratings than other municipal bonds because in many states they are backed by the state government rather than a city or agency.

Upper-income families who aren't eligible for the new tax break on U.S. Savings Bonds may be able to benefit from the state baccalaureate programs, which have so far refrained from imposing income restrictions.

Baccalaureate bonds are also attractive because they don't limit your choice of school as prepaid tuition programs do. You can use the money to go to any college, although some programs, like Illinois's, provide greater returns for those who choose an in-state school. Read the terms of the program carefully for restrictions on how the money has to be used. Some states have no strings attached. In others, the bonds have to be used for college or you forfeit the interest. You get only your initial investment back.

Baccalaureate bonds can be cashed in early if you need the money for something else, by selling them in the open market as you would other types of bonds. But as with any fixed-income investment, you risk selling at a loss if interest rates have gone up. What's more, baccalaureate bonds have not been very actively traded, so you might not get as good a price as you would with municipal bonds that are actively traded.

Twenty states have already enacted legislation authorizing the issuance of baccalaureate bonds: Arkansas, Colorado, Connecticut, Delaware, Hawaii, Illinois, Iowa, Kentucky, Louisiana, Missouri, New Hampshire, North Carolina, North Dakota, Ohio, Oregon, Rhode Island, Tennessee, Virginia, Washington, and Wisconsin.

Even if your state doesn't offer baccalaureate bonds, other municipal bonds offered in your state can still be attractive investments for college savings plans because of their tax advantages.

Because municipal bonds are tax-free no matter who owns them, you don't have to put them in your child's name to gain a tax advantage as you do with taxable investments. So there is no worry that your child will use the funds to buy a Ferrari rather than a college education.

One drawback of municipal bonds and other fixed-income investments is that if inflation accelerates, you won't be able to keep pace because the yield is fixed. So don't put all your money into zero-coupon bonds or other fixed-income investments. Those rates you lock in could well keep you short of your needs if inflation heats up.

Also beware that if you buy the bonds and then move to another state you may end up paying state and local taxes on the interest. Virtually all states tax interest on out-of-state municipal bonds.

Before investing in zero-coupon municipal bonds, make sure to compare yields on U.S. Treasury zero-coupon bonds, known as STRIPS. Treasury bonds are subject to federal income tax each year, but their after-tax return can sometimes be greater than that of municipal bonds. Treasury securities, which are backed by the U.S. government, are also considered safer than municipal bonds. Treasury bonds are exempt from state and local income taxes.

BANK CDs LINKED TO COST OF COLLEGE

To insure that your savings will grow fast enough to keep up with the rising cost of college, one bank offers a certificate of deposit that promises to keep pace with annual increases in college costs without limiting your choice of colleges.

The interest rate on the CollegeSure CD is adjusted each year to reflect the average rise in costs at 500 selected private colleges as computed by the College Board.

The CollegeSure CD is a creation of the College Savings Bank, a federally insured bank in Princeton, New Jersey, founded in 1987 to issue the CDs. The bank estimates how much it would cost to send your child to an average-priced college or a particular college you have in mind and then tells you how much you will need to deposit in order to reach that goal. The bank promises your investment will keep pace with college costs, whether they rise 5 percent or 20 percent a year.

There is a price for this guarantee. The CDs are priced to yield 1.5 percentage points less than annual college-cost inflation. Deposits of

$10,000 and up earn one percentage point less than the college-cost index. So if college costs are rising 8 percent, your return is only 6.5 or 7 percent, depending on the size of your deposit.

Another drawback is that the interest is taxable, and it's taxed each year even though you don't receive any of the interest until your child enrolls in college.

Because of the premium and the taxes, college-cost inflation would have to run a few points above inflation each year for you to come out ahead with the CDs. Presuming inflation doesn't get out of control, you could do better by investing your money in municipal bonds instead. There is no interest-rate premium to pay and no taxes to pay.

What CollegeSure CDs offer that municipal bonds and most other investments don't is protection against runaway college inflation. It's sort of a combination savings and insurance plan. The CD guarantees you will have enough to pay for college even if inflation gets out of control. While runaway inflation is not likely, the CD protects against the possibility.

Prepaid tuition plans offer similar protection. But CollegeSure CDs have fewer restrictions. Your child is free to go to any college. Even if your child doesn't go to college, you still get all your money and interest back. Although the CDs carry penalties for early withdrawal of principal, there are no restrictions on how or where the money is used. But you do pay a price for that flexibility. For more information, call the bank at (800) 888-2723.

BUILDING A BIGGER NEST EGG THROUGH TAX SAVINGS

Children are no longer the great tax shelters they used to be in the days before the Tax Reform Act of 1986. But they can still help reduce the tax bite on funds set aside for their college education.

Children under age fourteen still get preferential tax treatment on limited amounts of investment income held in their name. Once they turn fourteen, all their income is taxed at their own rate, rather than their parents'. So there is still some benefit to putting taxable investments in your child's name rather than your own. (Each parent can give each child up to $10,000 a year without incurring a gift tax.)

Some investments are more suitable than others. For children under fourteen, investments that generate taxable income each year, such as bank CDs or stocks with high dividend yields, should be limited since only limited amounts of investment income can be sheltered each year by the child. Any investment income in excess of $1,000 (this figure is indexed for inflation each year beginning with the 1989 tax year) is taxed at the parents' rate rather than the child's. For this reason, taxable zero-coupon bonds are no longer attractive for a young child's account either except in small amounts. You have to pay taxes each year on the interest that theoretically accumulates each year—even though you don't get any interest until the bond matures. So stick to tax-exempt zero-coupon bonds issued by state and local governments.

Investments that defer taxable income until the child reaches age fourteen—when the income is taxed at the child's rate—are also well suited to college savings plans. As mentioned earlier, U.S. Savings Bonds fit the bill. For those who don't qualify for the new tax break on the savings bonds, taxes on the interest can be deferred until the bonds reach full maturity. So if you buy savings bonds in your child's name that don't mature until after the child's fourteenth birthday, all the interest would be taxed at the child's rate rather than your own. (Remember: If you think you will qualify for the new tax break on savings bonds, buy the bonds in your own name.)

Growth stocks, which don't pay current dividends but offer the potential for long-term appreciation, are another way to take advantage of the special tax treatment of children. If there are no dividend payments there are no taxes to pay each year. And if you wait to sell the shares until after the child turns fourteen, the capital gain will be taxed at the child's rate rather than the parents'.

But stocks, particularly growth stocks, have to be approached with caution because they offer no guaranteed return and no guarantee that your principal will remain intact. If you invest in stocks, it should be done while the child is young so that you have the time to ride out market fluctuations and a chance to sell when the market is up. Once your child is within a few years of entering college, look for a good point to bail out. The reason is that the stock market goes up and down, sometimes staying down for years. Your stocks could be depressed just when you need the money to pay college tuition.

CUSTODIAL ACCOUNTS

Custodial accounts are the most common way of establishing investments in your child's name. Setting them up is easy. The paperwork takes only a few minutes. Your banker, stockbroker, or mutual fund will provide all the necessary forms.

Parents, who usually name themselves as custodians, manage investments in the account. But the money can be used only for the benefit of the child. Once the money is in the account, you can't take it back. Nor can you spend it on items that parents are legally expected to provide children, such as food, clothing, or shelter.

Why bother setting up a custodial account instead of just giving the child direct ownership of the stock or money? In the case of stocks, brokers are reluctant to deal directly with children since minors can't be legally held to contracts. If you set up a regular bank account in the child's name rather than a custodial account, the child could legally have direct access to the money at any age. It's the child's account, not yours.

With a custodial account, a minor child doesn't have access to the money. The adult custodian maintains control over it. However, the child does automatically gain clear title to all assets in the account when he or she legally becomes an adult, at age eighteen or twenty-one, depending on the state. So it's a matter of good faith—and upbringing— that your child will spend the money for college as intended.

If you are investing large sums in your child's name and are concerned about what he or she will do with the money, consult a tax lawyer or accountant about setting up a trust arrangement. It will cost a few hundred dollars to set up and a separate tax return for the trust has to be filed each year. But it can protect a college nest egg from being blown on sports cars or drugs.

Another option is simply to invest all your child's college funds in your own name. You won't save any taxes. But at least you'll have full control of the funds. No need to worry about your child squandering funds invested in his or her own name.

GETTING FAMILY AND FRIENDS TO CONTRIBUTE

Relatives and even friends can be a significant source of help in building a college nest egg. Let them know that you have established a college savings account for your child and encourage them to contribute money to it instead of giving another toy or doll on the child's birthdays.

When it comes to Bar Mitzvahs, graduations, and other major events in your child's life, friends sometimes ask what your child might like as a present. Use that opportunity to suggest a contribution to the child's college fund.

BRIBING YOUR KIDS TO GET HIGHER GRADES

Pushing your children to get better grades in high school will not only make them better people and get them into a better college, but it can also lead to thousands of dollars in financial assistance.

Even if you need to dangle a financial bribe—such as a car on high-school graduation—to spur your child to action, it can turn out to be one of the most profitable investments you make. Scholarships for academic achievement can be worth far more than a car.

What's more, students who stretch themselves in high school may be able to trim their college bills by up to 25 percent. It's not easy, but it can be done if the child takes advanced courses in high school. If the child does well enough on advanced-placement exams, he or she will be able to skip enough beginning college courses to graduate in three years instead of four. That will save a year's worth of tuition, fees, room, board, and the like—a lot of money for those who apply themselves in high school.

WAYS FOR CHILDREN TO SHARE THE BURDEN

Not all parents can afford to bear the entire burden of financing their children's college education. Children can—and should—pitch in. Sit down with them and explain that they need to share some of the re-sponsibility for financing their college education and then discuss how they can help.

Working after school, on weekends, or at least during the summer is the most common way they can help contribute. Earnings from part-time jobs need not be just for Saturday night dates or to buy cars or record albums. Part of it should be earmarked for college.

If you own your own business, you can put your children to work on your payroll. Their earnings will be taxed at their own lower tax rate and you will be able to deduct their salary as a business expense, just as you would any employee's. In addition, if the child is under 18, you won't have to pay Social Security taxes on the wages.

Sharing the burden can go beyond your child taking a part-time job. There are plenty of ways to put college within virtually everyone's reach, and they should be discussed with your child. Would your child be willing to go to a public university rather than a more expensive private college? Would your child be willing to start out at a community college to save money? Or would your child be willing to join ROTC or a cooperative education program in order to help ease the financial burden?

COOPERATIVE PROGRAMS: WORK AND LEARN

Cooperative education programs have attracted a growing number of students looking for a way to help finance their college education while gaining valuable work experience. Students go to school and work at a job in alternating semesters. Earnings from the job help pay part or all of their college expenses.

Co-op programs are not new. The concept originated in 1906. But with college costs increasing and government aid declining, cooperative education programs have become an attractive option to more and more students. About one thousand colleges now offer cooperative programs, with more than 250,000 students participating. The programs embrace a broad range of disciplines from engineering and computer science to the arts and the humanities. Pay averages $7,000 to $14,000 a year, depending on the field.

The program offers students more than a way to pay for college. The practical work experience gained during their college years gives them an edge in getting a job on graduation. Many get a job with the same company they worked for in the co-op program.

Some 50,000 employers participate in co-op programs, including IBM, Xerox, Digital Equipment, General Motors, Disney, Tiffany, Rockwell International, the Du Pont Company, Hughes Aircraft, Liz Claiborne, Exxon, and Texas Instruments. The federal government also participates, offering jobs in over thirty agencies ranging from the IRS to the CIA.

Typically, students work one semester or one quarter and go to school the next. In some programs, however, students work part of the day and study part of the day. Most colleges offer a few academic credits for each work period.

For more information on co-op programs, write for the "Co-op Education Undergraduate Program Directory," from the National Commission for Cooperative Education, 360 Huntington Avenue, Boston, Mass. 02115, or phone (617) 437-3778. The pamphlet is free.

THE MILITARY OPTION: ROTC

Children who are willing to spend at least four years on active military duty after college can get Uncle Sam to pay most or all of their tuition bill, fees, books, and a stipend of $100 a month by joining a Reserve Officer Training Corps program in college. ROTC programs are offered at more than five hundred colleges. High school students should apply early in their senior year.

Signing up for the program obligates you to drill periods and military-science classes during the school year, military training each summer, and four years of active duty after graduation.

Going to a military academy—West Point, Annapolis, or the Air Force Academy—is free. All expenses, including room and board, are picked up by the government. Competition for admission, however, is keen. High school students need to apply early in their junior year. A military academy appointment obligates you to at least five years' active duty.

COMMUNITY COLLEGES: AN ECONOMICAL BEGINNING

Community colleges offer an economical way to start a student on the road to a college degree. By starting out at a community college and finishing up at a four-year school, the cost of a college education can be cut sharply and you still get to list the four-year college as the place where you earned your degree.

Tuition and fees at a community college run about half the cost of a state university. What's more, room and board charges can be eliminated by living at home and commuting.

Community colleges have assumed a more important role in higher education over the past two decades. Since 1970, community college enrollments have more than doubled, and now account for nearly four of ten college students. Community colleges have benefited from soaring tuition costs at private universities, which in turn have created greater competition for spots at public universities. This trickle-down effect has helped boost community college enrollments.

If you want to transfer to a particular four-year university, find out the odds of being accepted as a transfer student from the community college you want to attend. Some community colleges are more revered than others in the eyes of university admission officers. Also ask the community college what percentage of its students go on to four-year programs.

9

WHY YOU NEED TO SAVE MORE FOR RETIREMENT

THE NEW REALITIES OF PENSIONS AND SOCIAL SECURITY

The days when Americans could count on their employer and the government to secure a comfortable retirement are slipping away. Financial security in old age will increasingly depend on how much workers themselves put away for their retirement years. Future retirees are likely to find that their pensions and Social Security no longer stretch far enough to provide a comfortable life-style in retirement. Threatening their long-term financial security are a variety of forces, including increased life expectancy, early retirements, shorter job tenure with a single employer, growing budgetary pressures to cut Social Security benefits, and efforts by companies to rein in their mounting pension costs.

Shifting the Burden to Employees: Struggling to control the ever-rising cost of providing for their growing legions of retired workers, more and more companies are making employees bear a larger share of the burden in financing their retirement. Growing numbers of companies are establishing "401(k)" plans and other retirement savings plans that require employee contributions. By offering these plans and encouraging employee participation by matching contributions, employers aren't under as much pressure to increase contributions to the company's main pension plan. In some cases, particularly in smaller firms, 401(k) plans are the company's only retirement plan and unless the employee makes a contribution, the company doesn't contribute anything to the employee's retirement. So employees who are relying strictly on their company providing for them in retirement are likely to find the pension insufficient—or even nonexistent.

Dropping Guaranteed-Benefit Plans: Many companies are dropping their defined-benefit pension plans, which typically guarantee a portion of your salary in retirement, and replacing them with defined-contribution plans,

175

which don't promise any particular level of benefit. Defined-benefit plans tend to be preferred by employees because the benefit is predetermined and fixed and the company is obligated to make sure the plan is sufficiently endowed to pay those benefits. With a defined-contribution plan, employees don't know what they'll wind up with at retirement. A company has only to promise to make a certain contribution to the fund each year, such as a percentage of profits in the case of a profit-sharing plan. (Under the terms of some plans, the company has no such obligation to make a contribution every year.) What you'll get depends on how much was contributed to the plan on your behalf and how well the funds were invested. If the investments fare poorly, so will you.

Scaling Back Pension Benefits: While defined-benefit plans are still widespread, some employers are trying to cut costs by tinkering with the formula that determines how much pension you'll get. Benefits under a defined-benefit pension plan are normally based on how much you earned in the final five years with the company. That's a good formula because your final years with the company are usually your highest-earning years. But some companies are figuring benefits using a longer period, sometimes averaging what you earned since you began work at the company. The new formula would reduce benefits you earned after the change took effect since it averages in your lowest-earning years.

Impact of New Compensation Schemes: New pay schemes being adopted at a growing number of companies are artificially holding down pension payouts under defined-benefit plans. Rather than increasing an employee's base pay, companies are handing out one-time bonuses and other forms of compensation. The problem is that the employee's base pay—not total compensation—is the figure used to determine the level of pension benefits.

Job-Hopping Reduces Benefits: With lifetime employment becoming the exception rather than the rule, workers can't count on receiving the same level of pension benefits that their parents earned by spending their entire career with a single employer. Pension benefits under a defined-benefit plan are based on years of service with the company, as well as your base pay. The formulas commonly used to determine the benefit heavily favor those with long-term service with the company. So, other things being equal, people who switched jobs during their careers will find their total pension payouts are substantially less than if they had stayed with one company for thirty years. Job-hopping won't be as serious a threat to pension benefits as it used to be, as a result of a recent change in the law that took effect in 1989. That change gives employees the right to pension benefits much sooner than before. Prior to 1989, most employees had to work ten years for their company before they established full rights to benefits that had accrued on their behalf from employer contributions to the pension plan. Now the law requires employers to provide a much shorter "vesting" period. Under the most common arrangement, employees can expect to acquire nonforfeitable rights to accrued pension benefits after completing five years of service. (Another arrangement gives employees partial vesting after three years of service and full vesting after seven years.)

Increased Life Expectancy: People are retiring earlier and living longer, so retirement funds have to stretch over a much longer period than in the past. Many Americans can expect retirement to last twenty-five years or more.

Greater Inflation Vulnerability: Longer retirement means a greater risk that inflation will erode your pension's purchasing power. Most pensions don't provide cost-of-living increases to retirees. According to a 1986 survey by the Labor Department, only 3 percent of pension-plan participants received automatic cost-of-living increases, and only about one-third received some kind of ad hoc increase to help keep up with inflation.

Weak Coverage in Service Sector: Pensions are not as widely offered by smaller companies and service businesses, where most of the job growth is expected to take place in the 1990s and beyond.

Social Security: Growing budgetary pressures make Social Security benefits a potential target for cutbacks, either by reducing cost-of-living increases or by making middle- and upper-income retirees pay more tax on their benefits.

Dual-Income Households: On the plus side of the retirement financing picture—and it is a very big plus—is the fact that more and more families consist of two wage earners, which means the prospect of two pensions and larger Social Security benefits. Two incomes also make it easier for a couple to set aside more savings for retirement.

THE SPECIAL PLIGHT OF BABY-BOOM RETIREES

Baby-boomers have even greater cause for concern about their long-term financial security. It will be much harder to support a comfortable life-style in retirement when the baby-boomers begin leaving the work force around the year 2010. The problem goes beyond any prospects for increased life expectancy.

Social Security Threat: Baby-boomers have good reason to fear that they won't receive the same level of Social Security benefits as retirees do now. The sheer size of the baby-boom generation will create enormous strains on the Social Security system. The Social Security trust fund is now actuarially sound and projected to run gargantuan surpluses over the next several decades so that a large reserve is available to pay benefits when the baby-boomers retire. But even if Social Security Administration projections prove accurate and Congress doesn't raid the fund for other purposes, the trust fund surplus is forecast to be exhausted while many baby-boomers are still alive. The working-age population at that time may not be willing or able to shoulder a large enough tax increase to fill the entire gap. When the baby-boomers retire, there will be just two workers for every retiree, compared to a three-to-one ratio now. Bear in mind that the Social Security surplus isn't stashed in a vault; rather the trust fund invests in special Treasury bonds that will have to be paid off by the government out of general tax revenues in the next century.

One cutback in benefits already scheduled is an increase in the standard Social Security retirement age of 65 for people born since 1938. Although retirees will still be able to receive partial benefits as early as age 62, the age for full benefits will increase gradually starting in the year 2000, reaching age 66 in 2009 and age 67 in 2027.

Medicare Threat: While Social Security is in no immediate danger of insolvency, the Medicare trust fund is projected to become insolvent around the turn of the century, raising the specter of cuts in the Medicare program, tax increases, or borrowing from the fund that is used to pay Social Security benefits.

Retirement Will Be More Expensive: With such a huge group of retirees all seeking retirement services at the same time, prices for everything from health care to retirement homes are bound to be pushed higher. Some services could be in short supply.

Less Home Equity: Baby-boomers can't count on appreciating home values as a source of retirement savings—at least not to the extent their parents did. Baby-boomers will be selling their homes to a much smaller pool of potential buyers, the "baby bust" generation, which portends depreciating home values rather than appreciating prices.

Less Family Support: Because baby-boomers are having fewer children— and many baby-boomers are choosing to have none—families probably won't be able to provide as much support as they do now for elderly relatives.

Declining Company-Paid Health Coverage: Faced with sharply rising costs of providing health insurance for retired employees, many companies are considering ways to reduce coverage for future retirees. Baby-boomers could well find that employer-paid health-care insurance for retirees is sharply reduced or phased out by the time they retire.

Low Savings, High Debt: The spendthrift life-style of baby-boomers is also threatening their own retirement security. Their high levels of indebtedness and low levels of savings portend difficulties later in having enough funds to finance a comfortable retirement.

TAKING A MORE ACTIVE ROLE

The implications of all these changes are clear: Individuals need to assume more responsibility for their own retirement security.

Although company pensions and Social Security may provide the foundation, they are rarely sufficient by themselves to assure a comfortable retirement. Even a pension that looks more than sufficient today may not look so grand after inflation takes its toll. At 5 percent inflation, money loses half its buying power in fourteen years. Only a small number of pension plans provide benefits that offer adequate protection against inflation in retirement. Personal savings have to fill that gap.

Most people wind up with insufficient retirement savings because they put away only whatever is left after the year's bills are paid. For many people, there's nothing left. The only way to ensure sufficient savings for retirement is to make retirement savings part of your household budget. Figure out what you need to save and then adjust your budget accordingly. Cutting back your life-style is not a pleasant thought. No one likes the idea of doing with a less expensive car or home. But the choice is either to live less lavishly now or live a frugal life in your golden years.

Assuming more responsibility for your long-term financial security also means paying closer attention to pension benefits when shopping for a job. Even if you don't intend to stay with the company for a lifetime, building a good pension income in this era of more frequent job changing requires amassing pension benefits from each employer. In job interviews ask about the company's retirement plans and take them into account when comparing job offers. When negotiating a compensation package, try to get your new employer to make up for at least part of the pension benefits you forfeit by leaving your old company early.

In an era of corporate cost-cutting, many employees in their fifties and sixties are receiving tempting offers of early retirement. But make sure you can afford to retire before you take a company up on an early retirement offer. If you're in doubt, consult with your accountant or financial planner to see whether you're getting a good deal and whether you have the resources to take early retirement. In weighing the offer, ask yourself how much time you would be buying if you turned down the incentive package. Would your job be secure until you reached normal retirement age? Or is it likely that the company might ask you in a year or two to take early retirement but without the extra financial incentives you're being offered now?

HOW MUCH YOU REALLY NEED TO SAVE

Building a retirement nest egg that will sustain you through today's longer life spans and inflationary environment is a much bigger task than commonly perceived.

To be safe, you have to assume that you will lead a long life. Life expectancy tables may be a safe bet for insurance companies to plan by, but individuals can't play the averages. If you are lucky enough to beat the averages and live to a ripe old age, you could find yourself woefully short of funds if your savings were based on actuarial assumptions. On average, men who reach age 65 can expect to live another 15 years and women can expect to live another 19 years. But to plan somewhat conservatively, you have to assume that you will live at least another 25 years, to age 90, because many people will.

Not only will your nest egg need to last that long, but it will need to be large enough to withstand the ravages of inflation.

After estimating what your pension and Social Security will provide and what your expenses will be, you'll have some idea as to what kind of gap personal savings has to fill. Most people are able to live on 60 to 80 percent of their preretirement income, since they don't have the expense of putting children through school, commuting to work, and life-insurance and disability-insurance premiums. Many retirees also have their mortgages paid off so they don't have to worry about monthly house payments.

The following chart shows how much you need to save each year in order to build a retirement nest egg that will provide you with supplemental income of $10,000 a year in today's dollars for twenty-five years and that will withstand the impact of inflation. Inflation is factored into the computations so that the next egg will provide you with the equivalent of $10,000 a year in today's purchasing power. In other words, if you figure you need $10,000 in today's dollars to supplement your pension and Social Security, don't worry about how inflation will affect the $10,000. The chart adjusts for inflation so that you'll have enough to offset completely the impact of inflation, which is assumed to be 6 percent a year. The chart assumes you will earn 7 percent a year, after taxes, on your savings.

Obviously, the figures are daunting and you may find it impossible to save anywhere near these numbers (let alone the additional amounts required if you estimate your supplemental income needs at more than

WHAT YOU REALLY NEED TO SAVE FOR RETIREMENT

Annual savings* required to assure $10,000 a year in real purchasing power in retirement from age 65 until age 90.

Current Age	Annual savings needed
25	$12,648
30	$13,650
35	$14,927
40	$16,658
45	$19,205
50	$23,413
55	$31,820
60	$57,128

*Assumes annual 6 percent inflation and annual after-tax return on investments of 7 percent.

Source: Seidman Financial Services

$10,000 a year). But these figures do provide a realistic assessment of how much saving is actually needed to provide even a small income supplement to last through twenty-five years of retirement and keep up with inflation.

For most people, coming up with enough savings will require a major alteration in household budgets and even life-styles. As the chart illustrates, the earlier you start the less you need to save each year. On the other hand, most people find it easier to save larger amounts as they become older and their income grows. To be sure, few people who are twenty-five years old can afford to put away $12,648 a year now. But they can put away lesser amounts now so long as they gradually accelerate their savings as their income grows and make up for any shortfall in savings from their earlier years.

It takes a lot of money to live twenty-five years in retirement, and saving that kind of money will require almost all Americans to make major sacrifices during their working lives and set aside much more money than they are used to.

IRAs, 401(K)'s, KEOGHs, AND SEPs

Workers can get help in saving for their retirement from both the government and employers.

Individual Retirement Accounts (IRAs) no longer provide a tax deduction for everyone but they can still be attractive for deferring taxes on some of your investments until retirement.

Employees at a growing number of companies can reduce their tax bill by earmarking part of their paycheck for a 401(k) plan. Many companies will even throw in matching contributions to help you along.

Self-employed individuals can earn substantial tax deductions by setting up Keogh retirement plans or Simplified Employee Pension plans (SEPs).

Because earnings in these special retirement accounts aren't taxed each year as they are in a regular savings account, you can build a larger nest egg. None of the money in these accounts is taxed until withdrawal.

To discourage you from trying to use these tax-sheltered accounts to save up for a yacht or a European vacation, a 10 percent penalty (on top of the regular tax due) generally is imposed on withdrawals made before age 59½.

IRAs: Any worker can put up to $2,000 a year of earnings into an Individual Retirement Account and have the money grow and compound tax-free until withdrawn. (One-income couples are allowed to contribute up to $2,250 a year.)

If you're not covered by a retirement plan at work you can also claim a tax deduction on your income tax return for the amount of your IRA contribution. (In the case of a married couple, if either spouse is covered by a retirement plan at work, then both are considered covered for IRA purposes.) But even if you or your spouse is covered by a retirement plan at work, you can still claim at least a partial deduction for an IRA contribution if your adjusted gross income is below $50,000 on a joint return or below $35,000 on a single return. (To get the full deduction, adjusted income has to be below $40,000 on a joint return or below $25,000 for a single's return.) Individuals have an entire calendar year, plus up until April 15 of the following year, to contribute to an IRA and claim a deduction for that contribution on the tax return due that April 15. For example, you would have until April 15, 1991, to make an IRA deposit and take the deduction on your 1990 tax return, due April 15, 1991.

Even if you're not eligible for an IRA deduction, it's worth considering contributing to an IRA anyway. The decision depends partly on your investment preferences, what other retirement savings options are available to you and how much money you have to invest.

If you're eligible to participate in a 401(k) plan and that's all you can afford to do, you'll find the 401(k) provides better benefits than an IRA. A nondeductible IRA doesn't stack up well against tax-exempt municipal bonds, either. Municipal bonds provide about the same after-tax return as a comparable investment in a nondeductible IRA. What's more, municipal bonds don't involve any early withdrawal penalty, or the paperwork or record-keeping requirements that nondeductible IRAs do.

But a nondeductible IRA can be advantageous if you're investing in something besides municipal bonds. IRAs can be used to shelter earnings from a wide variety of investments, from bank certificates of deposit to stocks.

Many members of Congress are pushing to restore the deductibility of IRA contributions for all taxpayers. But even if those efforts are successful, budgetary pressures are likely to prevent a full restoration. Under a proposal by the Senate's chief tax writer, for example, taxpayers who aren't eligible for an IRA deduction under the 1986 tax-reform rules would be allowed to deduct 50 percent of their contributions.

401(k) Plans: The 401(k) plan, sometimes known as a "Salary Reduction Plan" or a "cash-or-deferred arrangement," has been growing in popularity among employees since IRA deductions were curtailed by the Tax Reform Act of 1986. A fast-growing number of companies are establishing 401(k) plans for their workers. These plans offer employees the chance to save even more taxes than they ever could with an IRA. In addition, many companies encourage employees to participate in the plan by matching contributions. Some employers contribute as much as $2 for every dollar the employee contributes.

Under a 401(k), employees are allowed to earmark a portion of their salary to the plan each year. The money is automatically deducted from each paycheck. No income tax has to be paid on the amount contributed, which is the equivalent of receiving a deduction for a contribution to an IRA. But the tax savings from a 401(k) can be larger since you can earmark as much as 20 percent of your salary each year to the plan. The ceiling on annual contributions is adjusted for inflation each year. (In 1990 the ceiling was $7,979.) Bear in mind that these are the limits set by the tax law. For various reasons, employers often impose lower limits on contributions, such as 5 to 15 percent of salary.

Employees typically have to decide before the start of each calendar year how much of their salary they want to earmark for the plan, although most plans allow workers to change the amount one or more times during the course of the year.

Self-Employed Plans: Self-employed individuals, including those with income from a sideline business, can make even larger tax-deductible contributions to a Keogh retirement plan or a Simplified Employee Pension plan.

If you set up what is known as a "money-purchase" Keogh plan, you can make a tax-deductible deposit each year of up to 20 percent of your net self-employment earnings, up to a maximum of $30,000. This type of plan requires you to contribute a fixed percentage of your income each year. If you miss a year, the IRS will make you pay a penalty.

If you have a "profit-sharing" Keogh plan, which allows you to vary the size of your contributions from year to year, the tax-deductible limit is 13.043 percent of your net self-employment earnings, up to the maximum deposit of $30,000.

Still another type of Keogh plan, called a "defined-benefit" Keogh, lets you make even larger tax-deductible deposits. You are allowed to contribute as much as necessary each year to build a pension that will provide you with an annual retirement stipend of up to 100 percent of your income, subject to dollar limitations that are adjusted for inflation each year. (In 1990, the dollar ceiling on annual retirement benefits was $102,582.) How much you deposit each year depends on your age, your income, and actuarial assumptions about how fast your contributions will grow to reach your retirement income goals.

With Keogh plans, you have until the due date of your tax return—including filing extensions—to make a contribution to the plan and claim a tax deduction on your return. But the plan must have been set up by December 31 for the tax year in question.

Self-employed individuals who don't act by the December 31 deadline can still earn a last-minute deduction by contributing to a Simplified Employee Pension plan. SEPs can be set up anytime until April 15 for a contribution to qualify for a deduction. But with SEPs, deductible contributions are limited to 13.043 percent of net self-employment earnings, up to a maximum of $30,000.

If you contribute to a Keogh or SEP plan, you can still make contributions to an IRA but you won't qualify for any IRA tax deduction unless your adjusted gross income is below the prescribed levels ($50,000 on a joint return or $35,000 on a single return).

If you have employees, be aware that if you set up a Keogh or SEP plan for yourself, you also have to make retirement contributions for them.

REVERSE MORTGAGES: HOW ELDERLY HOMEOWNERS CAN CASH OUT WITHOUT MOVING OUT

Elderly homeowners who are struggling to make ends meet no longer need to sell their homes in order to tap into the equity. For house-rich, cash-poor senior citizens, the salvation may be a "reverse mortgage."

With a reverse mortgage, you receive monthly income for the rest of your life (or some specified period) and you get to stay in your home until you die. Not until you're dead and buried (or you sell the home) does the lender get repaid principal and interest from the proceeds of the sale of the house. (In the case of a couple, repayment doesn't have to be made until both spouses have died.)

How much you receive each month depends on your age and the equity value of your house. The older you are and the more valuable your home, the more you get.

As an example, a reverse mortgage on a $100,000 home under a new government program would provide around $200 a month for life if you took out the mortgage at age 65; $350 at age 75; or $600 at age 85. Some private plans provide larger payments.

Instead of receiving monthly income for as long as you live, you can choose to receive monthly checks for only a limited period, usually five to ten years. Since the period is finite, monthly payments are larger than the lifetime option. For instance, a 75-year-old taking out a 10-year fixed term would get almost $500 a month, instead of $350 a month for life.

The term option only makes sense if you need additional monthly income temporarily, such as if you're waiting to enter a nursing home or life-care community.

Another option is a "line of credit," which allows the homeowner to borrow as often as he or she desires, up to the maximum amount of the loan.

Reverse mortgages have been around for nearly a decade but lenders were reluctant to base lifetime commitments on actuarial assumptions. If the homeowner lives longer than expected, lenders still have to keep sending the monthly checks, even if the amount loaned exceeds the value of the home.

But reverse mortgages are expected to become more widely available as a result of the federal government's new involvement. Under a pilot program, the Federal Housing Administration is insuring reverse mortgages written by private lenders. That insurance will protect the lenders against the risk that proceeds from the home sale won't cover all the money loaned to the borrower. Borrowers must be at least 62 to qualify. To find out if a lender in your area offers an FHA-insured mortgage, you can call the agency at (800) 245-2691.

Besides the government effort, a few large financial firms have aggressively moved into reverse-mortgage lending, including American Homestead Mortgage Corporation of Mount Laurel, New Jersey (800 233-4762); Providential Home Income Plan of San Francisco (800 441-4428); and Capital Holding Corporation of Louisville, Kentucky (800 942-6550). These plans are worth comparing because the FHA-insured plans contain various limitations. For instance, the maximum amount of equity you can convert to cash under the FHA insurance program ranges from $67,500 to $124,875, depending on home values in the local area.

Before signing anything, consult with a lawyer familiar with reverse mortgages to review the terms. It's too large a commitment for any homeowner to take on without professional advice.

For a free list of names and addresses of lenders offering reverse mortgages, send a self-addressed, stamped, business-size envelope to the

National Center for Home Equity Conversion, 1210 East College Drive, Suite 300, Marshall, Minnesota 56258.

Keep in mind that there are other ways to earn cash from your house, such as taking in a roommate or, if zoning laws allow, making part of your home into a rental unit. Also consider the idea of moving to a smaller, less expensive home, and using profits from the sale to supplement your income.

10

SKILLS YOU WILL NEED TO
MAKE IT THROUGH THE 1990s

With American business venturing into ever more technical and specialized arenas, workers will need new skills in order to find jobs in the coming decade, stay employed, and advance their careers.

Success in the 1990s and beyond will demand increasingly higher levels of education and special skills, from computers to foreign languages, to deal with the new technological tools of the workplace and the changing needs of the marketplace.

Even professionals with the highest levels of education and skills will need to continue their education throughout their careers as advancing technologies redefine jobs and render knowledge obsolete at a quickened pace. Lifelong education will become a way of life in order to update skills and find new lines of work as jobs are displaced.

Employment prospects are growing darker by the day for occupations that require little formal education and few skills. Assembly-line workers are being replaced by "steel collar" workers—those increasingly sophisticated robots that make fewer mistakes, work harder and longer, don't gripe, and don't require the health or retirement benefits of human "blue collars." Other unskilled or semiskilled laborers are finding that work they used to do is now being done in countries where wages and living standards are lower. Keypunch operators and typists are losing work to optical scanning devices, which can read a document into a computer faster than the fastest typist.

Those who don't go beyond high school will face diminishing opportunities. Unskilled and semiskilled occupations are the most vulnerable to computer technology and to the transfer of jobs to lower-wage countries.

The fastest-growing jobs will be in the fields that require the highest levels of education and skills, especially science, engineering, accounting, computers, management, law, and health care.

Other fields will also require more education and higher levels of language, math, and reasoning skills. Clerical jobs that used to require only rudimentary skills are being eliminated by technology or else being transformed into more demanding positions, requiring the ability to use computers, analyze and interpret information, and then communicate those thoughts. Auto mechanics are dealing with increasingly complex electronic and computer systems in cars. And salespersons are peddling increasingly sophisticated products, be they electronics goods, financial services, or home appliances.

Precisely what kinds of education and skills you will need varies by occupation, but college is becoming a prerequisite for jobs with a promising future. So is a working knowledge of computers. Gaining an edge in a career also means learning specialized skills, such as fluency in a foreign language for a business world that is becoming more global in scope, or gerontology, for catering to a population that is rapidly aging.

GO TO COLLEGE

According to an analysis conducted for the U.S. Labor Department, more than half of the new jobs to be created in the 1990s will require some

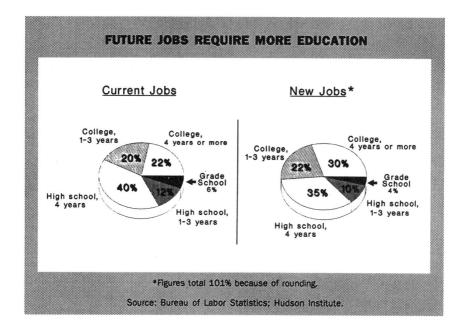

FUTURE JOBS REQUIRE MORE EDUCATION

Current Jobs

New Jobs*

College, 1-3 years
College, 4 years or more
20% 22%
Grade School 6%
40% 12%
High school, 4 years
High school, 1-3 years

College, 1-3 years
College, 4 years or more
22% 30%
Grade School 4%
35% 10%
High school, 4 years
High school, 1-3 years

*Figures total 101% because of rounding.

Source: Bureau of Labor Statistics; Hudson Institute.

sort of postsecondary education. Nearly a third will require at least a college degree.

The Hudson Institute, the economic think tank that conducted the study, said that these figures probably underestimate the need for advanced education because the numbers were based on the assumption that the new jobs created will require the same levels of education required for that occupation today. The trend, however, the institute said, has been toward higher education levels in each job category. Some labor experts think as many as three of four new jobs will require at least some college education.

In financial terms, the value of a college education has risen sharply over the past decade, leaving a wide gap in pay between those who attend college and those who don't.

When the baby-boomers graduated from college in the 1970s, the premium on a college education was relatively small because so many graduates were competing for jobs. Many of them had to settle for jobs that didn't even require a college degree. They were "underemployed," that discouraging buzzword of the 1970s. But Census Bureau surveys show college educations paid increasing dividends in the 1980s. Today college graduates have a big financial edge over high school grads, and even over those who went to college but didn't graduate.

In 1987, for example, white workers who attended four or more years of college earned 41 percent more than whites with only a high school education—double the 1978 figure. Those who attended one to three years of college earned only 16 percent more than the high school grads, according to the Census Bureau survey of workers between the ages of twenty-five and thirty-four years old. For blacks, the advantage was even more pronounced, with college graduates earning 49 percent more than high school grads, and those with one to three years of college earning 12 percent more than high school grads.

GETTING INTO COLLEGE WILL BE EASIER

Gaining admission to college should be somewhat easier over the next several years because of the shrinking numbers of eighteen-to-twenty-four-year-olds, the traditional college-age population. So far, the drop in enrollments has not been as sharp as demographics would suggest because a greater proportion of younger people, as well as a growing number of older people, are now going to college.

But education officials do expect to see a significant decline in enrollments as the number of high school graduates shrinks from 2.8 million in 1989 to around 2.5 million in the mid-1990s. Preliminary indications of a drop in enrollments came in 1989 when some of the most prestigious colleges saw applications drop 10 percent and more (although some of the decline may have been due to the soaring costs of tuition at private universities as well as to a more realistic attitude among students about their chances for admission to top schools, where competition is still keen).

The National Center for Education Statistics estimates that the number of bachelor's degrees awarded annually will drop from over one million in the early 1990s to fewer than 970,000 in the late 1990s. Not until late in the decade will enrollment declines reverse when the children of the baby-boom generation enter college.

As a result of shrinking enrollments and the increasing number of jobs requiring a college education, college graduates in the 1990s face a much more promising outlook than their predecessors did. Labor Department analysts predict 19 of every 20 graduates entering the labor force will find college-level jobs. That's in stark contrast to the job market over the past two decades when a glut of college graduates forced many of them to accept jobs that didn't require a college education.

Competition is also moderating for admission to professional schools in some fields. Medical school applications are down 27 percent from ten years ago, giving applicants the best chance of getting into medical school in decades. The latest figures show only 1.6 applicants for each medical school opening, compared to 2.2 applications a decade ago and 2.1 two decades ago.

Educators attribute the decline partly to demographics but also to the high cost of going to medical school, the predicted surplus of doctors by the year 2000, and promising opportunities in other fields, such as computer science and engineering. For many of the same reasons, dental schools saw similar declines in applicants.

Law school admissions offices, however, have been flooded with applications over the past few years. Not since the days following the 1973–74 Watergate hearings has there been such a swell of interest in the study of law. The TV series "L.A. Law" and the real-life intrigue of the Iran-Contra hearings on Capitol Hill helped spark some of the renewed interest. Another reason is that other top postgraduate professions have lost some of their allure. Some of the current crop of lawyers would have chosen medicine or business a few years ago. But the outlook for doctors has changed, and high finance lost some of its glamour in the wake of the insider trading scandals and the stock market collapse in 1987.

BECOME COMPUTER LITERATE

From the factory floor to the executive suite, virtually every job in the 1990s will require a working knowledge of computers as they spread farther and deeper into the workplace. Computers will become almost as commonplace as telephones. Engineers now design by computers. Managers and professionals are being equipped with their own and are expected to use them. Traveling salespeople are being given laptops. Librarians use computers for researching electronic databases. Teachers use them in classrooms. And clerical workers have long been at the vanguard of the computer revolution.

Computer literacy is an essential requirement for surviving in an age where computers play such a central role in the workplace and where they are spreading quickly to other parts of society. Lacking computer training today is akin to being a rocket scientist who still hopes to make do with his slide rule.

When computers were first brought into the workplace, companies provided in-house training to employees on how to use them. But employers are growing reluctant to hire new workers who aren't familiar with computers.

How much you'll need to know about computers varies with the job. But one night course at a community college should be enough to give most people a basic grounding in computers and the confidence to work with them. From there, it's a matter of refining your computer skills to your particular field. College students should make computers a part of their curriculum.

LEARN TO TYPE

Becoming a proficient typist is no longer just a need of would-be secretaries and word processors. It is part and parcel of the computer revolution. To use a computer, you need to type on a keyboard. It will be years before technology advances to the point where voice recognition systems become commonplace and you will be able to speak to the computer instead of typing on a keyboard. In the interim, those who need to hunt and peck will find their skills lacking for the job. Even professionals and managers can no longer rely on their secretaries to handle all the typing. With computer terminals spreading into every office, professionals and managers are increasingly expected to use the system to send their own memos and draft reports. As time goes on, more of them will lose their private secretaries. The trend is toward managers sharing secretaries.

Typing should be taken in high school. If you missed it, one semester of night classes can make you a proficient typist.

FOREIGN LANGUAGES OFFER AN EDGE IN GLOBAL ECONOMY

Anyone fluent in a foreign language will find his or her special talent of increasing value as business becomes more international in scope. The need for advertising, sales, marketing, financial, engineering, and managerial personnel fluent in foreign languages will grow as companies expand their markets overseas.

Foreign languages can also be helpful here at home. Growing international travel makes fluency in a foreign language a big plus for those who come in contact with foreign visitors, including hotel managers, desk clerks, flight attendants, restaurant workers, and switchboard operators.

A second language is also gaining value as labor shortages force businesses to rely more heavily on non–English-speaking immigrants. Managers and supervisors who speak a second language (Spanish is the most common) can establish a better rapport with workers and prevent the costly consequences of misunderstood instructions.

There's no simple rule for deciding which language to study since each company has its own needs. The best way to make that assessment is to find out whether companies in your chosen field need people with a specific language proficiency.

In general, Spanish is most in demand, but French, German, Italian, Portuguese, Japanese, and Chinese can be useful, depending on the position, according to the Labor Department.

The best way to learn a language is to take courses in it while you're in high school or college, where many curriculums require a minimum of two years of language study. Many colleges also offer study-abroad programs. Usually one year long, these programs are drawing increased interest from business majors. If you're working, there are plenty of ways to learn a language on the side. Night classes are offered by community colleges and through continuing education and extension programs at many universities. Private firms such as Berlitz offer group classes as well as individual tutoring. In major cities, cultural institutes, such as the German Goethe Institute, offer language courses.

Learning a language offers no guarantees that you'll land a job or get a foreign assignment. Companies weigh many factors when choosing someone for a foreign post. If they choose someone for a particular position who lacks fluency but is desired for other reasons, they'll send him or her to language school.

But fluency in a foreign language can provide a competitive edge at a time when the foreign-language needs of business are growing. And even though English is still the international language, fluency in a second language can only help in business relationships with foreign clients, customers, and workers.

GERONTOLOGY: A HELP IN MANY DISCIPLINES

As the elderly population swells over the next few decades, more and more of the nation's business and resources will focus on the needs of older people. They represent a growing share of America's wealth and political influence, and businesses will find the elderly a vast market with special needs.

While growing numbers of people are specializing in gerontology and earning degrees in the field, taking a course or two or more in gerontology may prove helpful in many professions, whether you are in health care, social work, engineering, or business. Few employers require courses in gerontology. But gaining an understanding of the aging process and the special needs of the elderly should prove valuable to engineers who will be creating or redesigning products specifically for the elderly; advertising and marketing managers who will need to promote those products; real estate developers trying to build housing for the elderly; psychologists and health-care workers who will be seeing more elderly patients; and others. As an indication of its growing importance, more than 1,000 colleges now offer gerontology courses, up from 600 in 1976 and only 150 in 1967. Thus, it shouldn't be hard to find a gerontology course in a formal college curriculum or a continuing education program.

THE VALUE OF AN MBA IN THE 1990s

A master's degree in business administration used to guarantee high salaries and a big edge in the race for top management positions. But its value has been diluted by the glut of students chasing after an MBA and by the streamlining of management ranks. Since the early 1970s, when the rage over MBAs began, the number of MBA degrees granted each year has more than doubled, to about 67,000 in the late 1980s. More are on their way. A couple hundred thousand are currently enrolled in MBA programs, either full-time or part-time.

It is now a buyer's market and many of the buyers are complaining about the kind of preparation MBA programs provide. In addition, one of the most lucrative havens for MBAs—Wall Street—was devastated in the aftermath of the 1987 stock market crash, forcing thousands of aspiring investment bankers with MBAs to lower their financial sights and look instead to insurance, commercial banking, accounting, manufacturing, electronics, and consulting.

For all these reasons, MBAs no longer command the luxurious starting salaries that led so many people to spend two years getting one in the first place. Engineers graduating with just a bachelor's degree are offered about the same starting salary as the average MBA. But an MBA can still provide an edge, particularly if you get into a top business school, whose graduates are offered starting salaries in excess of $50,000.

MBAs take on added value when you have prior work experience or an undergraduate degree in science or technology. Corporations pay premiums to get engineers and scientists with advanced business training to help manage the new technologies of the 1990s.

Some eight hundred colleges and universities have MBA programs, some of them offering classes at night or on weekends. These part-time programs allow executives to continue working while pursuing an MBA.

CONTINUING EDUCATION: A NEW LIFELONG
REQUIREMENT FOR WORKERS

With technology and jobs undergoing rapid change, workers will need to train and retrain throughout their careers in order to stay employed and advance their careers. Gone are the days when vocational school or college was enough preparation for a lifetime of employment in a given field. Jobs are constantly being altered by technology and the changing demands of the marketplace, making continuing education an essential part of life in the 1990s and beyond.

Workers will have to update their knowledge and skills as doctors have long had to do, attending symposiums throughout their careers to learn the latest medical advances and technologies.

Even in engineering, where job prospects are among the brightest, the Labor Department warned those in the profession of the dangers of not keeping up. "Engineers in high-technology areas such as advanced electronics or aerospace may find that their knowledge becomes obsolete rapidly," the Labor Department said in an assessment of the profession's employment outlook. "Even those who continue their education are vulnerable to obsolescence if the particular technology or product they have specialized in becomes obsolete. Engineers whom employers consider not to have kept up may find themselves passed over for promotions and are particularly vulnerable to layoffs."

Indeed, continuing education is no longer just a highbrow divertissement for the intellectually curious, but is essential to career survival.

ENTREPRENEURSHIP

Should you ever wish to start your own business, take courses in entrepreneurship. Chances are that the idea of becoming an entrepreneur will cross your mind at some point in your career. Most people toss the notion aside because they don't know where to begin. Others press forward to a disastrous conclusion because they are ill-prepared in the basics of what it takes to make a small business succeed.

With the explosion of new businesses in the 1980s, public and private colleges across the country began offering a broad selection of night and weekend courses for small-business owners and aspiring entrepreneurs. The offerings include courses in such basics as how to start a business, bookkeeping, marketing, and advertising. Other courses cover such topics as how to open a restaurant, how to market your invention, selling by mail, and exporting to foreign markets.

The thought of starting a business is likely to cross many more minds in the 1990s as large companies continue to trim their management ranks and baby-boomers get frustrated by clogged promotion ladders.

LEARN TO PLAY GOLF

If you're in management or sales and you don't know how to play golf, it may pay to learn. It could help your business. Golf is the most popular sport in business, and a lot of top executives routinely cut business deals out on the fairways. Golf is on the upswing with the aging of the baby-boom generation. The industry predicts the number of golfers could as much as double by the year 2000 if there are enough golf courses built for everyone to play.

11

THE JOB MARKET
OF THE 1990s

THE NEW CRITERIA FOR ASSESSING JOB OFFERS IN THE 1990s

Assessing a job offer in the 1990s requires different criteria from those in the past. Employment practices and benefits vary more widely than ever from company to company. Higher pay at one firm could easily be outmatched by a different mix of benefits at another.

Family circumstances are also more complicated and a more critical part of the equation. Whether a company requires frequent relocation for advancement, for instance, may now be pivotal for a person whose spouse is tied down in a professional career.

The new realities of the corporate world also mean viewing a prospective employer's outlook in a different light, assessing its vulnerability to takeovers, leveraged buyouts, foreign competition, restructuring, downsizing, and technological change.

Below are factors to consider in assessing a job offer in the 1990s.

Compensation and Benefits: Assess pay and benefits as a package. Benefits are minimal at some firms and represent more than 35 percent of compensation at others. So an offer of higher pay from one firm may be worth far less than an offer from another company that has a better mix of benefits. Assess the benefits package according to your own particular needs. Child care may be a valuable benefit to someone with young children but of no value to someone whose children are grown. In a similar vein, the type of pension plan offered can be of differing value depending on how long you plan to stay at the firm. Compensation also needs to be examined more closely in light of the new types of pay schemes proliferating throughout industry.

Is the Company Growing?: What are the long-term prospects for the company and the industry it's in? Are the company's businesses profitable? In particular, is the division or unit you'll be working for profitable? Or is it a drag on the rest of the company? If it's a drag, the division could wind up being sold or shut down. Go to the public library and read up on the company, in newspapers and business articles. If it's a public company, ask your stockbroker for any research analysis the brokerage firm may have published on the company. Browse through the company's annual report and, if possible, get hold of a copy of the company's "10-K" report, which is a more detailed financial report required by the Securities and Exchange Commission. (Many public libraries have copies of annual reports of local companies, and occasionally, some 10-K reports.) If the company made a recent offering of securities, try to obtain a copy of the prospectus, which contains loads of insights into the company's current business. All this research will not only help you decide whether you want to join the company, but your detailed knowledge about the company's operation should impress your job interviewers.

Is the Company a Takeover Target or a Candidate for Restructuring?: In researching the company, keep an eye out for any mention in newspaper articles or analysts' reports about the firm being a potential takeover target or in need of restructuring or cutbacks. Any such sign bodes ill for long-term job security with the firm.

Is the Company Loaded with Debt?: Has the company gone through a leveraged buyout or is it otherwise bogged down with so much debt that it has to struggle to make debt payments? If so, it could be forced to take drastic measures to cut expenses—perhaps your job—in order to stay afloat.

Job Stability: While job security is a vanishing dream, some companies do much better than others in protecting workers' jobs. Check the company's track record. Does the company offer retraining programs? If the company was forced to lay off workers in the past, how were they treated? Were they given generous severance payments and outplacement assistance?

Is the Job Important to the Bottom Line?: Is the job you are being offered an essential one or is it one that would be vulnerable in the event personnel cutbacks need to be made?

Room for Promotion: What are the prospects for promotion at the company? Is the corporate ladder clogged with able people? What is your next step and what can you expect over the long term? If the management bureaucracy is large, is it ripe for pruning?

Are You Likely to Be Transferred?: Ask about the company's policy on relocation. Will you be expected to relocate to another part of the country in the future? If so, is relocation compatible with your spouse's career? If you are hoping for a chance to move somewhere else in the company's organization, what are the prospects for a transfer?

Travel: Will the new job require travel? How much travel? Will it take you away from child-care or elderly-care responsibilities?

Is the Job a Good Springboard?: Will the job further your long-term career goals? Does the company provide education and training that will make you a more marketable commodity?

Flexible Work Hours: Does the company offer flexible work hours to accommodate any needs you have for child care or elderly care?

Parental Leave Policy: If you plan to have a child and want to take time off, does the company have a parental leave policy?

What Happened to the Person Who Had the Job Last?: Was the person who previously held the position promoted or hired away to a better job at another firm? Or is it a dead-end job, one that others have tried without success or without reward? If the person was promoted or left for a better job, the job is likely to have better prospects than if the previous person was fired for incompetence, was banished to some remote outpost, or had a nervous breakdown.

Are You Being Hired for a Dirty Short-Term Job?: Are you being invited to join a company to complete some dirty task that no one in-house wants to do, like closing down a division? What promises do you have for a position after you complete the task?

Title: Will the title you're being offered add to your prestige? Impressive titles are valuable on résumés.

Commuting: Will you have difficulty getting to your new job location? If you need to drive to work, does the company provide parking or will you need to spend $200 a month out of your own pocket to get a space in a private lot? Is mass transportation available?

Are You Their Spy?: Are you being hired just so the firm can pick your brain about a competitor (the company you used to work for)? After your new bosses have squeezed all the information about your former employer from you, will you still be valuable to them or will your mission be complete?

Amount of Overtime: Will the job entail overtime? How much? Will it entail working weekends? Will you be paid for the overtime?

Quality, Dynamism, and Congeniality of Your Bosses and Colleagues: These are people you will have to live with and live by. If they're incompetent, your job could be at risk, and if they're hard to get along with, your sanity could be at risk. If you can, try to talk with other people at the company or other people in the industry who may know something about the corporate culture at the company. Employment interviews don't always give you an accurate picture. Executives bend over backward to be gracious when they're trying to lure you to their firm. The yelling and the backbiting don't start until after you're on the payroll.

Work Environment: Physical surroundings at work can make a big difference in quality of life since you spend so much of your life at the office. When toting up the pluses and minuses, add extra points to a company that would give you a nice office rather than a tiny cubicle.

Moving to a Smaller Company: Consider all of the ramifications before moving from a big company to a small one. Small companies are a leading source of new jobs, and many of them entice talented scientists and professionals with stock options and other incentives that offer the potential for greater financial rewards. But bear in mind that job security and fringe benefits at smaller companies tend to fall short. Do you feel your skills are marketable enough to warrant the risk? If the company goes under, will you be able to land on your feet?

Family-Owned Businesses: If you are considering an offer of a management-level position at a family-run business with the hope of climbing to the top someday, investigate the family tree. If you are told that the owner is getting on in years and wants to retire, investigate further. Many owners who say they want to retire in a few years don't always step down when they say they will. And even if they do, they don't always let go of the reins. Ask if there is a specific timetable. If not, you could be waiting many more years than you thought to assume command. Find out if there are other family members waiting in the wings to take over at the first opportunity. If the owner should die, are the surviving members of the family interested in keeping the company or selling it?

THE EXPLOSION IN PART-TIME WORK

Part-time work, long common in the retail and restaurant business, is becoming commonplace in many other industries as well, from banking to health care.

For individuals, the explosion in part-time jobs offers new options for balancing work with other obligations and interests, such as caring for a young child or going to school. In the past, if you wanted to work part-time it usually meant leaving your company and settling for a job as a cashier, a waiter, or a security guard because businesses usually demanded full-time commitments for most types of jobs. Now it's becoming easier to work part-time without leaving your company or profession.

Virtually every sector of private enterprise has been increasingly turning to part-timers. The number of part-time workers—including freelancers, temporary employees, and other "contingent" workers—grew twice as fast as the overall labor force during the 1980s and now represent about 25 percent of the work force. According to the Conference Board, a business-sponsored research organization, an estimated 20 percent of all professional and technical personnel and nearly 10 percent of all managers are part-time.

One reason for the proliferation of part-time jobs is a shortage of qualified workers in many areas. Faced with a critical shortage of nurses, hospitals are trying to fill the gap by turning to people who only want to work a part-time schedule. Banks are going after part-timers for teller positions that can't be filled because of the dearth of entry-level workers.

Business is also making greater use of part-time help for special projects and to augment staff when business picks up. It's a more flexible, and usually cheaper, way to operate a business.

When the special project is completed or when business slacks off, the company doesn't have to go through the expensive and demoralizing process of cutting back permanent staff. The temporary workers and part-timers are simply let go. No need to pay any severance.

Part-time help is also less expensive to maintain. Part-timers usually get paid less and receive far fewer fringe benefits than full-time employees.

While the explosion in part-time work can mean new flexibility for many workers and businesses, it can sometimes mean real financial hardship. About one in four persons working part-time say they would prefer full-time work, a figure that has grown sharply over the past decade. And because wages and benefits tend to be far lower than what full-time workers get, a growing number of part-timers are forced to moonlight in order to make ends meet.

Of concern to labor unions is the potential for companies to make greater use of part-timers in order to undermine union influence and the pay levels of full-time workers.

Some members of Congress, voicing a dim view of the growing use of part-time workers, have introduced legislation that would require employers to provide a variety of benefits for contingent workers. Although many companies are starting to offer vacation pay and health insurance benefits to part-timers, most still aren't covered by health insurance or pension plans.

Some economists worry that the contingent work force has grown so large that massive layoffs of part-timers at the first sign of an economic downturn could snowball into a deep recession.

It's not all roses for businesses, either, which is why they haven't tried to put everyone on part-time or temporary status. Companies complain that many part-timers have poor attitudes and aren't as dedicated or well trained as full-time workers.

Nonetheless, the explosion in part-time work does open new doors for some people. For a growing number of professional women, a part-time schedule allows them to spend more time with their younger children without putting their career on hold.

Part-time work can also be a way station for individuals between jobs. Many companies use part-time or temporary positions as a way of recruiting good candidates for permanent positions. It gives the company a chance to see how you perform without any long-term obligation. It also gives you a chance to see what the company is like to work for without having to make any long-range commitment.

To make the most of such a situation, try to meet as many managers and other decision makers as possible. By making yourself visible to a wider group, you can improve your chances for landing a full-time position. Even if the department you are working for doesn't have a permanent position available, another department may.

Before taking a temporary job, be aware that any outplacement counseling you may have received through your old employer usually ends when you get work, regardless of whether it's temporary or permanent. If the temporary job doesn't work out, you'll be left to your own devices to find another job.

Another drawback to searching for jobs by taking a series of temporary positions is that prospective employers may look down on a résumé filled with short-term jobs.

THE EXPANDING ROLE OF "TEMPS"

It used to be that the only time a business called a temporary help agency was when things got truly desperate at the office, such as when a receptionist called in sick and no one else was available to fill in. But today, corporations are increasingly turning to "temps" to fill a variety of transient personnel needs rather than adding workers to their regular payroll. As part of the broader trend toward greater use of part-time help, temps are being used to handle special projects that are of limited duration and to augment staff when business picks up. Even the federal government started using temps in 1989.

Besides clerical workers, temps now include nurses, computer programmers, computer operators, accountants, paralegals, and home health aides. Even lawyers are becoming temps. Several agencies now specialize in placing legal temps with law firms that want to take on more work without hiring more lawyers or using another law firm.

Working through a temp agency is a way for individuals to achieve maximum flexibility in work schedules while pursuing other interests. You work only when you want to work. Working for a temp agency can also be a way to sample the job market, getting an inside view of companies to see where you might want to settle down. Temporary positions also give you a foot in the door. Many employers snap up temps they like for full-time positions. One drawback is that you never know whether the agency will have an appropriate assignment for you on any given day.

With surging demand for temps, temp agencies have been forced to scour the terrain for workers and offer fringe-benefits packages and training programs.

The Labor Department projects that the market for temps will grow much faster than that for the rest of the labor force in the 1990s.

RENT-AN-EXEC

In an age of management cutbacks, takeovers, and rapid change, the "temp" business has even expanded into the executive ranks. Companies can now rent an executive to fill a gap in depleted management ranks, handle a special project, fill in for a manager on parental leave, or head up a transition team until a takeover is completed. After going through the painful and costly process of laying off managers in the 1980s, many companies like the idea of being able to rent an executive rather than hire another manager who will have to be cut later.

For managers who have lost their jobs, becoming a temporary executive could provide a foot in the door to more permanent employment or at least a way to expand a résumé. Instead of trying to hunt for work while you're unemployed, you'll be able to earn money and also have a more attractive base from which to search for work.

In contrast to clerical temp assignments that often last no more than a day, temp assignments for executives tend to last several months. Salaries typically range from $25 to $100 an hour. Companies pay the temp agency's fee, which ranges from 20 to 30 percent.

Many outplacement firms, executive search firms, and personnel placement firms have sprouted into the rent-an-exec business. A few firms specializing in management temps have also sprung up recently.

Even chief executives can be rented. Demand for temporary chieftains comes mostly from smaller companies where the chief executive has taken ill or died, or when someone with expertise is needed to lead the company through a crisis of some sort. Who are these temporary chief executives? Some of them are in between jobs. Others are retired and yearn for another chance to take the helm of a company. Still others just like the idea of moving from company to company.

EMPLOYEE LEASING: RENT-A-WORK-FORCE

Taking the concept of temps a step further is the burgeoning practice of companies leasing an entire staff or department from an outside firm. A few hundred firms specialize in employee leasing and have farmed out hundreds of thousands of employees to small and medium-sized businesses, from hospitals to factories. Some larger companies are also starting to use leased employees to staff various departments.

Employers pay more for leased employees but the arrangement frees businesses from having to deal with all the paperwork and other personnel hassles. That's a big advantage for small businesses. All personnel matters are handled by an outside firm. It does the hiring, processes the payroll, handles all the government red tape, takes care of insurance matters, and provides the employees' fringe benefits.

Leased employees often get better fringe benefits than smaller companies can provide on their own. So leasing is a way for smaller employers to attract higher-quality workers.

Leasing used to be a way for employers to get around the requirements of providing pension and other benefits to employees. But the Tax Reform Act of 1986 tightened the rules. While the legislation didn't curtail employee leasing, it did make leasing more expensive.

Reliability of employee-leasing companies is another concern that has made some employers cautious about leasing arrangements. Some fairly large employee-leasing firms have gone bankrupt, leaving behind unpaid debts and employees without paychecks. The Internal Revenue Service has gone knocking on the doors of client companies to collect the leasing firm's unpaid tax and pension obligations.

ENTRY-LEVEL JOBS WILL GO BEGGING FOR APPLICANTS

In the 1990s young people will have a much easier time finding jobs than their baby-boomer parents did. Companies will be struggling to recruit enough workers to fill entry-level jobs. Employers, who have long had an abundant supply of young workers to draw from, will find a shrinking pool from which to recruit, and many companies will have difficulty finding enough people to fill all their positions.

At a time when businesses are expanding, the number of younger workers entering the labor force is dwindling. By 1995, the number of sixteen-to-twenty-four-year-olds in the labor force will be 16 percent, or 4 million, fewer than in 1980, according to Labor Department projections.

Evidence of widespread labor shortages can be easily spotted in the ubiquitous Help Wanted signs in front of fast-food restaurants, department stores, grocery stores, movie theaters, hotels, beach resorts, and other establishments that have long depended on plentiful supplies of teenagers and young adults.

The job picture is in stark contrast to the 1970s and early 1980s when the huge baby-boom population flooded the job market. Younger workers had to scratch for jobs and employers could be picky about whom they hired. And they didn't have to pay much to attract enough applicants.

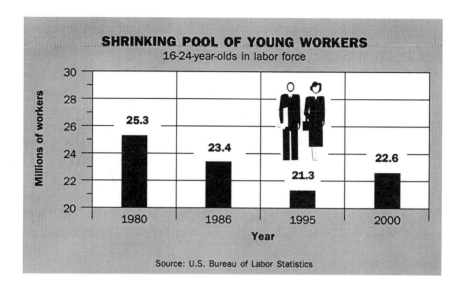

SHRINKING POOL OF YOUNG WORKERS
16-24-year-olds in labor force

Source: U.S. Bureau of Labor Statistics

Now businesses face a decreased pool of applicants and must pay higher wages and settle for workers they never would have given a second thought to before. They are turning to less-educated, less-motivated younger people. McDonald's and other fast-food chains are advertising for elderly workers to fill the gap.

The labor shortages have begun to spur demand for labor-saving technology. Automated checkout counters are being tested in a few grocery stores. Fast-food chains are experimenting with new gadgetry, such as automated beverage dispensers. Labor shortages have also prompted calls by some economists for more liberal immigration policies, even though Congress went through a lengthy ordeal to tighten them in 1986.

Overall, the labor force will continue to grow, but at a much slower pace—more slowly than at any time since the 1930s. The Bureau of Labor Statistics projects that the labor force will grow at a rate of only about 1.2 percent a year in the 1990s, compared to annual growth of 1.7 percent in the 1980s and 2.7 percent in the 1970s when the baby-boomers and increasing numbers of women entered the labor force.

The slowdown not only reflects the shrinking numbers of younger people but also a decline in the number of men aged fifty-five and older, who have increasingly opted for early retirement.

By the year 2000, the labor force is expected to reach 141 million, up 16 percent from 1988. During the same period, new jobs will be created at about the same pace. According to Labor Department projections, employment will rise 15 percent to 136 million. That is a slower rate of growth than was seen during the 1970s and 1980s.

Competition for qualified workers will be even keener than the numbers suggest because so many younger people lack the basic literacy, mathematics, and analytical skills demanded by the modern workplace.

THE NEW LABOR POOL: MOSTLY WOMEN AND MINORITIES

Not only will employers face a tighter labor market, but also a much more diverse mix of new workers. Job applicants passing through personnel offices will increasingly be women, disadvantaged minorities, and non–English-speaking immigrants.

While white males have long dominated the labor force, they will account for less than one third of new entrants to the work force, according to the Labor Department. Minorities will account for one of three new

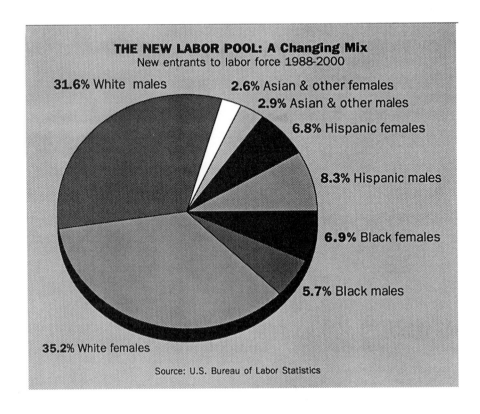

THE NEW LABOR POOL: A Changing Mix
New entrants to labor force 1988-2000

31.6% White males

2.6% Asian & other females
2.9% Asian & other males
6.8% Hispanic females
8.3% Hispanic males
6.9% Black females
5.7% Black males
35.2% White females

Source: U.S. Bureau of Labor Statistics

workers. In all, more than half of new entrants in the 1990s will be women.

With workers becoming a scarcer commodity, employers will have to dip deeper into the labor pool to find enough of them. Employers no longer have the plentiful supplies of labor that allowed them to ignore certain groups. Employers who don't develop more progressive attitudes and corporate cultures to attract and retain the best talent from minority groups will face serious shortages of qualified workers. If companies do adapt to the changing configuration of the work force, the tight labor market could offer an unparalleled opportunity for minorities to move into mainstream American economic life.

THE GREAT SKILLS DIVIDE: JOBS DON'T MATCH SKILLS

The 1990s could, nevertheless, make it tougher than ever for minorities, who tend to have less education than other groups, to gain a foothold. Indeed, the job market is likely to be characterized by a growing division between the jobs that will be available and the people available to fill them.

What's more, the plight of minorities could actually worsen since they are disproportionately concentrated in low-skilled jobs that are disappearing.

All of this portends a market in which higher-skilled jobs go begging for qualified applicants while people with less education and fewer skills compete for a shrinking number of lower-skilled jobs.

It is already visible. Classified ad sections in newspapers bulge with help-wanted ads for computer programmers, nurses, and other high-skilled professionals. Companies are forced to run the ads week after week because they cannot find enough qualified applicants to fill all the positions. But when a new factory announces plans to hire a few hundred blue-collar workers, thousands of job applicants are lined up around the block the next morning.

Such imbalances threaten to undermine America's competitiveness if industry withers from a shortage of skilled workers. Polarization is another risk as the economic gulf between the educated and the disadvantaged widens.

Yet there is reason for hope as the needs of business converge with those of the underclass. Growing concern over the shortage of skilled workers and its impact on America's ability to compete in the global marketplace could well be the impetus for business and government to make education and training a priority, thereby helping the disadvantaged and improving America's competitive position.

WOMEN NEARING EQUAL REPRESENTATION IN THE WORK FORCE

Women will continue to join the labor force in large numbers, albeit at a slower pace than in the 1970s and 1980s.

The slowdown doesn't portend any major shift toward neotraditionalist values. Rather, it is because women's participation in the labor force has already jumped to very high levels and is approaching that of men in most age groups.

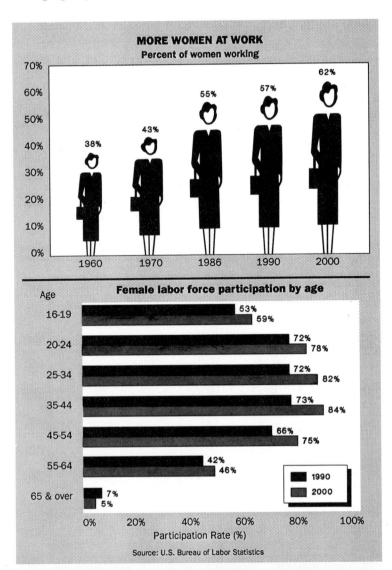

MORE WOMEN AT WORK
Percent of women working

Year	Percent
1960	38%
1970	43%
1986	55%
1990	57%
2000	62%

Female labor force participation by age

Age	1990	2000
16-19	53%	59%
20-24	72%	78%
25-34	72%	82%
35-44	73%	84%
45-54	66%	75%
55-64	42%	46%
65 & over	7%	5%

Participation Rate (%)

Source: U.S. Bureau of Labor Statistics

By the end of the century, more than 80 percent of women between the ages of twenty-five and fifty-four will be in the work force, compared to about 71 percent in 1986 and 37 percent in 1950. By the end of the century, women will make up more than 47 percent of the work force, reflecting a dramatic transformation of the role of women in the workplace. In the space of less than three decades, the situation for women has shifted from one in which the vast majority stayed home to one in which the vast majority now work.

But there are signs that the movement of women into the work force may be peaking, even in the face of the powerful social and economic trends that made work both a personal and financial necessity for most women.

One reason is that surveys and anecdotal evidence suggest that a large number of mothers with young children would prefer to work less than they do now in order to more adequately fulfill child-care responsibilities. Economic necessity and emotional commitment to their careers guard against any wholesale exodus. But with tight labor markets ahead, labor economists warn that should employers fail to become more accommodating to the needs of working mothers, they will not be able to attract enough qualified workers to fill their needs in the 1990s. Most of the recent increases in the numbers of women entering the labor force

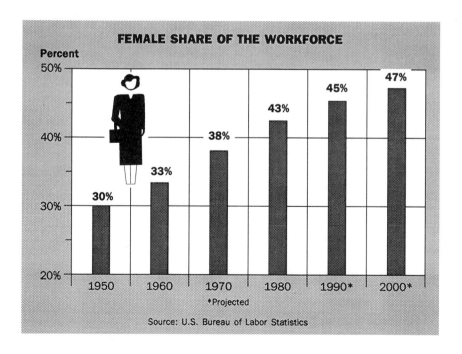

have resulted from rising participation rates of women with young children.

Corporations have been slow to respond, figuring they were able to draw a majority of women into the work force over the past couple of decades without changing much. But the new realities of the labor market are awakening more employers to the need to become more responsive to working women by providing more flexible work schedules, child-care assistance, and, increasingly, elderly-care assistance. Surveys show that sizable numbers of nonworking mothers with young children would be willing to work if reasonably priced child care were available.

The decades-old gap between what men and women earn should also continue to narrow as more women gain seniority and move into more financially rewarding occupations. One reason for the wage gap is that men have dominated some of the most lucrative professions, such as law, medicine, accounting, and investment banking, while women have been concentrated in lower-paid professions such as teaching and nursing. In increasing numbers, women are attending graduate schools and joining the ranks of lawyers, doctors, and bankers.

A MATURING WORK FORCE

If you gaze around at your coworkers, you may notice that the work force is getting older. With fewer young people entering the labor force, the median age of workers is projected to climb from 35.3 years in 1986 to 38.9 years in the year 2000. In the federal government, the trend is even more dramatic, with the average age of workers projected to climb from 38.6 years to 43.6 in the year 2000.

An older labor force implies a more experienced, stable, reliable, and productive work force. But a more mature work force also implies less flexibility in relocating and in learning new skills at a time when the economy demands flexibility. On balance, however, economists think an older work force will help boost productivity over the next several years.

A NEW ATTITUDE TOWARD OLDER WORKERS

Traditional attitudes toward the role of older people in the workplace are gradually falling away as companies come to grips with the new demographic realities. With shrinking numbers of younger people available for entry-level jobs and with labor shortages in many skill areas, a growing number of companies are turning to older workers and retirees to fill the gap.

The Travelers Corporation maintains a job bank to draw on retirees. Corning Glass Works calls on its retirees to help with special projects and seasonal demand. Other companies rehire their retirees for in-house training programs or to serve as consultants on various projects. Banks are hiring retirees for teller positions because they can't find enough young people to fill all the openings. For the same reason, fast-food chains are recruiting elderly workers to help behind the counter. And temp agencies are looking for retirees with skills in all sorts of areas.

Companies rehiring their retirees find a host of advantages: older workers are seasoned with decades of experience and don't have to be indoctrinated on the inner workings of the company or its people. They've worked with them for years. Other companies recruiting elderly workers find that they make good employees because they tend to be reliable, trustworthy, and motivated.

How widespread the practice of hiring older workers will become depends partly on retirees themselves. So far, relatively few have shown much desire for working past retirement. Rather, the recent trend has been toward early retirement. Social Security regulations also discourage retirees from working much. Until you reach age seventy, Social Security benefits are reduced if you are earning more than a minimal amount of income from a job.

But as more companies make accommodations for older workers by offering flexible and part-time schedules, more elderly workers are likely to be lured back into the work force to earn some extra money and to keep from getting bored in retirement.

At the same time, early-retirement offers are likely to become less common in the 1990s than they were in the 1980s when companies were aggressively trimming their payrolls. With the flow of young people into the job market slowing down, older workers will be encouraged to remain in the labor force longer rather than showered with incentives to leave early.

DISABILITY NO LONGER AS MUCH OF A HANDICAP

More job opportunities will open up for disabled persons in the 1990s as the economy shifts further toward services. Physical disability will become less of a handicap in the workplace as more jobs depend on mental rather than physical ability. Handicapped persons who may have been ignored when labor was plentiful will now get greater consideration in the face of tighter labor markets. Employers will be less concerned with their handicaps and more interested in what they know and their mental skills.

Technological developments will also help lower the barriers. "Telecommuting," for example, will provide new job opportunities to those whose handicaps prevent them from going to an office at all. In fact, telecommuting makes their physical handicaps invisible.

12

WHERE THE JOBS WILL
BE IN THE 1990s

In the 1990s, changing consumer needs, technological advances, and foreign competition will alter the employment outlook in virtually every occupation.

Doctors, who used to be in short supply, will soon be facing an overcrowded market. Stenography, once a sure ticket to employment security, is now being rendered obsolete by office automation. Meanwhile, teachers and airline pilots, who faced a glutted market in recent years, will soon be in short supply. Similar shifts are occurring in every field.

Reflecting the economy's continuing drift toward services, nine of every ten new jobs in the 1990s will be in service industries, including health care, legal services, financial services, education, computer processing, and management consulting.

Of the twenty fastest-growing occupations, half are in health care. Booming demand for health services created by an aging population will result in nearly three million new jobs by the end of the decade for all

WHERE THE JOBS WILL BE CREATED
1988-2000

Sector	Millions of jobs to be added or lost
Services	+ 16,668,000
Manufacturing	− 316,000
Construction	+ 760,000
Agriculture	− 134,000
Mining	− 16,000
Other	+ 1,145,000

Source: U.S. Bureau of Labor Statistics

sorts of health professionals, from nurses and physical therapists to optometrists and home health aides.

Jobs in the computer field will also grow rapidly as computers spread further into the workplace and into the home.

More teachers will be needed because of rising student enrollments, and later in the decade colleges will find the need to replace tens of thousands of retiring faculty members. Electrical engineers will be needed to design new generations of computers and electronic gadgetry. And more biologists will be needed for the burgeoning field of biotechnology.

Retail-industry employment is not growing as fast as that in computers or health-care services. But in terms of sheer numbers, retailing, which is one of the largest employment sectors, will offer the most new

FASTEST GROWING OCCUPATIONS
Projected growth in employment 1988-2000

Occupation	Percent growth	Numerical growth
Paralegals	75%	62,000
Medical assistants	70	104,000
Home health aides	68	160,000
Radiologic technologists and technicians	66	87,000
Data processing equipment repairers	61	44,000
Medical records technicians	60	28,000
Medical secretaries	58	120,000
Physical therapists	57	39,000
Surgical technologists	56	20,000
Operations research analysts	55	30,000
Securities and financial services sales workers	55	109,000
Travel agents	54	77,000
Computer systems analysts	53	214,000
Physical and corrective therapy assistants	53	21,000
Social welfare service aides	52	47,000
Occupational therapists	49	16,000
Computer programmers	48	250,000
Human services workers	45	53,000
Respiratory therapists	41	23,000
Correction officers and jailers	41	76,000

Source: U.S. Bureau of Labor Statistics

jobs. More sales clerks will be needed as sales volume grows and as retailers place increased emphasis on customer service and expand their store hours.

Despite the recent resurgence of America's manufacturing prowess in world markets, jobs in the nation's factories are shrinking. So are jobs on farms and in mining. Although generations of Americans have looked to manufacturing for secure, well-paying jobs since the Industrial Revolution, the manufacturing sector now offers dim hopes for future job opportunities. The era of blue-collar opportunity is over. U.S. manufacturing, which lost two million jobs through the early and mid-1980s, is still shrinking, and payrolls by the year 2000 are projected to list 316,000 fewer names than in 1988.

While manufacturing output is expected to grow about as fast as the

OCCUPATIONS WITH GREATEST NUMBER OF OPENINGS
Projected employment growth 1988-2000

Occupation	Numerical growth	Percent growth
Retail salespersons	730,000	19%
Registered nurses	613,000	39
Janitors & cleaners	556,000	19
Waiters & waitresses	551,000	31
General managers & top executives	479,000	16
General office clerks	455,000	18
Secretaries (except legal & medical)	385,000	13
Nursing aides, orderlies & attendants	378,000	32
Truck drivers	369,000	15
Receptionists & information clerks	331,000	40
Cashiers	304,000	13
Guards	256,000	32
Computer programmers	250,000	48
Food counter, fountain & related workers	240,000	15
Food preparation workers	234,000	23
Licensed practical nurses	229,000	37
Teachers, secondary school	224,000	19
Computer systems analysts	214,000	53
Accountants & auditors	211,000	22
Teachers, elementary school	208,000	15

Source: U.S. Bureau of Labor Statistics

overall economy, heavy investments in automation equipment and the shedding of inefficient operations will lead to substantial productivity growth—which means more goods produced with fewer people.

Manufacturing won't be devoid of employment opportunities; they just won't be blue-collar opportunities. Even though overall employment levels are projected to shrink by 316,000, manufacturers will still be adding several hundred thousand engineering, scientific, management, and technical positions.

FASTEST DECLINING OCCUPATIONS
Projected decline in employment 1988-2000

Occupation	Percent decline	Numerical decline
Electrical & electronic equipment assemblers	43	173,000
Broadcast technicians	31	8,000
Gas and petroleum plant/system occupations	24	7,000
Railroad brake, signal and switch operators	23	9,000
Farmers	23	266,000
Stenographers	23	36,000
Telephone and cable TV line installers and repairers	21	27,000
Directory assistance phone operators	21	7,000
Central office & PBX installers & repairers	21	15,000
Telephone station installers and repairers	20	12,000
Chemical plant and system operators	20	7,000
Railroad conductors and yardmasters	20	5,000
Furnace operators and tenders	17	11,000
Timber fallers and buckers	17	6,000
Farm workers	16	153,000
Chemical equipment controllers, operators and tenders	15	11,000
Locomotive engineers	15	2,000
Able seamen, ordinary seamen & marine oilers	15	3,000
Machine builders and other precision machine assemblers	15	8,000
Central office telephone operators	15	6,000

Source: U.S. Bureau of Labor Statistics

Blue-collar jobs aren't the only occupations affected by technological advances. Many white-collar workers, from stenographers and drafters to keypunch operators and mailroom clerks, will find employment prospects shrinking because of the spread of office automation equipment.

Other professions are suffering from overcrowding. Even though jobs for doctors, dentists, lawyers, entertainers, and writers are growing, the large number of people in those professions makes competition keen.

Budgetary constraints will make job opportunities in government limited. Federal employment is expected to remain flat because of the large budget deficits. Payrolls of state and local governments are expected to expand moderately, mostly because of the need for more teachers.

Below are more detailed assessments of the employment prospects for selected occupations. Employment projections are drawn from forecasts made by the Labor Department's Bureau of Labor Statistics for the 1988-to-2000 period.

ACCOUNTANTS AND AUDITORS

For those with a high aptitude for crunching numbers, there are few professional opportunities more promising than accounting. The supply of accounting graduates falls short of the demand. As the economy grows, so will the number of businesses whose books need to be kept and audited, and the number of individual and corporate tax returns that need to be filed. With more changes in the tax laws likely as Congress struggles to bring down the towering deficit, accountants will see even more business. The profession always does well when the tax laws change since change breeds more complexity and confusion. Accountants will benefit from the increasing globalization of business, which requires dealing with a multitude of international laws, and thus entails more complicated auditing and tax planning services. Accountants will also benefit as the demand for personal financial planning grows. Baby-boomers will be reaching the age when they need to start saving more for their children's college education and their own retirements, and many of them can be expected to turn to their accountants for help. Employment of accountants is expected to grow 22 percent, which translates into an additional 211,000 jobs.

AIRLINE PILOTS

Airline pilots used to be in abundant supply. Commercial airlines were able to pick and choose from a huge reservoir of military pilots trained during the Vietnam war. Today, however, airlines are facing future shortages of trained pilots because of the growth in air travel and an expected wave of retirements. Many of the pilots hired during the late 1960s—a period of great growth in the industry—will soon become subject to government-mandated retirement at age sixty.

In addition, the airlines' traditional sources for new pilots are drying up. The military no longer turns out as many pilots, and with boosts in military pay and other retention incentives, fewer military pilots are defecting to commercial airlines. At the same time, civilian flying schools are attracting fewer students. The cost of flight instruction has skyrocketed, due in part to the sharp rise in liability insurance premiums. The number of student pilots fell 28 percent between 1979 and 1987.

Employment of pilots is expected to rise 31 percent, adding another 26,000 cockpit positions. Many more than that will need to be hired to replace retiring pilots.

AIRPLANE MECHANICS

Airplane mechanics are also in short supply. Airlines are worried about whether they will be able to find enough qualified mechanics to maintain their growing fleets and perform the extra maintenance required on aging aircraft. Additional mechanics will also be needed to replace a large number of mechanics due to retire in the 1990s.

ARCHITECTS

Demand for architects should continue to rise, although employment growth is expected to be slower than in recent years. Commercial and residential construction activity is not likely to be as frenzied as it was in the 1970s and 1980s. Employment of architects is expected to grow 25 percent. Competition will continue to be keen for positions in the prestigious architectural firms.

AUTO MECHANICS

Good mechanics are always in demand, and those with formal training should find plenty of job opportunities. But it's a slow-growing field.

On one hand, people are keeping their cars longer and those older cars require more maintenance and repair. In addition, more sophisticated electronics and emission control systems being installed in cars are making autos more complicated to repair.

On the other hand, the field is expected to show below-average growth because new models are becoming more reliable and in less need of repair. In addition, more and more gasoline stations are shifting from full-service to self-service and getting rid of their repair shops. Most of the new job openings for auto mechanics are expected to be in independent and car-dealer repair shops. Employment is forecast to grow 16 percent.

BIOLOGISTS

The commercial promise of biotechnology will open new doors for biologists over the next decade and into the twenty-first century. Biotechnology has expanded research opportunities in almost all areas of biological research. Employment is expected to grow 26 percent, or by about 15,000 positions.

CHEMISTS

Employment opportunities for chemists will expand moderately in the decade ahead. The best opportunities will be in the promising fields of biotechnology and pharmaceuticals. Employment is expected to grow 17 percent.

CHILD-CARE WORKERS

Jobs for child-care workers will be abundant in coming years as more women with preschoolers enter the labor force. Although the number of young children will shrink, a larger proportion of them will have mothers who are working. Employment of child-care workers is expected to grow 28 percent. Job openings will be much higher than that because turnover in the field is high. Most child-care workers earn menial wages but those who manage day-care centers or open their own can earn far more.

In contrast to the growing demand for child-care workers at day-care centers, Labor Department analysts think that employment of nannies and other child-care helpers who work in private households will decline 8 percent. The reasons: the shrinking number of toddlers and the trend toward formal child-care programs rather than private help at home.

COLLEGE PROFESSORS

Over the next ten to fifteen years, colleges face the prospect of having to replace hundreds of thousands of retiring faculty members. The huge crop of college faculty hired during the 1960s to accommodate the surging enrollments of the baby-boom generation will begin retiring by the late 1990s. At the same time, enrollments are expected to start climbing again as children born to the baby-boom generation reach college age.

Colleges foresee problems in recruiting enough faculty because the supply of new academics is shrinking. Fewer people are getting doctorates, particularly in engineering and some other sciences. Meanwhile, demand from private industry for PhDs is growing.

While some colleges are already preparing for the retirement wave by chasing after top talent now, faculty positions at many other colleges could remain tight until retirements begin en masse, because student enrollments are expected to decline through the mid-1990s.

COMPUTER OPERATORS

As computerization spreads to more and more business applications, additional computer operators will be needed to run all the equipment. Employment is expected to grow 29 percent, adding another 80,000 jobs. These figures actually represent a slowdown in job growth from previous years, reflecting the slowdown in large computer installations. Computer operators work mainly with large computer systems, but more and more companies have been opting for desktop computers rather than mainframes. Computer operators tend to earn less than computer programmers and systems analysts, but academic requirements also tend to be less for computer operators. Many computer operators get their training from trade schools or community colleges.

COMPUTER PROGRAMMERS

Expanding use of computers throughout society will create a voracious appetite for computer programmers. Employment is projected to increase by 48 percent, or some 250,000 new computer-programmer positions.

Competition for entry-level jobs, however, is increasing as a result of the proliferation of computer-programming courses in community colleges and universities. So employers can now afford to be more selective. The best job prospects are for college graduates trained in a variety of programming languages and those who have also taken courses in fields where programming applications are in demand, such as accounting, management, engineering, and science.

Programmers skilled in artificial intelligence are in critically short supply. The shortage is so severe that American recruiters have been forced to scour European artificial-intelligence centers to fill U.S. positions. Top programmers can earn from $50,000 to $100,000.

COMPUTER SERVICE TECHNICIANS

With computers rapidly proliferating in the workplace and at home, more people are going to be needed to install and repair them all. Computer service technicians should be one of the fastest-growing occupations. Employment is expected to grow more than 61 percent.

Openings should occur at computer manufacturers, as well as at companies that maintain large computer installations. Independent service facilities are also growing rapidly and represent an attractive opportunity for entrepreneurs.

Training usually entails at least one or two years of vocational school or college.

COMPUTER SYSTEMS ANALYSTS

Computer systems analysts are the masterminds behind the computer systems used by corporations and government. As new applications for computers develop in the 1990s, there will be a need for hundreds of thousands more of these computer experts.

Strong demand is likely to push pay up even higher from the $25,000-to-$50,000-a-year salaries that most systems analysts already enjoy. Employment is expected to jump 53 percent, or about 214,000 jobs.

Systems analysts figure out how to computerize various kinds of tasks. If a company wants to computerize its payroll, its inventory, or whatever, the computer analyst is brought in to figure out how it can be done. The analyst determines what sort of information needs to be collected, how it's to be processed, what the end result is to be (issue checks to employees or warn the purchasing manager when inventories are running low, for example), and what kind of hardware and software is needed. The best job prospects go to those with a college degree in computer science.

DATA ENTRY KEYERS

The computer revolution created hundreds of thousands of office jobs for people to keypunch data from paper into computers. But technology is already threatening to make the occupation obsolete. The amount of data is growing, but more and more of it is being punched into the system by other people. In the banking industry, for instance, customers themselves are punching transaction data right into the computer system every time they use an automated teller machine. Salesmen, who once filled out written orders and sent them to the office for input into the computer, are now entering the data right into their laptop computers. Optical scanning devices, which automatically "read" data into a computer, will also be spreading into more and more offices. Another threat on the horizon is voice-recognition computer systems. As the technology advances in the 1990s, voice systems will allow more and more people to input data to a computer simply by speaking into a microphone or telephone mouthpiece.

In addition, as telecommunications networks expand and improve, more and more data entry jobs may be lost to workers in foreign countries where wages are lower.

In all, employment is projected to shrink by 5 percent, for a loss of 21,000 jobs.

DENTISTS

Despite major advances in dental health over the past decade, lots of dental work will need to be performed in the 1990s as the population gets older and more people have the incomes and the insurance coverage to better afford dental care.

Elderly people have retained their teeth longer than previous generations because of better care, and that guarantees lots of restorative work for dentists in the years ahead. As baby-boomers reach middle age, large numbers of them will also require intensive dental treatment. Not all baby-boomers benefited from the recent advances in dental care that have been successful in reducing tooth decay in their children.

Employment in the profession is projected to grow 13 percent, but competition for patients should be stiff because of a surplus of dentists. In the 1960s and 1970s, dental schools expanded, resulting in a glut of dentists. Since then, a few dental schools have closed their doors and enrollments have declined. But the number of new graduates still exceeds those retiring from the profession.

Even if declining enrollments ultimately bring supply closer in line with demand, dentists in the twenty-first century will have patients with much healthier teeth. On the horizon are promising new advances that would prevent cavities from ever developing.

These same forces shadow the prospects for dental hygienists and dental assistants. Labor Department projections forecast 19 percent growth in jobs for hygienists and 19 percent growth in employment for assistants because of the rising demand for dental services and the increasing use of support staff in private practice. But labor analysts caution that should patient loads fall, dentists might decide to perform more support functions themselves. That would cut back on the demand for dental hygienists and assistants.

DIETITIANS AND NUTRITIONISTS

As Americans grow older and more health conscious, dietitians and nutritionists will be needed in greater numbers to serve the expanding diet-planning requirements of hospitals, nursing homes, retirement communities, and company "wellness" programs. Employment is expected to grow 28 percent.

DRAFTERS

Demand for drafting services is growing but technology is picking up the slack. The spread of computer-aided design (CAD) systems has offset the need for hiring more draftsmen. Employment is expected to grow only about 12 percent, and many experts think that fewer draftsmen will be employed as CAD systems proliferate.

Using CAD, a draftsman or engineer sits at a computer workstation and draws the design on a video screen. Drafters with experience in CAD systems will have the best employment prospects.

ENGINEERS

People who can design and put the new technologies of the 1990s to work will be a hot commodity in the job market for years to come.

As an illustration of the strong demand, about half of on-campus job offers in recent years were made to engineering majors, even though they accounted for less than 10 percent of the graduating class, according to the College Placement Council.

Electrical Engineers: In greatest demand will be electrical engineers. Their talents will be needed to help put more sophisticated electronics systems into automobiles, household appliances, computers, factory robots, and an expanding array of technological gadgetry. The darker side of the picture is that many electrical engineering jobs are in defense-related industries, where layoffs are inevitable as military spending is pared over the next several years. Nevertheless, employment of electrical engineers is expected to grow 40 percent.

Mechanical Engineers: Modernization and automation of the workplace is projected to create employment growth of 19 percent for mechanical and industrial engineers. Their skills will be needed to design new machinery to streamline operations and improve productivity in an increasingly competitive global business environment.

Civil Engineers: More civil engineers will be needed to help design and engineer the repair and expansion of the nation's aging infrastructure. Employment is projected to grow 17 percent as civil engineers are called on to modernize and expand roads, bridges, and airports in order to relieve growing traffic congestion, build new disposal systems to handle the nation's mounting waste, and design other building projects required by an expanding economy and growing population.

Aerospace Engineers: Defense cutbacks will dim employment prospects for aerospace engineers, but the civilian sector will need more of them to meet the growing demand for new planes by commercial airlines. Overall employment is expected to grow more slowly than other occupations because of military cutbacks.

Petroleum Engineers: With oil prices depressed, petroleum engineers have had a tough time in the job market. Prospects should improve somewhat later in the decade when oil prices are projected to rise enough to stimulate more exploration. But over the very long term—which anyone picking a career has to consider—petroleum engineers must consider the increasing efforts to develop alternative sources of energy in order to reduce the nation's reliance on fossil fuels.

Nuclear Engineers: Nuclear engineers won't see many new jobs created anytime soon since few, if any, new nuclear plants are likely to be built in the United States this decade because of public concerns about the safety of nuclear power.

Other Opportunities: Engineering can prove to be a good background for people who eventually want to head up technology companies. Many engineers go on to get graduate degrees in business with an eye toward moving into management.

FARMERS

Since the Industrial Revolution, jobs on the farm have been on the decline, and employment is expected to drop by another 390,000 by the end of the decade as more family farms go out of business. One remaining growth area is wage and salary positions in large farming operations, where there is demand for highly trained farm managers.

FLIGHT ATTENDANTS

As the airlines add more and bigger planes to their fleets to accommodate growth in air travel, flight-attendant employment is expected to increase 39 percent, adding 34,000 new slots. Federal Aviation Administration regulations require one flight attendant for every fifty seats. Competition for those jobs, however, is expected to be stiff. It's a glamour occupation that draws lots of applicants.

HEALTH-CARE ASSISTANTS AND TECHNICIANS

Rising demand for health-care services not only means more jobs for doctors and nurses, but also more jobs for medical technicians and other health-care workers who provide some form of assistance or auxiliary service in the treatment of patients. Although pay for technicians and assistants tends to be much lower than for medical professionals, the educational requirements are also much less.

The fastest growth is projected for medical assistants, who help physicians in various routine office and clinical tasks. Employment is expected to swell 70 percent. Jobs for physical and corrective therapy assistants and aides, who help physical therapists in rehabilitating patients, are projected to grow 52 percent. Radiologic technologists, the people behind the X-ray camera and other diagnostic equipment, can expect a 66 percent increase in positions. Jobs for recreational therapists, who use arts and crafts, music, and other recreational activities to help treat patients, are expected to grow 37 percent.

Rapid employment growth is also projected for other specialties: respiratory therapists (41 percent growth); surgical technicians (56 percent); and lab technologists (19 percent). Jobs for nursing aides, orderlies, and attendants are expected to grow 32 percent.

HEALTH SERVICE MANAGERS

Health service managers—the people who run hospitals, HMOs, outpatient clinics, nursing homes, and the like—face a bright future as the health needs of an aging population grow and the industry diversifies. The field, which has traditionally been the preserve of health administration graduates, now attracts growing numbers of MBA graduates, particularly those with some sort of health service background.

HOME HEALTH AIDES

The pay is generally low and the work can sometimes be stressful. But home health aides, who provide personal care, household help, and emotional support to elderly or disabled people, will find abundant job opportunities with the rapid expansion of home health care. It is one of the few occupations with relatively low skill requirements whose job opportunities will expand substantially in the 1990s. Many home-health-care agencies will hire unskilled workers and then train them, or provide opportunities for outside training while they're employed. Employment is expected to surge 68 percent.

HOTEL-MOTEL MANAGERS AND ASSISTANTS

Increased business and personal travel will lead to expanding job opportunities for hotel managers, assistants, and other employees. Those with college degrees in hotel management will have the best prospects. Graduates of top hotel-management schools, such as Cornell University's School of Hotel Administration, commonly receive several job offers.

Promotions tend to be very rapid for good workers in the industry. Salaries for assistant hotel managers average $35,000 to $40,000. Hotel employees also receive some nice perks. Many hotels offer free or discounted meals to their employees while on the job, and larger chains give employees free rooms at any of their hotels for vacations.

But running a hotel is a demanding occupation. Staying late and working six- or seven-day weeks is not uncommon. If you are working for a large hotel chain, moving up the management ladder usually entails relocation.

INSURANCE AGENTS

Insurance sales are expected to increase as more people reach the age when family responsibilities, health concerns, and homeownership create the greatest need for insurance protection. But jobs for insurance agents won't grow as fast as sales because a lot of the new policies will be sold through group plans. In addition, a rising volume of insurance is being sold by direct mail and telephone. Employment is projected to grow 14 percent.

LAWYERS

Demand for legal services is growing rapidly, but so is the supply of new attorneys. Law school applications have been surging even though the field is already crowded. As a result of the competition, many new lawyers may be forced to take relatively low-paying jobs, jobs that entail fairly tedious and routine legal work, or settle for a career in a small-town practice.

Legal services is a growing field, spurred by increasing business activity and a growing population. Growing legal action in such specialized areas as employee benefits, consumer protection, the environment, and safety is also expected to contribute to growing demand for legal services, according to Labor Department analysts.

At the same time, a rising segment of the population can now afford legal services thanks to the emergence of prepaid group legal service plans and the proliferation of storefront legal clinics that offer such basic services as wills, uncontested divorces, and personal bankruptcy at relatively low cost.

Starting salaries for lawyers can still exceed $75,000 a year. But those are the bounties paid by top New York law firms to students who graduate at the top of their class from big-name law schools. Although employment in the field is expected to grow 31 percent, many of the new jobs for lawyers will be at the lower end of the spectrum and carry much lower pay.

In the past, many students went to law school because a law degree offered so many career options. If they didn't practice law, their law degree would make them attractive candidates for other jobs in business. Banks, insurance firms, and government agencies have long turned to law school graduates to fill various business, management, and administrative slots. But there are signs of change. Law school graduates are no longer greeted as warmly in the corporate marketplace. Part of the reason is competition from the flood of MBA graduates, whose training is more tailored for specific business assignments. Law school graduates are also encountering an image problem. Some executives think lawyers are too confrontational and too narrow-minded to come up with the creative solutions needed to compete in today's business world.

LEGAL ASSISTANTS: PARALEGALS

At billing rates of $75 to $350 an hour, lawyers—and their clients—have been concerned about how so much of their valuable legal time and so much of the client's money is spent researching cases and drafting routine documents. Lawyers could handle more clients, and do it more economically, if the routine legwork and groundwork were handled by assistants. That thinking gave birth in the late 1960s to what is now the most rapidly growing occupation in America: legal assistants, more commonly known as paralegals. Employment is expected to surge 75 percent, reaching 145,000 positions by the year 2000.

But competition is also increasing. It used to be that high school graduates could find work as paralegals, but law firms are increasingly looking only at those who have undergone formal paralegal training in college. Hundreds of colleges offer paralegal programs. Most of them require only two years to complete. Others require four years of study.

Paralegals sit in the shadow of lawyers in terms of pay, prestige, and responsibility; the occupation is not a substitute for those aspiring to be a lawyer. Paralegal salaries average less than $25,000 a year.

LIBRARIANS

Jobs for librarians are not expected to grow much during the 1990s, but many opportunities will open up because a large proportion of librarians will be reaching retirement age in the next several years.

Competition for jobs is also easing. The number of college graduates with library science degrees has dropped to about half the level of the mid-1970s.

The best opportunities are for librarians with the skills and specialized knowledge to work in libraries maintained by law firms, research laboratories, ad agencies, professional associations, medical centers, and government agencies. Demand is also growing for librarians in the burgeoning computer database field.

Overall, employment of librarians is projected to grow 10 percent.

MAILROOM CLERKS

Tales abound about successful executives who started their careers in the mailroom. But such legends will need to start someplace else in the future. Mailroom clerks are increasingly being replaced by robotic devices as well as by the spreading use of fax machines and "electronic mail."

MANAGEMENT CONSULTANTS

With the business world becoming more competitive, companies are increasingly turning to outside consultants for advice on how operations can be streamlined, costs reduced, and products improved. Opportunities in consulting are best for those with a graduate degree or expertise in a particular industry. Major consulting firms regularly woo top-ranking MBA graduates of the best business schools with the highest salary offers. Starting salaries in excess of $60,000 are not uncommon for top graduates.

Employment of management consultants is projected to grow 35 percent, but consulting is a competitive field. Many professionals and managers from business and government try to launch new careers as consultants in hopes that their experience, expertise, and contacts will prove a marketable commodity. But many of those who start up their own consulting firms fail for lack of clients.

MEDICAL RECORDS TECHNICIANS

Medical records technicians, the people who handle all the medical records at hospitals and other health facilities, face a bright outlook, with employment expected to grow 60 percent. Accurate, timely, and complete medical records play a critical role in the drive to manage health-care costs, particularly as more health-care facilities operate as for-profit institutions. Most employers hire technicians who have completed a two-year associate degree program in the field.

NURSES

If you want a career where you can always be sure of a job, become a nurse. The pay and the hours may not always be great, but the work can be satisfying and your services will always be in demand. Nurses are in critically short supply and the shortages are expected to get worse as the aging population creates much higher demand for health services.

Employment of registered nurses is expected to grow 39 percent, or by 613,000 positions. Employment of licensed practical nurses is projected to expand 37 percent, or by 229,000 jobs.

Salaries are finally beginning to respond to the surging demand, with income now averaging more than $25,000 and top pay for experienced RNs exceeding $40,000.

OCCUPATIONAL THERAPISTS

Colleges can't turn out enough occupational therapists to fill the growing demand for their rehabilitative services. Occupational therapists, who help disabled individuals develop the necessary skills to become self-reliant, will be needed in much larger numbers as the elderly population rapidly increases and as medical advances save the lives of more and more younger people with debilitating conditions from accidents and birth defects. Demand for cardiac rehabilitation should also increase as the baby-boom generation moves into the age group where they are at high risk of heart attacks and strokes. Employment is projected to increase 49 percent by the year 2000. Occupational therapists earn between $25,000 and $30,000 a year on average. Certification requires a bachelor's degree in occupational therapy.

OPTOMETRISTS

An aging population holds great promise for optometrists. People tend to pay visits to their eye doctors more frequently once they reach age forty-five. That's when a lot of people start to have trouble reading the fine print in newspapers and the faraway signs on highways. Aging also brings a higher incidence of more serious vision problems, such as glaucoma.

At the same time, greater use of computers and video display terminals is expected to send more people to eye doctors with eyestrain complaints.

Employment is projected to grow 16 percent. In addition, one in four optometrists are age fifty or older, so a large number of openings will occur as a wave of retirements takes place.

One threat to the long-term job outlook for optometrists and others in the eyeglass industry is an experimental laser procedure that can cure near- and farsightedness without the need for eyeglasses. The procedure, known as "eye sculpturing," is undergoing review by the Food and Drug Administration. Of course, even if the laser procedure passes muster, it remains to be seen how many people will be willing to undergo a surgical procedure and pay an ophthalmologist an estimated $1,000 to $2,000 per eye to satisfy their vanity.

PHARMACISTS

Pharmacists face a promising future as the population gets older. Rapid growth of the elderly population will spur demand for prescription drugs and pharmacists to dispense them. On average, those over the age of sixty-five use twice as many prescription drugs as younger people. Scientific advances should also increase the number of drug products available. Employment is projected to grow 27 percent.

PHYSICAL THERAPISTS

Physical therapy is one of the fastest-growing occupations and therapists will find more rehabilitative work than they can handle with an aging population. Employment is expected to surge 57 percent. The number of new graduates from college degree programs is expected to fall short of the number needed to fill all the job openings.

Physical therapists use massage, exercise, heat, and a variety of other methods to treat people with physical disabilities resulting from accidents, strokes, heart attacks, and other ailments.

Salaries start at around $25,000 a year but supervising therapists can earn over $40,000.

PHYSICIAN ASSISTANTS

Physician assistants, an occupation dating back only to the mid-1960s when physicians were in short supply, are expected to be in growing demand in the 1990s as the health services industry expands and attempts to cut costs. Physician assistants are more economical to use than physicians in a variety of primary-care tasks. They are trained to interview patients, conduct physical examinations, make diagnoses, establish treatment plans, and in some states they are authorized to prescribe medicine. They also assist physicians in more complicated medical and surgical procedures. Physician assistants generally go through a formal two-year program. About half of those entering the program already have a bachelor's or master's degree. Although physician assistants go through considerable training and their authority is extensive in many states, their income prospects are much less than those of physicians. On average, earnings ran $34,000 in 1988. Employment is expected to grow 28 percent. Demand is expected to outstrip the supply of new graduates.

PHYSICIANS

An aging population means more business for doctors, but practicing medicine isn't what it used to be.

For one thing, medicine is getting to be a crowded field. Studies forecast a surplus of doctors in the years ahead, forcing physicians in some lucrative specialties to fight for patients in large metropolitan areas.

Doctors are also beginning to lose some of their autonomy. Health insurance trends are driving many doctors out of private practice and into salaried positions at health maintenance organizations. Others are finding their fees capped or second-guessed by insurance arrangements and Medicare restrictions.

All of this means that income prospects, while still at the upper end of the pay spectrum, are not as bright as they used to be. Doctors who are willing to go into less lucrative specialty fields, such as internal medicine, or work in rural areas or inner cities should find less competition and more business. Overall, employment is projected to grow 28 percent.

Getting into medical school is easier now than it was during the 1970s and 1980s, when applications from the huge baby-boom generation flooded admissions offices.

PODIATRISTS

The fast-growing elderly population will spur demand for podiatrists in the years ahead. Older people tend to have more severe foot problems. Podiatrists who specialize in sports medicine are also likely to reap more business from maturing baby-boomers who stick to jogging, tennis, and racquetball. Employment is expected to grow 35 percent.

POLICE OFFICERS

Employment opportunities for police officers are expected to expand moderately to meet the needs of a growing population and citizen demands for greater resources in the fight against drugs and street crime. But budgetary constraints will limit the growth of police departments and force them to use lower-paid civilian employees—rather than police officers—for parking enforcement and various administrative positions. Increasingly, private security firms are also taking over some routine police functions, such as crowd surveillance at airports and concerts and even security in courtrooms.

Employment is expected to grow about 13 percent. Applications far exceed the number of openings, but many police departments complain of having trouble finding enough qualified candidates among those applicants.

Corrections officers will also be needed in greater numbers to supervise an expanding prison population. Many states are under court order to build new prisons and expand existing facilities in order to ease overcrowded conditions. Federal proposals also call for new prisons as part of the escalating war against drugs. Employment is expected to surge 41 percent.

PSYCHOLOGISTS

Psychologists should find expanded opportunities in the 1990s as the workplace becomes more stressful and an aging population creates greater demand for counseling. Schools are also expected to increase their psychological counseling programs for students. And midlife crisis could become a national epidemic as the huge baby-boom generation enters middle age. Overall, employment in the field is expected to grow 27 percent. The best prospects go to those with PhDs. Graduates with master's degrees will face stiff competition, while those with only a bachelor's degree will find few opportunities.

PUBLIC RELATIONS SPECIALISTS

Public relations is an expanding field. A growing number of businesses and trade associations are recognizing the need to gain higher visibility as part of their overall marketing strategy. While large corporations and national trade groups used to be the primary users of public relations services, small businesses and professional associations are generating growing demand for public relations firms. Employment of public relations specialists and publicity writers is expected to grow 15 percent.

REAL ESTATE AGENTS

Real estate agents, who prospered from a booming housing market in the 1970s and 1980s, face a weaker market in the 1990s. But most job openings should arise from the need to replace people who leave the profession. In this fiercely competitive field, hordes of people go out and get a license (about 1 out of every 75 residents in California has a real estate license) and then get discouraged when they can't close enough deals to make a living. Real estate is very much a local game, and the best prospects will be in fast-growing-population areas.

RESTAURANT AND FOOD SERVICE MANAGERS AND WORKERS

The restaurant industry is already struggling to find enough help, and the situation is expected to grow worse during the 1990s as the pool of younger workers continues to shrink. Employee turnover in the restaurant business also is very high. Many fast-food chains are offering salaries far in excess of the minimum wage, an array of fringe benefits, and flexible work schedules in order to attract applicants. Retirees are also being courted to fill the gap left by the dwindling numbers of younger people.

Restaurant managers, however, won't find the business growing the way it did in the 1970s and 1980s. The industry's rapid expansion has left the market saturated. In addition, many people aren't going out to eat as often as they used to. Restaurants now have to contend with take-out food and microwave ovens in competing for customers whose busy lifestyles leave less time for cooking.

Fashionable restaurants are also being hurt by corporate cost-cutting. Many companies have tightened the belt on expense accounts, particularly after the Tax Reform Act of 1986 scaled back the deduction for business meals and entertainment expenses. (Only 80 percent is now deductible.) The corporate cutbacks have forced some restaurants to cut back their staffs, making competition for jobs at luxury restaurants even tougher than usual. Competition for jobs of all sorts at expensive eateries has always been keen because the earnings can be substantial.

In the long term, some analysts see the potential for the restaurant business to rebound once the baby-boomers' children grow a little older. Parents with toddlers tend to stick close to home. A growing elderly population may also help sit-down restaurants, since many retirees are dining out more frequently.

In the meantime, food-service managers should find expanded employment opportunities in nursing homes, residential care facilities, and other health-care institutions as the elderly population grows.

Job opportunities will be best for those with a bachelor's degree or associate degree in restaurant and institutional food services management.

RETAIL SALESPERSONS

Jobs should be plentiful in retailing in the 1990s even though the fastest growing segments of the retail business—self-service discount stores, warehouse outlets, mail-order, and electronic home shopping—employ relatively few salespeople.

Many department stores, boutiques, and specialty retailers are placing renewed emphasis on personal service as a way to compete against the discounters. So to pamper customers, many full-service stores have been adding sales workers. Additional sales staff will also be needed as more stores expand their hours to accommodate the growing ranks of working women.

Retailing offers plenty of opportunities for both part-time and full-time employment. In fact, retailers are having trouble finding enough part-timers and are being forced to rely more on full-time help. Turnover is always high in retailing. And shrinking numbers of younger workers will exacerbate the labor shortages. Competition for jobs in the most fashionable stores, however, is usually keen.

But be aware that the 1990s will be tumultuous times for many retailers. An aging population portends slower growth in consumer spending, and many regions are already "over-stored." In addition, some of the larger retail chains, burdened with debt from the wave of takeovers and restructurings of the 1980s, could be forced to cut back on customer service and close down some of their stores to stay afloat. Retailers also face growing competition from home shopping—mail order, videotex and cable TV.

Competition among retailers will be fierce and there are likely to be casualties as the industry undergoes radical change. Mass merchandising is a dying strategy. Department stores can't just offer a broad array of goods anymore and hope to prosper. To survive in the 1990s, retailers will either have to compete on the basis of price or else compete by offering customer service or a specialty line of merchandise.

A college education is becoming essential to those aspiring to management positions in the retail industry. Large retailers prefer to hire college graduates for management trainee positions.

SECRETARIES

Good secretaries are always in demand. Turnover is high and employers always complain about a shortage of first-rate secretaries. But employment growth is projected to be slow because of the spread of office automation.

Increasingly, managers are performing many of the clerical tasks that they used to rely exclusively on their secretaries to do. They are drafting letters and reports on their own personal computers. They are sending their own memos through electronic mail systems. And their phone calls are being answered by "voice mail" systems. As a result, more and more lower-level managers and professionals are being forced to share secretaries.

Secretaries should try to work for senior executives. Even though top executives can be more demanding, secretaries in the executive suite tend to be paid more than those working for lower-level managers. Top executives have the clout to get you more money, and job security is better at the top. Though lower-level managers and professionals will increasingly be expected to do without private secretaries, senior executives are not likely to give up their secretaries, no matter how much automation spreads into the executive suite.

Employment in the field is expected to grow only about 13 percent by the year 2000, so replacement needs will be the main source of jobs for secretaries. Several hundred thousand secretaries leave the labor force or transfer to other occupations each year. Among specialists, legal secretary employment is projected to grow 25 percent and jobs for medical secretaries are expected to surge 58 percent.

Early in the twenty-first century, advances in artificial intelligence and voice-operated computer systems could cut even further into the demand for secretaries.

SECURITY GUARDS

Jobs for security guards will be plentiful. Demand for guard services at stores, offices, plants, and public places is growing rapidly due to increased concern over vandalism, terrorism, theft, and other crimes. Businesses also have more to protect than they did before. Computers and other high-tech equipment are vulnerable to sabotage and theft. Private guards are also taking on some of the routine duties that police officers used to perform, such as monitoring crowds in shopping centers and other public places.

Employment of guards is expected to grow 32 percent. Turnover is also high. Competition will be keenest for in-house jobs, which typically offer higher pay and better benefits than jobs at private security firms.

SOCIAL WORKERS

More social workers will be needed to handle the problems of a rapidly increasing elderly population. Demand is expected to be particularly strong in elderly services and in mental health counseling. In addition, more social workers are likely to be needed to deal with the plight of the homeless, a problem gaining increased attention in the political arena. Employment is projected to grow 29 percent.

STENOGRAPHERS

With dictation machines in widespread use, the steno pool is rapidly going the way of the manual typewriter. Jobs for stenographers are rapidly disappearing as sophisticated dictation equipment makes its way into more and more offices. Employment is expected to shrink 23 percent, according to the Bureau of Labor Statistics, one of the sharpest declines projected for any occupation.

One area where shorthand reporters are still in strong demand is government. Federal and state courts are adding reporters to handle the rising volume of criminal and civil cases, although some states are experimenting with videotape machines to record court proceedings. Another pocket of demand is in the growing number of conventions, conferences, and symposiums, for which stenographers are hired to transcribe the proceedings.

STOCKBROKERS

It may be some time before Wall Street sees individual investors return with the kind of enthusiasm they displayed prior to the 1987 stock market crash. Yet employment opportunities for stockbrokers are expected to rebound in the years ahead as baby-boomers reach the age when they need to invest more for their children's college educations and their own retirements. Stocks, bonds, and mutual funds are bound to be a part of those portfolios. Competition for Wall Street jobs, however, is always keen because the earnings potential is high.

Electronic trading services that allow investors to buy and sell securities from their home computers could cut into the demand for brokers. Some major Wall Street firms recently launched electronic trading services to the chagrin of their brokers. Brokers fear that they will lose customers to these computer services, which offer the advantage of discounted commissions.

TEACHERS

Rising enrollments and greater public emphasis on quality education should create brighter employment prospects for teachers in the 1990s.

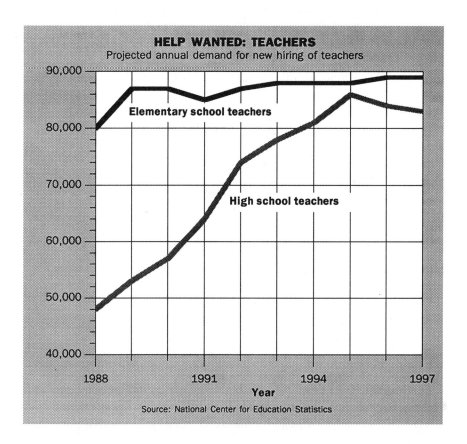

HELP WANTED: TEACHERS
Projected annual demand for new hiring of teachers

Source: National Center for Education Statistics

Demand for new schoolteachers is expected to rise steadily through the mid-1990s to accommodate rising enrollments. According to U.S. Department of Education projections, annual hiring will increase 22 percent between 1990 and 1995, when it will peak. Children of the baby-boom generation are now making their way through the school system.

Most of the increased demand is at the high school level. School districts are expected to increase their yearly hiring of high school teachers by more than 50 percent through 1995.

Demand for teachers will vary greatly by geographical area. Teaching opportunities in the South and West, where population is growing the fastest, are expected to be much greater than in other regions.

Demand will also vary by subject matter. High school principals reported in surveys that they had the most trouble finding qualified science, math, and foreign-language teachers.

Ultimately, national concern over the quality of education is likely to lead to higher pay scales as school boards try to improve their schools by recruiting the best teachers. In fact, school districts may have to compete with private industry for good teachers. Corporations are spending billions of dollars on training and retraining workers in subjects ranging from remedial English to highly technical computer applications.

TRAVEL AGENTS

Travel agents will find expanding employment opportunities as spending on both personal and business travel increases in the 1990s. Individuals are traveling more and relying more than ever on travel agents to translate the complicated maze of air fares and vacation options. Businesses are also relying more on travel agencies to help keep their travel costs in line. Employment is expected to surge 54 percent.

VETERINARIANS

Demand for veterinary services will increase with the growth in the pet and livestock population and the greater use of scientific methods for raising and breeding farm animals. But the supply of veterinarians is expected to exceed demand, leading to increased competition for jobs and animal patients. Veterinary school enrollments, while expected to decline slightly, have surged over the last 20 years. Job growth is projected at 26 percent.

WORD PROCESSORS/TYPISTS

If you browse through any newspaper's classified section, you'll find an abundance of help-wanted ads for word processors, but demand is expected to shrink sharply.

Advances in optical scanning devices are occurring so rapidly that it's likely that we will see widespread commercial application in this decade. If a machine can automatically read and type documents, you don't need human word processors. At the same time, professionals and managers are doing more of their own word processing.

Farther down the road is the threat from voice-activated computers. Speak to the computer and it will automatically type what you say. The technology may not be perfected in time to make such computers commercially widespread by the end of the decade, but once they do spread into the workplace the need for human word processors will be sharply reduced.

So while there may be plentiful jobs in this large field for several years to come because of high turnover, its long-term prospects are dark. Employment through the year 2000 is projected to shrink 6 percent.

OBTAINING MORE INFORMATION

For more details about each profession, consult the *Occupational Outlook Handbook*, published by the U.S. Department of Labor's Bureau of Labor Statistics. Updated editions come out every two years. The handbook contains a wealth of information about each occupation, including earnings, training requirements, employment prospects, and the nature of the work.

Almost every library has a copy of it. Copies can also be purchased from the Superintendent of Documents, U.S. Government Printing Office, Washington, D.C. 20402. Phone: (202) 783-3238.

OUTLOOK FOR OVER 250 SELECTED OCCUPATIONS

OCCUPATION	EMPLOYMENT GROWTH 1988–2000 PERCENT	EMPLOYMENT GROWTH 1988–2000 NUMBER	PROJECTED EMPLOYMENT 2000
ENGINEERING			
Aerospace engineers	13%	10,000	88,000
Chemical engineers	16	8,000	57,000
Civil engineers	17	32,000	219,000
Electrical engineers	40	176,000	615,000
Industrial engineers	18	24,000	155,000
Mechanical engineers	20	44,000	269,000
Nuclear engineers	3	430	15,000
Petroleum engineers	7	1,000	18,000
Architects	25	21,000	107,000
Surveyors	12	12,000	112,000
Engineering technicians	28	204,000	926,000
Drafters	12	39,000	358,000
COMPUTERS, SCIENCE, MATH			
Computer systems analysts	53%	214,000	617,000
Computer programmers	48	250,000	769,000
Computer operators	29	80,000	354,000
Peripheral EDP equipment operators	29	12,000	54,000
Agricultural & food scientists	21	5,000	30,000
Biological scientists	26	15,000	72,000
Foresters—conservation scientists	8	2,000	30,000
Actuaries	54	8,000	24,000
Statisticians	23	3,000	18,000
Mathematicians	19	3,000	19,000
Operations research analysts	55	30,000	85,000
Chemists	17	13,000	93,000
Geologists, geophysicists, oceanographers	16	7,000	49,000
Meterologists	30	2,000	8,000
Physicists & astronomers	12	2,000	21,000
SOCIAL SCIENCE, LAW			
Economists	27%	10,000	45,000
Psychologists	27	28,000	132,000
Urban & regional planners	15	3,000	23,000
Clergy	7	13,000	199,000
Directors, religious activities & education	10	6,000	62,000
Recreation workers	19	35,000	221,000
Social workers	29	110,000	495,000
Judges, magistrates, other judicial workers	18	7,000	47,000
Lawyers	31	181,000	763,000
Paralegals	75	62,000	145,000
TEACHERS, LIBRARIANS & COUNSELORS			
Teachers, preschool	30%	72,000	309,000
Teachers, elementary	15	208,000	1,567,000
Teachers, high school	19	224,000	1,388,000

OCCUPATION	EMPLOYMENT GROWTH 1988–2000		PROJECTED EMPLOYMENT 2000
	PERCENT	NUMBER	
College faculty	3	23,000	869,000
Instructors, adult (nonvocational) education	18	41,000	268,000
Instructors, vocational education & training	7	16,000	255,000
Librarians, professional	10	14,000	157,000
Counselors	27	33,000	157,000
Teacher aides & educational assistants	21	145,000	827,000
Library assistants & bookmobile drivers	6	6,000	111,000
Curators, archivists, museum technicians & restorers	17	3,000	19,000

HEALTH

OCCUPATION	PERCENT	NUMBER	PROJECTED EMPLOYMENT 2000
Dentists	13%	22,000	189,000
Dietitians & nutritionists	28	11,000	51,000
Optometrists	16	6,000	43,000
Pharmacists	27	44,000	206,000
Podiatrists	35	6,000	22,000
Physician assistants	28	14,000	62,000
Physicians & surgeons	28	149,000	684,000
Registered nurses	39	613,000	2,190,000
Occupational therapists	49	16,000	48,000
Physical therapists	57	39,000	107,000
Recreational therapists	37	10,000	35,000
Respiratory therapists	41	23,000	79,000
Speech pathologists—audiologists	28	15,000	68,000
Veterinarians & veterinary inspectors	26	12,000	57,000
Dental hygienists	18	16,000	107,000
Emergency medical technicians	13	10,000	86,000
Licensed practical nurses	37	229,000	855,000
Lab technologists	19	46,000	288,000
Medical records technicians	60	28,000	75,000
Radiologic technologists	66	87,000	218,000
Opticians, dispensing & measuring	31	16,000	65,000
Surgical technicians	56	20,000	55,000
Dental assistants	19	31,000	197,000
Medical assistants	70	104,000	253,000
Nursing aides, orderlies, attendants	31	405,000	1,703,000
Physical & corrective therapy assistants & aides	52	21,000	60,000

MANAGEMENT

OCCUPATION	PERCENT	NUMBER	PROJECTED EMPLOYMENT 2000
Education administrators	19%	62,000	382,000
Financial managers	19	130,000	802,000
Food service & lodging managers	29	161,000	721,000
General managers & top executives	16	479,000	3,509,000
Marketing, advertising & public relations managers	26	105,000	511,000

OUTLOOK FOR OVER 250 SELECTED OCCUPATIONS *(continued)*

OCCUPATION	EMPLOYMENT GROWTH 1988–2000 PERCENT	NUMBER	PROJECTED EMPLOYMENT 2000
Personnel, training & labor relations managers	22	38,000	208,000
Property & real estate managers & administrators	19	43,000	267,000
Purchasing managers	14	36,000	289,000
MANAGEMENT SUPPORT			
Accountants & auditors	22%	211,000	1,174,000
Claims examiners, property & casualty insurance	23	7,000	37,000
Inspectors & complicance officers (except construction)	14	18,000	148,000
Construction & building inspectors	14	8,000	64,000
Cost estimators	15	26,000	194,000
Employment interviewers, private or public employment service	40	33,000	113,000
Personnel, training & labor relations specialists	21	53,000	305,000
Loan officers & counselors	22	37,000	209,000
Management consultants	35	46,000	176,000
Underwriters	29	30,000	134,000
Wholesale & retail buyers (except farm products)	6	13,000	220,000
WRITERS, ARTISTS & ENTERTAINERS			
Artists & commercial artists	27%	58,000	274,000
Dancers & choreographers	19	2,000	13,000
Designers	28	86,000	395,000
Musicians	9	22,000	251,000
Camera operators, television & motion pictures	29	3,000	14,000
Photographers	18	17,000	111,000
Producers, directors, actors, entertainers	30	24,000	104,000
Public relations specialists & publicity writers	15	14,000	105,000
Radio & TV announcers & newscasters	19	11,000	67,000
Broadcast technicians	−31	−8,000	19,000
Reporters & correspondents	16	12,000	82,000
Writers & editors, including technical writers	25	55,000	274,000
MARKETING & SALES			
Cashiers	13%	304,000	2,614,000
Counter & rental clerks	28	67,000	308,000
Insurance sales workers	14	58,000	481,000
Real estate brokers	20	14,000	84,000
Real estate sales agents	16	50,000	361,000
Real estate appraisers	20	8,000	49,000
Retail salespersons	19	730,000	4,564,000

OCCUPATION	EMPLOYMENT GROWTH 1988–2000		PROJECTED EMPLOYMENT 2000
	PERCENT	NUMBER	
Travel agents	54	77,000	219,000
Securities & financial services sales workers	55	109,000	309,000
Stock clerks, sales floor	15	174,000	1,340,000

FINANCIAL RECORDS PROCESSING

Billing, cost & rate clerks	3%	11,000	333,000
Billing, posting & calculating machine operators	−10	−9,000	89,000
Bookkeeping, accounting & auditing clerks	1	20,000	2,272,000
Payroll & timekeeping clerks	−2	−4,000	172,000
General office clerks	18	455,000	2,974,000

ADMINISTRATIVE SUPPORT

Adjustment clerks	20%	47,000	278,000
Loan & credit clerks	27	41,000	192,000
Bill & account collectors	31	46,000	195,000
Insurance adjusters, examiners & investigators	20	29,000	175,000
Insurance policy processing clerks	9	15,000	186,000
Welfare eligibility workers, interviewers	12	11,000	102,000
Central office phone operators	−15	−6,000	36,000
Directory assistance operators	−21	−7,000	26,000
Switchboard operators	24	62,000	316,000
Duplicating, mail & other office machine operators	10	17,000	181,000

INFORMATION CLERKS

Hotel desk clerks	26%	29,000	142,000
Interviewing clerks, except personnel & social welfare	18	23,000	152,000
New accounts clerks, banking	19	21,000	129,000
Receptionists & information clerks	40	331,000	1,164,000
Reservation & transportation ticket agents & travel clerks	28	37,000	170,000

MAIL & MESSAGE DISTRIBUTION WORKERS

Mail clerks, except postal service	1%	2,000	137,000
Messengers	19	24,000	147,000
Postal mail carriers	9	25,000	310,000
Postal service clerks	4	16,000	396,000

DISPATCHERS, DISTRIBUTION, SCHEDULING

Dispatchers	14%	29,000	231,000
Meter readers	−9	−4,000	45,000
Order fillers, wholesale-retail	8	17,000	224,000
Stock clerks, stockroom	8	63,000	841,000
Traffic, shipping & receiving clerks	10	55,000	591,000

OCCUPATION	EMPLOYMENT GROWTH 1988–2000		PROJECTED EMPLOYMENT 2000
	PERCENT	NUMBER	
CLERICAL RECORDS PROCESSING			
File clerks	10%	27,000	290,000
Order clerks	−2	−4,000	289,000
Personnel clerks	9	12,000	141,000
Bank tellers	5	24,000	546,000
Court clerks	21	9,000	51,000
Data entry keyers	−5	−21,000	410,000
First line supervisors-managers	12	137,000	1,319,000
Statistical clerks	−2	−1,000	76,000
JANITORIAL			
Institutional housekeepers	37%	51,000	189,000
Janitors & cleaners	19	556,000	3,450,000
SECRETARIAL			
Secretaries	17%	571,000	3,944,000
Stenographers	−23	−36,000	122,000
Typists & word processors	−6	−61,000	924,000
FOOD PREPARATION			
Cooks, except short-order	24%	263,000	1,362,000
Short-order & fast-food cooks	14	89,000	719,000
Food preparation workers	23	234,000	1,260,000
Bartenders	22	92,000	506,000
Dining room & cafeteria attendants & barroom helpers	29	130,000	578,000
Food counter workers	15	240,000	1,866,000
Hosts & hostesses	31	56,000	239,000
Waiters & waitresses	31	551,000	2,337,000
Butchers & meat cutters	4	12,000	269,000
PERSONAL SERVICE OCCUPATIONS			
Barbers	0%	0	76,000
Hairstylists & cosmetologists	12	74,000	683,000
Child-care workers	28	186,000	856,000
Flight attendants	39	34,000	123,000
Home health aides	68	160,000	397,000
Social welfare service aides	52	47,000	138,000
Amusement & recreation attendants	24	42,000	217,000
PRIVATE HOUSEHOLD WORKERS			
Housekeepers & butlers	−3%	−1,000	33,000
Cleaners & servants	−3	−13,000	464,000
Child-care workers, household	−8	−28,000	347,000
PROTECTIVE SERVICES			
Firefighters	10%	24,000	257,000
Police detectives & patrol officers	13	68,000	583,000
Guards	32	256,000	1,050,000
Correction officers	41	76,000	262,000

OCCUPATION	EMPLOYMENT GROWTH 1988–2000		PROJECTED EMPLOYMENT 2000
	PERCENT	NUMBER	
AGRICULTURAL			
Farmers	−23%	−266,000	875,000
Farm managers	22	29,000	160,000
Farm workers	−16	−153,000	785,000
Gardeners & groundskeepers	24	182,000	943,000
CONSTRUCTION			
Bricklayers & stone-masons	16%	26,000	193,000
Carpenters	16	175,000	1,257,000
Electricians	18	96,000	638,000
Highway maintenance workers	9	15,000	190,000
Painters & paperhangers	16	70,000	501,000
Plumbers, pipefitters, steamfitters	18	73,000	469,000
Roofers	19	24,000	147,000
TRANSPORTATION			
Aircraft pilots & flight engineers	31%	26,000	108,000
Air traffic controllers	15	4,000	31,000
Bus drivers	17	88,000	593,000
Taxi drivers	26	28,000	137,000
Truck drivers	14	382,000	3,024,000
Locomotive engineers	−15	−2,000	13,000
Railroad brake, signal & switch operators	−23	−9,000	29,000
Railroad conductors & yardmasters	−20	−5,000	21,000
Able seamen, ordinary seamen & marine oilers	−15	−3,000	19,000
Ship captains & pilots	−7	−1,000	13,300
Ship engineers	−12	−1,000	6,000
Parking lot attendants	14	7,000	54,000
Service station attendants	7	23,000	331,000
VEHICLE & EQUIPMENT MECHANICS & REPAIRERS			
Aircraft mechanics	17%	18,000	124,000
Auto body repairers	26	56,000	270,000
Auto mechanics	16	126,000	898,000
Bus & truck mechanics	16	43,000	312,000
Farm equipment mechanics	1	1,000	55,000
Mobile heavy equipment mechanics	14	16,000	124,000
Heating, air conditioning, refrigeration—mechanics, installers	17	38,000	263,000
Office machine & cash register servicers	1	1,000	57,000
Industrial machinery mechanics	16	75,000	538,000
Maintenance repairers, general utility	19	202,000	1,282,000
PRECISION METAL WORKERS			
Jewelers & silversmiths	16%	6,000	41,000
Machinists	9	36,000	433,000
Sheet metal workers	4	11,000	257,000
Tool and die makers	4	7,000	159,000

OCCUPATION	EMPLOYMENT GROWTH 1988–2000		PROJECTED EMPLOYMENT 2000
	PERCENT	NUMBER	
ELECTRONIC EQUIPMENT INSTALLERS & REPAIRERS			
Central office & PBX installers, repairers	−21%	−15,000	59,000
Data processing equipment repair	61	44,000	115,000
Electrical power line installers & repairers	17	18,000	122,000
Electronic home entertainment equipment repairers	13	6,000	49,000
Electronic repairers, commercial & industrial equipment	17	13,000	92,000
Telephone & cable TV line installers & repairers	−21	−27,000	100,000
PRECISION TEXTILE, APPAREL & FURNISHINGS WORKERS			
Sewers, hand	−11%	−2,000	14,000
Custom tailors & sewers	12	16,000	146,000
Shoe & leather workers-repairers	0	0	32,000
OPERATOR, FABRICATOR & LABORER OCCUPATIONS			
Machine tool cutting & forming setters, operators & tenders	−6%	−45,000	747,000
Welders & cutters	−5	−16,000	309,000
Printing press operators	15	35,000	274,000
Sewing machine operators	−13	−97,000	666,000
Electrical & electronic assemblers	−44	−103,000	134,000
MATERIAL MOVING & EQUIPMENT OPERATORS			
Crane & tower operators	11%	7,000	66,000
Excavation & loading machine operators	10	8,000	84,000
Grader, dozer & scraper operators	11	10,000	96,000
Hoist & winch operators	10	1,000	14,000
Industrial truck & tractor operators	−5	−21,000	400,000
Operating engineers	13	21,000	179,000
HELPERS, LABORERS & MATERIAL MOVERS, HAND			
Freight, stock & material movers, hand	2%	21,000	905,000
Hand packers & packagers	−12	−75,000	560,000
Helpers, construction trades	14	78,000	633,000
Machine feeders & offbearers	−13	−31,000	218,000
Refuse collectors	0	0	126,000
Vehicle washers & equipment cleaners	7	15,000	230,000

Source: U.S. Bureau of Labor Statistics

13

THE CHANGING FACE
OF AMERICAN BUSINESS

New technologies, foreign competition, demographic trends, and life-style changes promise to reshape American business in fundamental ways.

Following is a guide to some of the trends that will be shaping selected industries in the 1990s. It is intended to give investors, entrepreneurs, and anyone thinking of starting a business a long-term perspective of the opportunities and dangers that lie ahead in various fields. (Many other industries, such as energy, environmental services, biotechnology, and airlines, are covered elsewhere in the book.)

ADVERTISING: SPLINTERED MARKETS

In an increasingly competitive environment, businesses will need to spend more on advertising in order to differentiate their products and expand their markets. But they will be doing it in much more diverse ways than before.

While broadcast TV, magazines, and daily newspapers remain the dominant vehicles for advertisers, many companies are devoting a growing portion of their advertising budgets to alternative media, such as cable TV, direct marketing, promotions, in-store advertising, specialized publications, telemarketing, and videotex.

One reason for the growing diversity is that the traditional mass-market outlets are no longer as powerful as they used to be. Network TV is the best example. With the growth of cable TV, network audiences have steadily declined, so companies that continue to rely solely on network TV for their advertising campaigns are no longer getting their message out to a sizable share of households. In addition, the growing number of ads on television (resulting partly from the increase in fifteen-second commercials) has led many advertisers to wonder if their messages are being lost in the clutter. What's more, advertisers fear that many of their commercials are being electronically "zapped" or "fast-forwarded" now that remote control devices and VCRs are widespread.

To get their message seen and heard, some advertisers are trying to find openings wherever they occur in the American landscape—on posters in classrooms, in specialized magazines in doctors' offices, and on shopping carts in grocery stores.

Companies have also found that alternative media allow them to more narrowly target their messages than ever before. Targeting specific audiences is becoming more important as companies come out with products aimed at specific groups—be they computer users or senior citizens.

Specialized entertainment channels and programs on cable TV, such as Spanish-language networks and business news shows, let advertisers more narrowly target specific television audiences than they could on broadcast TV. Eventually, many cable-TV subscribers will be equipped with interactive devices that let them instantly order a product they see advertised.

Videotex, a small but growing market, can narrow an audience much further. These services could be programmed so that if, say, you used the system to make airline reservations, an advertisement from a hotel chain might pop up in a corner of your screen. If you liked their pitch, you could instantly ask them to send a brochure or even reserve a room for your trip. Audio-information services provide a similar opportunity; a brokerage firm that wanted to target stock-market investors could advertise on a telephone hotline offering stock quotes.

Traditional media have not been sitting idly by. Increasingly, they are trying to provide more targeted outlets. Many newspapers and magazines, for example, have been developing "zoned" editions, where local news and advertising content are distinct to each geographic region.

And broadcast television is likely to remain a foundation of mass-market advertising, because its audiences are still the largest, and it is still the most cost-effective way of reaching a mass audience.

AGRICULTURE: NO RETURN TO THE BANNER DAYS

Farming may be recovering from its long slump, but the recent rise in exports, land prices, and income doesn't presage a renaissance for the agricultural sector.

America is no longer the "breadbasket of the world." Despite famines in parts of Africa and elsewhere, agricultural production in developing countries has been steadily increasing. Many of the countries that U.S.

farmers used to sell crops to have become self-sufficient. Some of them have become so sufficient that they too have become exporters, in direct competition with U.S. farmers.

Global food supplies are growing faster than demand and that trend is expected to accelerate as developing countries reform their agricultural policies and invest more heavily in mechanization and new technologies. Advances in biotechnology are expected greatly to increase crop yields by the turn of the century, putting even more downward pressure on crop prices.

At the same time, federal farm subsidies are being threatened by growing budgetary pressures.

Agriculture in America is increasingly the domain of large corporate farmers. Family farms are continuing to disappear from the rural landscape; the survivors are mainly those who have either become very large or who have second incomes from sources off the farm.

ALCOHOLIC BEVERAGES: A NEW TEMPERANCE

Growing health consciousness and tougher drunk-driving laws have led to a new sobriety among Americans. People are drinking less wine, beer, and hard liquor.

Alcohol consumption declined slowly but steadily in the 1980s and industry analysts expect further declines in the 1990s, reflecting the trend toward healthier and more moderate life-styles among Americans. The "three-martini" business lunch became an anachronism more than a decade ago, and even a single glass of white wine at lunch is becoming a rare phenomenon in some circles. In today's competitive environment, executives need to stay alert throughout the business day, which means doing without a drink at lunch.

Even after work, growing health consciousness and tougher drunk-driving laws have helped reduce drinking among adults. Legislatures have raised the legal drinking age in many states, which has helped hold down alcohol consumption among younger people.

Many liquor companies saw the writing on the wall and diversified into other businesses. Several brewers and liquor companies have moved into more sober product lines, including soft drinks, fruit juices, and bottled water. Nonalcoholic beverages have benefited from the decline in alcohol consumption. (Even so, soft drinks are expected to experience slower growth in the 1990s because of slowing population growth and slow growth in fast-food restaurants.)

Premium liquors and wines have also benefited. Apparently, Americans figure that as long as they're drinking less they may as well enjoy the finer labels. According to Commerce Department estimates, shipments of premium and super-premium wines surged 20 percent between 1984 and 1988, a period in which overall wine consumption was down. This trend has helped smaller wineries in northern California producing higher-quality wines and has forced the largest U.S. vintners to promote their better-quality wines more heavily.

Growing demand for vintage wines might seem to offer good reason for individual investors to stock up on fine wines. If you select wisely, and if Americans continue to display an affinity for vintage wines, your investment should appreciate nicely as the wine ages. Trouble is, you will have a tough time finding a way to cash in on your profits. Virtually every state (Illinois and California are exceptions) prohibits individuals from selling wine without a liquor license. It is also illegal for a retailer to buy wine from a private party. So your only outlet is selling at wine auctions, which are held infrequently and only in a few cities.

APPAREL: LESS DRIVEN BY FADS

Apparel should benefit from the aging of the baby-boom generation since the thirty-five-to-fifty-four-year-old age group traditionally spends the most on clothing. Although they don't buy as much apparel or respond as much to fads as younger people, they buy higher-priced clothing. As a result, the fashion business is likely to become much less driven by fads and volume than it was in the 1970s and 1980s. Apparel sales should also be helped as increasing numbers of women enter the labor force.

Overall, apparel sales are expected to continue growing but at a slower rate than during the 1980s, when the industry benefited from the mass migration of women into the work force and their need to purchase new wardrobes for work.

APPLIANCES: FEWER NEW HOUSEHOLDS

The appliance industry faces two major problems in the 1990s: fewer new households being formed and the absence of a blockbuster product like the microwave oven to give business a lift.

With new households being created at a slower pace, demand for new refrigerators, ovens, and dishwashers won't be as strong. Appliance makers are hostage to demographics; while you may be able to convince a family to buy a second television for their home, a second refrigerator or a second oven isn't something most families need. As a result, manufacturers face the challenge of trying to persuade more Americans to trade up to a better oven, refrigerator, or dishwasher.

As more women go to work, the demand for timesaving appliances should increase. Trouble is, the market for the biggest timesaving appliance—the microwave oven—became saturated in the 1980s when the vast majority of households bought one.

AQUACULTURE: RISING SEAFOOD DEMAND

Fish farming, or aquaculture, has experienced rapid growth over the past decade as a result of growing demand for seafood by health-conscious Americans and mounting concerns about pollution of the nation's waterways. Fish farming is done in clean, controlled waters—in freshwater ponds and in tanks or floating cages near shore. Aquatic animal husbandry is expected to account for a growing share of seafood production in the 1990s and an even bigger share of the dollar volume, because fish farming tends to focus on the more expensive species, such as shrimp, oysters, salmon, and sea bass.

AUTOMOBILE MANUFACTURERS: ROUGH DRIVING CONDITIONS

American carmakers, who returned to strong profitability in the 1980s, face an uphill battle in the 1990s.

U.S. car sales aren't expected to grow much. Competition from foreign manufacturers is intensifying. And tougher fuel-efficiency and environmental standards portend costly changes in design.

Car sales, which averaged around 10.5 million a year in the late 1980s, are projected to grow at a slow rate during the 1990s because of the shrinking size of the sixteen-to-thirty-four-year-old population, which represents the bulk of first-time car buyers. Industry analysts expect annual sales to peak at under 12 million a year by the late 1990s.

At the same time, competition is growing fiercer. Japanese carmakers are expected to gain an even larger share of the American market. What's more, the Japanese are making inroads into the lucrative luxury-car market, where models have the highest profit margins.

Should the government continue to mandate tougher fuel-economy standards, American carmakers may be forced to sell fewer luxury cars even though an aging population is expected to boost demand for larger cars. (Luxury cars tend to have lower mileage ratings and thus drag down a company's fuel-efficiency average.) Japanese manufacturers, who sell a greater proportion of smaller, fuel-efficient cars, should be in a better position to exploit the luxury market if tougher mileage standards are imposed.

Legislative proposals for cleaning up the urban environment would mandate other costly challenges for the automakers as well, including reduced tailpipe emissions and accelerated development of cars that run on alternative fuels.

CABLE TV: WILL ANYONE SPOIL THE PARTY?

For cable TV, it's prime time. Freed of regulatory strings since 1984, cable TV operators can charge their growing list of subscribers whatever they can get away with. Cable operators' costs are way down, too. Most of the expense of building their systems is now behind them. Cable TV is also gaining new revenue sources, such as pay-per-view and commercial advertising. As the cable viewing audience grows, so do advertising revenues.

The cable TV picture is so bright that the telephone companies are begging regulators for a chance to get into the business. At the same time, some members of Congress are threatening to put a regulatory clamp on steep rate hikes.

Industry analysts think that cable companies would still be able to operate profitably even if only moderate rate increases were permitted. And while the entry of phone companies into the cable business represents a serious long-term threat to cable companies, experts say it will take many years for the phone companies to wire homes with fiber-optic cable.

Regardless, cable TV will have to work hard to sustain growth. Cable TV is already in a majority of households, and how fast it attracts new subscribers and additional revenues from here on in will depend more and more on how well it can compete against broadcast networks, videocassettes, and home satellite services.

CELLULAR PHONES: WILL GROWTH MATCH EXPECTATIONS?

In a few short years, mobile cellular phones have become an essential tool of business and an essential toy for the idle rich who get restless sitting in traffic.

No one doubts the cellular phone business will continue to have spectacular growth in the 1990s. The only question is whether the growth will be as phenomenal as the industry expects.

From more than 3 million cellular users in 1989, industry analysts see the number reaching 10 to 20 million by the mid-1990s. By the year 2000, 30 to 40 million Americans will have portable phones, according to one forecast.

Cellular companies have been plowing their earnings into building and expanding their networks to accommodate the growth. Switching their systems over to digital technology in the next few years will vastly expand capacity and should help bring service charges down. That, in turn, should attract more subscribers. While the cost of cellular phone equipment has been dropping rapidly, the average cellular phone bill still runs about $125 to $150 a month.

As prices for equipment and service drop, cellular phones should make their way into more briefcases and cars. Cellular phones may well become commonplace in taxicabs, on tables in fashionable restaurants, and as factory-installed options on new cars. But with radio frequencies a scarce resource, capacity limitations are likely to keep cellular technology from supporting a mass consumer market. Cellular systems simply will not be able to handle the volume needed to put a cellular phone into everyone's pocket.

Even if cellular service charges were to drop by more than one third—as many analysts expect by the late 1990s—it remains to be seen whether businesses and consumers will find as much need for a portable phone as the industry anticipates. It may take some savvy marketing to persuade a lot of people of the need for telephonic portability.

Another concern of cellular operators is whether the government might decide to allow an additional competitor into each market after capacity is increased. Today no more than two operators are allowed in a market.

New technologies are another worry for cellular companies. In Great Britain, for example, pedestrians carrying hand-held cordless phones will soon be able to make calls in many public locations; low-powered transmitters are to be set up in train stations, shopping malls, airports, and other heavily traveled areas. The system, called Telepoint, won't allow users to roam very far or receive incoming calls. So it's far less flexible than cellular. But calling charges on Telepoint are a fraction of the cost of cellular. Of greater concern to cellular operators are advanced versions of the Telepoint concept. In development are systems, known as personal communications networks or PCNs, that would give users a greater degree of mobility than with Telepoint and the ability to receive calls as well as make them. In the United States, Millicom, Inc., a New York communications company, recently received FCC permission to conduct pilot tests of PCN systems in Houston and Orlando, Florida, beginning in 1992. (For more on cellular phones, see chapter 22.)

CHILD CARE: HELP FOR WORKING MOTHERS

Child care should be one of the growth industries of the 1990s as more women enter the labor force. Even though the number of preschoolers is projected to decline, more of their mothers will be working.

With a tighter labor market, a growing number of companies will be forced to offer child-care assistance in order to attract and retain enough qualified workers. About half the new workers in the 1990s will be women of childbearing age.

To meet the demand for child-care services, day-care centers are expected to multiply. Although most young children of working parents are still cared for at home by a relative or at someone else's home, the trend has been toward formal day-care programs.

The child-care industry is still dominated by mom-and-pop operations, but chains are a growing force in the market. The largest chain is Kinder-Care Learning Centers, Inc., a publicly traded company that runs more than 1,200 child-care centers across the country.

CONSUMER ELECTRONICS: A PAUCITY OF NEW BLOCKBUSTERS

Consumer electronics will have a tough time repeating the blockbuster decade of the 1980s, when such revolutionary products as VCRs, cellular phones, camcorders, compact disk players, and facsimile machines made their big splash.

Some evolutionary products, like compact disk players with recording capability and high-definition television, as well as continued sales of camcorders, cellular phones, laser-disk players, and facsimile machines, are expected to provide steady, albeit slower, growth for the industry in the years ahead. And as baby-boomers enter their peak earning years and spend more time at home, analysts anticipate they will spend the money to upgrade their home-entertainment systems, with big-screen TVs, laser-disk players, and other audio-video advances.

As with the home appliance industry, electronics manufacturers will have to find new ways to induce people to upgrade their equipment because there will be both fewer new revolutionary products and fewer first-time buyers. VCRs, for instance, have reached saturation with two of three households now equipped with one; VCR sales declined for the first time in 1988. Continued growth will depend on people trading up to VCRs with advanced features, such as enhanced-image super-VHS recorders or recorders that allow you to program the unit by telephone.

Consumer electronics has been increasingly dominated by foreign manufacturers, and American industry is worried that it will lose even further ground with the arrival of High-Definition TV (HDTV). HDTV is viewed by some in the electronics industry as the blockbuster consumer electronics technology of the 1990s. Industry forecasts of HDTV sales range from $10 billion to $20 billion a year by the late 1990s in the United States alone. Whether American consumers will rush out in such large

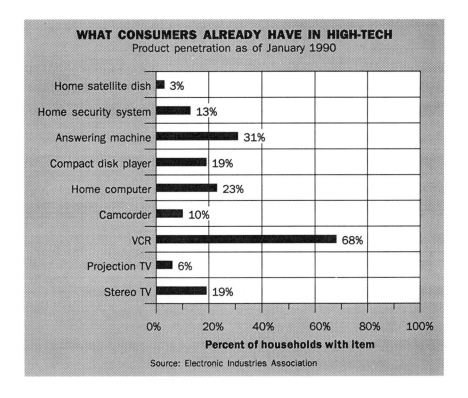

WHAT CONSUMERS ALREADY HAVE IN HIGH-TECH
Product penetration as of January 1990

Item	Percent
Home satellite dish	3%
Home security system	13%
Answering machine	31%
Compact disk player	19%
Home computer	23%
Camcorder	10%
VCR	68%
Projection TV	6%
Stereo TV	19%

Percent of households with item

Source: Electronic Industries Association

numbers to buy one is questionable; the first sets are expected to sell for $2,500 and up. Regardless, HDTV technology and standards are critical in a wide range of other electronics products, from computers to VCRs. So if America is unable to be competitive in HDTV technology, it could lose other markets as well. American manufacturers are attempting to forge joint ventures to develop HDTV, but they are already far behind the Japanese and the Europeans.

CONVENIENCE STORES: FACING NEW COMPETITORS

Since the 1950s, convenience stores have dominated fast-food shopping, offering salvation for people too rushed or too late to get to the supermarket. Today they are facing a bevy of new competitors. The main source of trouble is the thousands of service stations that have converted their repair garages into convenience stores, providing the same assortment of foods and accessories previously only offered by late-night stores like 7-Eleven. Full-service supermarkets are also extending their hours, with many of them staying open as long as or longer than convenience stores.

DEFENSE INDUSTRY: THE PARTY'S OVER

Following the biggest military buildup in U.S. peacetime history, the defense industry is heading for much leaner times. With the Cold War coming to an end, Pentagon spending is a major target for cutbacks as budget planners struggle to reduce the huge federal deficit. Defense experts see the potential for huge cuts in military spending as a result of the revolutionary changes in Eastern Europe and a receding Soviet military threat. If the situation persists, defense spending could be reduced by a third to a half by the end of the decade, according to some estimates.

Peace portends troubles for military contractors. But there may be some beneficiaries. As new weapons systems are scaled back, the Pentagon is likely to modernize and upgrade existing systems with more sophisticated electronics, benefiting defense electronics firms.

Some military electronics companies also stand to benefit from progress in arms control negotiations between the U.S. and the Soviet Union. Arms-reduction treaties that require verification would lead to greater investments in electronic surveillance systems to insure compliance.

EDUCATION: TRAINING ADULTS IS A GROWTH BUSINESS

The need for job training, retraining, and updating skills should make educating adults a growth industry in the 1990s.

Adult education is already keeping college enrollments from slumping sharply at a time when the number of new high school graduates has dropped. If you walk around campuses these days you will notice that the student body is much older than it used to be. Adults aged twenty-five and over represent around 40 percent of college enrollments, and the figure is expected to rise in the 1990s. In 1972, only about 28 percent of college students were over twenty-five. Colleges are adding a wide variety of continuing education and extension courses to attract adult students.

Corporate programs to train and retrain workers are also growing rapidly. Many corporations are contracting with local school districts, community colleges, and private firms to provide employee training. Businesses have been forced to make education a top priority as they find a growing proportion of young workers ill equipped to meet the demands of the modern workplace. Corporate training now goes beyond traditional business-related subjects to more basic ones—from basic English to remedial reading—to make up for the failings of the public education system and the need to rely more on immigrant workers. Many of these entry-level workers can't speak or read English well enough to operate today's complex machinery or communicate with English-speaking coworkers and supervisors when they need help or something goes wrong.

Elementary and high school education will also expand during the 1990s. Enrollments are projected to surge as the offspring of the baby-boom generation make their way through public and private schools.

FINANCIAL SERVICES: THE MIXED PICTURE

An aging population should benefit the financial services industry in the 1990s. Elderly Americans have large nest eggs to invest. Baby-boomers will need to begin saving more for their children's college education as well as their own retirement. And people with established careers and family responsibilities account for a large portion of life insurance sales.

But competition in the industry should intensify as deregulation continues to blur the distinction between financial services firms.

Insurance companies—some of which have expanded into financial planning and brokerage services—now worry that Congress will soon allow banks to start selling insurance. Wall Street securities firms, which offer a wide array of financial services, want to get into banking. And bankers are seeking permission to enter securities underwriting, a major source of revenue for the brokerage industry. (Instead of borrowing from banks, major corporations have increasingly turned to the securities industry to issue commercial paper or other securities on their behalf. Banks have been lobbying hard for the right to underwrite securities in hopes of recapturing some of the corporate business.)

In the banking industry, geographic barriers are also tumbling. Reciprocity agreements between states as well as new federal rules allowing banks to acquire out-of-state savings and loan associations have paved the way for further consolidation of the banking industry. Many bankers expect the number of players to shrink dramatically in the 1990s, with larger banks acquiring smaller ones in an effort to expand their geographic reach.

Besides heightened competition, financial services companies face numerous challenges. Wall Street brokers have been in retrenchment ever since individual investors were scared away by the stock market's 500-point nose dive on October 19, 1987. Luring them back will take time. On several occasions since the crash, the market has fallen more than 100 points in a single day, giving many investors fresh reason for being cautious.

In addition, the investment banking departments at Wall Street brokerage houses probably won't find takeover activity to be as frenzied as it was in the 1980s. The wave of leveraged buyouts helped buoy many Wall Street firms at a time when the brokerage side of the business was sluggish due to the stock market crash. Takeovers will be harder to finance in the 1990s with investors taking a more cautious view of high-risk "junk bonds," the securities used to help finance many of the mergers and buyouts of the 1980s.

Some commercial banks that lent heavily to help finance those corporate buyouts could face heavy losses in the 1990s if the economy slips into recession. Many of the companies that were bought out won't have enough cash flow to repay their huge debts if business slows down. Banks that stretched their lending standards too far to take advantage of the lucrative buyout business could face sizable losses. Third World debt and sour real estate loans are other problems that will continue to confront major banks. As for the beleaguered savings and loan industry, it is likely to be a shadow of its former self by the end of the century.

Life insurance companies face the threat of Congress scaling back the tax advantages of cash-value life insurance policies. As one of the few tax shelters left in the wake of the Tax Reform Act of 1986, cash-value policies—such as whole life and universal life—are considered vulnerable in future revenue-raising efforts. The tax advantages are a major selling point of these investment-oriented policies.

Another threat life insurance companies face is the increasing number of AIDS cases. Profits in the future could be severely affected as the disease takes its toll on more and more lives and insurers are forced to pay out billions of dollars in AIDS-related claims.

Property/casualty insurers face the threat of tighter government regulation. They fear that the consumer revolt that led to passage of legislation in California rolling back auto insurance rates could spread to other states.

Always looming as a threat to the financial solvency of property/casualty insurers is a major earthquake jolting a large city. If a catastrophic earthquake struck Los Angeles, which geologists say is a real possibility within the next thirty years, damage could reach $69 billion, according to government estimates. Insured losses could eat up a substantial portion of the industry's reserves and lead to a wave of insolvencies.

Tremors could ripple throughout the financial community. Massive liquidations of stocks, bonds, and other insurance-company assets to pay earthquake claims could send the financial markets into a nosedive. And mortgage lenders could face massive defaults if there was widespread destruction of uninsured real estate property.

FOOD PRODUCTS: CONVENIENCE AND HEALTH

Convenience and health are the prime forces shaping the diets of Americans. As more women enter the labor force, foods that are quick and easy to prepare are becoming a higher priority. And, as the population grows older, health is becoming an increasing concern, as reflected in the growing demand for low-cholesterol and high-fiber foods.

These trends may be the salvation of food producers in an era of slow population growth. Whereas this slowdown is bad news for an industry that counts on growing numbers of mouths to feed, changing lifestyles should create increased demand for higher-valued food products, such as prepared microwave meals.

Some food producers are also counting on technological breakthroughs, such as Procter & Gamble's "Olestra," a no-calorie, no-cholesterol fat substitute. Olestra, which is undergoing FDA review, could find its way into a wide range of foods, such as french fries and pies, that many people on diets must now avoid.

FUNERAL HOMES: DEATH ISN'T A GROWTH BUSINESS

Death is one of life's inevitables, but it's not going to be a growth business any time soon. The number of deaths that occur each year is not projected to rise much through the end of the century. What's more, American attitudes toward traditional funerals are changing. More and more people are opting for cremations and simpler memorial services in place of big funerals and expensive caskets.

In a few cities, as many as a third to a half of all funerals involve cremation. Overall, cremations now represent about 17 percent of the business, up from about 10 percent in 1980. By the year 2000, the industry predicts nearly one of four deaths will involve cremation.

Funeral homes aren't just worried about the fact that cremations bring in less revenue. A growing number of states no longer require that cremations be handled by traditional funeral homes, opening the door for businesses that specialize in low-cost cremations. Nor can funeral homes count on rising volume to fill the gap. Despite an aging population, people are living longer. Deaths have held steady at around 2 million a year since the 1970s, and the Census Bureau projects the figure will only edge up from about 2.2 million in the early 1990s to just over 2.3 million a year by the late 1990s. Not until the next century will the number start climbing significantly, reaching almost 3 million by 2020 and 4 million in 2050.

Since the death rate remains out of their control, funeral homes have tried peddling new products. The most notable is a prepaid funeral policy, sort of a "pay now, die later" insurance plan. (Unless you're worried that there won't be funds available to pay funeral expenses when the time comes, you can generally do better investing the money on your own.)

GAMBLING CASINOS: OTHER STATES ARE INTERESTED

Gambling is thriving in America, but that has Nevada and Atlantic City casinos worried. The expansion of various forms of legalized gambling across the country and in Canada could mean economic trouble for Nevada and New Jersey in the 1990s. Not only are big-stakes lotteries a threat, but resistance to the idea of casino gambling has been eroding among voters in some states with the expansion of other forms of legalized gambling. Casino gambling is already permitted in parts of Canada, in several Caribbean nations, on cruise ships departing U.S. ports, in Deadwood, South Dakota, and on some Indian reservations in the United States. And the list is about to get longer. Iowa, for one, has authorized riverboat gambling beginning in 1991, and Illinois recently approved a similar measure to keep up with its western neighbor. Casino proposals are being considered in several other states, as well. Expansion of casino gambling would help boost the fortunes of companies that manufacture slot machines and other gaming equipment.

GROCERY STORES: ONE-STOP SHOPPING

Grocery stores have long relied on rapid population growth to spur volume in what is one of the most competitive businesses with the narrowest of profit margins. But with population growth slowing and with Americans spending more of their food dollars on prepared meals, the supermarket industry is being forced to take a different tack. In an attempt to capitalize on growing customer demand for convenience, grocery stores are rapidly evolving into one-stop shopping marts, offering an ever wider array of merchandise, from gourmet take-out to video rentals.

By adding salad bars, bakeries, take-out meals and nonfood merchandise, grocery stores have been able to defend against growing competition from fast-food restaurants, build customer traffic, and fatten profit margins. Grocery stores traditionally operate on the slimmest of profit margins—about 1 percent of sales. Prepared foods and nonfood merchandise offer considerably higher margins.

Grocers are also becoming smarter managers. Bar-code scanners at the checkout stand are used for more than ringing up prices at the cash register. Scanning systems can be programmed to provide a detailed listing of what's selling and what's not, giving supermarket managers the information needed to make quick decisions on product mix, advertising campaigns, and how much shelf space to devote to each product.

One growing problem grocers will face in the 1990s is a shortage of entry-level workers. The problem is critical because grocers are becoming more service-oriented, requiring more people to staff the gourmet take-out, the bakery counter, the video-rental section, and all their other new departments.

HEALTH CARE: BITTER MEDICINE

Efforts by employers, insurers, and the government to contain the spiraling costs of medical care are revolutionizing the health-care industry.

The days when you could go to the doctor or hospital of your choice, get whatever treatment you needed, and count on your company's health insurance plan to pick up virtually the entire tab with few questions asked are coming to an end.

Struggling to control the skyrocketing costs of company health plans, employers are making workers shoulder more of the burden, requiring second opinions on expensive treatments, and steering employees to doctors and hospitals that have agreed to work for fixed or discounted fees.

For employees, the corporate cost-cutting drive is leading to higher out-of-pocket expenses, new restrictions on coverage (such as limits on mental health counseling and preapproval for hospital admissions), and strong financial incentives to seek care only from doctors who are part of a preferred provider organization (PPO) or to enroll in a health maintenance organization (HMO). PPOs are networks of doctors and hospitals that have contracted with an employer to provide services for employees at discounted fees. HMOs agree to provide comprehensive medical care, from routine checkups to major surgery, for a fixed monthly premium. If the HMO's primary-care physician won't approve a procedure you think you need or let you consult with a specialist, you have to pay to go to an outside doctor. Under some arrangements, you'll pay 20 to 30 percent of the bill; in other cases you have to pay the full cost.

Though some companies still give employees the option of sticking with traditional health insurance coverage under which they have free choice of doctors, the employee's out-of-pocket costs are much higher than under HMO or PPO plans. As costs rise, more and more employees will migrate to HMOs and PPOs.

Employees aren't all taking the changes in stride. Many companies have met stiff resistance and even labor strikes when employees have been asked to foot more of the bill and accept new restrictions on health coverage. Another concern is whether the quality of health care will suffer, even though employers contend much of the effort to control costs is aimed at curbing the rise in doctors' fees and eliminating needless tests and procedures. For instance, some doctors worry about the inherent conflict of fixed-fee arrangements. Doctors never had to think twice about ordering another test or keeping you in the hospital a couple more days since fees were based on whatever services were provided. But when a hospital or HMO is receiving only a fixed amount for treating you, each additional test or day in the hospital is affecting the institution's bottom line.

Even employers have been frustrated that their efforts to date have hardly put a dent into the rising costs. But companies are swimming against strong currents. The 1990s are unlikely to bring respite from the spiraling cost of health care—barring a radical overhaul of the system. Demand for health-care services will surge as the population ages and as the number of AIDS cases swells. Promising new medical technologies are also on their way, but they will be costly.

What's more, companies are shouldering the burden of the government's effort to control Medicare costs. Hospitals are charging privately insured patients more in order to make up for what they lose in treating Medicare patients. Medicare provides only fixed payments for most treatments regardless of the actual cost of treating the patient. And those reimbursements haven't kept pace with the rising costs.

With no relief in sight, some major employers have begun to think a radical overhaul of the health-care system may be the only solution, and a few have even endorsed the idea of some form of national health-care system. With an aging population, the debate over how to meet the nation's growing health-care needs without emptying the pocketbooks of American businesses and individuals is certain to heat up. While socialized medicine is not expected anytime soon in this country, the concept of a national health-care system is likely to be debated in the next several years as Congress considers proposals to address the pressing problem of how to protect the 37 million Americans who don't have any health insurance.

In the meantime, hospitals will continue to struggle in the face of inadequate Medicare reimbursements, a glut of hospital beds, and new competition from outpatient facilities. Many kinds of tests, treatments, and emergency-room services that hospitals have traditionally provided are now being performed in doctors' offices and other less expensive settings, such as urgent-care centers and surgical centers. These alternative care facilities are equipped to handle minor injuries and illnesses and certain types of surgical procedures, but they don't need all the expensive equipment and staffing that hospitals do.

Some private hospital companies have been able to improve their financial situation by aggressively cutting costs, building outpatient volume, and expanding into more profitable specialty areas, such as psychiatric care and drug and alcohol rehabilitation programs. Some private analysts believe the financial climate will get better as growing numbers of elderly persons and new medical technologies involving complex procedures increase admissions. Vacancy rates will also decline as the number of hospitals contracts.

Public and nonprofit inner-city hospitals have been hit the hardest. These are the hospitals that end up providing care for most of those Americans without insurance and that have shouldered the costly burden of dealing with the victims of the drug epidemic and the AIDS crisis. Rural hospitals are also suffering large losses and many are being forced to close their doors.

HMOs have also sustained large losses and undergone forced mergers in recent years as a result of overexpansion and stiff competition. But many analysts believe HMOs are entering the 1990s in better shape and that the growing movement toward HMOs will allow them to raise rates enough to permit profitable operations.

(For more on health care, see later sections in this chapter on home health care, medical equipment and supplies, nursing homes, and pharmaceuticals.)

HOME FURNISHINGS: HELP FROM COCOONERS

Furniture makers won't be able to count on the housing market to boost sales since the number of younger adults is shrinking and household formation is expected to slow down. So the middle-aging of the baby-boom generation is likely to be the salvation of the home furnishings industry. Upgraded furnishings are expected to be a high priority of baby-boomers as they entertain at home more frequently. Spending on household furnishings is traditionally high among middle-aged consumers.

The bottom line is that furniture makers are expected to see sales continue to grow but at a slower rate than that of the 1980s.

Competition for baby-boomers' dollars should be fierce. Department stores are trying to cash in on the aging of the baby-boomers by expanding their home furnishings departments, providing new competition for specialty furniture stores.

HOME HEALTH CARE: A BENEFICIARY OF COST CONTAINMENT

With rising medical costs pressuring hospitals to shorten most patients' stays, home health care is one of the fastest-growing sectors of the health-care field.

Home health care is the beneficiary of the industry's increasing emphasis on cost containment as well as of technological advances that now permit more types of medical treatments to be performed at home. Patients also tend to prefer recuperating at home where they can be with their families rather than being stuck in a hospital bed or nursing-care facility.

Care provided in a home is usually far less expensive than that provided in institutions, which is why Medicare and private insurers are so fond of home health care. For instance, the average cost of care for an AIDS patient in 1987 averaged $94 a day at home versus $773 a day in a hospital, according to industry estimates.

While high costs are forcing hospitals to discharge patients sooner, technology has made it possible for patients to go home to recuperate. Microchips make possible a broad array of medical monitoring and infusion therapy equipment for the home. (Infusion therapy involves the administration of antibiotics, chemotherapy, nutrients, and other fluids by intravenous injection or feeding tubes.)

Home health care, although still a small portion of total health-care spending, has been growing at a rate of about 20 percent a year. Not only do firms that provide home nursing services stand to benefit, but also companies that provide home infusion services and makers of home health-care products and medical equipment.

INFRASTRUCTURE: REBUILDING AMERICA

The decay and neglect of America's infrastructure are becoming ever more visible, from collapsing bridges to clogged freeways. Spending on infrastructure has declined over the past two decades, and by most estimates, tens of billions of additional dollars will need to be spent each year in the 1990s to rehabilitate decaying bridges, deteriorating roadways, antiquated water and sewage treatment facilities, overcrowded prisons, and other older structures.

The Federal Highway Administration estimates that 44 percent of all highway bridges are either structurally deficient or obsolete, while more than 25 percent of interstate pavement and over 40 percent of other roadways are deemed in need of resurfacing or reconstruction.

After a two-year study, a government panel recently concluded that the nation's infrastructure was "insufficient to meet the demands of future economic growth and development" and recommended that annual public works spending be increased by 100 percent.

A decaying infrastructure implies long-term opportunities for a range of businesses, including engineering and construction contractors with expertise in public works projects, cement producers, construction equipment manufacturers, and parts of the steel industry.

As the infrastructure continues to decay, major rehabilitation will become an ever-more pressing need. But timing is always uncertain in public works projects, particularly in an era of budget constraints.

MEDICAL EQUIPMENT AND SUPPLIES: NEW TECHNOLOGY AND NEW MARKETS

Manufacturers of medical equipment and supplies are benefiting from the proliferation of alternative care facilities. More and more diagnostic and surgical procedures are being performed in doctors' offices, ambulatory-care centers, and other outpatient facilities. That has vastly expanded the market for the kinds of medical equipment and instruments that used to be ordered mainly by hospitals, which are now on tighter budgets. Home health care is also providing a new outlet for medical equipment and supplies. Even with cost-containment pressures, technological innovations in areas such as laser surgery, which is more cost-effective than scalpel surgery, are expected to keep medical equipment sales in this country and overseas strong.

NURSING HOMES: AN INSATIABLE DEMAND

With the aged population growing rapidly and advances in medical technology prolonging the lives of more and more people, the number of Americans requiring nursing-home care will jump dramatically in the 1990s and beyond.

Thousands of additional nursing homes will be needed to meet the demand. According to some estimates, one nursing home a day would have to be built through the end of the century to fill projected needs.

The primary age group for nursing-home care—age eighty-five and over—is the fastest growing segment of the population. According to Census Bureau projections, the over-eighty-five group will increase 42 percent in the 1990s, reaching 4.6 million in the year 2000. More than one in five Americans over eighty-five requires nursing home or hospital care.

Translating this surging demand into profits is another story. Nursing homes face a regulatory quagmire, rising costs, and relatively low reimbursement rates from Medicare and Medicaid.

PHARMACEUTICALS: GROWTH FROM AN AGING POPULATION

An aging population and an array of new products should create growing demand for pharmaceuticals in the 1990s.

As the elderly population swells, so will pharmaceutical sales, since spending on drugs increases sharply with age. On average, each elderly person uses about ten prescription drugs a year at a cost of more than $300 a year.

At the same time, advances in medical technology and biotechnology are expected to give birth to a wide variety of new drug products in the 1990s.

In addition, more prescription drugs are expected to become available over the counter, offering new growth opportunities for drug companies. With health-care costs rising, Americans are increasingly turning to self-treatment for everyday health problems, and using home diagnostic tests such as blood glucose and pregnancy tests.

But competition in the drug industry is also picking up. Drug companies have been squeezed by growing competition from lower-priced generic drugs as well as the emergence of innovative products from biotechnology companies.

Over the past two decades, the number of generics on the market has tripled, and that number is expected to surge in the next several years as patents expire on scores of expensive brand-name drugs. Once patents run out, anyone can make clones of the drug. Companies that market generic drugs are expected greatly to expand their share of the prescription drug market in the 1990s.

Druggists also stand to benefit from the growing demand for pharmaceuticals. But mail-order companies are starting to make significant inroads.

Mail-order sales of pharmaceuticals have been growing 30 to 40 percent a year. People with chronic diseases and large prescription needs have been attracted in growing numbers to mail-order companies, whose prices are often 20 to 30 percent below what retail druggists charge. Mail-order companies have low overhead and are able to command volume discounts from manufacturers.

PHOTOGRAPHY: THREAT FROM ELECTRONIC CAMERAS

Traditional photography faces formidable challenges from new technologies in the years ahead. Electronic still cameras, which let you take snapshots without film or developing, have recently invaded the American market. Images are recorded on a tiny magnetic disk and can be instantly viewed on your home TV set. The early models, produced by some of Japan's leading electronics manufacturers, are expensive, and the picture quality doesn't measure up to conventional film-based photography. But while electronic photography may not pose an imminent threat, chemical-based photography could face serious competition if engineers are able to improve the picture quality and bring down the cost of "filmless" cameras. Analysts believe that day is years away, but engineers have already demonstrated the capability for major improvements in image quality on more expensive electronic models designed for commercial use.

Eastman Kodak, the leading name in consumer photography, is not sitting idly by; the company has been working on its own version of an electronic camera as well as diversifying into other businesses. Polaroid is also developing an electronic camera.

While still photographers may be a different breed, consumers already have shown their proclivity for electronic photography by embracing camcorders for taking home movies.

Electronic photography poses a dire threat to the photofinishing industry. One-hour photofinishing labs would be devastated if filmless cameras ever caught on in the mass consumer market. Consumers wouldn't have to sacrifice paper prints with filmless photography; electronic camera makers plan to offer color printers as an option.

Regardless, photofinishing minilabs aren't likely to proliferate as quickly as they did during the 1980s; from 1980 to 1988, minilabs were installed at an average annual rate of 50 percent. Some 15,000 of them now dot the American landscape.

REAL ESTATE CONSTRUCTION: A SLOWDOWN IN BUILDING

Demographic trends portend a slowdown in housing construction. With shrinking numbers of young adults and with households being formed at a slower pace, America simply won't need to build as much housing.

Government and private analysts assume that the slowdown will be greatest for multifamily housing construction, which includes apartments, town houses, and condominiums.

Commercial construction is also expected to remain slow for years to come. A glut in vacant office space will take years to absorb in many markets.

Hotels are suffering from high vacancy rates resulting from the over-building that occurred during the 1980s. In resort areas, villa and condo rentals are eating into the hotels' share of package vacations. New construction is expected to focus on all-suite hotels and moderate- and budget-priced lodging.

Far fewer shopping malls will be built in the 1990s. Aggressive building over the past two decades has left America "over-malled" and the mergers of department store chains in the 1980s have left fewer big names as potential anchors for large regional malls. In the 1990s, the focus is expected to be on renovations of existing malls and construction of smaller shopping centers in new residential areas.

Retirement housing should be one of the fastest-growing segments of the real estate construction industry in the 1990s. A burgeoning elderly

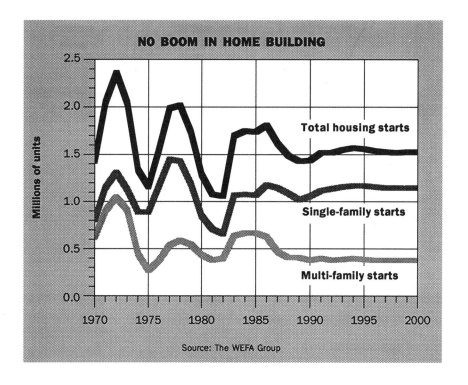

NO BOOM IN HOME BUILDING

Source: The WEFA Group

population promises a growing market for residential developments that cater to the special needs and desires of retirees.

Rental retirement housing offers investors the potential for higher returns than conventional apartments provide. One reason is that residents of retirement communities tend to be less transient than younger people; once settled into a retirement development, residents tend to stay put. As a result, established retirement developments tend to have relatively low vacancy rates and rents aren't as sensitive to competition (residents aren't as prone to move out if the rent is raised a bit more than at nearby developments).

But investors need to be cautious. Retirement housing isn't an instant ticket to riches. For one thing, some cities already suffer from a glut of retirement housing. Demand turned out to be weaker than developers expected, particularly at the luxury end of the market.

Real estate developers also learned that it takes longer to lease retirement housing than conventional apartments. That can be fatal if your investment partnership borrowed a lot of money to build the complex and didn't make provision for a lengthy lease-up period. Once construction is completed, the partnership would have high mortgage payments to make with little income coming in. If the partnership projections are based on assumptions of quick rentals, beware.

To avoid the risk that rental income won't cover mortgage payments in the early stages, some developers are offering investors deals in which little or no money is borrowed. The trade-off is that the profit potential of all-cash or mostly cash projects is lower than in highly leveraged deals.

TEMPORARY HELP: A NEW CORPORATE TREND

Temporary-help firms are benefiting from the growing reluctance of corporations to increase the size of their permanent staffs when business picks up. Instead, corporations are increasingly turning to temps for a variety of transient personnel needs.

But all the extra business that temporary help agencies are garnering isn't showing up on their bottom line. A shortage of qualified workers has forced temporary help agencies to engage in costly recruiting campaigns and training programs. To attract candidates, some agencies have been forced to expand their fringe benefits packages, and to pay bounties to employees who refer friends to the agency.

14

TAXES IN THE 1990s: HOW TO HANDLE YOUR FINANCES IN AN ERA OF RISING TAXES

NOWHERE FOR TAXES TO GO BUT UP

Given the towering budget deficit, federal taxes have nowhere to go but up in the 1990s, and that prospect has important implications for the investments you make and for the strategies you need to employ to minimize your tax burden.

Despite the rancorous partisan debate over the need for new taxes, few on Capitol Hill truly believe that spending cuts alone will be enough to reduce the deficit. The prevailing view on both sides of the political aisle is that sizable tax increases will soon be needed in order to meet the yearly targets of the Gramm-Rudman-Hollings balanced-budget law. Even President Bush's 1990 and 1991 budget proposals contained assorted provisions to raise taxes by billions of dollars, although he chose to call the revenue proposals by other names (such as "user fees") in order to stay semantically true to his pledge of "no new taxes."

What's more, the deficit problem is larger than commonly perceived; the true extent of the budget deficit is being masked by a growing surplus in the Social Security trust fund (to help pay benefits to the baby boomers in the next century) and by accounting gimmicks that hide tens of billions of dollars in government financing "off-budget."

All that appears to be in question is which taxes will be raised, how much they will be raised, and how soon they will be raised.

Despite uncertainty about what's in the offing, it's important to assess the realm of possible tax changes and their potential impact on financial decisions you make now.

COPING WITH THE THREAT OF HIGHER INCOME TAX RATES

With personal income tax rates at their lowest level in more than a half century, growing budgetary pressures would suggest that tax rates can only go higher. Indeed, most tax advisers are planning their clients' affairs on the assumption that Congress will have no choice but to raise income tax rates.

Yet the prospect for higher rates is far less certain than is commonly suggested. Although many Democrats feel that raising rates would be the fairest way to increase taxes, resistance by the Bush administration and Republican lawmakers is so strong that raising rates must be considered a last resort. Raising rates is too visible a way to raise revenue in an era when voter sentiment still runs strongly against higher taxes. So the more likely approach is to raise revenues by less obtrusive means, such as curtailing deductions and raising excise taxes. Few voters ever remember who was responsible for imposing tighter restrictions on some deductions (which politicians can usually explain away as an effort to make the system fairer by closing "loopholes") or for adding a few pennies onto a pack of cigarettes or a gallon of gasoline. But everyone would remember who was at the helm when tax rates were raised, and if they didn't, political opponents would certainly refresh voters' memories. There's no disguising a rise in tax rates as anything but a tax increase.

Those are lessons learned from the 1980s. President Reagan was able to maintain a harsh anti-tax reputation throughout his two terms in office even though he put his signature on three major tax-increase bills—in 1982, 1984, and 1987—none of which tampered with income tax rates.

Nonetheless, the possibility of a boost in tax rates can't be ignored. Should a consensus be reached that the deficit poses a serious enough threat to warrant a major tax increase, then a boost in marginal tax rates could become part of a compromise package.

Most proposals focus on raising the top tax bracket by a few percentage points. One often-mentioned proposal would make higher-income taxpayers pay a 33 percent rate on all income beyond a certain level, rather than the current scheme under which the 33 percent rate applies to only a limited amount of income, with the rest taxed at 28 percent.

In summary, the assumption that has to be made in devising tax-saving strategies is that tax rates are almost assuredly not going any lower but they could well go somewhat higher. That means adopting a much different strategy from the one that was widely employed in the 1980s when tax rates kept declining. In those days, the prospect of lower rates encouraged people to find ways to defer income to a future year so that it could be taxed at a lower rate. Employees asked their bosses to delay giving them their Christmas bonus until after the New Year. Executives and sports celebrities arranged elaborate deferred-compensation schemes. Investors put money into Treasury bills that wouldn't mature or pay interest until the following year. And people who ran their own businesses delayed sending out year-end bills to make sure customer payments didn't arrive until after January 1.

Following such strategies now, however, could mean deferring income into a future year when tax rates are higher. So with the possibility of higher rates in the future, it may pay to realize income sooner rather than later to take advantage of the low rates while they last.

CAPITAL GAINS TAXES: PROSPECTS FOR LOWER RATES

Capital gains tax rates are a different story. They are likely to stay where they are or even decline.

President Bush has made lower capital gains taxes a top legislative priority, contending that it would help spur investment. His crusade has the strong support of Republicans as well as some Democrats in Congress. A bill that would have temporarily reduced the top capital gains rate to 19.6 percent for assets held longer than one year was approved by the House of Representatives in 1989. But efforts to win approval for a similar measure in the Senate were blocked by Democratic leaders who argued that cutting capital gains taxes would disproportionately help the wealthy and exacerbate the deficit problem.

President Bush vowed to continue to campaign for lower capital gains taxes until the battle is won. But even if his initiative fails and a consensus is reached to raise income tax rates, capital gains are likely to be exempt.

Congress can be expected to retreat to the old method of providing preferential treatment for stocks and other investments that were held a certain amount of time. In fact, Congress indicated its intention to do just that when drafting the Tax Reform Act of 1986, which eliminated the preferential treatment of capital gains. Congressional tax writers left intact the statutory structure of capital gains in the tax code to, in their words, "facilitate reinstatement of a capital gains rate differential if there is a future tax rate increase." (Capital gains are currently taxed like wages and other ordinary income, at rates of 15, 28, or 33 percent.)

So with capital gains tax rates likely either to remain at their current levels or to decline, there's no need to rush into unloading long-term stock holdings or certain other investments in order to beat a rise in income tax rates. What's more, the chance that capital gains tax rates could decline offers incentive to hold off selling a stock or a parcel of raw land on which you have a big gain.

Of course, tax consequences should be only part of the decision. If you think your stock is headed into the gutter, waiting to dump it might cost you much more than you stand to save in taxes.

Also be aware that there remains uncertainty over whether Congress would bestow preferential capital gains treatment on all the same investments that used to be accorded special treatment. The capital gains measure approved by the House in 1989 applied to securities, commercial and residential real estate, and timber. But it wouldn't have restored preferential capital gains treatment for collectibles, such as artworks, antiques, or rare stamps.

If you are shopping for real estate, watch developments on the capital gains front closely. Provided real estate is included, a cut in the capital gains rate would likely prompt a wave of property sales. Many people have held off selling appreciated real estate, waiting for a drop in rates. Not many principal residences are likely to be involved since homeowners are allowed to defer paying capital gains taxes on the sale of a principal residence indefinitely (so long as they buy another home that costs as least as much). But vacation homes, which don't qualify for the deferral, as well as investment properties, could well flood the market, depressing prices for a while.

TAKE DEDUCTIONS NOW BEFORE THEY DISAPPEAR

If personal income tax rates go up, deductions will become more valuable, and that prospect might seem to offer incentive to hold off paying deductible expenses until that time. (If the 28 percent bracket were increased to 33 percent, for instance, deductions would be worth 33 cents on the dollar rather than 28 cents.) Trouble is, some of those deductions may be scaled back or abolished by the same tax bill. In fact, the odds of deductions being scaled back are greater than the odds of tax rates being raised. So, unless you're vulnerable to the "alternative minimum tax," the safest bet is to claim deductions while they're still around to claim. (The alternative minimum tax effectively reinflates the tax bills of higher-income individuals who try to take advantage of too many tax breaks. If you fall prey to the alternative minimum tax, you generally want to defer deductions to a future year because most deductions aren't allowed in the minimum tax computation. In addition, you generally want to accelerate income into a year you expect to be hit by the alternative tax because the income will be taxed at a rate of 21 percent rather than the higher regular rates of 28 or 33 percent.)

FOCUS ON ECONOMICS, NOT TAX BENEFITS OF INVESTMENTS

With the prospect that many tax benefits will need to be scaled back by Congress in its search for new revenues, investors need to focus more closely on the economic soundness of a prospective investment rather than the tax benefits. If an investment deal doesn't have a prayer of being profitable without the tax benefits, look elsewhere because the tax benefits may not survive intact.

DON'T BET YOUR HOME ON THE MORTGAGE DEDUCTION

Growing budgetary pressures raise the specter that the home mortgage interest deduction could once again be vulnerable in a revenue-raising effort. The deduction for mortgage interest is one of the most fertile fields to farm for revenues.

As sacred and as politically sensitive as the mortgage deduction may seem to be, Congress has already demonstrated its willingness to tamper with it. The first encroachment came in the Tax Reform Act of 1986, when the mortgage deduction was restricted to first and second homes and new limits were placed on the deductibility of home-equity loans. A year later, Congress went a step further and limited the mortgage interest deduction to the first $1 million in debt used to acquire a first and second home. Never before had there been any limit on the cost of a home. Although relatively few homes are affected by the $1 million cap, the real estate industry fears that the decision could pave the way to a lower cap, just as the medical expense deduction has been steadily tightened over the years. Before tax writers on the House Ways and Means Committee approved the $1 million cap, there was serious discussion in a closed-door session about a $500,000 mortgage cap.

Some proposals go much further. The Congressional Budget Office, outlining various spending and revenue options for reducing the deficit, offered a few suggestions for scaling back the mortgage deduction, including one that would limit mortgage interest deductions to $20,000 a year on a joint return (or $12,000 on a single return). A $20,000 limit would cover only the first $200,000 or so of a couple's mortgage debt. While that kind of ceiling would affect only the most luxurious homes in many communities, the impact of such a cap would be widespread in high-priced real estate markets such as New York and California. It would put downward pressure on property values since the out-of-pocket cost of monthly payments would go up if part of the mortgage weren't deductible.

Vacation homes stand to be hurt the most. When you're financing two homes, $200,000 in mortgage debt doesn't stretch very far.

If recent history is any guide, it's likely that a new cap would not apply to any existing mortgage debt you have. In the past, Congress applied the new restrictions only to new mortgage obligations. But while a cap might not affect your monthly mortgage payments, it would affect the value of your home since a future buyer would be subject to the new cap.

Cutting back the mortgage deduction, especially to a significant extent, is not high on anyone's list. But it is a possibility and thus has to be considered a potential threat to property values. The higher the value of your home, the more vulnerable it is to a change in the mortgage deduction. Congress would be less reluctant to lower the cap to, say, $500,000 than it would to $200,000.

Vacation homes are much more vulnerable than principal residences, not only to an overall cap but also to proposals that put special deductible limits on second homes. Because vacation homes are considered luxuries and are owned by only a small percentage of Americans, an assault on second-home deductions could be expected to draw less political flack than one that would affect deductions for principal residences.

What are the ramifications?

- Don't borrow too heavily against the equity in your home. Should property values decline because of tighter limits on mortgage deductions, you may not be able to sell the home for enough to pay off all your first and second mortgage debt.
- Buy a vacation home for pleasure, not for speculation. Vacation home prices have never recovered from the beating they took when the Reagan administration proposed, as part of its original tax reform blueprint, abolishing the mortgage deduction for second homes. Think of a vacation home as you might a pleasure boat. People buy a boat for enjoyment, not with an eye to selling it someday at a profit; in fact, they assume the boat probably won't fetch as much as they originally paid for it.
- Be especially cautious about speculating on higher-priced homes as investments. They are the most vulnerable to new mortgage restrictions.
- In considering how much to spend on a principal residence, assume the worst will happen on the tax front: that property values will decline—or appreciate more slowly than in the past—because of new

limits on mortgage deductions. So be cautious about buying more home than you need. As an investment, it may turn into a money-losing proposition.

THE THREAT TO PREFERRED STOCK PRICES

Preferred stock could lose some of its appeal under one revenue-raising proposal being considered by congressional tax writers. Corporations have long had a big incentive to invest their spare cash in preferred stock of other corporations. Corporations are allowed to claim deductions for most of the dividend income they receive from investments in other companies' stock. So the dividend tax break encourages companies to buy preferred stock, which offers higher dividends than common stock.

But in recent years congressional tax writers have threatened to scale back the tax break, which would force companies to pay more tax on dividend income. Such a move would have a depressing effect on the market for preferred stock, since the tax break has helped fuel corporate demand for preferred stock and has thus kept prices artificially high.

If the tax break is curtailed, investors holding preferred stock could see the value of their shares decline.

TAXING CASH-VALUE LIFE INSURANCE POLICIES

Cash-value life insurance policies, such as whole life and universal life, were among the few investments to escape unscathed in the Tax Reform Act of 1986, and are thus considered a potential target in future revenue-raising efforts. Investors are able to defer paying taxes on the annual buildup in the cash surrender value of these policies.

Based on past proposals relating to insurance products, any change in the tax treatment of "inside buildup" is likely to apply only to new policies sold as of a given date. So people who buy policies before the tax writers begin their hunt for new revenue targets are not likely to be hurt.

TAXING AWAY MORE SOCIAL SECURITY BENEFITS

Upper-income retirees should be prepared for a possible cutback in Social Security benefits. Making higher-income retirees pay more tax on their

Social Security benefits is an often-mentioned proposal for reducing the deficit. Since 1984, upper-income retirees have been required to pay tax on as much as half their benefits. Various proposals call for subjecting more of their benefits to tax, or limiting cost-of-living increases.

Under current law, retirees face paying tax on part of their Social Security benefits if their income exceeds $32,000 on a joint return and $25,000 for single persons. For purposes of the threshold test, income is defined as adjusted gross income plus tax-exempt interest and half of your Social Security benefits. If your income tops those base amounts of $32,000 or $25,000, then you have to include in taxable income either the amount by which your income exceeds the base figure or half of your Social Security benefits, whichever is less.

MOTORISTS FACE HIGHER GASOLINE TAXES

Motorists can expect to see gasoline taxes rising in the 1990s, if not at the federal level then at least at the state level. State and local governments are groping for new revenues to underwrite the expansion and improvement of their traffic-clogged roadways.

At the federal level, boosting gasoline taxes is mentioned in virtually every discussion about ways to reduce the deficit. The chief tax writer in the House, Representative Dan Rostenkowski, the Illinois Democrat who is chairman of the House Ways and Means Committee, supports the idea. So does Alan Greenspan, the chairman of the Federal Reserve Board.

Most proposals call for a 10- to 15-cent-per-gallon hike in the federal excise tax. Some proponents have argued for a hike of as much as 50 cents a gallon, contending that many other industrialized countries levy more than twice that much tax on gasoline. Each penny increase in the gasoline tax would raise an additional $1 billion in revenue for the federal government.

Not only would a higher gasoline tax help reduce the deficit, but it would also help increase energy conservation and help reduce pollution. Motorists would be encouraged to drive less or buy more fuel-efficient cars and trucks.

But a higher gasoline tax would hurt the trucking industry. It would also hurt people who have to commute long distances to work. That's why lawmakers from Southern and Western states, where constituents tend to drive long distances, oppose any increase in the gasoline tax.

As an alternative, many of those lawmakers prefer the idea of imposing a tax on imported oil. An oil import fee of around $5 a barrel is favored by lawmakers from oil-rich states such as Texas because it would drive up domestic oil prices and thus help American oil producers. Proponents argue that an oil import fee is much more effective than a gasoline tax in promoting energy conservation and reducing the nation's dependence on foreign oil. But an oil import fee has its downside. While gasoline taxes primarily affect motorists, oil import fees raise the cost of oil for all purposes, from manufacturing to heating homes. Because home heating fuel prices would be driven up, legislators from the Middle West and Northeast, where it gets cold in the winter, don't like oil import fees.

Because of the geographic split over the two kinds of energy taxes, some tax writers think a compromise solution might be to spread the burden by enacting both an oil import fee and higher gasoline taxes.

COST OF SMOKING AND DRINKING GOING UP

Alcohol and tobacco are also prime targets for both federal and state lawmakers, adding to the woes of the tobacco and alcoholic-beverage industries.

Faced with cuts in federal aid and a rising demand for services, many states are just as hungry as the federal government for new revenues, and excise taxes on cigarettes and alcohol are a convenient place to start. These "sin taxes" are easy for politicians to rationalize on the grounds that raising them also helps promote laudable social and health policy objectives.

FILING YOUR RETURN BY COMPUTER: IS IT WORTH THE COST?

If you want a taste of the future and a quicker refund check, you can take your income tax return down to a participating tax preparer or financial institution and have it sent by computer to the Internal Revenue Service. Electronic filing of returns, which began in 1986 as a pilot program in various parts of the country, has been expanded to all fifty states.

For the taxpayer, electronic filing offers the advantage of speedier refunds and reduced odds that your return will be bungled by IRS employees. The revenue service claims electronic filing cuts the waiting period for a refund check by up to three weeks. Officials also say it greatly minimizes the chance of the agency making a mistake in processing your return since electronically filed returns bypass employees who keypunch the data from paper returns into IRS computers, a process that is a major source of errors. Tests showed that electronic filing reduced the chance of error to 3 percent from 20 percent. So electronic filing reduces the chance that you'll receive an erroneous query from the IRS asking you to explain some mistake on your return that was actually made by one of its employees.

The IRS has been promoting electronic filing because it saves the agency money, time, manpower, and costly mistakes that can breed a host of other problems. IRS officials have grand hopes for electronic filing. Eventually, they see almost everyone using the system either through their tax preparer or their own home computer. But that day is probably somewhere in the next century.

For now, electronic filing is available only through participating tax preparers and financial institutions and it can be used only by taxpayers expecting a refund. Assorted technical problems, including the method by which taxpayers owing money can make payments electronically, need to be resolved before everyone will be able to take advantage of electronic filing and do it through a home computer.

Thousands of tax preparers and financial institutions have signed up with the IRS to file electronically, so it won't be hard to find someone who can transmit your return—even if you prepare it yourself. But electronic filing doesn't come free. The IRS doesn't charge anything, but tax preparers and other firms usually charge an extra fee for sending your return electronically. Fees typically range from $25 to $45.

Unless you're due a large refund or desperately need the money in a hurry, electronic filing may not be worth the cost. It would take a refund of more than $10,000 to justify a $35 fee, assuming you could profitably put the money to use by getting it back three weeks sooner. (In an account yielding 6 percent interest, the $10,000 would earn nearly $35 during the three-week period.) It would take a refund of more than $7,200 to recoup a $25 fee, and more than $13,000 to earn enough interest to justify a $45 fee. Relatively few people are due such large refunds.

TAX-EXEMPT BONDS: A HEDGE AGAINST HIGHER RATES

Tax-exempt municipal bonds could prove to be a good hedge against any rise in income tax rates. If tax rates go up, the tax exemption would become more valuable since it would shelter income from higher taxes.

That isn't to say that municipal bonds are out of harm's way. Congress has tampered with the tax-exempt status of municipal bonds several times in recent years. Since 1984, middle- and upper-income retirees have had their municipal bonds taxed indirectly; tax-exempt interest is counted as income in determining how much, if any, tax they have to pay on their Social Security benefits. In 1986, Congress took away the tax exemption for new issues of municipal bonds that are used for certain private purposes, such as sports stadiums. Other private-purpose bonds issued after August 7, 1986—mainly industrial development bonds, student-loan bonds, and housing bonds—were made subject to the alternative minimum tax.

If recent history is any guide, Congress would be reluctant to make previously issued bonds directly subject to tax. In drafting the Tax Reform Act of 1986, Senate tax writers soundly defeated a proposal that would have made interest from all types of municipal bonds—both new and previously issued—subject to the alternative minimum tax. Senators strongly objected to the idea of taxing previously issued bonds—which would have caused prices of existing bonds to plummet—but they didn't rule out the possibility of making new issues subject to the minimum tax in the future.

As part of the 1986 tax act, Congress decided to make everyone report on their tax return all of the tax-exempt interest they receive each year—even though most people don't have to pay a cent in taxes on the interest. One reason for the new reporting requirement, according to the legislation, is so that Congress will "have the information available when it considers possible tax changes in the future."

Municipal bonds pay lower interest rates than comparable taxable bonds but the tax exemption can make the return of municipal bonds higher. The higher the tax bracket you are in, the more valuable the tax exemption is. As you can see in the chart on the following page, a municipal bond paying 8 percent interest is equivalent to a taxable bond paying 11.1 percent interest to someone in the 28 percent tax bracket. If you live in a state which has its own income tax, the tax exemption would be even more valuable. Interest is generally exempt from state and local taxes in the state where the municipal bonds are issued. But virtually all states impose taxes on out-of-state bonds held by residents.

Despite the advantage of the tax exemption, municipal bonds are not for everyone. Most people in the 15 percent tax bracket—and even some investors in the 28 percent tax bracket—may find that taxable bonds provide a higher return after taxes. Treasury bonds, for instance, are subject to federal taxes but are exempt from state and local taxes. Even people in the 33 percent bracket will find that tax-exempt money market funds don't always provide a better after-tax return than taxable money funds.

When comparing investments, always calculate the return after taxes (including state and local taxes), and then look carefully at the bond's other features, such as its safety.

Beware of bond funds that seem to offer tantalizingly high yields. A high-yielding bond fund may not reflect the acumen of the fund managers but rather a portfolio loaded with high-risk bonds. Getting 14 percent interest may be wonderful. But how long the party lasts is the question. There is no free lunch, particularly when it comes to high-yielding "junk bonds."

Just as people get paid extra for cleaning up the insides of contaminated nuclear reactors, investors are rewarded with high yields for pouring money into junk bonds. Junk bonds owe their name to the precarious financial position of the companies that issued them. Traditionally, junk bonds were associated mainly with well-established companies that wound up in troubled financial waters with the very real possibility of capsizing. Junk bonds were also associated with young, emerging companies that had just set sail and thus lacked the track record to give investors enough confidence that they would receive interest payments on time and ultimately get back all their principal.

More recently, junk bonds became synonymous with the wave of leveraged buyout deals on Wall Street. Although many of the buyouts have involved well-known corporate giants, these companies don't look as sturdy by the time the deal is done. To finance these kinds of takeovers, the people doing the acquiring end up borrowing heavily against the assets of the company being acquired. So while the company may have been in fine financial shape before the takeover, it now has a mountain of extra debt on its books that needs to be paid off. That may

COMPARING TAX-FREE VERSUS TAXABLE BONDS

A tax-free municipal bond that yields:

Tax Bracket	5%	6%	7%	8%	9%	10%
	is equivalent to a taxable bond yield of:					
15%	5.9%	7.1%	8.2%	9.4%	10.6%	11.8%
28%	6.9%	8.3%	9.7%	11.1%	12.5%	13.9%
33%	7.5%	9.0%	10.4%	11.9%	13.4%	14.9%

not be a problem so long as business remains strong. But if business falls short of projections, then the company may be forced to default.

Despite the risks, many investors felt that so long as they diversified in a lot of junk bonds, the higher yields would more than make up for the losses from any defaults. Whether that would hold true if the economy slowed down or slipped into recession is the question. If business conditions soured, defaults would certainly rise, and if investors panicked, all junk-bond prices could plummet.

Even if the economy doesn't slide into recession, junk-bond holders face another risk around the mid-1990s when the first wave of ten-year junk bonds issued during the leveraged buyout frenzy of the mid-1980s come due. It's likely that many of those companies won't have the money to retire the debt, so they'll be forced to try to refinance the debt with a new junk-bond issue. Such new debt may not receive as welcome a reception the next time around, particularly since there will be many more bonds outstanding than there were in the mid-1980s. These fears could send junk-bond prices tumbling.

Junk bonds are easy to pick out in the bond tables of newspapers. Bonds that yield a lot more than the average are junk bonds. Junk bonds traditionally yield three to seven percentage points more than Treasury bonds. You can also spot junk bonds by looking at their credit rating. Generally, junk bonds are considered those graded BB or lower by Standard & Poor's, a leading credit rating agency, or Ba or lower at Moody's Investors Service, the other leading credit agency.

But even high-grade corporate bonds have to be approached with caution these days. Overnight, a high-grade bond can be turned into a low-grade bond if a new pile of debt is heaped onto the company's balance sheets to finance a buyout. (Such risks are one reason why diversity is always important in investing.) Some bonds now contain provisions to protect bondholders in buyout situations, but these "protective covenants" are difficult for most investors to analyze and don't cover every exigency.

Be aware that a certain breed of municipal bond—industrial development bonds—is subject to similar risks. These bonds are issued by municipalities (usually to encourage a business to locate a factory or some other facility in the local area). But the bonds are effectively backed by the corporation. So if the company runs into financial troubles or becomes the target of a leveraged buyout, the value of the bonds could be affected.

Contrary to popular perception, many municipal bonds aren't backed by the full faith, credit, and taxing power of the local government. When a jurisdiction builds a toll road or bridge, for instance, the bonds used to finance the project would typically be repaid from toll revenues. If traffic on the new facility falls short of projections, bondholders could find interest payments falling short. Similarly, bondholders could get hurt if the facility is damaged or destroyed in an earthquake, hurricane, or some other disaster. That's why it's important to know what insurance or other protections the bond accords investors in the event of a catastrophe—especially if the facility is located in a region vulnerable to earthquakes or hurricanes. Find out what would happen to interest payments if the bridge is damaged in an earthquake and no toll revenues come in for the weeks or months or years it takes to rebuild. Or what would happen to bondholders if a public hospital they financed is destroyed by a hurricane and city fathers decide that it's not worth rebuilding because there are now other hospitals in the region that can fill the gap?

15

THE ECONOMY OF THE 1990s: SLOWER SAILING IN CALMER SEAS

America's economy appears to be headed for slow but steady growth in the 1990s. Forecasts by leading private and government economists agree that the economy is destined to expand at a slower rate than in any decade since World War II. But economists also see the 1990s as a decade of tranquil prosperity—a period of relatively moderate inflation, low unemployment, rising living standards, a higher savings rate, faster productivity growth, shrinking trade and budget deficits, stable or even easing interest rates, and steadier growth.

Demographic changes should make the average household better off than the economic projections suggest. As more women enter the labor force, an increasing number of households will have two paychecks. And with the aging of the huge baby-boom population, more Americans will be in their peak earning years.

As the economy becomes more service-oriented, it will be less prone to the wrenching ups and downs of an industrial-based economy. Forecasters also see the 1990s as devoid of the kind of shocks that jolted the economy in the seventies and eighties, a period in which several major industries were deregulated, inflation surged into the double digits, the dollar plummeted, and energy prices skyrocketed in the wake of two oil crises.

In the decade ahead, the U.S. economy will become even more closely intertwined with the global economy. Exports and imports, which represented only 10 percent of U.S. gross national product (GNP) in 1955, accounted for nearly 26 percent in 1987 and are expected to surpass 32 percent by the year 2000. As a result, America's economic health is becoming increasingly dependent on what happens in foreign capitals and how well American businesses meet the challenge of increasing competition from abroad. With trade barriers crumbling and new industrial powers emerging, more players will be competing in everyone else's backyard.

THE MODERATE-GROWTH SCENARIO

No economic miracles are in sight that would foster a decade of exuberant growth like that of the 1950s or 1960s. The nation's budget and trade deficits, inflation, interest rates, and foreign competition are too high and productivity, investment, and world economic growth are too low to foster another period of booming growth.

Most major forecasters project economic growth averaging around 2.5 percent a year during the 1990s after adjusting for inflation. That's far short of the 3.3 percent annual growth in GNP of the 1950s and the 3.8 percent rate of the 1960s, and even shy of the 2.8 percent rate of the 1970s and 1980s.

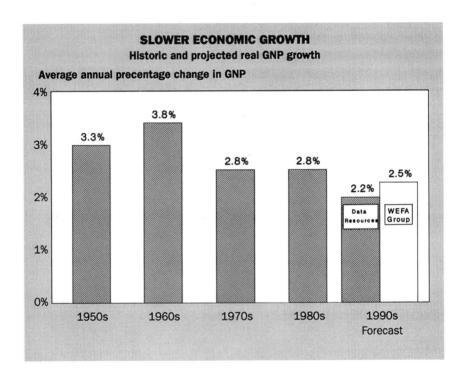

SLOWER ECONOMIC GROWTH
Historic and projected real GNP growth

Average annual precentage change in GNP

WHY INFLATION IS EXPECTED TO REMAIN MODERATE

Intense foreign competition, a worldwide surplus of labor and raw materials, and a determination on the part of central banks to keep inflation in check should help keep price increases moderate through the 1990s.

Most major economic forecasters see inflation held to around 5 percent a year through the end of the century.

Several forces are tempering inflationary pressures. Fierce competition from foreign producers is a powerful discipline, preventing American businesses from raising prices too far. As American automakers, steel producers, and many other manufacturers have learned, setting prices is no longer an insular affair in Detroit or Pittsburgh or any other U.S. city; prices are set in the international marketplace. If American carmakers charge too much, consumers can simply drive down the block to a dealer selling cars made in Japan, South Korea, West Germany, France, Italy, or Great Britain.

This intense competition also makes a wage-price spiral less likely. Even though tighter labor markets in the United States are putting upward pressure on wages, American business is committed to holding the line in order to compete with foreign manufacturers. U.S. companies are adopting new compensation schemes to limit increases in base pay and they are shipping production work overseas to developing countries where wages are lower. At the same time, unions have been losing membership and influence and their power to press wage demands has been further weakened by increasing foreign competition.

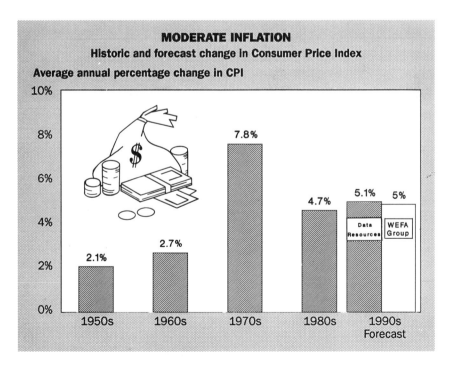

MODERATE INFLATION
Historic and forecast change in Consumer Price Index

Average annual percentage change in CPI

1950s: 2.1%
1960s: 2.7%
1970s: 7.8%
1980s: 4.7%
1990s Forecast: Data Resources 5.1%, WEFA Group 5%

The Federal Reserve has also demonstrated its commitment to keeping inflation in check. After a decade on the front lines of the battle against inflation, the central bank seems determined to prevent a repeat of the inflationary spiral of the 1970s. In addition, the financial markets have proven an effective discipline on policymakers to make sure that inflation remains under control. When investors perceive an inflationary threat, they quickly push up bond yields, and set in motion a self-correcting mechanism for fighting inflation: Fears of inflation send interest rates higher, slowing down the economy to prevent inflation from raging out of control.

Fighting inflation also has much more grass-roots support today than it did a decade ago. More and more Americans have a direct stake in protesting a steep rise in inflation because of the growing prevalence of adjustable-rate mortgages and home-equity loans. Every inflationary surge is reflected in the borrower's next monthly payment. Even those without such a direct stake remember well the double-digit inflation of the late 1970s and the wrenching recession it took to wring inflation from the system. With that memory, investors get jittery when inflation threatens to reach even 6 or 7 percent.

INVESTMENT IMPLICATIONS OF MILD INFLATION

Inflationary expectations bear heavily on the performance of many investments. Some investments thrive on high inflation; others do poorly. In an environment of moderate inflation, collectibles, precious metals, diamonds, real estate, and other "tangible" assets lose an important prop. These investments tend to do best when inflation runs high, as was the case during the 1970s and early 1980s when investors poured their money into fine art, diamonds, gold, and all sorts of other hard assets as a refuge from the ravages of inflation. While other factors can influence the performance of tangible assets, particularly real estate, high inflation can be a driving force.

In contrast, stocks, bonds, and other traditional financial assets tend to fare better in a lower inflationary environment. Most forecasts show interest rates remaining fairly steady during the 1990s, on the assumption that inflation will remain tame and that continued progress will be made in reducing the federal budget deficit.

A RISING STANDARD OF LIVING

Personal incomes should continue to rise steadily through the 1990s, slowly improving the lot of most Americans as the economy expands.

Even beyond this gradual improvement, baby-boomers should be living increasingly well in the 1990s as they approach their peak earning years and most families benefit from two wage earners. What's more, many baby-boomers will inherit appreciated real estate and other assets from their aging parents. Thus the baby-boom generation, who struggled to launch their careers in a crowded job market and then struggled to buy homes at a time of skyrocketing prices, will finally begin to reap the kind of financial fruits that previous generations enjoyed. But they're largely the result of having two spouses working, of fewer children, rising real estate values, and gifts from parents.

The post-baby-boom generation should also do well, reaping the benefits of being a relatively small group. Entry-level jobs will be plentiful and the so-called baby-bust generation will enjoy higher pay because so few of them are around.

UNEMPLOYMENT: EASING CONCERNS

A tighter labor market should keep unemployment well below the levels of the seventies and eighties. Even though jobs are expected to be created at a slower rate in the 1990s, the labor force will also be growing at a slower rate.

Forecasters see the jobless rate averaging about 5 percent during the 1990s, compared to more than 7 percent during most of the 1980s and above 6 percent during the 1970s.

Shrinking numbers of young people entering the labor force should help reduce the unemployment rate, because teenagers and young adults tend to have high jobless rates.

Another reason is the more mature work force. Older workers don't change jobs as often as younger people do and they tend not to be laid off as often.

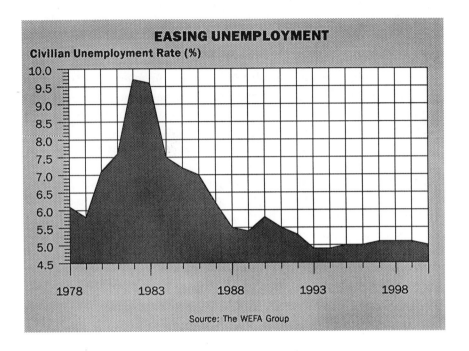

EASING UNEMPLOYMENT

Civilian Unemployment Rate (%)

Source: The WEFA Group

A HIGHER SAVINGS RATE—FINALLY?

An aging baby-boom population offers hope that personal savings in America will finally begin to climb from its abysmally low rate, one of the lowest in the industrialized world.

A higher savings rate would foster lower interest rates and nourish the economy with capital that businesses can use to expand and modernize their factories, laying the groundwork for future growth.

Age has a lot to do with saving habits. Younger people, particularly those under thirty-five, don't do much saving; they tend to spend more money than they make, raising children, buying a house, cars, furniture, stereo systems, and the like. But once they move into their forties, they start to become big savers, setting aside funds for their children's college educations and their own retirement. And so as the baby-boom generation approaches the age when people traditionally save more, economists see the potential for a boost in national savings.

It remains to be seen whether baby-boomers, notorious for their spendthrift ways, will follow tradition. Many economists suspect that baby-boomers won't be able to save much for a while because they waited until a later age to have children and because high housing costs take up so much of their income. As a result, many economists believe the savings rate will only inch up.

For most of the postwar era, the savings rate averaged 6.8 percent of after-tax income, and then declined sharply in the mid-1980s, reaching a forty-year low of 3.2 percent in 1987.

Sooner or later, the baby-boom generation will provide a more substantial boost to the savings rate. It is only a matter of time before they start setting more money aside for their children's college educations and for their own retirement needs.

A LESS LAVISH SHOPPING SPREE

If Americans save more, consumer spending—a major engine of economic growth in the 1980s—will grow at a slower pace in the 1990s.

Personal income won't be rising fast enough to sustain the recent rate of consumer spending. Nor can consumers keep borrowing at the record pace of the 1970s and 1980s to finance more lavish shopping sprees. Their income simply won't support adding more debt at that rate.

Per-capita consumption, a gauge of material living standards, is expected to rise more slowly than in any period since World War II. The WEFA Group forecasts real per-capita consumption to rise at an annual rate of only 1.2 percent a year in the 1990s, compared to 2.2 percent during the 1980s.

So if gauged strictly from a materialistic perspective, American living standards will experience slower growth in the years ahead. This also means that consumer spending won't be propelling the economy to the extent it did in previous decades.

Nor will government spending be a major engine for growth as it was during the 1980s. Large deficits built up during the past decade when spending far exceeded revenues now pose a constraint on new government programs and are forcing drastic cuts in existing programs.

Fueling economic growth in the 1990s, economists say, will be productivity improvements, exports, and business investment.

A REBOUND IN PRODUCTIVITY

Productivity improvements, a key to rising living standards and economic growth in the 1990s, should outpace the lackluster 1970s and 1980s as a result of higher rates of business investment and a more seasoned work force.

Increasing foreign competition and a shortage of entry-level workers have led American manufacturers to invest more in productivity-enhancing machinery and equipment and to take steps to make their organizations more efficient.

Productivity gains in the service industries, which have been elusive in recent years, are finally expected to materialize as a result of increased automation and growing competition in many service industries.

A more mature work force should also help boost productivity. With shrinking numbers of young people entering the labor force, the work force will be dominated by seasoned workers with lots of experience and skills.

Government and private forecasters expect productivity to increase at an average annual rate of 1.2 percent in the 1990s, compared to less than 1.0 percent in the 1980s.

THE COMEBACK OF "MADE IN AMERICA": NARROWING THE TRADE GAP

American-made goods, from computers to agricultural equipment, have received a much warmer reception in overseas markets since the dollar's plummet made U.S. goods more price-competitive. Assuming a continued decline in the value of the dollar against major currencies and further productivity improvements, the trade deficit should continue to narrow. Exports are expected to grow much faster than imports during the 1990s, producing a substantial improvement in the serious trade imbalance of the mid-1980s.

Most economic forecasts assume the dollar will continue to decline but at a much slower rate than in the last several years. A lower dollar makes American goods relatively cheaper in countries with stronger currencies. A lower dollar also makes America a more attractive haven for foreign investors, as evidenced by the Japanese and European buying spree of U.S. companies and real estate in recent years. That trend should continue.

For Americans, a shrinking dollar means imported goods—be they Japanese cars or German wines—become more expensive. If you travel abroad, you'll find the dollar doesn't stretch as far.

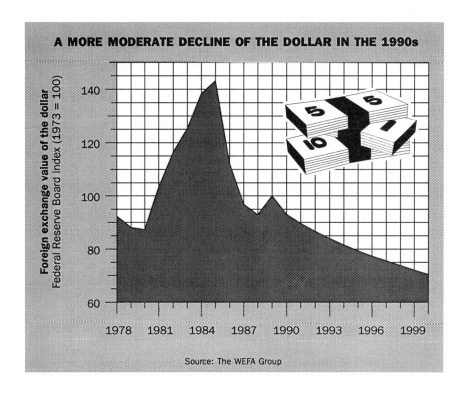

A MORE MODERATE DECLINE OF THE DOLLAR IN THE 1990s

Foreign exchange value of the dollar
Federal Reserve Board index (1973 = 100)

Source: The WEFA Group

WHY THE ECONOMY SHOULD BE LESS VULNERABLE TO RECESSION

As the economy becomes more diversified and more dominated by service industries, the nation should become less susceptible to severe recessions and the roller-coaster boom-and-bust business cycles that have characterized America's economic history.

Structural changes in the economy may go far to explain why the economic expansion that began in 1983 is the longest in peacetime history.

Services are increasingly dominating economic activity and the demand for services is much steadier than that for goods. Over the past thirty years, the goods-producing sector was in recession six of those years while the service sector never went into a recession. Consumers may put off buying a car or a washing machine if economic prospects look bleak, but they are not as likely to cancel visits to their doctor, lawyer, or barber.

At the same time, the economy is not as likely to experience the kind of booming growth that the goods-producing sector has sometimes sparked in the past. Demand for services is much steadier.

An economy-wide slump is also seen as less likely than in the past because the economy has become more diversified and thus better able to withstand shocks. In the past, a slump in a leading sector of the economy often pulled the rest of the economy down with it in domino fashion. But over the past several years, the economy has shown its resilience in the face of severe slumps in the oil and agriculture sectors, as well as the stock market crash of 1987. Rather than a general recession, some economists see the prospect of "rolling recessions" that are limited to particular industries at any one time.

Furthermore, many of the excesses that can turn a boom into a bust are now being wrung from the system before they have a chance to do harm. For instance, companies have become better at managing inventories, so the economy is not as vulnerable as it used to be to excessive stockpiling. The corporate restructurings and cost-cutting of the 1980s have also eliminated a lot of the bureaucratic fat and inefficient operations from organizations. What's more, businesses have become much more cautious about expanding their payrolls or adding plant capacity.

LOOMING THREATS: WHAT COULD GO WRONG

Despite the relatively sanguine outlook, there are lingering problems that, if left unresolved, pose serious threats to the stability of the U.S. economy in the decade ahead.

Growing U.S. dependence on imported oil makes America vulnerable to another energy-price shock, although most oil analysts believe the more likely scenario is for a gradual rise in oil prices during the 1990s. (See chapter 20, Living with Higher Energy Prices Again.)

Mounting Third World debt makes the risk of defaults a looming threat to the health of major U.S. banks, the American economy, and the global economy. But all parties involved, including the debtor nations, have a stake in working out plans to avert the debacle of default.

Another concern is the mountain of debt that corporate America has taken on in the past several years, making more businesses vulnerable in the event of an economic downturn. If the economy were to slip into a recession, many companies would be unable to make the interest payments and be forced into bankruptcy.

The towering federal deficit is another threat. Just as Congress is struggling to shrink the deficit, an economic downturn would send the deficit soaring again as tax revenues fell and social insurance payments rose. Such a situation could put the government into a state of policy paralysis. Tax cuts, a traditional remedy for a slumping economy, might be seen as doing more harm than good. They could cause the deficit to rise even further, frightening the financial markets into bidding up interest rates and bidding down the value of the dollar.

These risks do not necessarily represent the likely course of events. But they do offer reason for investors to diversify in the event that the unexpected happens.

16

THE NEW WORLD ECONOMY

The world economic order is changing. Western European nations are about to lift trade barriers and create a unified marketplace that is almost as big as the United States and Japan combined. In the Pacific Rim, new industrial powers are emerging in the shadows of Japan and South Korea. Hong Kong is headed for a new life under China. And in the Soviet Union and in Eastern European countries, socialist ideology is being replaced by free-market economic ideas that only a few years ago would have been denounced as heretical.

EUROPE: A REVOLUTION IN 1992

If all goes as planned, Europe will become a truly common market by December 31, 1992. The hundreds of barriers that have hampered the free flow of goods and services between the twelve member nations of the Common Market will be lifted and the European Economic Community will become one huge, integrated market of 320 million consumers.

The idea of a common market was established back in 1957, but achieving it has been a long and arduous process. Tariffs were abolished in 1968 but hundreds of barriers to free trade remained.

EUROPEAN UNITY 1992
12 nations of the European Economic Community

Belgium	Luxembourg
Denmark	The Netherlands
France	Portugal
Greece	Spain
Ireland	United Kingdom
Italy	West Germany

Once the barriers are lifted, a French company will be able to sell goods in Germany or Italy or Great Britain as easily as a New York firm can sell goods to people in Connecticut. No longer will trucks waste hours going through customs at each border. Nor will insurers be barred from selling products in each other's markets. Nor will companies need to waste millions of dollars redesigning their products to meet each country's peculiar technical standards; a product that passes muster in one country is good enough for the rest.

After being divided economically since the Roman Empire, European nations finally realized that the trade barriers they had erected to protect their individual economies had kept prices too high for consumers, inhibited economic growth, and kept their corporations from becoming world-class competitors. Companies were unable to exploit economies of scale by expanding efficiently into other markets. When economic unification is finally achieved, car manufacturers will no longer need to redesign cars for each country in order to conform to particular headlight,

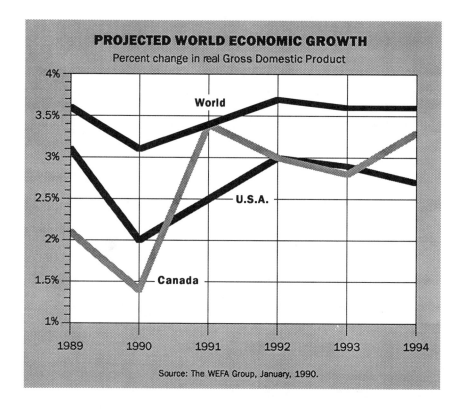

PROJECTED WORLD ECONOMIC GROWTH

Percent change in real Gross Domestic Product

Source: The WEFA Group, January, 1990.

pollution-control, and wiring standards. Food and drug makers will no longer need to get approval from each country before selling. Without controls on currency flows, insurance companies will be able to sell policies throughout Europe and Europeans will be able to invest their money in any country they like.

Companies that already have strong transcontinental operations, such as food and consumer-products companies, should see their costs quickly reduced as layers of bureaucratic red tape are peeled away, product standards become uniform across Western Europe, and distribution costs are lowered by deregulation. Leading companies in financial services and other protected industries will be presented with lucrative new opportunities as they win the freedom to sell their products across national borders. Trucking companies and other common carriers will find new opportunities for expansion once the regulatory road is smoothed for the free movement of goods. Deregulation may even help countries such as Spain and Portugal, who lack the industrial might of many of their Eu-

EUROPE
Projected economic growth
Percent change in real Gross Domestic Product

Country	1989	1990	1991	1992	1993	1994
Austria	4.7	2.3	0.7	1.5	2.5	3.0
Belgium	5.0	2.4	2.7	3.1	2.8	3.2
Denmark	0.7	0.8	1.6	2.9	2.7	2.4
Finland	4.0	1.7	2.5	2.8	2.8	2.8
France	3.6	2.6	2.9	3.2	3.2	3.2
Germany	3.9	3.5	2.1	2.7	2.9	3.1
Greece	2.0	1.2	3.0	3.2	3.4	3.1
Iceland	-0.4	-1.3	0.2	0.7	0.8	0.1
Ireland	4.6	3.3	3.0	3.6	3.2	2.8
Italy	3.4	2.8	2.7	3.3	2.9	2.8
Netherlands	3.8	2.8	3.0	2.7	2.9	2.5
Norway	2.3	1.2	2.2	1.6	3.8	3.7
Portugal	3.8	2.8	3.2	3.4	3.7	3.8
Spain	4.7	4.6	4.3	4.7	4.7	4.5
Sweden	1.8	1.1	2.5	2.7	2.4	2.1
Switzerland	3.0	2.5	1.2	2.1	2.2	2.2
Turkey	0.8	3.2	1.5	3.7	2.9	2.5
United Kingdom	2.2	1.4	2.1	2.6	2.3	2.0

Source: The WEFA Group, January, 1990

ropean neighbors; low labor costs are making Spain and Portugal magnets for new plants and factories in a unified Europe.

But as the economic barriers are lifted, many companies that now are protected will face new competition. Smaller companies may not be able to survive against industrial Goliaths from other countries.

American companies have been expanding their presence in Europe in preparation for 1992. Companies without a strong foothold are linking up with European companies in joint ventures partly out of fear that Europe will decide to build protectionist walls around its new free-trade empire, giving companies inside an advantage over outsiders.

One price of admission Europe is likely to demand of outsiders is reciprocity. If U.S. companies are to be allowed to play in Europe's free market, then European companies should have more access to America's backyard. This could bring new competition in the United States from European companies in such industries as banking and airlines.

While investors have begun placing their bets on the new Europe, the benefits won't appear overnight. For one thing, under the timetable, the deadline for lifting all barriers is December 31, 1992. So an integrated Europe probably won't be a reality any sooner than 1993, assuming that member nations can agree on eliminating all the remaining barriers by the deadline, which is not certain.

Moreover, deregulating Europe is bound to be similar to deregulation of the airline industry in the United States, where airlines entered into costly fare wars trying to force out smaller players and capture market share. Consumers were the first beneficiaries of airline deregulation. Not until years later did the airline industry finally realize the benefits of deregulation.

THE NEW FACE OF EASTERN EUROPE

The political and economic reforms sweeping through the Soviet Union and Eastern Europe represent a historic turning point, and if allowed to continue, should gradually draw increased investment from Western businesses. But the fruits of Soviet leader Mikhail S. Gorbachev's economic reforms will be slow in coming, as will those of the new freedoms in Eastern European countries. It will take many years for most of them to modernize their industries, build confidence in their currencies, and convince investors that the political reforms are lasting.

In the long term, Eastern Europe offers considerable promise. The spread of democracy opens vast new markets for many types of goods

EASTERN EUROPE
Projected economic growth
Percent change in real Gross Domestic Product

Country	1989	1990	1991	1992	1993	1994
Bulgaria	0.5	2.2	1.1	2.0	2.1	2.2
Czechoslovakia	1.5	2.7	2.8	3.2	3.5	3.8
East Germany	2.2	2.2	2.4	2.7	2.9	2.2
Hungary	1.0	1.6	1.7	1.9	1.9	1.9
Poland	-2.2	-0.6	2.8	4.3	4.6	4.6
Romania	1.0	1.0	1.9	2.3	2.5	2.8
Soviet Union	2.5	1.0	1.9	2.2	2.6	3.2
Yugoslavia	2.0	1.5	0.8	1.1	0.8	1.3

Source: The WEFA Group, January 1990

and services from the West. Eastern Europe also offers a source of relatively skilled, low-wage labor for Western companies seeking a low-cost manufacturing base for exporting products to the rich Western European markets.

But while there is plenty of pent-up demand in Eastern Europe for Western goods, affording them is another matter. And while Eastern European workers are relatively well-educated and trained and work for a fraction of the wages that their Western European counterparts earn, managers face the formidable challenges of motivating them and teaching them Western ways of doing business. Western companies also have to contend with outmoded plants, chronic supply shortages, and antiquated communications and transportation networks. Repatriating profits will also be tough in the early stages since Eastern European currencies largely have no value outside their countries.

What's more, the transition from socialism to capitalism carries the risk of political setbacks. The transition will involve painful adjustments that could lead to new economic crises and social tensions. The move to freer markets portends layoffs and unemployment in countries that have long boasted of guaranteed employment for every worker, and the lifting of price controls on such heavily subsidized staples as food and gasoline. Soviet leaders fear secession by several rebellious republics.

East Germany has the most promising outlook as it heads for re-unification with West Germany, a combination with awesome economic potential. Though the union will entail economic and social costs in the short run, a united Germany could well turn out to be to the 1990s what

Japan was to the 1980s. West Germany is already the world's largest exporter.

After East Germany, Czechoslovakia and Hungary have the most promising economic outlooks. Czechoslovakia has a relatively solid industrial base and relatively little foreign debt. Hungary has been experimenting with capitalist policies for several years and has been aggressively wooing Western business, although it is saddled with large foreign debts.

Poland was quick to implement radical economic reforms, but it faces formidable challenges; the economy is plagued by large foreign debts, high inflation, and low productivity.

THE RISE OF THE PACIFIC RIM

While American businesses are now focusing on Europe, more and more of their attention will inevitably be drawn to the other side of the globe. Along the Pacific Rim, new industrial powers are emerging that pose both competitive threats to American business and fast-growing markets for U.S. businesses to tap. Although starting from a smaller base, the

FAR EAST
Projected economic growth
Percent change in real Gross Domestic Product

Country	1989	1990	1991	1992	1993	1994
Australia	4.2	1.2	2.9	3.9	3.7	3.6
China	4.0	3.9	9.6	10.6	9.6	9.6
Hong Kong	3.2	3.7	3.6	5.7	5.5	3.1
India	5.4	5.1	5.2	5.3	5.3	5.3
Indonesia	5.9	5.7	5.5	5.7	6.0	5.9
Japan	5.0	4.3	4.7	4.2	3.9	4.2
Malaysia	8.2	7.6	7.1	6.8	6.6	6.2
New Zealand	0.5	2.1	2.2	2.6	3.3	2.1
Philippines	5.6	4.6	5.3	5.7	5.6	5.7
Singapore	9.0	7.3	6.8	6.0	5.2	5.0
South Korea	6.3	6.7	7.6	8.1	7.5	7.0
Taiwan	6.9	6.7	7.5	6.9	6.8	7.1
Thailand	10.6	10.1	9.6	7.3	6.4	5.8

Source: The WEFA Group, January 1990.

economies of the Pacific Rim are growing far faster than those of Europe.

Japan's global economic influence is expected to continue to expand in the 1990s even though it faces major challenges in sustaining rapid economic growth. Its population is aging, labor supplies are tight, and social services will demand an increasing share of its resources. Its reliance on imported energy makes the nation susceptible to rising oil prices, and it faces increasing competition from its neighbors along the Pacific Rim. And there is the ever-present risk of a major earthquake that could devastate Tokyo and its industrial complex, as one did in 1923. Barring such a catastrophe and despite all the other challenges Japan faces, economic growth is expected to continue to be strong, albeit somewhat slower than in the 1980s. Japan has a highly educated and dedicated work force, a modern industrial base, and well-established research and development into such promising fields as space-age materials, super-computers, industrial automation, high-definition television, and other consumer electronics.

South Korea is the fastest-growing foreign competitor of American manufacturers and is poised to become another major world competitor in the 1990s, rivaling Japan's ascent in the 1980s. Singapore, Taiwan, and Hong Kong have shown the same kind of remarkable growth as Japan and South Korea.

Following hard on their heels, Thailand, Malaysia, and Indonesia are rapidly becoming industrial centers.

One uncertainty in the Pacific Rim is China, the largest enclave of consumers in the world and a nation with the resources, and an entrepreneurial tradition going back many generations, to someday become a world economic power. China's political upheavals in 1989, however, make its future course in the 1990s unpredictable.

Also uncertain is the future course of Hong Kong, long a major financial center linking East and West. In 1997, the British lease on the colony runs out and control of the territory reverts to China. Although Beijing has promised that Hong Kong will be allowed to continue its capitalist system for fifty years, the Chinese government's bloodied repression of the democracy movement in June of 1989 cast doubt on those assurances.

LATIN AMERICA'S CONTINUING WOES

Latin America, once one of the fastest-growing regions of the world, holds enormous potential in the long run. But until the Third World debt crisis is solved, most of these economies will remain bogged down under the weight of huge foreign debts, inflation, social unrest, and political instability. Brazil, one of the world's biggest markets, is plagued by triple-digit inflation. Colombia, one of the strongest economies in the region, is in the midst of a guerrilla war with the country's drug lords.

LATIN AMERICA
Projected economic growth
Percent change in real Gross Domestic Product

Country	1989	1990	1991	1992	1993	1994
Argentina	-5.2	1.6	1.8	1.6	1.4	-2.7
Brazil	1.2	3.7	8.7	6.8	5.2	2.0
Chile	9.3	4.8	4.3	5.2	4.9	3.7
Colombia	1.9	3.0	3.3	3.4	3.3	3.6
Ecuador	-0.3	2.3	2.6	3.4	2.8	3.1
Mexico	3.1	4.3	3.7	2.9	5.0	5.8
Peru	-13.5	2.0	5.0	6.1	3.1	1.4
Uruguay	0.3	4.3	3.1	2.7	3.9	3.4
Venezuela	-4.2	1.1	5.5	6.4	7.1	4.4

Source: The WEFA Group, January 1990

Mexico, with an abundance of cheap labor and with new governmental reforms aimed at encouraging foreign investment, can be expected to attract more American factories to its borders. But absent debt relief, Mexico will find its economic prospects constrained.

Chile, which is probably in the best economic shape of any country in the region, starts the 1990s in political transition, from the dictatorship of General Augusto Pinochet to an elected democratic government, which faces public pressure for more social spending.

INVESTING OVERSEAS

Over the past decade, growing numbers of American investors have poured money into overseas investments, both to diversify their American portfolios and to capitalize on some of the special opportunities abroad. Indeed, a number of foreign economies, such as those of South Korea and Japan, have outpaced growth in the United States, and prospects are that many countries will experience faster growth than the United States in the 1990s as well.

Investing in overseas stocks is often as easy as buying American securities. Stocks of hundreds of the world's leading corporations can be bought and sold on the U.S. stock exchanges, where foreign shares trade mostly as American Depositary Receipts (ADRs). ADRs are negotiable receipts issued by major American banks to simplify the trading of foreign securities and the payment of dividends. ADRs trade just like regular shares of stock, the only difference being that the actual stock certificate is held in the country of issue, usually at the foreign branch office of the American bank that issued the ADR.

Another option is to invest in an international mutual fund. Some funds invest in securities from around the world, while others confine their investments to a particular region, such as Europe, or even a particular country, such as Japan or South Korea.

Mutual funds offer diversity, because they invest in a wider range of stocks than most individuals can afford. Mutual funds also provide professional management, of special value in overseas investing since it's much harder to keep close track of political and economic developments abroad. Information and research reports on foreign companies aren't as widely available as those on American stocks.

In some cases, mutual funds are the only way to invest in a particular country. Some countries, such as South Korea, restrict direct investments by foreigners, so the only way to participate is through a mutual fund. That's why many of these funds that offer exclusive access to a market sell at premiums above the value of the underlying investments; they're the only way for foreign investors to play in that market. (Beware that these premiums could shrink if the country decides to open up its markets to foreign investors.)

Most of these single-country mutual funds are "closed-end" funds, whose shares are bought and sold by investors on the open market. (By contrast, "open-end" funds deal directly with the shareholders, issuing an unlimited amount of new shares and redeeming existing shares as deposits and withdrawals are made by shareholders.)

By making a single-country fund closed-end, the fund manager doesn't have to worry about redeeming everyone's shares if the country's economy sours. If such funds were open-end, the fund manager would be forced to sell stocks in the fund to pay off shareholders at the very worst time—when the market is collapsing.

Single-country funds are among the most volatile of mutual funds because share prices tend to follow the rising and falling tides of a single economy. The problem is that investment analysts frequently come to the same view about a country's prospects at the same time, so fund

MIDDLE EAST
Projected economic growth
Percent change in real Gross Domestic Product

Country	1989	1990	1991	1992	1993	1994
Bahrain	4.2	2.8	2.0	4.3	3.6	3.5
Iran	7.4	5.0	4.3	6.5	3.8	6.2
Iraq	10.8	4.5	12.3	9.4	5.4	3.3
Kuwait	30.2	12.7	5.8	4.4	7.6	3.5
Oman	4.5	2.5	2.4	1.8	3.3	3.0
Saudi Arabia	1.1	1.4	1.0	3.6	3.1	2.1
United Arab Emirates	25.0	1.4	7.4	5.4	8.5	4.5

Source: The WEFA Group, January 1990

AFRICA
Projected economic growth
Percent change in real Gross Domestic Product

Country	1989	1990	1991	1992	1993	1994
Algeria	3.2	3.1	1.0	2.6	1.9	2.2
Cameroon	1.8	0.9	2.3	3.5	3.7	3.6
Egypt	2.3	2.3	2.0	2.3	3.1	3.0
Gabon	4.5	3.5	2.8	3.1	2.4	2.4
Ghana	3.1	3.7	4.3	4.0	4.5	4.2
Ivory Coast	0.9	2.3	3.6	3.5	3.6	3.8
Kenya	3.8	2.6	2.8	3.3	3.7	4.0
Libya	2.4	1.7	1.8	4.2	5.1	5.7
Morocco	3.4	4.0	3.3	4.1	3.8	3.7
Nigeria	2.1	0.4	2.2	4.2	4.1	2.6
South Africa	2.1	0.4	2.9	2.7	3.1	1.9
Tunisia	2.9	4.1	4.0	3.6	4.1	4.2
Zaire	1.6	1.5	2.7	2.7	3.2	2.3
Zimbabwe	4.2	3.3	3.1	4.0	2.7	3.2

Source: The WEFA Group, January, 1990.

investors tend to bail out at the same time. That's why many investors prefer multi-country international funds, which offer greater diversity and give fund managers the discretion to scour the world for investment opportunities.

Foreign investing tends to be more of a roller-coaster ride than investment in American stocks. Most foreign stock markets are puny compared to the American stock market. Their stocks tend to be thinly traded, and thus can be subject to wild price swings. What's more, profits can easily be wiped out by fluctuations in currency exchange rates.

Foreign Bonds: Foreign bonds gave American investors glittering returns in the 1980s, but prospects aren't quite as bright for the 1990s. Interest rates on top-grade foreign bonds are often about the same as or even lower than those offered in the United States. What made foreign bonds such stellar performers in the 1980s was the sharp decline in the value of the U.S. dollar. Thus, their effective yields were enhanced as the foreign currencies in which they were denominated appreciated in value relative to the dollar. Most economists believe the value of the dollar will continue to fall in the 1990s, but not as steeply as in the 1980s.

COUNTRIES RANKED BY POPULATION
Projected population 1990–2000
(in millions)

	1990	2000
1. China	1,115	1,242
2. India	850	1,013
3. Soviet Union	291	312
4. U.S.A.	250	268
5. Indonesia	191	227
6. Brazil	158	195
7. Japan	124	129
8. Nigeria	119	161
9. Bangladesh	116	145
10. Pakistan	113	145
11. Mexico	87	104
12. Vietnam	68	86

Source: U.S. Census Bureau

17

AMERICA'S MECCAS FOR THE 1990s: WHERE THE GROWTH AND OPPORTUNITIES WILL BE

How well you live in the 1990s will depend to a significant degree on where you live. Population and economic growth are expected to vary sharply across the country. While the Farm Belt is losing population and the industrial Northeast is growing slowly, the Far West and the Sun Belt are mushrooming with new settlers and new businesses.

Despite vast stretches of economic despair in the South and major pockets of prosperity scattered through the North, America's future growth is clearly headed southward and westward. It is the Far West and the South to which population is migrating, where fast-growing high-technology and service industries are clustered, and where businesses are choosing to expand their operations. More than half of the nation's population growth in the 1990s is projected to occur in three Sun Belt states (California, Texas, and Florida) and most of the decade's fastest-growing job markets are expected to be sprinkled in the western and southern regions, from the Los Angeles Basin to the Florida Gold Coast.

As an indication of the magnitude of the geographic shift, the Northeast, once the most populous region, will soon become the least populated. While New York State's population is projected to expand by about 200,000 during the 1990s, California is expected to add more than 4 million, and Florida and Texas are expected to pick up an additional 2.5 million residents each.

What's more, the explosive growth in the Far West and the slowdown in the Northeast are creating a bicoastal economy. New York City still reigns as the nation's leading financial, communications, and cultural center, but its growth is slowing and its dominance is eroding; Los Angeles, meanwhile, is a fast-growing commercial and international trade center positioned as the gateway to the burgeoning Pacific Rim.

FASTEST-GROWING JOB MARKETS
1988-2000 Forecast

Metropolitan Statistical Area	Percent Growth	Numerical Job Gain
1. Fort Myers, Fla.	61.1%	113,000
2. Naples, Fla.	55.7%	39,000
3. Fort Pierce, Fla.	53.6%	52,000
4. Anaheim-Santa Ana, Calif.	50.8%	807,000
5. West Palm Beach-Boca Raton-Delray Beach, Fla.	49.1%	260,000
6. Orlando, Fla.	45.5%	313,000
7. Ocala, Fla.	45.5%	35,000
8. Bryan-College Station, Tex.	43.5%	27,000
9. Santa Rosa-Petaluma, Calif.	43.4%	89,000
10. Boulder-Longmont, Colo.	41.3%	62,000
11. Las Vegas	41.3%	169,000
12. Oxnard, Ventura, Calif.	41.3%	135,000
13. Fort Lauderdale-Hollywood-Pompano Beach, Fla.	41.2%	284,000
14. Bradenton, Fla.	40.2%	33,000
15. Fort Collins-Loveland, Colo.	40.2%	39,000
16. Portsmouth-Dover-Rochester, N.H.	39.7%	71,000
17. Phoenix	39.3%	491,000
18. Sarasota, Fla.	38.8%	64,000
19. Fort Walton Beach, Fla.	38.5%	30,000
20. Santa Fe, N.M.	38.2%	26,000

Source: NPA Data Services Inc.

BOOMTOWNS OF THE 1990S

Most of the fastest-growing job markets, according to forecasts by NPA Data Services, Inc., of Washington, D.C., are second-tier cities that are adding jobs at a rapid rate to relatively small employment bases. These boomtowns tend to be magnets for high-tech and service businesses, offering affordable room to expand, proximity to major metropolitan areas, affordable housing, and attractive amenities to lure an ample supply of educated and skilled workers—the lifeblood of tomorrow's growth industries.

Southern Florida tops the list of the fastest-growing job markets. Florida has been drawing more than retirees, tourists, and new attractions at Walt Disney World to its sun-drenched shores. Low taxes, low wages, major airports, seaports, and enough golf courses to keep any chief executive officer happy have been strong magnets for high-tech, service, and entrepreneurial enterprises. And the warm weather, affordable housing, and promise of good jobs are drawing thousands of new settlers to Florida each week.

California is another strong draw for people and jobs. In northern California, Silicon Valley, a hotbed of high technology, is expected to continue to have strong job and population growth, albeit at a slower pace than in the 1970s and 1980s when the electronics industry was rapidly expanding. In southern California, traffic congestion, pollution, high housing costs, and defense cutbacks may prevent Los Angeles from repeating its explosive growth of the 1980s. But the region is still expected to be one of the fastest growing in the nation, with both population and jobs being pushed farther into the suburbs, making boomtowns out of once-sleepy communities like Anaheim and Oxnard.

The major earthquake that jolted northern California in 1989 heightened awareness of the seismic threat facing the state and could slow the inflow of new settlers and jobs. Some businesses may well choose to

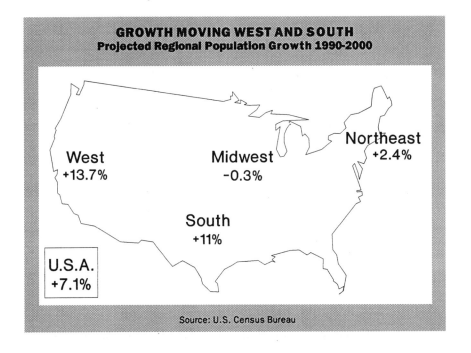

GROWTH MOVING WEST AND SOUTH
Projected Regional Population Growth 1990-2000

West +13.7%

Midwest -0.3%

Northeast +2.4%

South +11%

U.S.A. +7.1%

Source: U.S. Census Bureau

expand or relocate at least part of their operations elsewhere. But California is a hard state for businesses to leave or ignore in their expansion plans. It has a huge internal economy (one of the largest in the world), a rapidly growing population, and, with geological assurances that it won't fall into the ocean, California has the geographic advantage of being the first mainland stop for expanding trade with the Pacific Rim.

Other western cities, such as Phoenix, Seattle, Portland, and Sacramento, are also likely to benefit from the western migration, advertising themselves to high-tech and service firms as lower-cost alternatives to Silicon Valley and Los Angeles.

The fast-growing job markets of the 1990s are different from the boomtowns of a decade or two ago. When oil was booming and basic manufacturing was expanding, the fastest-growing cities were those that were rich in natural resources, like Houston and Denver, or smaller communities that offered cheap land, cheap labor, and tax incentives to lure new factories. But oil prices aren't expected to rise much in the near future and the growth businesses of the 1990s are looking for much different locations. High-tech and service firms don't care as much about cheap land and tax incentives as they do about having a reservoir of educated and skilled workers to draw from.

That's why the fastest-growing job markets are expected to be in metropolitan areas or university towns that offer the social and cultural amenities to attract an ample supply of skilled and educated workers.

THE URBAN CENTERS

Major metropolitan areas will continue to dominate the job market of the 1990s. Most of the cities expected to have the largest actual gains in employment in the 1990s are the large urban centers that currently have the most jobs. Of course, that doesn't necessarily connote economic dynamism since a city with a large employment base can have a large increase in jobs without growing very much, as is the expectation for Chicago and Philadelphia, where job growth is expected to be below the national average. Many other cities with large employment gains—including many of those that experienced rapid growth during the 1980s, such as Los Angeles, Boston, Baltimore, Miami, and St. Louis—are expected to achieve employment growth that runs no better than about the national average for the 1990s.

Houston and Dallas are expected to add a large number of jobs at a rapid rate. But their quick growth largely reflects a recovery from the oil bust of 1985 to more normal growth patterns. Both cities are resurging with more diversified economies. Depressed real estate prices are also helping to lure corporate headquarters offices from high-cost northeastern cities.

By contrast, Anaheim, San Jose, Fort Lauderdale, and Orlando are examples of booming cities creating large numbers of jobs at a rapid pace.

Anaheim, as a suburb of Los Angeles, is also an example of where growth in major metropolitan areas is occurring the fastest: on the suburban fringes.

People are moving to suburbs in search of more affordable housing and to escape the problems of the inner city, and businesses are moving to the suburban fringes in search of cheaper and roomier quarters.

CITIES WITH LARGEST PROJECTED EMPLOYMENT GAINS
1988-2000 Forecast

Metropolitan Statistical Area	Numerical Job Gains	Percent change
1. Los Angeles-Long Beach	822,000	15.8%
2. Anaheim-Santa Ana, Calif.	807,000	50.8%
3. Washington D.C.-Md.-Va.	730,000	26.5%
4. Atlanta	613,000	33.7%
5. Houston	607,000	33.6%
6. Dallas	604,000	36.0%
7. San Diego	493,000	34.3%
8. Phoenix	491,000	39.3%
9. Boston-Lawrence-Salem-Lowell Brockton, Mass.	401,000	16.2%
10. Seattle	400,000	30.1%
11. San Jose, Calif.	388,000	36.7%
12. Tampa-St. Petersburg -Clearwater, Fla.	383,000	34.4%
13. Denver	348,000	32.8%
14. Riverside-San Bernadino, Calif.	319,000	32.6%
15. Minneapolis-St. Paul	315,000	21.2%
16. Nassau-Suffolk, N.Y.	314,000	20.7%
17. Orlando, Fla.	313,000	45.5%
18. Chicago	295,000	8.2%
19. Sacramento, Calif.	289,000	34.7%
20. Fort Lauderdale-Hollywood- Pompano Beach, Fla	284,000	41.2%

Source: NPA Data Services Inc.

With fax machines, computers, and advances in telecommunications, many businesses are no longer tied to expensive downtown office space. If prices get too expensive, they can easily relocate at least part of their operations to cheaper space out in the suburbs. In the Washington, D.C., area, the most rapid growth is taking place in suburban Virginia. In the Atlanta area, the fastest growth is taking place in Gwinnett and Cobb counties. In New York City, Wall Street firms have shifted many of their back-office operations to less costly quarters in suburban New Jersey.

One of the greatest economic challenges facing New York and other high-cost cities in the 1990s is trying to keep firms from fleeing to less costly areas. The recent relocation announcements by the Exxon Corporation, the Mobil Corporation, and J. C. Penney cited the high cost of operating in Manhattan as a reason for moving their corporate headquarters to other cities. NPA Data Services projects that New York City employment—hit hard by the cutbacks on Wall Street in the wake of the 1987 stock market crash—will decline slightly in the early 1990s, but then edge back up in the latter half of the decade as the financial services industry rebounds. Wall Street securities firms and major banks should benefit from the globalization of the international marketplace. For the region as a whole, employment is forecast to expand about 7 percent during the decade.

The Los Angeles–Long Beach area recently surpassed New York City (including Westchester County) in terms of both jobs and population. (If northern New Jersey, southern Connecticut, and Long Island are included in the count, the greater New York region is still number one, with an estimated 18.6 million residents and 10.8 million jobs in 1990. But the sprawling Los Angeles economic region, with an estimated 14.9 million residents and 8.9 million jobs in 1990, is projected to add population and jobs at several times the rate of New York during the decade.)

STATE POPULATION WINNERS & LOSERS

State	Projected Population 1990	Projected Population 2000	Percent Change
Alabama	4,180,000	4,410,000	5.5%
Alaska	580,000	690,000	19.2%
Arizona	3,750,000	4,620,000	23.1%
Arkansas	2,430,000	2,530,000	4.2%
California	29,130,000	33,500,000	15.0%
Colorado	3,430,000	3,810,000	11.0%
Connecticut	3,280,000	3,450,000	5.1%
Delaware	670,000	730,000	10.2%
Florida	12,820,000	15,420,000	20.3%
Georgia	6,660,000	7,960,000	19.4%
Hawaii	1,140,000	1,350,000	17.9%
Idaho	1,020,000	1,050,000	3.0%
Illinois	11,610,000	11,580,000	− 0.3%
Indiana	5,550,000	5,500,000	− 0.9%
Iowa	2,760,000	2,550,000	− 7.6%
Kansas	2,490,000	2,530,000	1.5%
Kentucky	3,740,000	3,730,000	− 0.3%
Louisiana	4,510,000	4,520,000	0.1%
Maine	1,210,000	1,270,000	4.9%
Maryland	4,730,000	5,270,000	11.5%
Massachusetts	5,880,000	6,090,000	3.5%
Michigan	9,290,000	9,250,000	− 0.5%
Minnesota	4,320,000	4,490,000	3.8%
Mississippi	2,700,000	2,880,000	6.6%
Missouri	5,190,000	5,380,000	3.7%
Montana	800,000	790,000	−1.4%
Nebraska	1,590,000	1,560,000	− 2.0%
Nevada	1,080,000	1,300,000	21.1%
New Hampshire	1,140,000	1,330,000	16.7%
New Jersey	7,900,000	8,550,000	8.2%
New Mexico	1,630,000	1,970,000	20.5%
New York	17,770,000	17,990,000	1.2%
North Carolina	6,690,000	7,480,000	11.8%
North Dakota	660,000	630,000	− 4.7%
Ohio	10,790,000	10,630,000	− 1.5%
Oklahoma	3,280,000	3,380,000	2.8%
Oregon	2,770,000	2,880,000	4.0%
Pennsylvania	11,830,000	11,500,000	− 2.7%
Rhode Island	1,000,000	1,050,000	4.6%
South Carolina	3,550,000	3,910,000	10.1%
South Dakota	710,000	710,000	0.8%
Tennessee	4,970,000	5,270,000	5.9%
Texas	17,710,000	20,210,000	14,1%
Utah	1,780,000	1,990,000	12,1%
Vermont	560,000	590,000	5,1%
Virginia	6,160,000	6,880,000	11.7%
Washington	4,660,000	4,990,000	7.2%
West Virginia	1,860,000	1,720,000	− 7.3%
Wisconsin	4,810,000	4,780,000	− 0.5%
Wyoming	500,000	490,000	−2.6%
Washington, D.C.	610,000	630,000	3.2%
United States	**249,890,000**	**267,750,000**	**7.1%**

Source: U.S. Census Bureau.

18

URBAN GRIDLOCK

COMMUTING TO BECOME A LONGER, COSTLIER AGONY

From the Ventura Freeway in Los Angeles to the Beltway in Washington, D.C., America's roadways are approaching gridlock. Traffic is swelling beyond the capacity of the nation's thoroughfares, and neither sufficient funds nor sufficient space for roadway expansion are expected to become available to prevent traffic congestion in many American cities and suburbs from reaching crisis dimensions in the 1990s.

TOP 15 URBAN AREAS OF TRAFFIC CONGESTION

1984	2005
1. Houston	1. Charlotte
2. New Orleans	2. Houston
3. New York	3. Detroit
4. Detroit	4. San Antonio
5. San Francisco	5. Dallas
6. Seattle	6. Miami
7. Los Angeles	7. New Orleans
8. Boston	8. Seattle
9. Charlotte	9. Boston
10. Atlanta	10. San Francisco
11. Minneapolis	11. Washington D.C.
12. Dallas	12. Baltimore
13. Norfolk	13. Phoenix
14. Chicago	14. New York
15. Denver	15. Los Angeles

Note: Projections assume no future improvements.
Rankings based on total delays per million vehicle miles traveled.

Source: U.S. Department of Transportation

Without major improvements, freeway commutes in major urban areas will take more than 50 percent longer by the end of the decade than they do today, according to various government and private studies. On urban freeways, where the average speed is now 30 to 40 miles per hour, growing congestion is expected to slow speeds down to 20 to 30 miles per hour by the year 2000.

Traffic jams are no longer confined just to urban centers. Suburban sprawl has brought all-day traffic snarls to once-sleepy bedroom communities where city dwellers used to seek refuge from urban traffic and pollution. No more. Congestion in the suburbs is increasing at a faster rate than in central-city areas. And in many metropolitan areas, rush hour is an all-day affair; traffic is nearly as congested at noon as it is at 8:00 A.M. or 5:00 P.M.

Growing congestion means Americans will be spending more time and more money driving to and from work. It will aggravate pollution and threaten new development. It will erode property values of homes located along noise-ridden routes of swelling traffic as well as homes in outlying areas requiring intolerably long commutes. It will add billions of dollars in wasted fuel and lost productivity each year as salespeople and delivery trucks waste valuable hours stalled in traffic. It will force more employers to stagger work hours. It will affect where people choose to live, how they get to work, where they work, and where economic development takes place.

Traffic congestion already tops the list of citizen concerns in many communities, and as the problem grows worse, politicians will face difficult choices on how to prevent their roadways from becoming gridlocked parking lots and roadblocks to economic development.

Mass Transit: No Longer Seen as Panacea

Few cities have major mass-transit projects on the drawing boards, but even if more did, mass transit doesn't appear to be the solution to the traffic mess in most metropolitan areas. Subways and heavy rail systems used to be viewed as the panacea for traffic congestion in the days when most people worked downtown. Fixed rail lines could be built along heavily traveled corridors leading in and out of the city center.

But commuting patterns have changed. Downtown is no longer where most people work; businesses have migrated to outlying areas in such large numbers in recent years that a majority of metropolitan jobs are now located in the suburbs. Offices and factories are now sprinkled all over metropolitan areas, from downtown to distant suburbs, and commuting patterns have become helter-skelter. While many people still go from suburb to downtown, others commute from city to suburb, and still others travel from suburb to suburb. Transportation patterns now look like a child's doodle rather than a neat hub-spoke bicycle tire conducive to mass transit. With job locations so widely dispersed and trips beginning in so many diverse locations, the mass transit solution becomes more complicated. For the same reason, car pools are failing to attract much interest.

All this means that reliance on the auto is growing, rather than diminishing. It is far from what science fiction writers imagined. Futuristic visions of everyone being whisked to work downtown on sleek high-speed monorail systems didn't figure that factories and offices would migrate to the suburbs.

Road Building Won't Catch Up to Demand

No one seriously believes America will be able to build itself out of traffic jams. Highway construction has lagged far behind traffic growth. Whereas the number of cars increased 54 percent between 1970 and 1985, the number of miles of roads and highways increased by only 4 percent. Federal and state governments have failed to come up with enough money to prevent the existing road system from deteriorating further, let alone expand it. With the interstate highway system scheduled for completion in 1991, the federal government, constrained by huge budget deficits, hasn't shown much interest in any major new road-building effort. State capitals, struggling through their own period of fiscal austerity, aren't eager to embark on any budget-busting road-building programs either.

But construction faces more than financial roadblocks. Finding room to expand existing highways and build new roadways is proving next to impossible in many cities overgrown with development. Paving over developments of $200,000 homes is not a realistic option.

Band-Aid Solutions

With a paucity of traditional options, traffic engineers are looking at patchwork solutions to the traffic crunch. In situations where freeway expansion is constrained by space, highway shoulders are being sacrificed to make way for one or two additional traffic lanes. Adding second decks, although expensive, is another option being considered for some clogged freeways hemmed in by development.

Lack of government financing has even led private enterprise to give serious thought to building and operating toll roads. Private toll roads, which are common in Europe and the Far East, are already on the drawing boards in Virginia, Colorado, and Illinois. The Virginia project would connect Dulles Airport with Leesburg, Virginia. In Colorado, a 200-mile private tollway would run from Pueblo to Fort Collins. And in the Midwest, plans call for a 400-mile tollway between Chicago and Kansas City.

Ferry service has been revived in Boston and New Jersey, and other coastal cities are considering the same. Underutilized Amtrak and freight-train tracks are also being reassessed as relatively low-cost ways to start commuter rail lines, as was recently done between West Palm Beach and Miami.

Some communities are soliciting the help of employers to stagger work hours and promote ride sharing among employees. Most such programs are voluntary. But in some cases, employers are required by local ordinance to reduce the number of employees driving to work alone during rush hours. In Pleasanton, California, for instance, a local ordinance requires employers and developers to reduce single-occupancy car trips during the rush hours by 45 percent over four years.

Employer involvement is bound to make flexible work hours more common. It may also lead to more employees being allowed to "telecommute" from home, one or more days a week.

Voters in a growing number of communities have taken more drastic steps, approving ballot initiatives to ban development that breeds more traffic. While the anti-growth movement offers a quick and easy solution to mounting traffic congestion, it can also lead to a community's economic stagnation, stopping the flow of jobs and additional tax revenues.

High-tech Solutions: Automated Tollbooths

Given the prospect of relatively little in the way of new roads in the 1990s, traffic engineers are looking to technology for ways to make traffic flow more smoothly on existing roadways.

Automated tollbooths, which have undergone successful tests in the United States and Europe, represent one solution to the backups that routinely occur at toll plazas on bridges and tollways. All a motorist needs is a special identification tag to display under the fender or inside the windshield. At the tollbooth, an electronic radio device scans the tag, which contains information on the owner's identity, and the computer records the toll charge. Depending on the system, the toll may be charged to the driver's credit card or to a prepaid account, or the driver may receive an itemized bill from the tollway authority every month or so.

There is no need to stop at the tollbooth. The identification tag can be scanned while you cruise through the toll plaza.

An automated toll system is already in place at Dallas's North Tollway. After being successfully tested on the San Diego–Coronado Bridge, an automatic collection system was scheduled to be installed on San Francisco's Golden Gate Bridge. A system was also planned for the Dulles Toll Road in suburban Washington, D.C.

"Smart Streets," "Smart Cars"

High technology also offers hope for easing traffic conditions on city streets. A goal of traffic engineers is to make streets electronically smart enough to monitor themselves and transmit information on road conditions to traffic control centers and motorists.

In Los Angeles, New York, and some other cities, sensors are being embedded in streets and highways to monitor traffic flow. The information from these sensors is then relayed to central computers to adjust the timing of traffic lights.

On the horizon are systems that transmit the information gathered from the street sensors—along with advice on less-congested alternate routes—to motorists. Europe is in the midst of a major test of such a system. In London and West Berlin, information on traffic conditions is transmitted to thousand-dollar navigating computers on board test vehicles.

This is how it works: The driver punches in his destination on the device, which figures out the optimal route based on up-to-the-minute traffic information. As the car starts moving, so does an arrow on the dashboard-mounted computer display screen, pointing in the direction the driver should be going. When the car approaches an intersection where the driver needs to make a turn, an electronic voice tells the driver to get into the right or left lane. As the driver reaches the intersection where the turn is to be made, the electronic voice says, "Turn right" or "Turn left."

Along the way, the on-board computer digests incoming traffic information and modifies planned routes as traffic conditions change.

In the United States, a much smaller experiment is under way in Southern California.

A more primitive system, using radio broadcasts and billboard-type message signs along the highway—rather than on-board computers—is planned for the mid-1990s in the San Francisco Bay Area.

An Early Entry in Navigating Your Way

In the United States, it will probably be many years before you can count on being guided around town by dashboard navigation systems linked to "smart streets." But a new computerized device is making its way into some commercial vehicles in the United States as well as some personal autos in Europe and Japan to help drivers find their way through unfamiliar neighborhoods. The system won't steer you away from congested areas since it doesn't communicate with smart streets or traffic operations centers. All the device does is guide you to your destination.

Using a compact disk to store its maps, the computerized device guides you to your destination on a video screen. Once you tell the system where you are and where you want to go, the system keeps track of where you are along the route by assessing the car's speed and the turning angles of the front wheels.

An early entrant to the field is Etak, Inc., of Menlo Park, California, whose U.S. licensee is the General Motors Corporation. Its European licensee was scheduled to begin selling the navigation device in Germany for about $3,000.

It will probably be years before prices drop enough to attract a mass market for the device. In the face of a $3,000 price tag, pulling to the side of the road to look at a 50-cent paper map will probably do for the time being for most people.

THE HIGHER COST OF DRIVING TO WORK

Driving to work is destined to become not only a much longer agony in the 1990s but also a much more expensive proposition. As congestion grows worse, and state and local governments look for ways to help finance transportation improvements, drivers will face higher tolls, higher parking fees, higher gasoline excise taxes, and higher registration fees.

Imposing higher charges directly on motorists can also be rationalized as a means of encouraging more people to join car pools or use public transit.

Parking fees are already climbing. In dense downtown areas, parking-lot fees are being driven up as the number of cars increases. But supply and demand may be only the beginning of spiraling parking costs. Some local governments have their eye on parking fees as a way to reduce traffic. In the Los Angeles Basin, a radical plan to reduce air pollution calls for the elimination of free parking and the imposition of higher parking fees on cars that carry only one person. The plan also calls for sharply higher registration fees for families with more than one car. Other cities may well be forced to take similar drastic measures to meet federal clean-air standards.

Growing congestion also makes the federal income tax exemption for employee parking vulnerable. Traffic planners have long argued that the exemption should be repealed because it encourages people to drive to work. Company-paid parking is one of the few fringe benefits that remains exempt from tax. If the exemption were repealed, motorists could end up paying hundreds of dollars a year in extra taxes for their company-paid parking spots.

The $15 Toll

Crises often demand radical solutions, and some traffic planners think the only way to resolve the traffic mess is to impose exorbitant fees on motorists who drive during peak periods. A stiff toll would force motorists to consider alternatives, such as car pools, public transit, or working staggered hours so they could commute during off-peak periods. Traffic congestion would quickly be eased, and drivers willing to pay the steep price could cruise to work during rush hour.

It has worked before. Facing chronic congestion in its downtown area, Singapore required motorists to purchase special stickers in order to gain access to downtown streets during morning rush hour. Overall traffic was cut by 40 percent.

Rather than taking up Singapore's sticker approach in this country, traffic planners are looking at high-tech ways of pricing roadways. They envision cars being equipped with electronic identification tags (such as those used for automated toll collection) that could be read electronically by roadside equipment. Drivers would receive a monthly bill.

In California, Randall Johnston Pozdena, an economist at the Federal Reserve Bank of San Francisco, recently proposed the idea of charging peak-period highway tolls of 65 cents a mile in central urban areas, 21 cents a mile in suburban areas, and 17 cents a mile in fringe areas. For off-peak hours, the highway toll would range from 3 to 5 cents a mile.

For a 25-mile rush-hour commute, including five miles through a central urban area, a driver would pay almost $15 round-trip. For the price, the driver would get a speedy trip on an unclogged road, said Pozdena. Citing previous research on road pricing, he said average rush-hour speeds on properly priced California highways would increase to 48 mph from 15 mph today.

To be sure, the concept of rationing roadways based on price faces considerable political hurdles. But when traffic congestion reaches crisis proportions and cities struggle to find ways to meet clean-air standards, economic rationing of the roadways may appear a more feasible alternative.

IMPLICATIONS FOR HOMEOWNERS AND COMMUTERS

Coping with traffic congestion in the 1990s will depend more and more on where you choose to live. People who live far from work will find commuting consuming more of their time, more of their money, and more of their peace of mind. People who live along thoroughfares will find noise steadily growing worse as traffic increases. And people who choose to live far from mass transit in congested urban areas will be foreclosing an option that is bound to become more important as driving becomes more time-consuming, expensive, and aggravating.

As traffic congestion becomes more of a concern, property values will also become more sensitive to traffic patterns. Homes that are convenient to mass transit, close to work centers, and protected from the sights and sounds of congestion are likely to be most in demand as congestion gets worse.

When shopping for a home, don't just consider how long a commute you would face today; estimate what it will be like in the future. What may seem a tolerable commute now may not be in a few years. As a case in point, many Americans have been migrating to the fringes of urban regions in search of affordable housing. But the attraction of these outlying developments may be temporary. Homes currently within marginally tolerable commuting range of work centers may not be a few years from now. As congestion worsens and turns 90-minute or 2-hour trips into 2 ½- or 3-hour journeys, commuting may stretch beyond tolerable limits.

Property values could well erode unless new employment opportunities open up closer to these remote residential developments.

Homes that aren't conveniently located near mass transit facilities may also suffer. Even if mass transit isn't an attractive option now, it may be in the future. As congestion turns hour-long downtown commutes into ninety-minute and two-hour nightmares, many drivers are likely to look at subways and park-and-ride transit systems in a new light. Choosing to live in a location convenient to public transportation gives you an option should road conditions become intolerable.

Noise Pollution: The Sound of Congestion

As traffic congestion gets worse, so will the noise. Cars are actually quieter than they used to be, but any technical improvements have been offset by the increased amount of traffic. Residents who live along major thoroughfares will find noise a growing problem.

Noise barriers along freeways are becoming a commonly used method of shielding residential developments from the worsening drone of traffic. Resident requests for new installations are growing rapidly.

When shopping for a home, pay special attention to traffic noise. If you're looking on a weekend, come back during the week to see how bad the noise is during the hours you'll routinely be at home. Then try to assess what the future holds. If the property is situated along any throughway, expect the noise to get worse. Even back roads are vulnerable as motorists seek alternatives to congested main arteries. So even if a through street seems quiet now it may not be in the future. Cul-de-sacs provide the best protection from growing congestion.

Why the Parking Spot in Front of Your Home May Disappear

One cheap, quick, and simple way to widen a thoroughfare to accommodate more traffic is to ban parking on the street, at least during rush hours. Without lifting a jackhammer, you can widen a roadway by one or two lanes overnight. As traffic engineers look for ways to squeeze more traffic onto major thoroughfares and funnel more of it onto less-used arteries, No Parking signs will be posted on more and more streets.

While no-parking zones may help alleviate traffic congestion, they will create new parking headaches for residents who don't have a driveway or garage.

Prospects that more streets will be made into no-parking zones need to be taken into account when shopping for a new house or apartment in the 1990s. If the street is a thoroughfare, it is a potential target for a no-parking zone, at least during rush hours.

MORE ELDERLY DRIVERS ON THE ROAD

As America grows grayer, the number of elderly drivers on the road will increase sharply, posing a new traffic hazard. Elderly drivers, particularly those over seventy-five, tend to have slower reaction times and many have problems reading traffic signs, seeing clearly at night, and gauging traffic flow when making a left turn or merging into traffic.

Drivers over the age of seventy-five are about twice as likely to be involved in a crash as the average motorist, and are more likely to sustain serious or fatal injuries than other drivers involved in accidents of equal severity, according to a recent two-year study by the National Research Council.

No justification was found in the study to restrict driving on the basis of age alone. The study said that most elderly motorists are likely to be capable and safe drivers and the threat they pose to traffic safety is small compared to that from teenage drivers, who are responsible for far more accidents.

But the panel did urge tougher screening of driver's-license applicants of all ages. That could put the brakes on the practice of renewing licenses by mail. The panel's recommendations could also spur more restricted licenses for some elderly people, such as a daylight-only driving permit for those who have trouble seeing well at night.

Larger and brighter road signs are also in the future, since about 40 percent of drivers age sixty-five or older have trouble reading today's signs. Communities will also feel pressure to improve public transit for the elderly, particularly in suburban areas where elderly people have no choice but to drive because mass transit is so sparse.

One recommendation offered by the panel for elderly people: Buy an automobile equipped with air bags. They offer an extra measure of protection to elderly drivers who are at greater risk of sustaining serious injury in an accident.

In choosing a place to live, retirees should look for a location that is convenient to shopping and recreational facilities, as well as public transit. It will reduce their dependence on the automobile.

BUYING VERSUS LEASING YOUR CAR

Why buy a car when you can lease one for less cash down and lower monthly payments? That's a question more and more Americans are asking these days as they leave car showrooms in sticker-shock and grieving the loss of tax deductions that used to make car ownership more affordable.

Leasing has become the new wave in car financing, applying to nearly one of every ten new cars on the road today. And the numbers are growing rapidly. So with car prices rising and Uncle Sam no longer willing to help out with tax breaks, why would anyone want to own an asset that depreciates the moment it's driven off the showroom floor?

Because in the long run, it's generally cheaper to buy than lease. Despite all the hoopla over leasing and the enticing newspaper ads pointing out how you can get behind the wheel of a luxury car for less cash, ownership remains the better bargain for most people.

To be sure, leasing has its advantages. Lease payments are lower than monthly car loan payments, which means you don't have to come up with as much cash each month or you can lease a more expensive car for the same monthly outlay. Up-front costs are also lower. You can usually drive a leased car out of the showroom for a security deposit as small as a few hundred dollars. No need to shell out 10 to 20 percent of the purchase price as a down payment.

Leasing's drawback is that when the lease expires, you don't own the car. You have to start all over again. That's the catch. The value of the car at the end of the lease more than offsets any savings you reaped from leasing. Even if you diligently invest in a bank account every penny you save by leasing, ownership still turns out to be cheaper in the long run.

How much cheaper depends on how long you plan to keep the car, how many miles you put on it each year, how you finance it, how good a deal you get on the car versus the terms of the lease, and what you do with the cash you save by leasing.

If you plan to keep the car for many years and put a lot of mileage on it, buying is much cheaper because the cost of the car is effectively depreciated over a longer period than the standard lease term and because leases entail extra charges for above-average mileage. Quite simply, it's cheaper to buy a car and nurse it into old age than it is to buy or lease one every three or four years.

Leasing contracts are also complicated. If you're not careful, you can be hit with numerous extra charges—such as for driving too many miles, excessive wear and tear, and early termination of the lease—that can make leasing far more expensive than it appears at first glance.

When Leasing Becomes More Competitive

While leasing is more expensive in the long run, it's cheaper in the short run, which is why some people like leasing.

Lower up-front costs make leasing appealing to people who can't— or don't want to—make a big down payment. Lower monthly payments make leasing attractive to people who are trying to cut their monthly outlays or get behind the wheel of a more expensive model for the same monthly cost as buying.

Leasing may also make sense for people who like to trade in their cars every few years. Most leases run three to five years. If costs are compared over a four-year period, leasing may run only several hundred dollars more than outright purchase of a mid-priced car, as you can see from the example of a $14,000 car in the following chart.

Although the example is intended to be fairly typical of leasing deals,

BUYING vs. LEASING
Comparing four-year costs on a $14,000 car

	Lease	Finance	All cash
Down payment* or lease security deposit	$280	$2,800	$14,000
Sales tax (5%)	—	$700	$700
Total monthly payments**	$12,880 ($268.33/mo.)	$13,764 ($286.76/mo.)	—
Forgone interest***	$60	$845	$3,168
	$13,220	$18,109	$17,868
Less: Refunded security deposit	$280	—	—
Residual value	—	$5,600	$5,600
TOTAL NET COST:	**$12,940**	**$12,509**	**$12,268**

  * Assumes 20% down payment for financing option.
 ** Car loan rate of 10.5%.
***Assumes cash paid up front as well as higher cost of monthly car loan payment could have earned 5% after taxes.

the economics can vary greatly depending on the specific terms of the lease and how you take advantage of the extra cash flow.

Talk to people who lease their cars, and they'll brag about the thousands of dollars they didn't have to tie up in a big down payment as well as the money they save each month on lease payments. Indeed, all that extra cash can be profitably invested and the interest earned has to be calculated as a saving. In our example of the $14,000 car, this "opportunity cost" amounts to $845 of forgone earnings if the car is financed. The figure assumes that the down payment, the sales tax, and the extra $19 in monthly payments could be profitably invested over four years at an annual after-tax return of 5 percent. On an all-cash deal, the opportunity cost would be $3,168 in forgone interest. If, however, your opportunity cost is more than 5 percent a year—say you're a small business owner in need of working capital and would otherwise have to borrow money from the bank at 15 to 20 percent interest—then leasing becomes the better deal. Opportunity cost assumptions heavily influence the bottom line in a lease-or-buy decision.

In reality, however, most people aren't so diligent about investing the money saved. They spend the extra cash for other purposes, such as a better stereo system, a nicer vacation, or lottery tickets. If forgone interest isn't counted, leasing suddenly becomes much more expensive than buying.

For the most part, taxes are no longer a consideration in the lease-or-buy decision on a personal car. The sales-tax deduction is long dead. And interest deductions on car loans are being phased out. There's one exception: If you're willing to put your house up as collateral, you can salvage the interest deduction by financing your car purchase with a home-equity loan. If you do, take the tax savings into account when comparing leasing and buying costs.

Advertised Bargains versus the Reality

When browsing through newspaper advertisements, beware of monthly payments that seem irresistibly low. Touting artificially low monthly payments is a common tactic in the leasing business. Not until you read the fine print at the bottom does it become clear that to get the advertised price, you must pay thousands of dollars up front. This down payment is called a "capitalized cost reduction." As in buying a car, the more you put down, the lower your monthly payment. But if you make a large initial payment you lose an important advantage of leasing: lower initial costs.

Leasing lets you drive away for as little as the first month's payment plus a refundable security deposit, which usually amounts to one or two months' payments. Sales tax, title, and license fees can often be included in your monthly payments instead of paid up front.

Monthly Payments and Residual Values

Monthly lease payments are based on the difference between the original value of the car and what the car is expected to be worth in the used-car market at the end of the lease. The car's anticipated value at the end of the lease, known as "residual value," varies from about 25 to 50 percent of the original value, depending on the car and the length of the lease. Some cars hold their value better than others. You'll get the best deal by leasing a car that tends to hold its value over time.

Not every dealer arrives at the same estimate of residual value, so it pays to shop around. The residual-value estimate is crucial to your lease payments.

Closed-End versus Open-End Leases

Under the most common lease arrangements, known as "closed-end" leases, you don't have to worry about what your car is worth in the used-car market when you turn the keys back in to the dealer at the end of the lease. If your car fell out of favor and is worth less than the residual value that the leasing company originally placed on the car, that's the company's tough luck. You can't be charged for the difference. The company assumes the risk.

Under an "open-end" lease, you assume the risk. If your car is worth less than the estimated residual value specified in the contract, you pay the difference. In exchange for assuming this risk, your monthly payments are comparatively lower than under closed-end leases. But the risk is large enough that most consumers prefer the closed-end deal.

Hidden Costs

Even if the monthly payments and residual-value figures seem attractive, there are numerous other charges that can wreck the economics of a leasing deal.

One such demon is the excess mileage charge. If you put more than 15,000 to 18,000 miles a year on the car, the dealer will usually charge you 8 to 15 cents a mile for any excess mileage. If you expect to drive farther than the prescribed limits, negotiate a higher limit in the contract. The price you pay for a higher limit should be less than the excess mileage charge. To make sure it's cheaper, run the numbers on your pocket calculator.

If you want to get out of the contract early, it's costly. Regardless of whether you're simply bored with the car or the car has been racking up huge repair bills, you'll usually pay early-termination charges that can run into the thousands of dollars. The earlier you break the lease the stiffer the charge. That's mainly because in the first few years, the car depreciates more than is covered by the monthly payments. (Some companies impose penalties on top of this depreciation shortfall.)

Read the terms of the lease carefully and check your insurance policy, because if your car is stolen or totaled in an accident some contracts require you to pay early-termination charges on top of the amount reimbursed by the insurance company for the cost of the car.

When you return the car to the dealer at the end of the lease, you'll be charged for any damage beyond reasonable wear and tear. Make sure the contract spells out clearly what damage you're responsible for, because language such as "excessive wear and tear" is too vague.

Also find out where the car has to be returned at the expiration of the lease and consider whether you are likely to be in the same area at the end of the lease. Leases usually require the car to be returned to the original leasing agent. If you move, you may end up having to take a drive across the country to return the car. If you expect to move, find a dealer who allows you to return the car to an affiliated dealership anywhere in the country.

Many dealers also impose a "disposition charge" at the end of the lease to pay for the cost of preparing your car for sale. A $250 charge is not unusual.

Virtually everything in a car lease is negotiable, and the only way to come up with the best deal is to shop around and haggle as you would if you were buying a car. Compare the terms, the total costs, and any appealing options such as low-cost maintenance and service or an option to buy the car at the end of the lease at an attractive price.

AUTO INSURANCE: HOW TO SAVE HUNDREDS OF DOLLARS IN PREMIUMS

There appears to be no end in sight to the relentless climb in auto insurance rates. Growing traffic density makes cars more prone to bump into each other. Rising car prices boost the cost of fixing dented fenders. And holes in most no-fault laws are failing to stem bodily injury lawsuits.

But there are ways to slash auto insurance premiums by hundreds of dollars a year without assuming much additional risk.

Buying the Right Car

Which car you buy has a big impact on how much you'll pay for insurance. Insurers base the premiums on how well the car holds up in a crash, how expensive it is to repair, how tempting it is for thieves, and whether it's the kind of car that inspires you to drive as if you were in time trials for the Grand Prix.

Premiums on high-performance "muscle" cars and flashy sports cars can run 100 percent more than those on a boring sedan because they tend to be driven more aggressively. So if you're trying to discourage your twenty-year-old son from buying a hot rod, get him a few quotes from your insurance agent. Such high-performance cars can boost premiums by $1,000 or more a year. Luxury cars are also more expensive to insure because parts and repairs are more expensive.

Another factor is weight. Heavier cars tend to be less costly to insure than lighter models because they tend to suffer less damage in crashes.

Foreign-made cars tend to cost more to insure than their American counterparts because parts are generally more expensive. As the dollar loses further ground to the Japanese yen and the German mark, foreign parts will become even more expensive.

Thieves have their preferences, too, and if your car is a coveted model, your premium for comprehensive coverage will reflect that. Thieves are particularly fond of sports cars and luxury models.

Before buying a car, check with your insurance agent and find out what the premiums will be. It may help narrow down your choices.

Higher Deductibles

Premiums on collision and comprehensive coverage can be cut sharply by raising the deductibles. Collision premiums can be cut by 20 to 35 percent by raising your deductible from $100 to $500, and you'll save up to 45 percent if you raise it to $1,000. Paying for smaller damages out of your own pocket can also preclude hikes in your premiums since you'll have fewer blemishes on your insurance record. If you do opt for higher deductibles, though, make sure you have enough money set aside in savings in case of an accident to pay for the first $500 or $1,000 in repairs.

Drop Collision on Older Cars

If your car is getting on in years and has a low resale value, it may pay to skip collision coverage altogether. You may end up paying more in premiums than the car is worth. Keep in mind that if your car's totaled, the most you will get is the depreciated market value of the car. The insurance company may not even give you enough to get the car repaired if repair costs amount to more than the depreciated market value. As a rule of thumb, consider dropping collision coverage once the car reaches its fifth or sixth birthday.

Special Discounts

Insurance companies offer special discounts for a variety of reasons that can substantially cut your premiums.

Students are eligible for various discounts if they maintain good grades, take driver training courses, or attend college away from home.

Equipping your car with a burglar alarm will reduce premiums on comprehensive coverage by up to 15 percent in some states. Air bags or automatic seat belts will reduce your medical coverage premiums by 10 to 30 percent or more.

Various other discounts are available for members of car pools, senior citizens, nonsmokers, farmers, motorists who take a defensive driving course, and females who are at least thirty years old and are the sole driver in the household.

You can also save money by insuring your entire family on one policy rather than insuring teenage drivers separately.

Don't count on your insurance agent to mention all the available discounts. Remind the agent of discounts that you know you're eligible for, and then ask if there are any discounts that you may have overlooked.

Also make sure to inform your agent when any changes occur that might affect your premium, such as when you stop using your car to commute to work.

What Not to Skimp On

Liability Coverage: Don't try to cut costs by opting for low limits on bodily injury or property-damage liability coverage. First of all, you won't save very much. Second, liability coverage is the most critical part of your auto insurance policy; it is your shield against the potentially ruinous costs that can arise from major accidents involving serious injury or death in which you're at fault. Even in no-fault states, the injured party still has the right to bring suit. If you own a house or other assets, the minimum liability coverage usually recommended is $100,000 per person and $300,000 per accident.

If you have substantial assets to protect against big court awards, you can supplement your basic auto and homeowners' liability coverage with an "umbrella" policy. A $1 million umbrella policy runs about $100 to $200 a year.

Property damage liability coverage, which pays for damage you cause to someone else's car or other property, should be at least $25,000. Even though most states require only $5,000 or $10,000, that won't go very far if you run into a Porsche or BMW or many other new cars these days. Besides, boosting coverage from $10,000 to $25,000 costs only about $10. It costs only a few dollars more to raise coverage to $50,000.

Medical Payments: Even if you're covered by a separate health insurance plan, don't try to save money by dropping the "medical payments" portion of your auto policy as some financial advisers suggest. Your health insurance policy may cover you and your family, but it won't help any other passengers in your car injured in an accident. Medical payments insurance pays your medical bills as well as those of any passenger injured in an accident regardless of who was at fault and without anyone having to wait to sue for liability damages. The minimum generally recommended is $10,000.

If you live in a state with no-fault laws, you are often required to buy Personal Injury Protection, or PIP. PIP is more comprehensive than medical payments coverage in that it usually reimburses for lost wages and some other expenses in addition to medical bills.

If your car is equipped with an air bag—as more and more new models will be—many insurance companies will reduce your PIP or medical payments premiums by up to 30 percent. In dollar terms, the discount's not a big deal—usually $10 to $20 a year. But it does provide some financial incentive for ordering air bags as an option on models where they aren't standard equipment. The rest of the incentive is the comforting knowledge that you will have a better chance of surviving a crash and escaping serious injury with an air bag.

Uninsured-Motorist Coverage: Uninsured-motorist coverage is also worth having because a growing number of drivers on the road are going without insurance due to the high rates—even though that's illegal in most states. Uninsured coverage reimburses you for bodily injury accidents caused by a driver who doesn't carry insurance. Generally, the minimums of your own liability insurance should apply to uninsured coverage—$100,000 per person and $300,000 per accident.

"Underinsured-motorists" coverage is also more important these days because rising insurance premiums have led many drivers to cut back their liability coverage to the minimums required by law. If your damages exceed the other motorist's coverage, your insurer picks up the excess—up to the limits of your underinsured-motorists coverage.

19

AIR TRAVEL GRIDLOCK: CHRONIC CONGESTION, HIGHER FARES

Imagine if every day of the year were like the Christmas travel season and you will have a picture of what air travel will grow to be like in the 1990s. More anguishing delays, more crowded planes, and higher fares are destined to result as growing passenger traffic places ever-increasing strains on a system already suffering from insufficient capacity. Air travel will approach gridlock for lack of new airports, runways, gates, terminals, parking lots, and curbside unloading areas.

Only one new major airport is planned for the 1990s, yet passenger traffic is projected to surge 65 percent. U.S. airlines now carry around 500 million passengers a year. By the year 2000, annual passenger traffic will exceed 800 million, according to Federal Aviation Administration projections.

As a National Research Council panel concluded in a recent report: "The present airport system would be overwhelmed and could not function without intolerable delays, if at all."

In 1986, 11 airports were classified by the FAA as prone to serious delays, and that number is expected to reach 29 by 1996.

Aviation experts see scant hope that the crisis can be averted, even if more new airports were authorized today. Planning and constructing a new airport can take a decade or more. The only one now in the pipeline is in Denver. Scheduled for completion in 1993, Denver's facility will be the nation's first major new airport since 1974. FAA officials believe ten more major airports are needed by the year 2000 but won't be built.

Runway expansions are planned at several airports, but many older airfields have no room to expand because residential and commercial development now hugs the airport perimeters. Proposals for new airports have languished for lack of available sites, a lack of public funding, opposition from local residents, and sometimes even opposition from airlines who don't want to pay the higher landing fees that are needed to finance construction. The airline industry is lobbying the federal government to take the lead in an airport-building program using the multibillion-dollar surplus in the Airport and Airway Trust Fund, which is financed almost entirely by surcharges on passengers.

The price that Americans will pay for a lack of new facilities will be more congestion, more delays, more inconvenience, and higher fares. Although fares lagged behind inflation since the industry was deregulated in 1978, most aviation experts expect fares to keep pace with inflation from now on.

Airlines are in a better position today to raise fares. Over the past decade, major carriers used the freedom of deregulation to consolidate their positions, creating what is widely perceived as an unregulated oligopoly. The eight largest airlines now control more than 90 percent of the U.S. market. Moreover, single carriers control nearly two thirds of passenger traffic at fourteen major hubs.

Nor is there much chance that any feisty new competitors will emerge to challenge the major carriers with deep discount fares, as People Express once did. A shortage of landing slots and gates at major airports effectively keeps out new entrants. An airline that owns the rights to the gates can keep out the biggest of competitors.

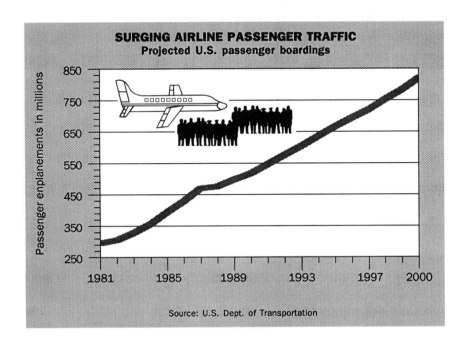

SURGING AIRLINE PASSENGER TRAFFIC
Projected U.S. passenger boardings

Source: U.S. Dept. of Transportation

Higher operating and capital costs will also drive up fares. Airlines will need to spend tens of billions of dollars over the next decade to replace aging aircraft, meet new noise regulations, and expand their fleets with bigger planes to accommodate growing passenger traffic.

It will take larger planes and more crowded ones to sustain even

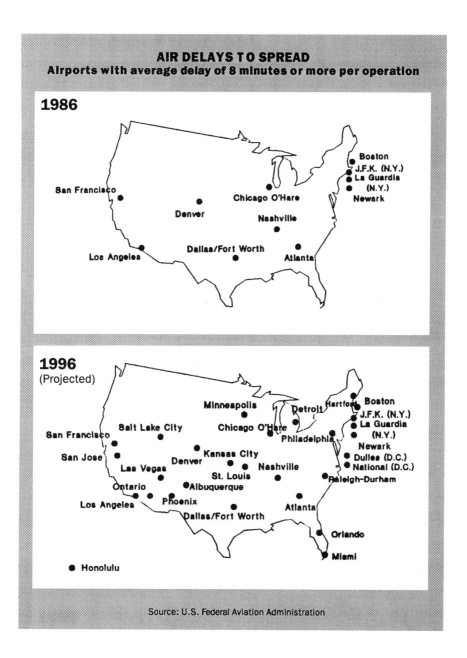

AIR DELAYS TO SPREAD
Airports with average delay of 8 minutes or more per operation

Source: U.S. Federal Aviation Administration

moderate growth in air traffic. Some stopgap measures are also being taken to squeeze more capacity out of existing facilities. The FAA has allowed planes at some airports to land simultaneously on closely spaced parallel runways. Several airports are building high-speed runway turnoffs that get landing planes out of the way more quickly. FAA officials are also looking at the possibility of using some military airfields for com-

AIRPORTS TO GET MORE CROWDED
Passenger boardings
(in millions)

Airport	Actual 1987	Forecast 2000	Rank 2000
Chicago: O'Hare	28	42	1
Atlanta	24	31	4
Los Angeles	21	26	5
Dallas/Ft. Worth	21	35	2
Denver	16	33	3
New York: Kennedy	14	22	6
San Francisco	14	19	8
Newark	12	18	9
New York: La Guardia	12	15	16
Miami	12	18	10
Boston	12	17	12
St. Louis	10	16	15
Detroit	10	17	11
Honolulu	9	15	18
Minneapolis/St. Paul	9	16	14
Phoenix	9	20	7
Pittsburgh	9	17	13
Washington D.C.: National	7	9	27
Philadelphia	7	14	21
Houston	7	14	20
Las Vegas	7	14	19
Orlando	7	15	17
Seattle-Tacoma	7	11	23
Charlotte	6	11	22
Memphis	5	9	26
Washington D.C.: Dulles	5	10	25
San Diego	5	9	28
Salt Lake City	5	10	24
Tampa	5	9	29
Kansas City	5	8	30

Source: Federal Aviation Administration

mercial traffic. In the longer term, new aircraft that can take off vertically and don't need airport runways hold promise for short-haul routes between major cities.

Air travel congestion is also spurring greater interest in other forms of travel and communications. Teleconferencing, whose time has yet to come, could gain wider use as a substitute for some travel. Major companies have been installing their own private TV networks, and new telecommunications technology will in several years permit high-quality, low-cost video communications on a wider scale.

Some states are also exploring high-speed passenger rail service for short-haul commutes between major cities. One such system would shuttle gamblers between Las Vegas and Los Angeles by the late 1990s. Florida is considering a high-speed system to serve Miami, Tampa, and Orlando. In Texas, a proposed high-speed system would link Houston and Dallas. In Ohio, a high-speed line would link Cincinnati, Columbus, and Cleveland. But the United States is far behind other countries in developing high-speed rail. High-speed rail networks are undergoing vast expansion in Europe. France, which has operated a high-speed rail line between Paris and Lyons since 1981, recently inaugurated service between Paris and Le Mans with cruising speeds of 186 miles per hour. The French are also working on a new line that will connect Paris and London once the English Channel tunnel is completed in 1993. Spain will have high-speed rail service linking Seville and Madrid by 1992. And both Japan and Germany are working on prototypes of magnetically levitated trains that could reach speeds of 300 mph. Despite their promise, none of these alternatives is likely to provide much salvation for American travelers in this century.

In the meantime, flight delays are expected to become chronic, making air travel an even more frustrating, uncertain, and costly experience. Already, many business travelers fly to their destination the night before because they can no longer be certain of getting there on time the same day. Such practices will become more commonplace.

Delays may not always be evident. Airlines have been adding extra time to their schedules to give the appearance that more of their flights are arriving on time—even though it now takes longer to get from one point to another because of air traffic congestion.

TIPS FOR COPING WITH AIR TRAVEL CONGESTION IN THE 1990s

Coping in an age when delays, lost baggage, and missed connections become routine as air travel congestion becomes chronic will require new strategies on the part of travelers. Here are some ways to assure getting to your destination on time, with the least frustration, and in the most comfort.

Fly Direct: If money isn't a concern, take nonstop or direct flights whenever possible. Growing air traffic congestion will lead to more frequent delays and increase the odds that you or your luggage will miss a connecting flight.

If You Have a Connecting Flight: When making reservations, try to leave sufficient time between connecting flights. Growing congestion will make it harder for travelers to make tight connections. If you have a choice of flights, avoid those that connect at airports prone to delays. Your travel agent should know which airports are currently suffering the worst delays.

Avoid Delay-Prone Flights: When making reservations, ask your travel agent whether your particular flight is prone to delays. The computer reservation system contains such information for each flight. Even an airline whose on-time performance is above average can have particular flights that are routinely delayed because of the airports used.

If Timing Is Critical: If you have an important business meeting or social function to attend, leave enough room in your travel schedule for delays. Consider traveling the night before. You will be assured of getting to your meeting on time and won't be frazzled from rushing and worrying over delays.

Baggage: Baggage problems are likely to increase in the future, especially with connecting flights. So always be prepared for the worst: that your checked baggage will be delayed or lost. If you are going on a short trip and can get by with a garment bag, carry it on board; don't check it. If you need to check luggage, carry essentials on board with you, including any suit or dress needed for a business or social function.

Avoid the Busiest Times: If your schedule permits, avoid flying at the busiest times. That's when delays are the worst and planes are the most crowded. The busiest times are late afternoons, when business travelers are trying to get home after a day's business. Early weekday mornings are also busy on a few heavily traveled commuter routes, including flights between New York and Washington, D.C., Boston, or Chicago, and between Los Angeles and San Francisco. Sunday and Friday evenings are also busy. Sundays are busy because business people are heading for Monday morning meetings and vacationers are returning for Monday's work. Friday evenings are busy because business travelers are trying to get home and vacationers are trying to get out of town for the weekend. Thursdays have also become busy recently, apparently because business people are trying to get home a day earlier and because of the trend toward long-weekend vacations. That leaves Tuesday, Wednesday, and Saturdays (particularly Saturday afternoons) as the least busy travel periods. Saturdays, however, can be very busy on routes to vacation destinations.

Avoid Daytime Crowds: If your schedule permits, consider taking night flights, which are usually less crowded. But bear in mind that flying at night doesn't mean you'll avoid delays—even though the skies seem much less crowded at night. In fact, the greatest risk of delay is at night. The reason is that a domestic airliner averages five flights and 3,500 miles per day, according to Travelmation Corporation, a travel management firm in Stamford, Connecticut. So by late in the day, the plane has been subjected to the greatest risk of delay. If, for some reason, the plane experiences delays throughout the day, you may have a long wait for your night flight. If you decide to fly at night, ask your travel agent whether your particular flight is routinely subject to delays.

Confirming Rental Car and Hotel Reservations: If you are renting a car or a hotel room, ask for a confirmation number when you make the reservation. Reservations sometimes get lost and if the hotel is booked up or the rental agency is out of cars you may be out of luck unless you can provide some proof of your reservation. With business travel increasing, many hotels and car rental agencies will have trouble making last-minute accommodations for those without confirmed reservations. If the hotel doesn't issue confirmation numbers, ask for the reservation clerk's name so you can prove later that you made a reservation.

Guarantee Your Hotel Room for Late Arrival: Even if you plan to arrive early, flight delays can make you a late arrival. If the hotel's booked, you lose your room. Hotels usually won't hold a room after 6:00 P.M. unless your reservation is guaranteed with a credit card for late arrival.

If you cancel your travel plans, make sure to let the hotel know in time. Otherwise your credit card will automatically be charged for a night's stay. Beware that some hotels now require notification of canceled reservations by 4:00 P.M. rather than 6:00 P.M. Make sure to find out in advance what the deadline is.

Prepare for Long Delays: Accept flight delays as a way of life in the 1990s and find something interesting to do while you're waiting instead of agonizing over the delays. At the least, take reading materials along.

If you travel a lot on one particular airline, consider membership in an airline club. Dues typically run $100 to $150 a year. Airline clubs are a nice place to relax, watch television, read, and have a drink. Many now offer an array of business services as well, including computers, photocopiers, and fax machines. If you tend to travel on different airlines, however, membership in one airline club won't help much. In most major airports, the distance between one airline's club and another airline's departure gates is too great to make the club a convenient oasis for short layovers.

A growing number of airport terminals contain business service centers where stranded travelers can have access to workstations equipped with typewriters, computers, telephones, copying machines, and the like. Prices run around $20 an hour for use of a personal computer.

FLIGHTS TO BECOME MORE CROWDED: TIPS ON GETTING THE BEST SEAT

Planes are already crowded, and as the decade progresses airline cabins are projected to become even fuller as passenger traffic swells. Since airport capacity constraints will prevent airlines from adding a lot of extra flights, the extra traffic will have to be squeezed onto existing flights.

Gone are the days when you could board many flights and find a whole empty row in which to stretch out, or at least a vacant seat between you and the next passenger. But there are ways to improve your chances of getting a seat with more room to stretch out and maneuver.

Getting a good seat requires more than just hoping the airline computers will be kind to you. Hope is likely to land you in a center seat.

Try to get your seat assignment when you make your reservations. The earlier your reservations are made, the better choice of seats you'll have. If you wait until you get to the airport, you're stuck with what's left, and on crowded flights that usually means a center seat. Window seats are the most popular, since you get a view and you rub elbows with only one other person. Aisle seats go next, although some people prefer them over window seats because you can stretch an elbow into the aisle when there aren't any food or beverage carts rolling through the cabin.

But there are a few rows in the main cabin that offer extra room. For the most leg room, ask for the row adjacent to the emergency exit. Manufacturers build extra room into exit rows so people can escape quickly and easily in an emergency. One drawback is that on some planes, these seats are right near the kitchen galley, so you'll hear a lot of clanging of glasses, chipping of ice, and flight attendant conversation. (Restrictions bar young children, as well as certain handicapped persons, from sitting in exit rows. So if you're taking small children you will probably be asked to move if you get assigned exit-row seats.)

Another section with extra room is the row immediately facing the bulkhead. Besides extra leg room, you won't have to worry about the person in front of you reclining his seat to encroach further on your cramped space. There is no one in front of you. One drawback on longer flights is that you may not have a good view of the in-flight movie since the screens are usually located on the bulkhead. Another problem is that

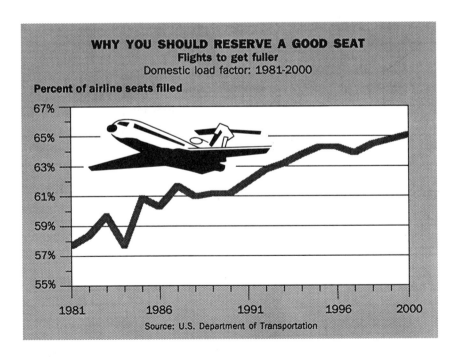

WHY YOU SHOULD RESERVE A GOOD SEAT
Flights to get fuller
Domestic load factor: 1981-2000

Percent of airline seats filled

Source: U.S. Department of Transportation

you may have to fight with the people seated behind you for space under your seat for carry-on luggage. Passengers are supposed to put their carry-ons under the seat in front of them (or in the overhead compartments). But with bulkhead seats, there's only a bulkhead in front of you, no seats.

Keep an eye out the next time you're on board and mark down the seats you like. Your travel agent should also be able to help since computer reservation systems contain diagrams of aircraft seating configurations.

If you are traveling with a companion, one way to increase your chances of having an entire row to yourselves on planes with three-across seating is to request the window seat for one of you and the aisle seat for the other. Center seats are the last to be assigned. So if the plane isn't crowded, you stand a good chance of having the center seat empty. If not, nothing is lost. The unfortunate person assigned the center seat will certainly be willing to switch seats so that you can sit next to your companion.

Flying during off-peak times also increases your chances of getting a better seat since those flights tend to be less crowded. On longer flights, the extra comfort may be worth adjusting your schedule.

If you find yourself assigned to a bad seat when you check in for a flight, don't give up hope. On a typical flight, several people with good seats reserved will be "no-shows." So ask the gate agent to hold your ticket until they free seats reserved by no-shows. Some of the best seats in the house often become available a few minutes before departure.

Upgrading to First Class: One way to avoid congestion in the main cabin is to upgrade to first class, and there are ways to do so without great expense. Members of frequent-flier clubs can upgrade to first class by using their mileage award coupons. If you don't want to waste the award on an upgrade, many frequent-flier clubs allow members to upgrade to first class for only $15 to $50 above the full coach fare so long as a seat is available. For people traveling on a full-fare ticket, the cash premium can be a good deal since by sitting in first class you won't have to pay for your drinks or a movie headset, you'll get a better meal, more room to stretch out, and perhaps most important, a more conducive atmosphere to work in.

What's more, traveling first class increases the odds that you'll meet someone of influence on your trip and pick up some valuable professional tidbit or contact. Celebrities, top executives, and politicians don't sit in coach. A lot of people looking to advance their careers will pay thousands of dollars to join country clubs to meet the kinds of contacts who routinely fly first class. One advantage of flights is that you have a captive audience.

Besides frequent-flier deals, super-saver discounts are sometimes available on first-class tickets. On some routes, first-class super-saver tickets cost only about 25 percent more than the super-saver coach fare.

Be aware that first class isn't always the isolated refuge that it used to be. Today, more and more travelers are using frequent-flier awards and discount fares to upgrade to first class in order to get away from the congestion in back. On some flights, first class is more crowded than the coach section, where empty seats allow travelers room to stretch out. So if you're planning a last-minute upgrade to first class, it pays to check with the ticket agent to see if the flight's going to be less crowded in coach. If so, you may find sitting in coach more peaceful, roomier, and cheaper than first class, even though you may not meet anyone famous.

DELAYED? LET YOUR CAR RENTAL COMPANY KNOW

Not every car rental company is patient when it comes to holding reservations for customers who don't show up on time. Some of them will wait all day for you. But others, contending that a lot of people with reservations never show up, wait as little as thirty minutes or an hour after your promised pickup time before giving your car away to someone else if they're short on cars.

With the prospect of more flight delays, the odds of being left stranded by your car rental company are sure to grow, making it more important than ever for travelers to take steps to ensure that their car will be there when they get there.

When making the reservation, check the company's policy for holding reservations and under what circumstances you'll need to call to notify of any delay.

In most cases, you won't have to call at all if the car company has your flight number. If you're late, most car rental companies will check your flight to see if it's been delayed and, if so, hold your reservation. So remember to give the flight number when making your car reservation. If you book the car through a travel agent, make sure the agent passes on your flight number to the car rental company. All too often an agent will forget to do that.

If you miss your flight or otherwise change your itinerary, let the car rental company know. For if your scheduled flight arrives and you're not there, the car rental company has no choice but to assume you're not going to show up.

TIPS FOR FINDING THE LOWEST FARES

Air fare bargains are getting harder to find. In contrast to the early years of deregulation when airlines struggled to fill up seats in the face of fierce competition, major carriers now realize they can compete without so much discounting. With passenger traffic rising and competition in many markets diminished, airlines are reducing the number of discount tickets they issue as well as raising base fares. Discounts are still easy to obtain if you are going on vacation and can purchase your tickets weeks in advance. But airlines have made it tougher for travelers who can't make plans that far in advance or abide by the numerous restrictions that go with many discounted fares.

Nonetheless, if you know where to look and are willing to be somewhat flexible, you should still be able to find some kind of discount—even if you need to travel on short notice and can't be tied down to a lot of restrictions.

One-Stop versus Nonstop: Taking a nonstop flight is the quickest way to get to your destination. But it can also be the most expensive, particularly on the longer routes. So taking a one-stop or connecting flight can substantially reduce your travel costs—even if you're making travel arrangements at the last minute. Taking a connecting flight doesn't necessarily mean it will take a lot longer to get to your destination. Many stopovers are less than an hour. So for only an extra hour of travel time, you can save as much as a few hundred dollars. Few people earn that kind of money for an hour's work. But keep in mind the greater potential for delay with one-stop and connecting flights. If you miss the connection, will you still be able to get to your appointment on time?

Fly When Others Don't: Flying during off-peak periods can yield substantial savings. When is off-peak? That depends on the route. On routes dominated by business travelers, weekends and weekday nights are usually considered off-peak. If you're headed for a tourist destination, weekdays and weekend nights are usually considered off-peak.

Shop Around: Not all airlines charge the same fare, so it pays to shop around. Smaller carriers, such as Midway, Southwest, and America West, sometimes offer lower fares than larger carriers competing on the same route. An airline that offers infrequent service on a particular route also often charges less than competitors with more frequent service. Also watch for promotional fares when an airline begins new service on a route.

Plan as Far Ahead as Possible: The deepest discounts require purchasing tickets two weeks or a month in advance. But there are still some discounts available for those who purchase tickets a week in advance, and occasionally just two or three days in advance. It depends on the airline and the route. Regardless, you should book as far in advance as possible because discount tickets are limited on each flight. Discounted seats on holiday flights can sell out months in advance.

Flexibility with Restrictions: Don't dismiss super-saver fares just because you need to keep your travel plans somewhat flexible. Not all super-saver tickets carry 100 percent penalties for canceling your reservation or changing your itinerary. For a little more money, you can often buy super-savers with only a 50 percent or 25 percent penalty. Even if you make a change in your itinerary, you will still end up paying less than if you traveled on an unrestricted coach fare. But before buying a ticket, find out how much advance notification is required for a change in plans and figure out how much flexibility you need. If you don't give enough advance notification, you may be stuck paying more than the penalty to switch flights.

Alternate Airports: Not all airports in a given city are created equal when it comes to fares. When flying to or from Chicago, for instance, flights using Midway Airport are often less expensive than those at O'Hare. So it pays to check fares at alternate airports. The New York City area has three airports to choose from. The Washington, D.C., area also has three. San Francisco has two. And in south Florida, there are airports in Miami, Fort Lauderdale, and West Palm Beach. Make sure the airport you choose is not so far out of your way that the extra cab fare wipes out what you save on the plane ticket.

Hidden-City Ploy: This ploy takes advantage of quirks in airline fare pricing on flights that stop at a major city—usually a hub—and then continue on to another destination. On occasion, you will find that flying to the hub itself is more expensive than flying on to the final destination. For example, take a flight that originates in Los Angeles, stops off in

Chicago, and then continues on to Toronto. Recently, the fare for Chicago-bound passengers was higher than for those traveling between Los Angeles and Toronto. So if your destination is Chicago, the trick is to buy a ticket to Toronto (the "hidden city"), but simply get off the plane when it lands in Chicago. Don't check your luggage, though, because it will be sent through to Toronto. Airlines contend this strategy violates their rules and passengers using it face the risk of having to pay full coach fare if they get caught. And airlines can easily catch passengers with round-trip tickets. So the ploy works only one way. If you wanted to avoid paying the full fare on the return leg of your Los Angeles–Chicago trip, you would have to find another "hidden city" beyond Los Angeles.

Buying Two Super-savers Instead of One Regular: Business travelers usually ignore super-saver tickets because they don't want to have to stay overnight on Saturday, a normal requirement of super-saver deals. They want to be home for the weekend with their family. So they end up paying full fare. But by buying two round-trip super-saver tickets you may be able to save hundreds of dollars off the regular fare without having to stay the weekend. This is the way it works: Say you're flying from New York to San Francisco on Tuesday, May 15, and you want to return Thursday, May 17. Buy a New York–San Francisco super-saver ticket with a departure date of Tuesday, May 15. (The return date can't be any earlier than the following Sunday, May 20, to fulfill the requirements, but it doesn't matter what date you choose because you're not going to use it.) Now buy a second super-saver, this time a San Francisco–New York round trip departing on Thursday, May 17, as you wanted. (Again the return date doesn't matter.) The recent cost of the two super-savers: $750, compared to full coach fare of $1,200. You save $450 without having to stay the weekend. What's more, if you scheduled the return dates on each super-saver just right you could take a second New York–San Francisco trip later for free.

Vacation Lull Periods: In planning vacations, look for slow traffic periods when fares are lower. For instance, major airlines usually cut their fares for travel to Florida during January and early February, a traditionally slow period sandwiched between the Christmas–New Year's crunch and the mid-February onslaught of winter tourists. Fares to Florida and other warm-weather destinations are also lower during the off-season, which extends from after Easter until Thanksgiving. For Europe, the cheapest fares are usually offered from November through March.

Don't Give Up on Discount Seats: If your travel is for pleasure and contingent on a discount fare, don't give up if you find that all the discount seats have been sold out. More may open up as the departure date gets closer. Seats on flights are apportioned to discount and business travelers based on past sales patterns. But the mix of seats on each flight is reexamined frequently. So if business-travel bookings on a particular flight are lower than usual, the airline will increase the allotment of discount seats on that flight.

Special Discounts: Some airlines routinely offer special discounts for children and senior citizens. Such discounts usually mean at least a 10 to 20 percent savings.

Find a Good Travel Agent: Develop a relationship with a good travel agent. Getting through the air travel maze in the 1990s will require an agent who knows the ins and outs of the computer reservation system and is willing to spend the extra time to find the best fare.

Finding Fares with Your Computer: Even if you have a good travel agent, it may pay to do some preliminary browsing of the available flights and fares on your home computer. The same reservation systems used by travel agents can be accessed through such consumer videotex services as CompuServe, Genie, and Prodigy. The reason for browsing yourself is that there is a limit to the amount of time a travel agent can devote to the often-conflicting goals of finding the cheapest fares and the flights you want. The lowest fares aren't always on the flights you prefer. So deciding on a compromise can be a time-consuming process. By searching the airline reservation system on your home computer, you can see for yourself what fares are available and what flights are available and spend the time thinking about what trade-offs you want to make. Even if you spend $10 or $20 an hour in access charges, it may be worth the expense since the savings can amount to hundreds of dollars. Once you spot the fare and flight you want, you can have your travel agent check to make sure you didn't miss a lower fare, and then make the reservation.

AIRCRAFT NOISE: QUIETER PLANES COMING, BUT STILL NOISY

A new generation of quieter planes is gradually coming into service, such as the Boeing 757 and 767, which are only about half as noisy as early versions of the 727. But aircraft noise will be of continuing concern to residents near major airports during the 1990s. The problem: While environmental regulations are expected to lead to a phaseout of older, noisier jets, this may not happen until the year 2000 or later. In the meantime, the total number of takeoffs and landings will be increasing as passenger traffic grows.

During the day, people who live near major airports may increasingly find two jets landing at once. At some airports, the FAA has allowed planes to land simultaneously on parallel runways as a way to increase airport capacity.

In addition, more flights are likely to be scheduled during nighttime hours because of daytime saturation. Even where noise restrictions limit nighttime flight operations, the quieter engines now coming into service allow airlines to meet some of those nighttime noise restrictions. So while nearby residents didn't have to contend with any nighttime noise before, they may in the future.

National Airport in Washington, D.C., is an example. National prohibits aircraft that exceed certain noise levels from taking off or landing between 10:00 P.M. and 7:00 A.M. Those noise restrictions were tantamount to virtually closing down the airport overnight. Only a relatively few flights could meet them. That satisfied neighboring communities just fine. But advances in engine technology have produced planes that can now meet the restrictions. Nearby residents fear night flights could multiply over the next ten to fifteen years even under existing noise regulations.

Prospective home buyers need to be aware that noise from jet aircraft is going to be a continuing concern for years to come. A home doesn't need to be hugging an airport to be affected. Houses located miles away from an airport can be affected if they are situated along the flight path. Visit the home during the day and at night to see what kind of noise you will have to live with. And then assume it will get worse before it gets better.

New battles between local property owners and airport authorities are already beginning to erupt over aircraft noise. But it is risky to assume that local residents will always win out at a time when the air travel system is running out of capacity.

Aircraft noise may not only make life miserable for you and your family, but it can also have a significant impact on property values. In a recent study on the impact of aircraft noise on residential property values, Marvin Frankel, a professor of economics at the University of Illinois, found that noise reduced property values by as much as 21.6 percent in suburban communities around Chicago's O'Hare Airport (see chart

EFFECT OF AIRCRAFT NOISE LEVELS ON RESIDENTIAL PROPERTY VALUES

NOISE LEVEL	MEDIAN PRICE REDUCTION*
LOW: awareness, occasional annoyance	1.6%
MODERATE: occasionally interferes with conversation, TV listening	5.5%
SUBSTANTIAL: often interferes with conversation and TV; may disturb sleep	13.0%
SEVERE: frequently disrupts conversation, TV and sleep; intense annoyance	21.6%

*Realtor estimates

Source: Professor Marvin Frankel, University of Illinois, Office of Real Estate Research

above). Three of four realtors surveyed said it took longer to sell a house where aircraft noise was a problem. The survey also indicated that one of three home buyers is not very well informed about noise in the area he or she is buying in, and as a result tends to bid higher than advisable.

BETTER TIMES FOR AIRLINES

Major airlines face an improved operating environment in the 1990s. Passenger traffic is rising and competition is diminished.

Consolidation of the industry over the past decade has eliminated much route duplication and has limited price competition. Unprofitable fare wars are unlikely to erupt as they did during the early 1980s when new airlines like People Express entered the newly deregulated skies. In most major cities, one or two carriers dominate airport gates and landing slots, making it nearly impossible for new airlines to gain access to airport facilities.

With passenger traffic rising, competition limited, and airport capacity strained, airlines will have an easier time raising fares and filling up their planes.

As a National Research Council panel concluded in a report on the future of aviation: "In this changed environment, it will be very difficult for small carriers to find niches in which they can survive and it will be virtually impossible for new carriers to be created. The panel expects never to see the likes of People Express again. This means there will be less likelihood of fare wars and less pressure to hold fares down. Markets dominated by one carrier or shared by two carriers are not likely to have fares set below costs as was often the case in recent years." (The National Research Council is an arm of the National Academy of Sciences.)

The FAA estimates that yields will increase 40 percent in the 1990s, from 12.46 cents per revenue passenger mile in 1990 to 17.44 cents in the year 2000.

But the outlook for airlines is not all rosy. They face considerable expense in the years ahead to modernize and expand their fleets. Major carriers are placing record orders for new planes in order to accommodate rising passenger traffic, replace aging aircraft, and meet proposed new noise regulations. Their fuel costs are also expected to escalate, with oil prices forecast to climb during the decade. And recession always looms as a constant threat to the health of the industry. The fates and fortunes of the airline industry are closely tied to the health of the economy.

Airport capacity constraints will also make it hard for airlines to expand their operations. Expansion through mergers will also be tougher than it was in the 1980s. Concerned about reduced competition after a decade of airline industry consolidation, the Bush administration has indicated it would give closer scrutiny to further mergers of the remaining Goliaths.

Airlines also face the threat of a return to greater government oversight. Debate is already under way on whether deregulation has created an oligopoly in which a few major carriers have gained too much dominance and stifled competition.

As a recent Commerce Department analysis of the long-term outlook for airlines warned: "A general upward spiral in passenger fares, coupled with reductions in public convenience, could lead to the reintroduction of federal oversight, reducing the industry's freedom and placing a damper on the performance of individual firms, if not the entire industry."

Few politicians or aviation experts expect airlines to be completely re-regulated. Instead, any future government role is likely to be limited to specific areas of concern, such as tougher antitrust enforcement, closer FAA supervision of airline scheduling, more rigorous enforcement of safety standards, and provision of more information (such as the on-time performance statistics that the government began publishing in 1987) to consumers.

Airlines also face new opportunities and challenges abroad. Major U.S. airlines have been forming alliances with foreign carriers and expanding their operations overseas, where passenger traffic is growing faster than in the United States. Worldwide passenger traffic is expected to grow about 5 percent a year in the 1990s, compared to about 4 percent a year in the United States, according to most forecasts. The Pacific Rim is expected to have the fastest growth.

But competition is also growing overseas. Europe is moving gradually to deregulate its own skies, an event that is likely to lead to a wave of mergers and the emergence of some giant European-based "megacarriers" able to compete for traffic around the globe. Given that prospect, U.S. airlines have been forming marketing agreements with European carriers in what many analysts foresee as the coming globalization of the airline industry. Most recently, several European carriers bought stock in U.S. airlines.

European carriers are also pressing for the right to move into American markets. They want reciprocity if U.S. carriers want the right to fly anywhere in Europe once deregulation is complete by the end of 1992. Foreign airlines are currently barred from providing domestic service in the United States.

Making money in the U.S. airline industry has been tough for many years. Net profit margins have been averaging only around 2 percent, although a few have done better. Despite all the challenges ahead, both at home and abroad, most analysts expect the healthier airlines will see their profit margins improve in the 1990s.

STRONG DEMAND FOR AIRPLANE MANUFACTURERS

Worldwide traffic growth and an aging airline fleet promise strong demand for new aircraft in the 1990s and beyond. Airlines are in the midst of a major buying cycle. Aircraft manufacturers are already sitting on a huge backlog of orders that should keep assembly lines busy for years to come. Airlines have been ordering record numbers of planes to accommodate traffic growth and to replace aging aircraft. About one of every five planes in the world's jet transport fleet was more than twenty years old in 1988; in the United States, more than one in four has reached its twentieth birthday. The average age of the world's fleet is twelve years.

Old does not necessarily mean unsafe. Even the oldest planes can be kept flying through additional inspections, increased maintenance, and modifications. But several recent incidents in which parts of older aircraft gave way in midflight raised concerns that inspections and modifications may not be enough to keep older planes flying indefinitely.

Although the recent retirement rate of older aircraft has been well below the historical average, advancing age will eventually lead to more retirements.

Tougher noise restrictions would also boost demand for new aircraft. Proposals to phase out older, noisier planes are expected to be adopted soon in the United States and in Europe. Although the timetable is still in question, federal regulations are expected to require a phaseout by the year 2000 or soon therafter. Airlines are lobbying for more time. In the United States and Europe, more than 3,300 aircraft would be affected by the new regulations, according to one government estimate. Not all of that would translate into new orders. Modifications can be made to older engines to bring the noise levels down to standard.

The Boeing Company commands more than 60 percent of the world's commercial aircraft market. The other two leading manufacturers are McDonnell Douglas, the nation's biggest military contractor, and Airbus Industrie, a four-nation European consortium.

According to Boeing's long-term forecast of the world airliner market, manufacturers will sell a total of 8,417 planes through the year 2005. In dollar terms, that is $516 billion in business, including the current $100 billion backlog.

Despite the strong demand for new aircraft, competition between the three manufacturers is intense and has resulted in narrower profit margins in recent years. The aircraft makers are also moving cautiously in stepping up production because the good times have been cut short before.

Should the airline business run into turbulence, manufacturers fear that airlines might do what they have done in past economic downturns: cancel their orders. Airlines order lots of planes when times are good, but if economic conditions have soured when it's time to take delivery, they don't want all the planes they ordered.

VERTICAL-TAKEOFF PLANES: A PARTIAL ANSWER
TO AIRPORT CONGESTION?

A new type of aircraft being developed for the military is also being eyed for commercial use as a way to help ease airport overcrowding. The "tilt-rotor" aircraft combines the vertical takeoff and landing features of a helicopter and the flying features of a fixed-wing turboprop with a cruise speed of 300 knots. Tilt-rotors are so named because the rotor blades can be positioned like a helicopter for takeoff and landing, and like a conventional aircraft for forward flight. Bell Helicopter and Boeing are developing the V-22 Osprey tilt-rotor for the military under a government contract, although the program has been threatened by defense budget cutbacks. A modified version for civilian use is expected by the mid-1990s. Aviation experts envision tilt-rotors being used for short-haul service between metropolitan areas, particularly in the crowded Northeast corridor.

If the concept is embraced, tilt-rotors could help lift the civilian helicopter industry out of its long recession.

20

LIVING WITH HIGHER ENERGY PRICES AGAIN

After a decade of cheap and plentiful oil, the energy outlook is darkening. By the mid-1990s, Americans can expect to come face to face again with the geological reality that oil is a scarce commodity held mostly by a few Middle Eastern countries.

Most government and private analysts expect oil prices to climb 50 to 100 percent or more by the year 2000. As worldwide energy consumption soaks up the current glut of oil, OPEC, which holds three quarters of the world's known reserves and almost all of the world's surplus production capacity, should once again be in a position to dominate the global oil market.

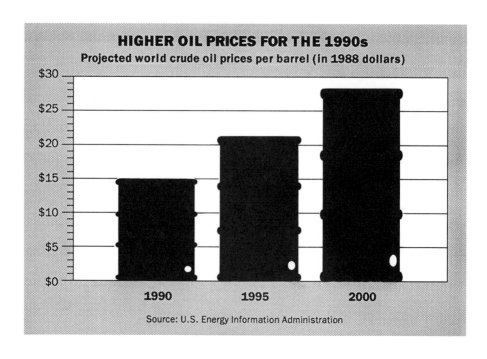

HIGHER OIL PRICES FOR THE 1990s
Projected world crude oil prices per barrel (in 1988 dollars)

Source: U.S. Energy Information Administration

America's dependence on imported oil is growing steadily and will soon exceed the record levels attained prior to the last energy crisis. This growing reliance on foreign sources threatens to make the nation vulnerable again to volatile energy prices and even the risk of another energy crunch should political tensions flare in the Middle East.

With America's appetite for oil projected to increase 7 percent in the 1990s, the United States has little choice but to turn to foreign sources of oil, which is getting harder and more expensive to find in this country. Even with the prospect of higher oil prices spurring more exploration in the 1990s, U.S. Department of Energy forecasts show a steady decline in domestic production through the end of the century.

Alternative energy sources are not likely to offer much help before the dawn of the twenty-first century. Not a single new nuclear plant has been ordered in more than a decade because of public concerns about safety. Coal is abundant and cheap but faces tighter restrictions because of growing concerns over acid rain and global warming. Solar power is making substantial progress but its promise as a significant energy source is not expected to be realized for another decade or two. And while scientists remain hopeful that nuclear fusion holds the key to a safe and inexhaustible supply of energy, no one expects it to become a commercial reality until well into the twenty-first century.

Higher oil prices, increased dependence on foreign crude supplies, and growing environmental concerns over the burning of fossil fuels are bound to accelerate development of alternative energy sources. But oil's role as the nation's primary energy source seems secure for the 1990s. Large-scale commercial applications of alternative energy sources are many years away.

Americans will face higher costs for driving a car, heating a home, and powering appliances in the 1990s. For investors, the prospect of higher oil prices later in the decade may eventually bring a rekindled interest in energy investments, ranging from companies that supply drilling equipment and services to those researching alternative energy sources. Higher energy prices would also help resuscitate the distressed economies of the nation's oil regions.

Energy conservation, which fell from the national consciousness when the price of oil collapsed in the 1980s, is bound to receive renewed attention as energy prices climb and the nation struggles to deal with the environmental and national security concerns of relying so heavily on oil. Perhaps most visibly, America's renewed love affair with big cars and big engines is likely to be short-lived, not so much because fueling them will be more expensive but rather because carmakers may be forced to cut back on their bigger models in order to meet higher federal fuel-efficiency standards.

THE ROAD TO HIGHER ENERGY PRICES

It is expected to be a few years before the worldwide oil glut is soaked up and excess production capacity is drained. Analysts see crude oil prices remaining under $20 a barrel (in 1988 dollars) during the early 1990s as OPEC continues its struggle to establish production and pricing discipline among its members, who now have plenty of excess production capacity and plenty of individual reasons for producing more than their quotas allow. But by the mid-1990s, according to U.S. government projections, oil prices will increase at an accelerated rate. By then, world demand is projected to rise to the point where OPEC members will be selling almost as much oil as they are capable of producing.

Analysts are hopeful that the rise in oil prices will be gradual and not nearly as severe as the last energy crisis. The Energy Department forecasts the world price of crude oil reaching $28 a barrel (in 1988 dollars) by the year 2000; many private analysts predict prices won't climb quite that far. (Keep in mind that these price figures would be much higher if they weren't adjusted for inflation and not denominated in 1988 dollars.) But these forecasts assume everything remains calm on the Middle Eastern front. Oil analysts recognize the growing vulnerability of the United States as it relies more and more on foreign suppliers.

DECLINING U.S. PRODUCTION

By all estimates, oil production in the United States is expected to decline sharply through the 1990s. The Energy Department estimates a 23 percent drop in domestic crude oil output.

The reason is that most of America's easy, large, and cheap oil discoveries have already been made. Finding new oil is a more expensive, more intensive, and riskier process; oil companies are forced to dig deeper, drill offshore, and look for smaller oil accumulations. That's why big oil companies have been focusing more on foreign exploration, where drilling is more fruitful.

Once world oil prices head higher, exploration and drilling in the

United States are expected to increase, but prices aren't expected to go high enough to sustain oil production at its current levels.

The lower forty-eight states have already been intensively drilled. Developing new reserves depends largely on drilling more holes in known fields for small oil deposits, and receiving government permission to drill in environmentally sensitive offshore regions of California.

Even Alaska is running out of oil. By 1995, production from the mammoth Prudhoe Bay field on the North Slope of Alaska is expected to be half of what it was in 1988. Even if the government opened the promising Arctic National Wildlife Refuge for development, Alaska production could still decline by as much as 25 percent during the 1990s.

Other non-OPEC countries are also expected to see their production fall in the 1990s, including the United Kingdom, where several North Sea fields will be exhausted.

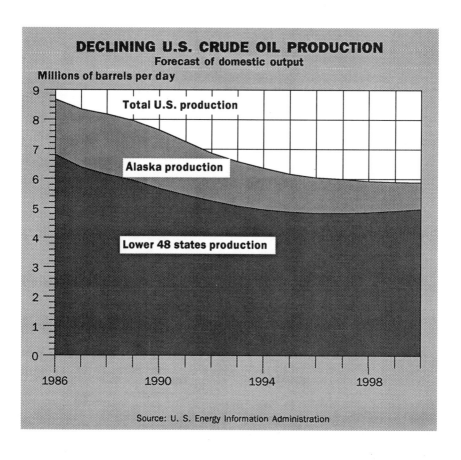

DECLINING U.S. CRUDE OIL PRODUCTION
Forecast of domestic output

Millions of barrels per day

Total U.S. production

Alaska production

Lower 48 states production

1986   1990   1994   1998

Source: U. S. Energy Information Administration

UNPRECEDENTED RELIANCE ON IMPORTS

With consumption rising and domestic production falling, heavier reliance on foreign oil is unavoidable. While imports accounted for only 36 percent of U.S. crude oil supplies in 1987, the Energy Department projects that the nation will be depending on foreign sources for a majority of its oil needs by the early 1990s. By the year 2000, import levels are expected to reach 59 percent.

That far surpasses the record 45 percent import level of 1977. Such heavy reliance on foreign oil carries the risk that OPEC will eventually regain control over the world oil market and be in a position to raise prices, cut supplies, or do both, as it did in 1973 and 1979.

Many analysts think that OPEC will not be as greedy next time around. The lesson learned from the oil price collapse of the 1980s is that raising oil prices too far can quickly boomerang.

The United States may also not be as vulnerable as it was in the 1970s because of the nation's growing crude oil stockpiles. The Strategic Petroleum Reserve, intended to provide a nest egg in case of another oil emergency, is already large enough fully to replace three months' imports (although the stockpile can be drawn down only at a rate equivalent to

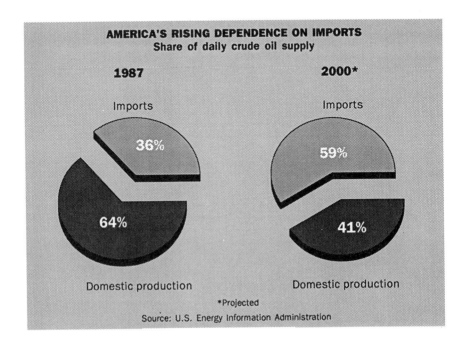

AMERICA'S RISING DEPENDENCE ON IMPORTS
Share of daily crude oil supply

1987

Imports

36%

64%

Domestic production

2000*

Imports

59%

41%

Domestic production

*Projected
Source: U.S. Energy Information Administration

half the daily imports). These supplies, as well as large stockpiles maintained by Japan and West Germany, may not only be sufficient to ease the impact of any temporary disruption in oil imports but also to discourage OPEC members from attempting to achieve some political objective by embargoing supplies.

BRIGHTER LONG-TERM PROSPECTS FOR THE OIL INDUSTRY

The long-term energy outlook suggests that though the oil industry will still be struggling with relatively low world oil prices through the early 1990s, there is light at the end of the tunnel. Rising oil prices should help improve the financial performance of domestic oil and gas producers. According to government forecasts, cash flow should start to increase in the early 1990s, with a substantial portion of it plowed back into exploration and development. That in turn should benefit oil-service firms that supply drilling equipment and technical services. Spending on drilling and equipment is expected to soar from about $9 billion in 1988 to more than $32 billion in 1995 and $57 billion by the year 2000, according to the Energy Department's forecast. Many private analysts expect a much more modest increase. Nevertheless, the general direction is clear: upward from the abyss.

Petroleum refiners, however, face numerous challenges in the years ahead, including the cost of meeting more stringent environmental regulations, adapting to a changing product mix as demand grows for alternative fuels, maintaining access to crude oil supplies as domestic production declines, and coping with slowing growth in demand. Demand for motor gasoline should level off in the 1990s as a result of expected increases in fuel-efficiency standards for automobiles and a slower rate of growth in the number of drivers.

On the plus side, refining capacity is expected to get tighter, leading to higher prices for refined products. The reason is that tougher environmental regulations will require more highly refined fuels, yet plans to build new refineries or expand existing facilities are running into opposition from environmentalists.

Higher oil prices would also help oil-patch states stabilize their depressed economies. But they're not likely to see a return to the boom times of the 1970s. Neither oil prices nor production are expected to reach the levels of a decade or two ago. Cities like Dallas and Houston are showing signs of revival because they have developed more diversified economies.

Investors will find that drilling for oil is riskier now than it used to be. Oil is getting harder and more expensive to find and the federal government no longer helps subsidize your investment. Investors in partnerships can no longer make use of tax write-offs to cushion the loss of a dry hole. Until you sell out, tax losses can only be used to shelter income from other tax shelters—not your other personal income. One exception applies to a certain type of oil and gas drilling venture in which the investors have a "working interest" in the partnership. Under the Tax Reform Act of 1986, investors with a working interest were given a blanket exception to the tough tax shelter restrictions and are allowed to use tax losses from the venture to shelter their personal income. But while conventional partnership arrangements limit your personal liability to the amount invested, working-interest partnerships entail far greater personal liability. Should problems develop, working-interest partners can be held personally liable for far more than their original investment.

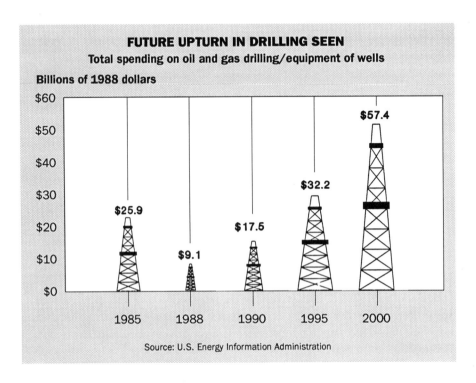

FUTURE UPTURN IN DRILLING SEEN
Total spending on oil and gas drilling/equipment of wells
Billions of 1988 dollars

Source: U.S. Energy Information Administration

ELECTRIC UTILITIES: HEADING FOR POWER SHORTAGES?

Electric utilities are buying cable-TV systems, investing in securities, and otherwise trying to diversify into businesses whose profits don't come under the watchful eye of state regulators. But one thing utilities aren't doing is building many new power plants. This lack of new generating capacity is raising fears that power shortages are on the horizon in many parts of the country.

Electricity consumption has picked up, and planned additions to generating capacity aren't expected to be sufficient to meet the rising demand, particularly in the East, Midwest, and Pacific Northwest. Unusually hot summers have already strained the peak load capabilities of utilities in some regions. In the past couple of years, many utilities saw electricity demand reach levels they hadn't expected until the 1990s.

Utilities are reluctant to embark on another aggressive round of building, fearful of being stuck again with excess generating capacity whose costs can't be recovered. In the 1970s, utilities engaged in a massive building program to accommodate what was then soaring growth in electricity consumption. But by the early 1980s, surging energy prices and a weakening economy slowed the growth in consumption, and utilities found themselves with an abundance of excess generating capacity.

State regulators contended the utilities were imprudent in expanding so fast and refused to allow them to recover all their construction outlays through customer rate increases.

As a result, utilities are now gun-shy about expanding their capacity to accommodate demand that may not soon be realized. Nor are they in a hurry to commit billions of dollars to new power plants while the acceptable fuel alternatives of the twenty-first century are still uncertain.

Many state regulators think that any shortfall in utility building can be made up through conservation programs and the construction of smaller power plants built by independent power producers that sell power to the utilities. But whether independent suppliers will be able to get over the regulatory, environmental, and financing hurdles to build enough generating capacity to handle the growing demand remains a question.

The gap that needs to be filled is large. Based on Energy Department forecasts, utilities have announced plans for new plants that would provide only 30 percent of what is projected to be needed during the 1990s in terms of additional generating capacity. As a result, utility analysts expect that plenty of additional orders for new plants will need to be made in the next several years.

The timing is uncertain. So is the type of equipment that utilities and other suppliers of electricity will end up ordering. But government analysts think the utilities will do it later rather than sooner and that much of the additional generating capacity will be met by gas turbines and combined-cycle units that use natural gas. Natural-gas–fired plants are smaller, cheaper, and quicker to build than nuclear or coal-fired steam generating plants. But gas is more expensive than uranium and coal, and so customers may end up paying higher electric bills as a result.

This scenario, although years away and subject to the risk of technological breakthroughs in alternative fuels, paints a bright long-term outlook for companies that make turbines and combined-cycle plants, as well as for natural gas companies.

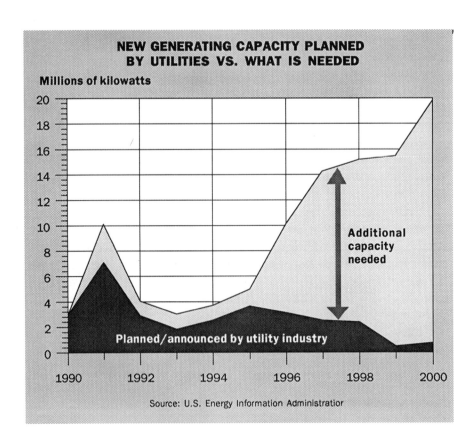

NEW GENERATING CAPACITY PLANNED BY UTILITIES VS. WHAT IS NEEDED

Millions of kilowatts

Additional capacity needed

Planned/announced by utility industry

Source: U.S. Energy Information Administration

NATURAL GAS: A CLEANER-BURNING FUEL

Greater use of natural gas by utilities and independent power suppliers is expected to help drive natural gas prices back up during the 1990s.

Natural gas prices are forecast to rise faster than those of crude oil, which is why many major oil companies are focusing their domestic exploration efforts on natural gas.

Natural gas has an environmental edge over both coal and oil. It releases relatively little in the way of particulate or sulfur emissions and it generates less carbon dioxide than any other fossil fuel. So efforts to reduce acid rain and atmospheric pollution would bode well for natural gas.

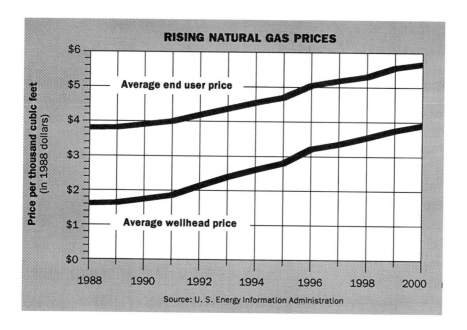

RISING NATURAL GAS PRICES

Average end user price

Average wellhead price

Price per thousand cubic feet (in 1988 dollars)

Source: U. S. Energy Information Administration

COAL'S ENVIRONMENTAL PROBLEM

Coal is the most abundant and cheapest domestic energy source available, but its potential for wider use is limited until technology can find a cost-effective way to eliminate emissions of sulfur dioxide and nitrogen oxide into the environment.

Proposed legislation to control acid rain would impose costly burdens

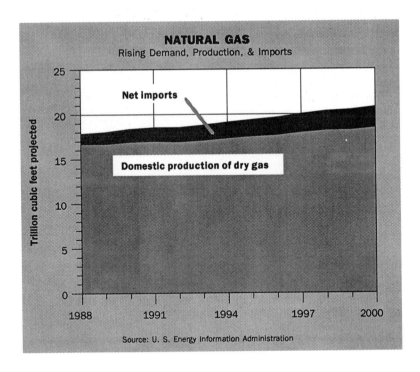

NATURAL GAS
Rising Demand, Production, & Imports

Net imports

Domestic production of dry gas

Trillion cubic feet projected

25
20
15
10
5
0

1988   1991   1994   1997   2000

Source: U. S. Energy Information Administration

on utilities that rely heavily on coal. Utilities would be forced to spend hundreds of millions of dollars on air pollution control equipment.

IS THERE A FUTURE FOR NUCLEAR?

The nuclear power industry has been moribund for years. Not a single new nuclear plant has been ordered by a U.S. utility since 1978. Nor are utilities likely to make any commitment to nuclear power without a radical change in public attitudes and answers to the problem of nuclear waste. But the nuclear industry is hoping for a rebirth and is trying to develop a new generation of safer and simpler reactors. Indeed, some of nuclear power's harshest critics are no longer as quick to foreclose the nuclear option. Growing concern about the greenhouse affect, acid rain, and other environmental dangers posed by the burning of fossil fuels has led many

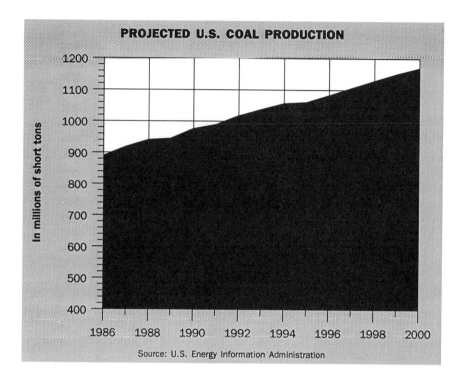

PROJECTED U.S. COAL PRODUCTION

In millions of short tons

Source: U.S. Energy Information Administration

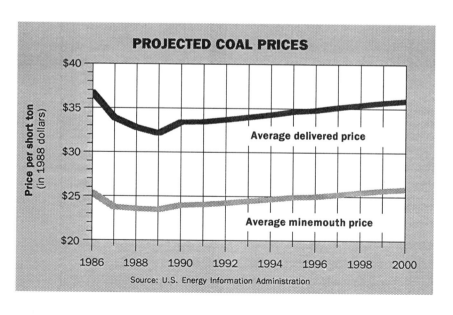

PROJECTED COAL PRICES

Price per short ton (in 1988 dollars)

Average delivered price

Average minemouth price

Source: U.S. Energy Information Administration

scientists and even some environmental groups to reexamine their opposition to nuclear power to see whether the next generation of nuclear reactors might be a less dangerous alternative than conventional fossil-fuel power plants.

Nevertheless, nuclear power is not expected to make a quick comeback. The anti-nuclear coalition that forced the recent shutdown of the Rancho Seco nuclear plant in northern California and prevented the start-up of the Shoreham nuclear plant on Long Island may not consider the new designs a significant improvement. Nor are utilities prone to rush into making new billion-dollar commitments while they face the risk of public protests, lawsuits, regulatory hassles and other obstacles that have led to costly delays in previous nuclear projects.

SOLAR ENERGY: RAYS OF HOPE

Solar energy offers great promise as an important energy source in the future and long strides are being made in developing the technology for large-scale commercial applications. But while researchers are coming closer to making solar energy competitive with conventional energy sources, solar power still costs two to four times more.

Utilities generate power at an average cost of just over 6 cents per kilowatt-hour. By contrast, solar power costs about 25 cents per kilowatt-hour, which is still twice as expensive as what utilities spend to get electricity from their least efficient plants.

When that gap will be bridged is uncertain, but many researchers believe it will be a decade or more before solar energy starts to make even a 1 percent contribution to the nation's electricity supply.

Despite all the progress and promise, not everyone has been satisfied with the pace of development. One of the industry's biggest players, Arco Solar, was recently sold by its parent, Atlantic Richfield, the large oil company. Executives felt the market wasn't growing fast enough. In 1988, the world market for solar cells totaled only about $125 million.

21

THE NEW
ENVIRONMENTAL AGE

Relegated to the back burner of civic consciousness in the 1980s, environmentalism is back with a new urgency. Mounting concerns about global warming, erosion of the ozone layer, acid rain, overflowing landfills, urban smog, toxic wastes, and water pollution promise to make cleaning up the environment a top national priority in the 1990s.

Cleaning up the environment will cost consumers and businesses many billions of dollars and impact many facets of American life. It will mean higher utility bills, higher prices at the gasoline pump, and higher costs for trash collection. For many Americans, it will mean separating trash under mandatory recycling programs; new incentives to use car pools and mass transit; and more frequent automobile emission inspections and costly maintenance. For residents of some of the nation's most polluted cities, environmental cleanup may mean new restrictions on wood-burning fireplaces, backyard barbecues, and power lawn mowers.

Cleaning up the environment will require heavy investments in pollution control equipment by electric utilities, chemical companies, oil refineries, factories, service stations, and even the corner dry cleaner. Automobile manufacturers will be forced to accelerate development of cars that run on alternative fuels, which oil refineries will have to produce and gas stations will need to sell.

Garbage and environmental control will be major growth industries of the 1990s. Tens of billions of dollars will be needed each year to clean up the nation's polluted air and waterways and to find ways of disposing of America's mounting garbage and toxic waste.

The new focus on the environment was assured long before President Bush unveiled his far-reaching clean-air plan and vowed to "make the 1990s the era for clean air." It was assured long before governments from around the world called for phasing out production of ozone-depleting fluorocarbons, or before hundreds of communities imposed mandatory recycling programs. The renewed commitment to cleaning up the environment was assured as evidence of the environmental damage boiled to the surface. Medical waste washed up on beaches and garbage scows sailed aimlessly across oceans in search of a dumping site. As doctors detected a rising incidence of skin cancer, evidence mounted that the protective ozone shield was eroding even faster than had been predicted. Local health departments issued more and more warnings on contaminated seafood and drinking-water supplies. And a succession of hot, drought-ridden summers brought attention to mounting scientific fears that pollution is leading the planet into a disastrous "greenhouse effect" scenario of steadily rising temperatures and sea levels. This time around, environmentalism is no passing political fad.

THE GARBAGE CRISIS

America is still number one in many fields, and trash production is one of them. America throws away more trash than any other industrial nation; an average of 3.5 pounds of it is generated each day by each man, woman, and child. But the day of reckoning is fast approaching.

Garbage is growing at a suffocating pace and municipalities are running out of places to put it all. Landfills have closed at a staggering pace over the past decade as stricter environmental regulations took effect and landfills filled up. At the end of 1989, fewer than 6,000 landfills remained

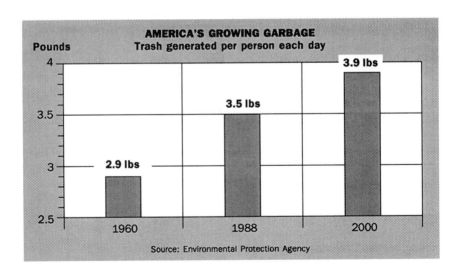

AMERICA'S GROWING GARBAGE
Trash generated per person each day

Pounds

4 —

3.9 lbs

3.5 lbs

3.5 —

2.9 lbs

3 —

2.5 —

1960   1988   2000

Source: Environmental Protection Agency

open, compared to more than 9,000 in 1984 and 30,000 in 1976. By 1995, the Environmental Protection Agency projects, only 3,000 landfills will still be open. Finding new sites for landfills has proven next to impossible as public officials have run into fierce opposition from community groups, none of which want a landfill in their neighborhood.

As a result, communities have been forced to turn to other, more expensive and less convenient options for disposing of garbage: recycling it, incinerating it, and reducing the amount of garbage people throw away by taxing or banning certain products.

With garbage growing and communities struggling for ways to get rid of it, companies with disposal sites or recycling facilities, the technology for solid-waste and hazardous-waste removal, and experience in getting through the sea of federal, state, and local regulations, should find a fast-growing market in the 1990s.

Burning It: Many local governments are considering huge incinerators as a way to solve the trash problem. Incineration can reduce the volume of garbage by 90 percent and its weight by 75 percent. Burning garbage also has a side benefit. The heat produced in the burning process can generate electricity, which can be sold to local utilities. That money, in turn, can help reduce the cost of garbage disposal. And so waste-to-energy plants have been making their way into a growing number of communities, and some analysts expect the industry to experience rapid growth in the 1990s. But there are hurdles. Incinerators have met tough resistance from environmentalists and community groups. Another drawback is that burning tends to be more expensive than recycling and landfills.

In addition, incinerators leave millions of tons of toxic ash to be disposed of. Getting rid of the toxic ash is no easy assignment. A ship left Philadelphia in 1986 and sailed the earth's seas for more than two years in search of a place to dump 28 million pounds of the city's incinerator ash. No one disclosed where the ash was finally dumped, but the ship was reportedly turned away by at least eleven countries on four continents. Disposal problems have led many communities to scrap plans for waste-to-energy plants.

Another potential impediment is the EPA, which has threatened to ban burning unless the municipality recycles 25 percent of its garbage.

Separating Trash to Become a New Household Ritual: Recycling, an idea that came and went in the 1970s, is returning as perhaps the most efficient and most environmentally sound solution to the growing waste problem. This time, the focus on recycling is spurred less by ecological concerns than by communities that are simply running out of landfill space. Ten states now have mandatory recycling laws and more than a thousand communities have instituted curbside pickup programs. Separating recyclable items from the rest of the trash is bound to become a commonplace ritual in American households in the 1990s.

Recycling can cut trash volume by up to 80 percent, extending the life of landfills and reducing burning and dumping costs. Cash from recycled material can also mean lowering overall disposal costs for the community. But it also may mean gluts on the recycling market. Recycling will be no easy business. Many could have trouble finding a market for their scrap. Gluts have hampered recycling efforts in the past. Many cities now find that they have to pay recyclers to take their newspapers, rather than get paid $50 a ton for them. The glut has led to legislative proposals in several states to tax virgin newsprint or to require newspapers to use a minimum amount of recycled newsprint. But inducements will also be needed to encourage paper companies to build more plants to recycle used paper.

Disposable Diapers: Cloth diaper makers and diaper services are trying to capitalize on the environmental wave to gain back some of the market share they lost to disposables over the past two decades. Disposables now account for about 80 percent of the market. Many state and local governments are considering legislation that would tax or ban certain nondegradable or unrecyclable products like disposable diapers, which would widen the advantage of cotton diapers. But makers of disposable diapers are not sitting idly by. Some smaller diaper companies have introduced disposable brands that they claim are biodegradable. Procter & Gamble, the leading maker of disposable diapers, has launched a pilot program to recycle used diapers into flowerpots and other products.

Plastic: Plastic is coming under increasing attack as the fastest-growing element of the waste problem and one of the most troublesome. With legislation under consideration in many states to ban or tax certain plastic products, its widespread use in packaging, bottles, diapers, fast-food containers, and grocery bags is threatened unless further progress is made in developing degradable plastics or recycling of plastics becomes widespread. Recycling of plastic waste lags far behind that of aluminum cans, glass bottles, and newspapers. Recycled plastic can be used to make a wide variety of products, including flowerpots, trash cans, toys, carpeting, foam insulation, and park benches.

Environmental Marketing: Many consumer product companies are attempting to cash in on the "green" movement by introducing lines of "environmentally friendly" products—such as bathroom tissue made from recycled paper and garbage bags and disposable diapers that are touted as being degradable. Other products, such as refillable spray bottles, are aimed at reducing the amount of garbage. Manufacturers have found that "green" products not only help win new markets but also that many shoppers are willing to pay a premium for products that seem to help the environment—even though some of the claims don't hold up to scrutiny by environmental groups. For example, there is considerable debate over whether degradable products actually do degrade in today's tightly packed landfills as well as claimed.

CLEANING UP TOXIC WASTES

Cleaning up toxic-waste dumps that American industry left behind promises to be an expensive and massive undertaking. Since 1980, when the federal government established the "Superfund" program to finance the hazardous-waste cleanup, only about three dozen of the nation's 1,200 most dangerous toxic-waste dumps have been cleaned up.

The Environmental Protection Agency, which was criticized during the Reagan administration for being slow to move, said that it would substantially increase the pace of cleanup in the 1990s. Along with state- and privately financed cleanup projects, hazardous waste should present golden opportunities for waste management companies in the years ahead, including some smaller firms that have developed special technologies for cleaning up hazardous waste. For instance, several dozen companies have developed—or are in the process of developing—microbes, or "superbugs," to devour various types of hazardous wastes, turning them into harmless by-products.

In addition, hazardous-waste companies, particularly those with expertise in nuclear waste, can look forward to the massive repair and cleanup of the nation's deteriorating nuclear weapons production plants. Some estimates for cleaning up radioactive and chemical pollution at the plants and upgrading them approach $100 billion over the next two decades.

CLEANING UP URBAN AIR

Reducing air pollution to safe levels in most cities by the end of the century, as the Bush administration has called for, will entail additional expenditures of $20 billion or more a year, technological innovations, and significant changes in the way Americans conduct their business and carry on their lives.

Utilities: Many of the utilities that use coal to generate electricity will be forced to spend hundreds of millions of dollars in the 1990s to reduce harmful emissions of sulfur dioxide and nitrogen oxide. These pollutants undergo chemical changes as they spew into the atmosphere and fall back to earth in the form of acidic rain, snow, fog, or dust. Acid rain is blamed for destroying marine life in lakes and streams and for damage to forests. Much of the pollution originates in the Midwest, but because the emissions travel long distances, a great deal of the damage occurs in the Northeast and Canada. For the utilities, controlling acid rain will require installing devices in smokestacks to reduce emissions or burning coal that contains less sulfur; each utility will have to calculate which is the less costly burden. But shareholders of utility companies that need to make heavy investments in pollution control equipment will find that pollution legislation is costly to the bottom line: Fitting a large coal-fired generating plant could cost as much as $500 million. Such measures could prove a bonanza for companies that make pollution control equipment as well as those that produce low-sulfur coal. Low-sulfur coal is produced mainly in the West and is more expensive and less abundant than high-sulfur coal, which is produced mainly in the East.

Electric Bills: For customers of utilities that need to reduce emissions, electric bills are projected to rise at least 5 to 10 percent.

Reducing Industrial Pollution: Industry would also be forced to invest heavily in pollution-control equipment to curb harmful emissions. Such measures may not only affect chemical companies, oil refineries, and other large manufacturing plants, but also smaller businesses, such as commercial bakeries and dry cleaners, that also add to the pollution problem. Reducing industrial emissions would be a boon to manufacturers of pollution control equipment. But it could also put pressure on the price of many goods and services, from donuts to dry cleaning, and perhaps force some smaller operators out of business.

More Auto Emissions Tests: Automobiles are the biggest source of urban smog and more states are expected to require better pollution control equipment on new cars and annual vehicle inspections to ensure that emission systems on older cars are well maintained. Motorists would be forced to spend more to keep their older cars tuned and their emission control systems functioning properly. With age, these systems tend to function less efficiently and require more maintenance. Such a move would be a boon to independent repair shops and service stations that perform emissions tests and make repairs. If you are buying a used car, make sure it can pass an emissions test. It can be expensive to make the repairs needed to bring a car up to standards. In some states, used-car dealers can't complete a sale until the car passes the emissions test.

Catalytic Converters: Makers of catalytic converters should also benefit from the move toward greater pollution controls. More stringent air pollution standards in Europe, Japan, and other parts of the world will increase the use of catalytic converters and their need for replacement.

Getting People Out of Their Cars: To meet air quality standards, many cities will have to encourage motorists to drive less by expanding mass transit, promoting the use of car pools, and encouraging or forcing employers to stagger work hours and allow more employees to work from home. Denver, Phoenix, Tucson, and Albuquerque have already instituted voluntary no-drive days. Higher tolls are also being considered in some metropolitan areas to reduce air pollution as well as traffic congestion.

Wood-Burning Fireplaces and Stoves: Wood-burning fireplaces and stoves are coming under tougher restrictions, and in a few urban areas, the crackling fires that warm hearts and home may be headed for extinction. Some western communities, including Denver and Albuquerque, already ban wood burning in fireplaces on days when pollution levels are high. The Metropolitan Air Quality Council in Denver also recommended that new wood-burning fireplaces be banned and that homeowners be forced to either seal their fireplaces or convert them to gas-burning before selling their home.

New EPA regulations impose progressively tougher pollution-control requirements on new wood-burning stoves in the early 1990s, and some cities have banned their installation.

Alternative Fuels: Cleaner-burning alternative fuels should have greater application in the 1990s. Pilot tests of fleets of cars and buses that run on methanol, for example, are already in progress in some cities, and the Bush administration has called for annual production of as many as one million alternative-fuel cars by the late 1990s. Methanol is the most likely alternative fuel. A gallon of methanol costs about the same as a gallon of gasoline but gets only about 60 percent of gasoline's mileage. So a methanol car would need a bigger fuel tank. It would also require more expensive parts since methanol is more corrosive than gasoline. Such alternative fuels are seen by environmentalists as only a stopgap measure until technology makes electric-powered cars practicable in the twenty-first century. Although methanol and natural gas reduce ground-level ozone pollution, they still emit other pollutants.

Oil Companies: For the oil industry, alternative fuels will mean spending billions of dollars on new refineries, storage tanks, tanker trucks, and service station pumps. Oil companies would also have to get more heavily involved in natural gas (the primary feedstock of methanol) or coal (a more costly feedstock), or possibly even corn farming if ethanol proves commercially promising as an alternative fuel. That's why major oil companies are working hard to come up with a reformulated gasoline that would meet clean-air requirements. Reformulated gasoline could be produced in the industry's existing refineries.

By the time alternative fuels come into widespread use there are likely to be far fewer service stations around because of the cost of complying with other new environmental regulations. Industry trade groups estimate that nearly a quarter of the nation's 112,000 service stations will be forced to close because of the heavy costs of complying with new rules aimed at protecting underground water supplies from leaky gasoline storage tanks. Under the regulations, station owners will be forced to replace leaking tanks, install new devices that detect leaks, and obtain liability insurance to cover potential damages in the event of a leak.

Automakers: Car manufacturers face tough and costly challenges in the new environmental age, including reducing tailpipe emissions, increasing the fuel economy of their fleets, and designing and selling cars that run on alternative fuels. These new environmental mandates threaten to bring an early end to America's renewed love affair with big and fast cars that made Detroit so prosperous in the latter half of the 1980s. Smaller cars have skinnier profit margins. Automakers are confident that they can build alternative-fuel cars in quantity. But they worry about a Catch-22 situation in trying to market them: Consumers will be reluctant to buy the cars until alternative fuels are widely available, and service stations will be reluctant to carry the fuels until there are a lot of alternative-fuel cars on the road. In addition, consumers would need some kind of incentive to buy an alternative-fuel car. A "flexible fuel" car, which can run on either gasoline or some alternative fuel, is expected to cost several hundred dollars more than conventional models that run on gasoline only.

The Los Angeles Example: A vision of what the future holds for urban America can be seen in southern California, which has mandated a comprehensive plan to clean up its air pollution over the next two decades. While southern California has by far the worst smog in the country, other cities with serious air pollution problems will likely be forced to adopt some of the same tough restrictions on everyday activities. Measures being phased in this decade include a ban on most free parking; a ban on gas-powered lawn mowers; a ban on barbecue starter fuels; a limit to the number of cars each family can have; increased registration fees for motorists with more than one car; restriction of all new tire purchases to radials, which throw fewer rubber particles into the air; and reformulation of paints, solvents, and deodorant sprays. In the next century, the plan calls for banning all gasoline-powered vehicles by the year 2007—technology permitting. Building a car that runs on electricity is no problem; the roadblock has been developing an affordable long-lasting battery that can store enough energy to allow the car to travel fast enough and far enough in between charges to make it practicable. Electric cars represent a serious threat to the oil industry in the next century but a vast new market for the electric utility industry.

THE GREENHOUSE EFFECT

Scientists have presented mounting evidence that carbon dioxide emissions from the burning of fossil fuels, and other industrial gases, are accumulating in the atmosphere to threatening levels. These gases trap the heat from the sun, much the way a greenhouse does. How much the earth will warm, and how quickly it will happen, are uncertain. So is the question of whether the global warming has already begun. But computer models predict that the earth's temperature will rise 3 to 9 degrees Fahrenheit by the middle of the next century, an increase humans have never experienced. This warming is predicted to cause a thermal expansion of the oceans and a melting of the polar ice caps, causing sea levels to rise by one to four feet.

That threat will force the United States, as well as countries around the world, to take bold steps over the next decade or two to mitigate the expected warming, including efforts to stop deforestation and to reduce sharply and eventually eliminate the use of fossil fuels.

Commercial development of electric cars and safer alternative energy sources, such as solar power, on a large scale is not likely until early in the next century. But, in a report to Congress, EPA officials have proposed some intermediate steps:

- A worldwide effort to increase average fuel efficiency of automobiles to at least 40 miles per gallon.
- Requiring all industrial countries to mandate installation of catalytic converters in automobiles.
- A halt to deforestation by planting at least as many trees as are cut down. (Some American communities are considering aggressive tree-planting programs as a way to reduce air pollution. Los Angeles, for instance, plans to plant up to 5 million trees over a five-year period. In its 1991 budget, the Bush administration proposed a nationwide program to plant a billion trees a year. Trees absorb carbon dioxide during photosynthesis.)
- Accelerated research to develop solar power.
- Imposition of fees on oil, coal, and natural gas to provide economic incentives to shift away from the use of fossil fuels.

THE ERODING OZONE LAYER

Mounting concerns over the destruction of the ozone layer have led to an international treaty, ratified by the United States and dozens of foreign governments, to reduce production of chlorofluorocarbons by 50 percent by mid-1998. Western nations are now pushing for a timetable to completely phase out the chemicals, believed to be the main culprits in eroding the atmospheric layer that absorbs harmful ultraviolet radiation from the sun.

Chlorofluorocarbons, known as CFCs, are widely used as coolants in refrigerators and air conditioners, as foaming agents to create plastic insulation, and as solvents in the manufacture of electronic components. CFCs are also used as aerosol propellants, an application banned in the United States but still widespread in Europe.

Chemical manufacturers are racing to develop substitutes. With

CFCs being regulated out of existence, the market potential for companies that can develop effective substitutes is enormous. For users, the replacements are likely to be more costly and require product redesigns. For example, some substitutes being considered for car air conditioners would require automakers to make costly design changes to the cooling system and possibly to the car itself.

Scientists warn that damage already done to the ozone layer will lead to a worldwide increase in cataracts and skin cancer in the decades ahead. The heightened risk of skin cancer should create a growing market for suntan lotions. But it could also dampen people's desire to spend as much time at the beach as they used to.

INDOOR POLLUTION

Staying indoors used to be considered a safe refuge from the harmful pollutants outside. But several new research studies suggest that you're more likely to get sick from pollution in your home or office than from breathing outdoors even in some of America's most polluted cities.

A five-year study by the Environmental Protection Agency found that air pollution levels in some offices, hospitals, nursing homes, and schools were as much as one hundred times higher than outdoors.

As scientific evidence mounts, indoor air pollution can be expected to draw increasing attention. Smoking bans will continue to proliferate. But while tobacco smoke is one of the worst culprits, scientists contend that indoor air pollution comes from a variety of sources, including cleaning solvents, pesticides, fumes from carpeting, furniture, photocopying equipment, asbestos, and radon. Indoor pollution has become worse in recent years partly because new office buildings have been designed with sealed windows to save energy.

If you find yourself feeling sick all day at the office and then improving when you get outside, indoor air pollution may be the culprit rather than mental anguish over your job. Headaches, runny noses, burning eyes, coughing, scratchy throats, dizziness, nausea, and upset stomachs are common symptoms of indoor pollution.

Coping with Pollution at the Office: Most people don't realize they're getting sick from indoor pollution and a lot of employers don't take individual complaints seriously. So if you suspect indoor pollution is making you sick, ask your colleagues if they are experiencing the same problems. It's much easier to get something done about an office pollution problem when many people register the same complaint.

Of course, getting rid of photocopying machines, typewriters, curtains, and all the other suspected sources of pollution is not likely to be considered a viable solution. Rather, efforts to mitigate the problem should focus on ways to improve ventilation. Sometimes, the ventilation system itself is the cause of the pollution problem. It can become contaminated with bacteria, fungi, or some other pollutant.

Some ventilation systems do no more than recycle indoor air, which may mean polluted air is simply being recycled around the office. Special equipment needs to be added to "scrub" the air clean.

Coping with Radon Pollution at Home: The Environmental Protection Agency recently recommended that homeowners test for the presence of radon, an odorless, colorless gas that is suspected of being responsible for up to 20,000 lung cancer deaths each year. The EPA estimates as many as 10 percent of homes contain high enough levels of radon to warrant immediate corrective action.

Radon is produced by the natural decay of uranium in soil and rocks and typically seeps into homes through drainpipes, sump pumps, and cracks in concrete floors or foundations. The EPA recommended that everyone living in detached houses or town houses or in apartments in the basement or on the first or second floor test for radon in living areas. (Engineers don't believe there's much chance of radon passing above the second or third floors of buildings.)

The easiest and most economical way to test for radon is to buy an EPA-certified do-it-yourself test kit available at hardware stores, supermarkets, and through mail order for $10 to $50. Depending on the model, the detector is left in place for from several days to as long as a year. Bear in mind that because radon levels vary widely over short periods, detectors that stay in place for longer periods generally give more reliable estimates of actual exposure. That's why some experts recommend doing a short- and a long-term test simultaneously; you get a quick indication of any radon problem with the short test and a more accurate measure with the long test. Follow-up tests are also recommended. Detectors have to be shipped to a laboratory for analysis, the cost of which is included in the purchase price of the detector.

Short-term testing can also be accomplished by calling in a radon technician. That's a more expensive route, but it's commonly used when a real estate sale is contingent on the results of a radon test.

If radon levels are marginal, some do-it-yourself measures, such as filling large holes in the basement floors and around pipes through walls, may be sufficient. But if that doesn't bring radon levels down, or if initial readings arc high, call a contractor who specializes in fixing radon problems. Try to stay away from hiring the same company that tests your home. Unscrupulous contractors have been known to rig the test results to show the need for thousands of dollars in repairs. Most radon repairs should amount to between $500 and $1,500.

Finding a reliable contractor takes some checking around. Some states are starting to certify radon contractors. And the EPA offers radon courses to contractors; a list of those who have passed the course can be obtained from your local EPA office.

The EPA can also provide you with a list of certified radon-testing companies, as well as two booklets: "Radon Reduction Methods—A Homeowner's Guide," and "A Citizen's Guide to Radon."

Before you buy a home, have it tested for radon. It's no different from checking for leaks in the roof or for termites. Even if your state doesn't require the test, insist on it because if there is a radon problem, repairs may be expensive enough to warrant an adjustment in the sales price.

The Radon Business: Hundreds of companies have moved into the radon detection and mitigation business as the radon problem has drawn increased attention. Most are small, privately owned companies. Theoretically, there is plenty of room for the business to grow. Only about 1 percent of homes had been tested for radon when the EPA issued its report in late 1988. But business prospects depend on whether homeowners stay concerned enough about the problem to get their homes tested and whether radon tests become a mandatory part of real estate transactions.

22

CONSUMER'S GUIDE TO PERSONAL ELECTRONICS IN THE 1990s

HDTV. IDTV. Recordable CDs. DATs. Videophones. Electronic filmless cameras. Cellular phones. Fax. A dazzling yet bewildering array of new consumer electronics is now available or soon to come. For the unwary buyer, it can be treacherous territory.

With HDTV on the horizon, will the video equipment you buy today make you sorry you did in a year or two? Are vinyl LPs about to become extinct? Does digital audiotape represent the future of home recording or is it headed for the same fate as eight-track tapes? If you want a mobile phone, do you buy a car phone, a portable phone, or a "transportable"? What features do you look for in a fax machine for your home office? Are radar detectors about to be rendered useless against new police weapons to nab speeding motorists?

This chapter is an attempt to sort out the new consumer technologies: what's here today and what's coming; which products are in imminent danger of being rendered obsolete by advanced technologies and which of today's technologies you can invest in with reasonable assurance that they won't be outmoded tomorrow.

THE NEXT GENERATION OF TV—HIGH-DEFINITION TELEVISION (HDTV)

For couch potatoes and videophiles, television is about to look much better. How much better? Next time you go to the movie theater, imagine being able to get the same kind of resolution and the same wide-screen dimensions on your home TV. That will give you a good sense of what High-Definition Television (HDTV) is all about. It will be available in Japan as early as 1990 or 1991, and in the United States as early as 1993 or 1994.

In the biggest advance in television technology since the advent of color, HDTV promises a picture that matches the clarity of 35-millimeter film. By doubling the number of horizontal scan lines that make up the TV image and widening the screen, television will bring cinemalike quality into your living room. No need to stand in a long movie line again.

Today's television picture standard consists of up to 525 horizontal lines, while HDTV technology generates up to 1,125 lines. The additional lines produce a much more detailed and sharper picture. As for screen size, current picture tubes are of squarish 4-by-3 proportions, while HDTV screens will match the 16-by-9 dimensions of wide-screen cinema. The difference in screen dimensions is roughly the difference between a letter-size sheet of typing paper and a legal-size sheet.

The price tag for the new technology is steep. Early HDTV sets are likely to run $2,500 to $4,000, although engineers think that mass production will eventually lead to models selling for as little as $1,000 or $1,500. Americans will still be able to receive broadcast programming on their conventional sets as they do now. But you won't see any difference in the picture unless you buy a specially designed HDTV set. The Federal Communications Commission, in setting the ground rules for an HDTV broadcast standard in the United States, decided that the nation's 160 million television sets shouldn't be rendered useless by the new technology. So the transition will be similar to when broadcasting switched from black-and-white to color.

HDTV

Conventional TV
Dimensions: 4 x 3
Resolution: 525 lines

High-Definition TV
Dimensions: 16 x 9
Resolution: 1,125 lines

The high price of HDTV sets is likely to make the transition slow, perhaps a decade or longer before significant numbers of American households have an HDTV set. By the turn of the century, only about one in four households will have an HDTV set, according to a marketing study commissioned by the Electronic Industries Association. Many analysts offer far lower estimates.

HDTV systems around the world will not share the same technical standard, which means TV sets designed for Japan's system won't work on America's HDTV system and vice versa.

Japan's HDTV system, which is scheduled to begin commercial broadcasts by 1990 or 1991, will deliver programming to Japanese homes via satellite. Europe also plans to deliver HDTV by direct-broadcast satellite (DBS). Satellite-to-home broadcasting is the easiest way to deliver HDTV because HDTV requires a broader bandwidth than is available on existing VHF or UHF channels, which are limited to a bandwidth of six megahertz. Satellite channels, which have several times more bandwidth, can more easily accommodate the HDTV signal.

Exactly how American broadcasters will transmit the HDTV signal on conventional channels is still under discussion. One option would require sending the added information for HDTV on a second channel. HDTV sets would be designed to blend the signals from the two channels. Another option would be to squeeze the signal into one channel, although that would result in something less than HDTV and fewer than 1,125 lines. The FCC will decide.

But TV stations are likely to be the last to start delivering HDTV signals. Many local stations will be reluctant to spend millions of dollars on equipment to broadcast HDTV in the early stages when only a tiny portion of their viewing audience has an HDTV set. Other programmers, however, will be eager to establish a niche.

HDTV will probably appear first on videocassette recorders and videodisk players. VCR standards are not regulated by the FCC. So if you rush out to get the first HDTV video recorder and TV set, make sure they will be compatible with the rest of the American HDTV system.

Home Box Office and other pay cable services that are in direct competition with video rentals are likely to follow soon after with HDTV programming. Cable systems could accommodate the larger bandwidth needs of HDTV by combining channels (although cable systems with small channel capacity would have to drop some existing services to make room for HDTV). Satellite-to-home broadcasts of HDTV are also on the drawing board.

What to Do While You're Waiting for HDTV to Arrive

Anything you buy now won't give you the enhanced picture of HDTV. So if you're about to spend a few thousand dollars on a state-of-the-art projection TV that you hope to cherish for years to come, think twice. Shortly, it won't be state-of-the-art any longer. Unless you can afford to spend a few thousand dollars on a TV every few years, buying now may preclude buying when HDTV comes out.

Big-screen TV is where HDTV really makes a difference. The additional scan lines give big-screen pictures much sharper detail. So the visual difference will be quite noticeable on projection TVs.

The difference is not so noticeable on smaller sets. In fact, some studies suggest that most people won't be able to tell the difference between an HDTV picture and a conventional picture on smaller screens. So if you're thinking about buying a smaller-screen TV for your bedroom or den, don't worry about HDTV. You won't be missing much if you buy a small set. You'll still be able to receive broadcast programming as you do now, according to the FCC plan. So none of your sets will become obsolete. What's more, few people can afford to buy an HDTV set for every viewing room in the house. With prices for HDTV sets in the thousands of dollars rather than the hundreds of dollars that conventional models cost, most households will probably choose to buy one HDTV set for the living room or family room and conventional sets for the rest of the house. By one industry estimate, it will be the late 1990s before smaller HDTV sets with screen sizes of 20 to 25 inches are introduced. In the early years, HDTV is expected to be a high-end product, with manufacturers turning out models with screen sizes of 30 inches and larger.

What about portable video cameras? HDTV camcorders will undoubtedly be available someday to capture your children in vivid detail. But your children may be grown by the time HDTV camcorders become affordable for consumers. It's not worth missing years of precious video of your children to wait for HDTV camcorders to arrive.

HDTV video recorders and players may appear soon, but the early models will be expensive, perhaps $2,500 or more. It may be several years before prices become affordable to most Americans. So if your old VCR wears out, you won't be alone if you spend a few hundred dollars on a conventional VCR to last you until HDTV prices come down.

IMPROVED-DEFINITION TELEVISION (IDTV): A STEP ALONG THE WAY

Don't confuse HDTV with Improved-Definition Television (IDTV), which is already on the market. IDTV uses internal circuitry and digital technology to make the current broadcast standard look sharper. But it doesn't add any more horizontal lines to the picture, as HDTV does.

Essentially, IDTV sets display pictures at twice the rate of ordinary TVs. On ordinary TVs, the picture is displayed in two sections: Even-numbered horizontal scan lines are displayed first, followed a fraction of a second later by the odd-numbered lines. On IDTV sets, the scan lines are displayed all at once, giving the viewer a more even and sharper image.

IDTV is a step along the way to better television pictures but it won't give you HDTV. IDTV is for those who can't wait until HDTV arrives for a sharper picture.

THE DIGITAL ERA: SAY GOOD-BYE TO THE VINYL LP

Vinyl LPs are about to join the Victrola and the 78 rpm in the technological scrap yard, supplanted by the superior-sounding compact disk and the more convenient audiocassette.

Vinyl LPs now account for less than 10 percent of all recording sales, and record dealers are giving them less and less space as they make more room for CDs, whose sales are exploding, and cassette tapes, which continue to enjoy heavy demand. Some record dealers have already evicted all vinyl LPs from their stores. And record companies are taking steps to hasten their demise by making it costlier for record stores to return unsold LPs.

In the face of the vinyl LP's imminent death, it would be folly for anyone to invest a lot of money in a new turntable unless you have a large library of albums that you play often or are one of those audiophiles who don't like the digital sound. If you want to build a durable collection of recordings for the future, the best bet is to invest in a CD player and build a collection around the CD format, which will be around for years to come. CDs are much more durable and offer far superior fidelity and clarity than vinyl LPs.

It may be a few years before vinyl LPs are issued a formal death certificate. After all, there are still some 80 million turntables in the United States alone. But as was the case with the now-dead eight-track tape, record-store selections of vinyl LPs will become more meager and obtaining certain new releases on vinyl will increasingly require special orders. Some releases will be impossible to obtain on vinyl. Several record companies have already stopped releasing new classical and jazz recordings on vinyl.

THE RECORDABLE COMPACT DISK: AN AUDIO-VIDEO REVOLUTION

If there is a budding technology with the potential to revolutionize home audio recording over the next few years, it is the compact disk recorder and erasable CD, which are expected to make their debut soon.

Using the same CD format and laser digital technology that revolutionized the record business in the 1980s, the new CD player/recorders will let you make perfect copies of original music recordings.

The erasable disks, which are expected to sell for about the same price as prerecorded CDs, can be recorded over time and again, just as with conventional audiocassette tapes. The difference is that the CD recorder should be able to produce much sharper fidelity with much greater dynamic range and frequency response because it uses digital technology. No background noise. No tape hiss. No scratches. No phonograph needle wearing down the album's grooves each time the record is played. No magnetic heads wearing down the tape.

Nothing comes in contact with the disk except a laser beam that reads the data. Thousands of tiny "pits" of digital data on the disk contain the information for reproducing the sound. To record on the CD, the laser first erases the disk by smoothing out the pits and then makes new pits during the recording.

Tandy, the corporate parent of the Radio Shack chain, plans to market a CD recorder/player and an erasable dye-polymer CD as early as 1991. Tandy expected the recorder to cost as little as $500. Other electronics manufacturers are also spending millions of dollars to develop the technology.

Recordable Videodisks versus VCR

Erasable disk technology also offers promise for video recording and could well challenge videotape as the recording medium of choice later in the 1990s. Prototypes have already been demonstrated. The big advantage: Disks don't deteriorate with use or age as videotapes do. Tape wears down a bit every time it's played and rubs up against the VCR's magnetic heads. Disks, touched only by a weightless laser beam, look as good after hundreds of plays as they do on the first.

Videodisk players, though currently lacking recording ability, are gaining popularity among videophiles because they offer high-resolution pictures, superb digital sound, and a large assortment of prerecorded material to choose from—on disks that won't wear out. Videodisks— often referred to as laser disks (LDs)—provide image resolution of 400 or more horizontal lines, compared to about 240 lines on a standard VHS cassette and about 330 lines on cable. Some tape formats, such as Super-VHS and ED Beta, now rival or even exceed the resolution of videodisks. (HDTV players and recorders will make all those resolution numbers look puny by comparison.) But videodisks have remained popular partly because of their greater durability, their digital sound, and the large catalog of prerecorded films, concerts, and documentaries available on disk—far more titles than now exist on the new tape formats.

Videodisks have other advantages over tape. With a videodisk you can switch to a particular scene almost instantly, in contrast to the lengthy rewind and fast-forward process of videotape. Videodisks also offer clear, rock-steady still frames, unlike the wobbly and streaky freeze-frames of videotape. The freeze-frame capability is one reason that videodisks have become popular in education and industrial training applications.

Videodisks are also expected to gain wider use as a way to browse electronically through museum collections, giving art lovers a chance to study works that may be hidden away in storage in the local museum or that are on display in museums across the country or abroad. A twelve-inch disk can hold over 50,000 still pictures on each side, and once videodisk technology is adapted to HDTV, the images will appear in breathtaking detail.

One drawback is that videodisks hold only about an hour of programming on each side, compared to several hours on tape. But the main drawback of videodisk technology has been the lack of recording capability. That should change in the next several years with the development of the recordable disk.

Most new videodisk players not only play the 12-inch videodisk, but also a shorter, 8-inch videodisk (which can hold up to twenty minutes on each side), the 4 ¾-inch audio compact disk, and the "CD-V" disk (sort of a CD version of the 45 rpm, holding up to 20 minutes of music plus 5 minutes of video).

Before spending $500 to $1,000 on a videodisk player, figure out where you'll get your supply of programming. Unless you plan to buy a lot of disks, make sure there is a nearby video rental outlet that carries a large selection of laser disks.

DIGITAL AUDIOTAPE RECORDERS: A CLOUDED FUTURE

If the recordable CD lives up to its billing, Digital Audiotape (DAT) recorders may never get much of a chance to audition for the American public. A $500 CD recorder would be less than half the price of a DAT recorder, a pioneering device whose American debut was delayed by the threat of lawsuits from the recording industry.

DATs, like the recordable CDs, can make perfect or near-perfect digital copies of other recordings. But CD recorders have the edge in price and durability as well as the advantage of being able to play the CD format, which is already well established in many home record libraries, with thousands of prerecorded titles to choose from. Prerecorded material for DATs is sparse, partly because of the recording industry's fight to keep DATs away from American shores.

Record companies complained to Congress that people would use DATs mainly to make perfect copies of a friend's CDs. The recording industry wanted Congress to require DAT recorders to have an anti-copying chip to prevent piracy. Government tests found that the chip degraded the overall sound quality of DATs—even on perfectly legal recordings—so the DAT issue was put on the legislative back burner. Meanwhile, the recording industry threatened to sue the first manufacturer who tried to mass-market DAT recorders in the United States.

A truce was finally reached in 1989 when manufacturers agreed to include circuitry in DATs that will prevent users from making a DAT copy of another DAT copy. That's the only limitation. DAT machines will still be able to make a copy of an original DAT recording, a compact disk, or any analog tape or phonograph album. In other words, if your friend just bought Michael Jackson's latest release on compact disk you could make a copy of the CD on your DAT. But if another friend with a DAT recorder asked to borrow your DAT copy of Michael Jackson, the circuitry in his machine would prevent him from copying it.

The delay in getting DATs into the American market gave recordable CDs extra time for development. To be sure, CD recorders are likely to meet the same opposition from the recording industry as DATs did. But however the dispute is finally resolved, recordable CDs are likely to prevail over DATs.

DATs, which have been around for some time in Japan and Europe, have only a few advantages over CDs. DAT cassettes, which are about half the size of conventional audiocassettes, hold up to two hours of music, compared to an hour on CDs. DATs also have a slight advantage as car stereos; tape decks aren't as vulnerable to dropouts on rough roads as CD players are. However, engineers have managed to build car CD players that do a good job of minimizing mistracks.

DAT car stereos have been around for a while, but they are only playback units, so the recording industry didn't consider them a threat. While DAT car stereos may be a dream to hear, finding enough DAT material to listen to is another story. There's little prerecorded music yet, and if DAT fails to catch on, the risk is that there won't ever be much prerecorded DAT music. That would make buying a DAT home recorder essential, so that you could make copies of CDs for your car DAT player.

DATs have some other drawbacks, as well. With a CD you can go to a specific track on the disk in an instant. But with a DAT, you still have to rewind and fast-forward the tape to get to the spot you want. While rewind and fast-forward on DATs are much faster than on conventional audiocassette machines, DATs are nowhere near as quick as the random-access capability of CDs.

DAT cassettes, encased in plastic as videotapes are, are less susceptible than CDs to dust, dirt, and mishandling. But DATs, like other recording tapes, are prone to sound distortions caused by the wear and tear of continuous playing and recording. CDs don't suffer the same fate. The beam of laser light doesn't do any damage to the disk.

MOBILE CELLULAR PHONES:
WHY THE PHONE YOU BUY MAY SOON BE OBSOLETE

Mobile phones, the latest status symbol of the busy executive, or anyone else who can afford the steep service charges, have become so popular that cellular phone companies are struggling to keep up with the growing volume of calls. Some areas of the country, such as New York and Los Angeles, are already facing capacity problems.

With projections that the number of mobile phone users will more than triple over the next few years, cellular companies are about to begin rebuilding their networks to squeeze more conversations into the limited number of radio frequencies allotted to cellular phone systems in each city.

Cellular companies are going to convert their cellular networks from analog to digital transmission, a conversion similar to that taking place in the music world. Analog LPs are being replaced by digital compact disks.

Switching to digital will allow cellular system operators immediately to triple or quadruple their system capacity, and eventually to increase it tenfold. Digital transmission will also improve reception, reduce costs, and make data transmission more reliable for those who want to hook up a portable facsimile machine or a laptop computer to their cellular phone.

But the switch to digital will also mean mobile phone customers will need to buy new equipment. Existing phones, which are analog, won't work on a digital cellular system any more than an analog LP will work on a CD digital player.

New equipment for transmitting conversations digitally between cellular radio towers and mobile phones is expected to be available for installation by cellular companies by 1991 or 1992. But analog phones won't be outmoded overnight. The conversion to digital cellular is expected to take place gradually, and both the analog and digital systems are likely to operate in tandem for a while.

Still, be aware that the analog phone you buy today will soon be superseded by a new generation of cellular phones designed for use on digital networks. Even though you should still be able to use your analog phone for a while after the digital system is in place, cellular operators are likely to offer customers inducements to use digital phones on the network. Cellular phones that can operate in either analog or digital mode are expected to be available by mid-1991.

The High Price of Telephonic Convenience

The convenience of telephonic portability doesn't come cheap. Cellular phones run from about $400 for a stationary car phone to more than $1,000 for a hand-held portable unit. That's only the beginning. Cellular carriers charge subscribers a monthly service fee ranging from about $30 to $45, plus phone calls. Phone calls are billed at the rate of 35 to 60 cents a minute during the business day. On weekends and evenings, the charge drops to about 25 to 40 cents a minute. Long-distance tolls are extra. That per-minute usage charge is not just for calls you make, but also for any calls you receive. That's why some people don't give their cellular numbers out. They let their secretary or paging service take the messages.

The average subscriber runs up monthly bills totaling $125 to $150, which is no big deal if your company is paying the tab, but it becomes an expensive luxury if you just want to chat at length with friends while driving around town.

Casual users can usually sign up for a special plan featuring a lower monthly service fee of $15 to $25. The trade-off is a much higher, peak-period usage rate of up to 90 cents a minute. Off-peak calls cost 20 to 30 cents a minute. These plans are "economical" if you don't make many cellular calls during business hours.

The high cost of cellular service is obviously the biggest deterrent to an even more rapid expansion of the cellular market. User charges are eventually expected to drop significantly, but not until cellular operators expand the capacity of their systems.

New technologies now in development could also make portable phones affordable to many more Americans by the mid- to late 1990s. These experimental systems, known as personal communications net-works (PCNs), are sometimes described as "poor man's cellular" because they would allow users to make and receive calls at lower cost, but with some limitations on mobility. PCNs are best suited to high-density urban areas because the systems require far more transmitter sites than cellular. A PCN transmitter, though smaller and less expensive than cellular equipment, operates at lower power and covers an area of only several hundred feet rather than several miles. How far a PCN user will be able to roam will depend on how ubiquitous the transmitter sites are and how far out the installations extend.

The shorter range of PCN transmitters does have some advantages. It will mean the handsets can be made smaller, lighter and less expensive than cellular phones since they won't have to send a signal as far. The shorter range will also make it possible for PCNs to accommodate more callers in a given area, and thus be able to offer lower rates to subscribers than cellular.

What to Look for in a Cellular Phone

There are three basic types of cellular phones to choose from: stationary car phones, which are the cheapest; portable hand-held phones, which are the most expensive but which can be used anywhere; and trans-portable models, which are sort of a mix between car phones and portables. Each has its advantages and disadvantages. Which one to choose depends on what you need it for and how fat your pocketbook is.

Car Phones: Stationary car phones are the least expensive way to go cellular. They also provide better reception than portables, particularly with a good antenna. Car phones deliver up to three watts of broadcast power, which is the maximum signal strength of mobile phones. The more wattage a phone has, the better the reception and transmission. Car phones are wired into your car's electrical system so you don't have to be concerned about battery charging as you do with portable phones. The only problem with conventional car phones is that they are stationary. You can't take them out of the car. Nonetheless, car phones are fine for people who spend a lot of time in their car and don't see any real need for a more portable unit. One of the more important options on a car phone to consider is the "hands-free" feature that will let you carry on a conversation without holding the telephone handset. The hands-free feature operates much like a speaker phone, with a microphone usually clipped to the sun visor. Some states have laws prohibiting motorists from holding a telephone handset while driving; doing so has caused accidents in the past.

Portables: Portables are hand-held models that weigh as little as twelve ounces and can be carried around and used like walkie-talkies. They also cost the most, provide the worst reception, and need frequent recharging. They deliver only 0.6 watts of broadcast power, which can sometimes lead to static reception and accidental disconnections. A portable can be used inside your car, but it won't work nearly as well as a car phone (although you can buy special equipment to hook a portable into your car's antenna and into the car's cigarette lighter.) Nonetheless, if you spend a lot of time away from your office and outside your car, a portable is the most convenient. You can pack it in your briefcase, take it on trips, make phone calls while you're dining at your favorite restaurant, take it to the beach while you're playing hooky from work, and you'll never be out of touch with the rest of the world. It is the closest thing yet to Dick Tracy's two-way wrist radio. The low power isn't as much of a problem now as it used to be because so many extra cell sites (transmitter/receivers) have been added to handle the growing volume of traffic. So unless you're doing a lot of traveling in fringe or hilly areas, you usually won't be far from a cell site in major cities. Battery power on a portable is a constraint, but sufficient in most situations. Between charges, newer models can be on standby, ready to receive calls for fifteen to twenty-four hours, and they will allow you to converse for ninety minutes to two hours. For most uses, that's plenty of time, especially if you're recharging the battery while you're in the car or in your office. If you anticipate longer use, you can carry around a spare battery pack, which weighs about six ounces. Battery makers are hopeful of being able to come up with longer-lasting batteries for cellular portables soon.

Transportables: Transportable phones are designed to snap easily in and out of a special mount in your car, giving you the power of a permanent car phone and the portability of a hand-held. Transportables provide clearer reception (delivering up to three watts of broadcast power) and longer battery life between charges than hand-helds. But transportables are heavier and bulkier. For use outside the car, the handset snaps onto a portable battery pack, which brings the weight of transportables up to five pounds or more. But the larger battery can support more than two hours of conversation and more than twenty-four hours of standby time. Because of their bigger batteries and stronger broadcast power, transportables are tremendously popular in the construction industry for use at building sites. Transportables are also popular among boat owners and golfers who take them from the car to their yacht or golf cart. In terms of price, they usually run a few hundred dollars less than portables.

FACSIMILE MACHINES: THE FACTS ON FAX

Fax machines permeated the American workplace and the American psyche almost overnight. With several million of them installed in offices across the country, fax transmission has moved into the business telecommunications mainstream. For a fast-growing variety of documents and messages, it has become the preferred method of delivery.

It's faster and cheaper than overnight mail. For the price of a phone call, you can transmit a document in seconds over regular phone lines to an office down the block, across the country, or around the world.

Fax technology has been around for generations. But until recently, the high cost of fax machines limited their use to urgent communications by large corporations. Today fax machines are affordable to even home-based businesses. For less than $500, you can buy a fax machine that will allow you to exchange important documents with fax machines at the largest corporations or transmit take-out orders to the corner deli.

Fax machines are already an essential tool in many businesses. And the threat of being left out of the mainstream will grow for those without fax machines as they become more common and fax delivery becomes routine for more types of information. By the end of the decade, 20 to 30 million fax machines will be installed in offices and homes, according to most projections.

When It Pays to Buy a Fax

If you send an average of at least one overnight letter a week, a fax machine can pay for itself in a couple of years. An overnight letter costs more than $8, while a fax transmission is the price of a phone call, and it's faster.

If your need for speed is infrequent, you may be able to get by without a fax machine by sticking with overnight delivery service or using a public fax machine when documents need to get there sooner.

You can also have people fax documents to you through a public fax service. But after a while, that becomes an inconvenience and perhaps even an embarrassment. Telling a business contact to fax your document to your neighborhood photocopy shop doesn't help instill confidence in your business. If you're a struggling artist, everyone will understand. But if you're trying to build a professional image for your business and you're in the type of business where fax transmissions are common, people will start wondering why you can't afford a $500 machine.

Nothing beats a fax for speed in transmitting documents. So if speed is an important part of your business, then a fax is a must. It's also a must if you deal with other businesses or customers who expect you to have a fax. If you start hearing the words "Can I fax it to you?" or "Can you fax it to me?" from important contacts or clients, then it's time to buy a fax. On the other hand, if you hardly ever need to send a fax, and no one needs to send you one, you probably don't need a fax.

Nor do you really need one if you're not running your own business. Fax is, and probably will remain, primarily a business form of communication. While faxing has found more personal uses, such as sending take-out orders to delis and musical requests to radio stations, most people will be able to cope without them. Deli owners and radio stations are not likely to stop taking phone requests.

If You Don't Have a Fax: The Burgeoning Public Fax Network

If you don't have a fax machine of your own, or you're away from your office, you can still send and receive faxes through the burgeoning network of fax machines available to the public.

Most print shops and photocopying outlets now offer fax service. The cost for sending a one- or two-page fax is about $3 plus long-distance charges. Faxes can also be received for about the same cost.

In what could evolve into the largest network, the Postal Service recently installed public fax machines in a few hundred post office lobbies across the country on an experimental basis. If the test proves successful, fax machines could become almost as commonplace in post offices as self-service postage machines.

Almost anywhere you travel these days you can find a fax machine. Public fax machines are springing up in airport terminals, hotel lobbies, and other public places. At self-service machines, all you need do is insert a credit card and dial the fax number. You can either send or receive documents.

If you have a personal computer with a modem, you can send text messages to another fax machine through one of the major electronic mail systems run by the long-distance telephone companies or online database services, such as CompuServe.

What to Look for in a Fax Machine

Good fax machines cost about $700 to $2,500, depending on the features. If you need a fax only to send and receive a few pages a day, you can get by with a lower-priced model. But when your fax needs expand, there is a variety of special features that can be helpful. Here are some guidelines to follow when shopping for a fax:

Technical Standard: Make sure the machine you buy is Group 3 compatible. If a dealer tries to sell you a Group 2 machine at a terrific price, tell him you will sell him a piece of the Brooklyn Bridge at a good price, too. Group 2's are obsolete models. Nearly all of the machines in existence today are Group 3 standard.

Document Feeder Capacity: With the lowest-priced machines, you have to feed documents one sheet at a time when transmitting, which means you have to baby-sit the machine each time you want to send a multipage document. Spending a little more money will get you automatic feeder capacity of five or ten pages. How much capacity you need depends on how many pages you tend to send. Feeder capacity on the biggest machines is 50 pages.

Resolution: The minimum resolution standards for fax machines are "normal" and "fine." Normal resolution, which is 200 horizontal lines by 100 vertical lines per square inch, is used for sending most types of business correspondence. If you want to send a sharper image, you can switch the machine to fine, which offers 200 by 200 lines per inch. The receiver's machine automatically adjusts to whatever resolution is being transmitted. Some machines also offer "superfine" sharpness, which is 200 by 400 lines per inch. But the superfine resolution is wasted if the receiving machine doesn't have the feature as well. Bear in mind that the higher the resolution, the longer it takes to transmit the document, making telephone charges higher.

Gray Scale: If you're going to send photographs or detailed graphics, consider getting "gray scale" capability. Images will be clearer and sharper because they'll be transmitted in varying shades of gray rather than just black dots. Using gray scale, however, slows down transmission.

Thermal versus Plain Paper: Plain paper is better than heat-sensitive thermal, but plain-paper machines are the most expensive.

Paper Rolls: Paper comes in rolls ranging from 98 feet to 328 feet. Short rolls are fine if you don't expect to receive many documents. But if you expect to receive a lot, it may pay to get a machine that accepts longer rolls. You won't worry as much about running out of paper, and longer rolls tend to be more economical.

Automatic Paper Cutter: Most lower-cost machines don't have this feature, and if you don't expect to receive much traffic you can live without an automatic paper cutter. But if you expect to receive a lot of transmissions, absence of a paper cutter will be readily apparent each morning when you walk into your office and find a seemingly endless stream of thermal paper flowing from your fax machine.

Mixed Phone Line: Fax machines don't require a separate phone line. But if it's going to share a line on which you converse, an automatic voice/data switch is needed. That switch figures out whether it's got a human or a fax on the line. If it's another fax calling in, your fax goes into action. If it doesn't hear any fax signals on the line, the fax figures it's for you and lets the phone ring.

Dialing: There is a variety of telephone dialing features that can be helpful if you regularly send a lot of documents. "Automatic redialing" is a common feature; if the fax number you're calling is busy, the machine will keep redialing until it connects. "Automatic dialing" gives you one-touch dialing to frequently called numbers. Another feature, called "broadcasting," lets you send the same document automatically to a number of different fax machines. To save on telephone charges, some machines can be programmed, using a "delay and send" feature, to automatically transmit documents after night rates go into effect. Another toll-saving feature, called "polling," will automatically call another fax machine and retrieve documents that have been left for you.

Photocopy Capability: Fax machines, including the lower-priced ones, can make photocopies. It's slow and the copies are no better than fax quality, but it may save you several hundred dollars if you were thinking about buying a personal copier for occasional use.

Fax Machines versus Computer Fax Boards

In the future, many fax machines are likely to be replaced by circuit boards inside personal computers. Instead of drafting the document on your computer, printing it out on paper, and then feeding the paper into a fax machine, you'll be able to transmit the document directly from your computer.

Faxing by computer is already feasible. But for what it costs to add the equipment needed to make your computer emulate all the features of a fax machine, you could buy a good stand-alone fax machine.

When computer users see ads in computer magazines showing fax boards selling for as little as $200, many of them think that that's the cheapest way to gain fax capability. But by themselves, fax boards—which are essentially modems that send fax-type signals—only let you transmit computer files. What if you want to send a newspaper clipping or some other paper document? To do that, you need a scanner, a device that inputs paper documents into your computer. A good full-page scanner costs as much as or more than most standard fax machines.

What's more, if you don't spend the money to buy a fax board that will operate independently in "background" from the computer's main processor, an incoming fax will interrupt whatever work you're doing on the computer. Sending a fax will also keep your computer tied up until the transmission is completed.

To be sure, computer faxing does have its advantages. With a laser printer, computer fax boards will produce sharper copies on plain paper than stand-alone fax machines, most of which use thermal paper. And if you're faxing material to another computer, images will arrive in much better shape. Images sent on standard fax machines get degraded when you put them through a relatively cheap scanning device on one end and they then come out the other end on thermal paper.

In addition, if you work mainly with computer files, it's more convenient to send documents right from your computer. No need to print the document on paper in order to send it. And you can view incoming fax messages right on your computer screen, although the text can't be edited; the fax transmission arrives as a graphics file rather than a text file.

RADAR DETECTORS: USELESS AGAINST NEW POLICE LASER WEAPON

For the millions of motorists who feel safe from the arm of the law with their dashboard radar detector, trouble is around the bend: Police departments may soon be equipping their highway patrols with a new laser speed gun that is invisible to radar detectors.

The new laser gun, developed by the International Measurement and Control Company, a Littleton, Colorado, firm that manufactures laser-based instruments, emits a much narrower beam than radar and is thus much better at homing in on a particular target among a group of cars in traffic. What's more, the new device gives police an edge against the growing numbers of motorists who have equipped their cars with antiradar devices, because the laser beam can't be picked up by radar detectors. Although an antilaser device could probably be built, the cost might be prohibitive for the mass consumer market—perhaps $1,500 or more. Radar detectors cost less than $300.

Police departments also have to pay more for the laser guns, which at a price of $3,000 each, cost up to three times as much as radar guns. As a result, laser guns may not completely replace radar guns. But even if police departments make laser guns a small part of their arsenal, motorists with radar detectors will be vulnerable since they won't know when they're speeding into a laser trap.

The laser guns were undergoing pilot tests in several states in late 1989, and were scheduled to be available for sale to police departments in 1990.

VIDEOPHONES

Videophones, whose arrival has been awaited ever since AT&T showed its "Picturephone" at the 1964 World's Fair, are finally a reality. While the reality may not measure up to everyone's imagination, the videophones do work over ordinary phone lines and are available for less than $250. A videophone call costs no more than a regular phone call.

If you expect full-motion color images like the ones you get through your television set, you will be disappointed. Videophones only produce black-and-white still-frame "snapshots." So you won't be able to see the caller's lips move in sync with the conversation and you won't be able to show off your latest magic tricks. Freeze-frame images are the best that currently available models can produce.

The Japanese-built videophones now on the market contain a tiny built-in TV camera and a small video display screen. To transmit a picture of yourself, all you need do is pose in front of the unit and press the "send" button. The image is frozen and transmitted to your caller's videophone. While the image is being transmitted, your conversation is interrupted, because the telephone line doesn't have enough capacity to transmit the audio and video signals from these units at the same time.

Some videophones allow you to store a limited number of previous images. So if you get a video call from your sister and you later talk to your parents, you can show them how your sister looks these days. An optional video printer allows you to make paper copies of the video image.

Pictures received on the videophone can also be recorded on standard audiotape since the video image consists of fluctuating audio tones. Some units have a built-in answering machine so you can receive video messages while you're away. (Conventional answering machines and portable tape recorders with automatic gain control can't record video images because the gain control prevents recording the various levels of gray.)

Videophones that produce color still-frame pictures are about to make their way onto the market. And videophones that produce moving pictures are expected to become commercially available in the early 1990s.

Developing videophones that transmit moving pictures over ordinary telephone lines has been difficult because of the limited capacity of copper wiring. Video images contain far more information than existing lines can handle in rapid sequence. Fiber-optic cable, with its vast capacity, can handle the job, but rewiring American homes with optical fiber will take into the next century to complete.

Compression Labs, Inc., the leading manufacturer of videoconferencing equipment, recently announced that it had developed a technology that can squeeze enough video signal through existing copper lines to permit color moving pictures as well as simultaneous audio transmission. This feat is accomplished by compressing the signal up to 6,000 times and transmitting only that part of each picture frame that moves. For example, assume the videophone camera is trained on your face. If your face is otherwise rigid except for a blink of your eyelash, the videophone would send only the video information relating to your blinking eyelash. The image of the rest of your face would remain static on the receiver's screen. The picture is repainted in this fashion at a rate of eight to fifteen frames per second. It's not up to the full-motion video standards of broadcast TV, but it does offer moving pictures along with simultaneous audio transmission.

Compression Labs plans to have a consumer version of the videophone on the market by 1992 or 1993 with an initial price tag of $1,500. Business models are expected to sell for $2,500 to $3,500.

Of course, the opportunity to reach out and visibly touch someone is limited to the number of people who have compatible videophones. While they aren't expected to become as pervasive as telephones anytime soon (many people abhor the thought of having to show their face on screen everytime they talk on the phone), there are potential applications that could make videophones more commonplace in the 1990s. Videophones can provide a way for families who live far apart (such as divorced parents who don't have custody of their children) to stay closer in touch. Videophones could also pave the way for new home-shopping services. For example, if you're looking for a new home, your real-estate agent could call you and transmit a picture of a home that just came on the market; if you don't like it, you haven't wasted a trip to the broker's office or to the home itself to see it. Or mail-order outlets might offer a service that allows people with videophones to call up and see a picture of the merchandise; no need to wait for a catalog to arrive in the mail or rely on just a verbal description. Videophones would also allow the deaf to communicate with each other using sign language.

With travel costs going up and the price of videoconferencing equipment coming down, videoconferencing is finally starting to pick up among larger businesses, particularly those with far-flung organizations. Using satellites, fiber-optic lines, or other special transmission networks, businesses can set up videoconferencing systems that provide full-motion video. Some organizations use the systems for meetings of executives in scattered office locations or for conferences between staff members in various cities working on the same product. Some advertising agencies have their clients hooked up to a videoconferencing network.

THE FILMLESS ELECTRONIC CAMERA: A COMING RIVAL FOR 35MM

Electronics manufacturers, hoping to revolutionize still photography as they did home movies, are beginning to come out with electronic cameras that produce snapshots instantly without film.

The cameras look like conventional 35mm still cameras. But instead of film, images are captured on tiny magnetic floppy disks, sort of miniature versions of the floppy disks used in home computers.

All you need do is snap your pictures, pop the disk into a special video player, and, *voilà*, your pictures can be instantly viewed on your TV set. (Some cameras don't require a separate player unit; an adapter is built right into the camera.) If you want to save some of the images for your scrapbook, you can print them out on paper on an optional color printer. Up to fifty images can be stored on a single disk.

Some of the biggest names in electronics and photography—Canon, Sony, Casio, and Konica—were among the first to introduce models for the mass market, starting at a bare-bones $600 or so. But the images produced by the early models don't measure up to the quality of traditional cameras. Manufacturers are working to improve the resolution.

If they can improve the image and make the cameras more affordable for the mass market, electronic still-imaging could well lead to a movement away from chemical-based photography, just as home movie cameras were supplanted by camcorders. Industry analysts believe it will take years for that to happen, but Kodak and Polaroid aren't sitting idly by. Both are developing electronic cameras of their own.

Although electronic cameras just recently made their debut in the consumer market, businesses have been using more expensive versions of the technology for a few years. Some newspapers use electronic cameras to snap late-breaking photos. The newspaper doesn't have to wait for the photographer to drive back to the office and then develop the film. Images can be sent by telephone right from the scene to the newspaper with no need to develop the picture.

PORTABLE VCR/TV

Among the latest in entertainment gadgetry to wash up on American shores from the Pacific is the portable VCR/TV, which Sony hopes will follow the immense successes of its portable audio Walkman and TV Watchman.

A number of Japanese electronics manufacturers have come out with battery-powered units combining a videocassette recorder with a small color television screen. With these, you can watch your favorite movie sitting on the beach or on your yacht; eliminate the boredom on your nightly train commute from the office; set the unit on the kitchen counter while you watch a cooking demonstration; take it to your client's office for a sales presentation; or give your kids something to keep them quiet on your next car trip.

Sony's version is about the size of a large paperback book and uses 8mm tapes. A unit made by Casio is about twice the size but uses standard VHS tapes. Although you can find prerecorded VHS tapes everywhere, there are relatively few in the 8mm format. Because 8mm tapes are much smaller than VHS cassettes, 8mm has proven an extremely popular format for camcorders; the smaller tape allows for smaller hand-held video cameras. But prerecorded tapes in the 8mm format haven't become widespread. Sony's recent acquisition of Columbia Pictures Entertainment, the Hollywood movie studio, is likely to increase the supply of 8mm programming. But as Sony found with its Beta videocassettes, video rental stores don't like to carry a lot of different formats.

With the retail price at around $1,000, these units will not become as commonplace as Walkmans anytime soon.

23

PRECIOUS METALS: LOSING THEIR GLITTER?

Precious metals may still be the classic hedge against various doomsday scenarios, but the underlying fundamentals of gold, silver, and platinum don't bode well for their investment mettle in other seasons. Gold supplies are swelling and new technologies threaten the underpinnings of the demand for silver and platinum.

GOLD: NOT AS RARE AS IT USED TO BE

Gold, worshiped for centuries because of its rarity and stockpiled by investors as a hedge against inflation and other economic storms, is no longer as rare as it used to be nor as certain a hedge against inflation.

Much has changed in the decade since gold fever infected small investors and sent the price of gold skyrocketing to $875 an ounce. World gold production has swelled. Inflation has moderated. World tensions have eased. And gold's performance since the 1980 peak has done nothing to perk investor demand. Gold prices plummeted. Languishing at the $300 to $500 level during most of the decade, gold prices lagged well behind inflation and other investments.

Investors who clung to gold all those years would have found themselves poorer and ravaged by inflation rather than protected from it. And instead of the heady prophecies of prices nearing $2,000 an ounce when gold fever swept the investment community a decade ago, gold analysts now offer predictions that run only into the hundreds of dollars.

Although gold fever didn't last, gold digging has. Worldwide gold output soared an estimated 60 percent during the 1980s as new discoveries and new low-cost technologies for extracting gold from ore spurred a vast expansion of global production capacity and lower costs. U.S. production capacity expanded sevenfold.

While supplies have been surging, demand has been lagging. Despite all the recent attention to heavy gold buying in the Far East, demand from Europe and the United States has been lackluster.

Gold's commercial uses are limited and analysts don't see anything that would cause a major surge in jewelry or industrial demand. Gold is primarily used for dentistry, jewelry, electronic components, painting, and pharmaceuticals. A study by the WEFA Group and Resource Strategies, Inc., a consulting firm, projected that consumer and industrial demand would rise less than 2 percent a year.

Even speculators have found better ways than gold to bet on inflation, such as currency futures where you wager on a harder currency than the American dollar to hedge against inflation. Gold hasn't been as sensitive to inflation in recent years, not even when inflation fears sent the stock and bond markets reeling. During the 1980s, gold prices lagged well behind inflation, while stock and bond returns skipped along well ahead of inflation.

Gold may still be a hedge against a severe bout of inflation, like the one that drove gold prices up in the late 1970s. But the inflation outlook for the 1990s is tempered. World tensions have also eased.

Speculators can't even count on social and political tensions in South Africa to fire up the gold market. While South Africa remains the world's leading gold producer and any disruption in production is likely to have repercussions, its share of the market has dwindled as mining capacity has increased in other parts of the world. In 1980, South Africa produced about 55 percent of the world's gold. Today it produces only about one third. Several important gold producers, including the Soviet Union, are desperate for hard currency to pay for imports and interest on foreign debts, and thus have great incentive to increase their exports of gold in the future.

Gold may still merit a small place in investment portfolios as insurance against unexpected economic or political disaster. But more and more investment analysts have come to the view that the fundamentals don't justify holding gold for other reasons.

Gold bugs who pour more than 5 percent of their investment portfolio into preparing for unlikely doomsday scenarios may well be risking funds needed for events that are far more certain, such as a child's college tuition bill and retirement.

SILVER: THE THREAT FROM FILMLESS CAMERAS

While demand for gold is based largely on investor emotion, silver is primarily an industrial metal. And a major underpinning of demand for silver—photographic film—faces an uncertain future. A new technology for taking snapshots electronically could eventually challenge conventional film-based photography. Photographic film is by far the largest user of silver, accounting for about 40 percent of worldwide silver demand.

Electronic filmless cameras, which record images on a small floppy disk rather than chemical-based film, recently entered the consumer market. The new cameras don't pose any significant threat to film yet because of their high cost and because the picture quality doesn't measure up to 35-mm film. But if engineers are able to improve the image and bring the camera's price tag down to more competitive levels, electronic imaging cameras could become a serious threat to conventional still photography, just as camcorders challenged home movie cameras. Industry analysts believe such advancements in electronic imaging are years away, but filmless cameras loom as a long-term threat to silver demand and silver's price.

Although a much smaller source of demand, silver flatware has been losing luster among consumers. High silver prices initially drove more and more consumers toward stainless-steel flatware in the 1980s. But changing life-styles also appear to be responsible for the trend away from silverware. With trends toward more informal entertaining and with more women working, fewer people have the time or inclination to polish silver.

On the supply side of the equation, silver supplies from mining and recycling were more than sufficient to meet consumption demand during the 1980s. What's more, silver production doesn't fluctuate much with demand. Most silver is merely a by-product of copper, lead, and zinc mining activities. So silver is sort of a bonus for miners extracting other metals.

PLATINUM: FRAGILE FOUNDATIONS IN CATALYTIC CONVERTERS

Platinum's future is also clouded by technological breakthroughs that could crack the major prop of its demand: catalytic converters for motor vehicles.

Platinum became the nouveau darling of precious-metal investors in the early 1980s, about the time that the glitter began wearing off gold and silver in the investment community. Platinum had much to offer speculators. For one thing, it was far rarer than gold or silver. For another, platinum was sensitive to political tremors since South Africa and the Soviet Union account for 95 percent of world platinum production. So any East-West rift or social or political upheaval in South Africa could threaten supplies and drive prices of platinum skyward. Moreover, platinum had a major and expanding source of demand in catalytic converters. Platinum was a critical ingredient of catalytic converters, and demand for converters was growing as air pollution standards around the world were tightened. But in late 1988, Ford Motor Company announced that it had developed a catalytic converter that didn't require platinum and that the new device would be included in as many as fifty thousand cars. Few details were given, but enough was said to send platinum prices into a tailspin.

Some metals analysts thought investors went too far in pushing platinum prices down, contending that it remained to be seen whether the platinum-free converters would be effective over a long period of time and in different sorts of engines. Nor was it known whether Ford would license the technology to competitors.

But the Ford announcement was enough to suggest that platinum's major source of demand was vulnerable. Few people thought a less costly replacement for platinum was possible anytime soon even though all the major auto companies have been trying to develop a platinum-free converter. Ford's announcement showed that it was possible and that it was coming sooner than anyone had expected.

INDEX

411